The Diary
of a
Country Parson

The Diary of a Country Parson

THE REVD JAMES *WOODFORDE*

Selected by
DAVID HUGHES
Engravings by
IAN STEPHENS

London
THE FOLIO SOCIETY
1992

Set in 'Monotype' Baskerville
by Gloucester Typesetting Services,
Stonehouse, Gloucestershire.
Printed by Butler & Tanner Ltd, Frome
on Hamilton Wove paper and bound by them
in quarter buckram with paper sides
marbled by Ann Muir.

Contents

Introduction

The facts are unexceptional. James Woodforde was born in June 1740 at Ansford in Somerset and three days later, being sickly, was baptised by his father who held the livings of both Ansford and Castle Cary. Like his father before him (his noted great-grandfather, Dr Samuel Woodforde DD FRS, had been at St Paul's) he attended Winchester College as a scholar on the foundation. At nineteen—his diary starts with this very achievement—he was elected a scholar of New College, Oxford; two years later he became a fellow, and within three days of being ordained deacon he took his degree of Bachelor of Arts. In 1763 he returned to Somerset where he looked after one or two local curacies until ordained priest at Wells in late 1764, whereafter he assisted his father at Castle Cary as curate. He took his MA in 1767, four years before his father's death, at which point— he was just over thirty—he moved into the parsonage at Ansford and looked after both the parishes for a little more than two years. He then returned to residence in New College, where he was appointed sub-warden and shortly afterwards a proctor. In the same year, 1774, he was presented by New College to the living of Weston Longeville in Norfolk but, taking his Oxford BD in 1775 as well as taking his time, he did not move to the living until May 1776. He died, having spent more than quarter of a century as a country parson in the same village, on New Years Day 1803, having written the last words of his diary, 'Rost Beef &c', in the middle of the previous October.

The young Woodforde began his diary purely as an account of his expenses; indeed money concerned him throughout his life. It seemed natural, a product of his careful upbringing perhaps, to review on paper how much life at any point was costing him. Even before the diary properly opens, he noted on various dates in early 1759 that he had spent thirty shillings on Swift's Works, eighteen pence on Joe Miller's *Jests* and five shillings on a ticket for the *Messiah*. Forty years later, in 1798, he is expostulating over having to pay almost three shillings for a quart of port that at New College in 1774 cost him only one and six. Such money worries are more of a product of temperament than of shortage; in Norfolk he cannot have found it difficult to keep open house, with two maids, two manservants, a boy and three horses, on an income of a little over £400 a year. Yet Woodforde was never rich except comparatively.

Had he stuck to such a limited record, however, his diary would have proved of cursory interest. Luckily at an early point he decided to expand the text beyond mere expenditure to cover his doings, his regrets, his feelings both waspish and fond about the people he encountered, the social events that opened up in him a vein of generous pleasure or fury, the almost daily card games he lost or won, his casual preaching and praying amid none too large a congregation at his lonely church, his dark fancies at night, the illnesses with scant hope of cure in ice-cold rooms, the hunts and the shoots and the fishing, the tangles with servants, and the irritations with such close relatives as his niece Nancy who kept him company and his nephew Bill who had his eye on the maids. It is fascinating in the journal to watch him over the years getting into his stride, almost as if he realised, with a gently gathering urgency, that his life was more real in the permanence of notes than in the transient flesh, even—or especially—if no one was ever to read those notes. After 1761 for sixteen thousand days he missed no entry except when illness forced his abstinence.

Yet in forty years he makes in the journal only one or two references to its existence. They touch a sympathetic nerve in the reader; he seems, as often, so vulnerable. The first occurs when he was leaving his familiar Oxford for the last time to take up residence in the unknown of Norfolk. On horseback he reached Thame for dinner only to discover to his mildly inexpressible consternation—we feel its shock to this day—that he had left behind in his vacated rooms the current little volume of the diary. At once he sent a man back and with the civil patience of his nature waited. His relief when hours later the notebook was trotted up is simply expressed: 'I was then quite happy—pd him for going o.2.6.' On another occasion on which he referred to the notebooks Woodforde, copying out a cure for cramp, suggested it should hardly earn a place in so modest a book as the one now under his pen. Such self-conscious mention of his millions of words was a rare event.

To read months or years of Woodforde at a sitting is to be overwhelmed after a while by the floods of calm that in those days flowed from time. Behind the words we hear an immense silence—a godsend we have lost for ever, save in pages such as these. The bald economy with which the parsonical pen very nearly writes off his days—only on occasion does he permit himself a flourish—is a sharp spur to the imagination of the reader. The setting has to be inferred from small hints. A nicely placed word is often enough to convey a feeling. Woodforde gives only a clue, just a slight adjective or a slighting one, to what the people he meets are like, and we are left to picture with accumulating pleasure some character who, thanks to the very exiguity of the manner of writing, springs into our minds fully clothed in the lineaments of personality. He has only to mention a carriage and we hear the rumble of wheels in the emptiness of that far night. We see what he sees with the utmost clarity for the simple reason that he uses so few words to describe it. And of course at the delineation of a dinner—immense quantities of food being in the mistaken view of most commentary about the parson the crux of his existence—our taste-buds quicken historically and our stomachs rumble two centuries back in time.

Today Weston Longville has modernised its spelling but hardly at all its atmosphere. Though only eleven miles from

Norwich, where Woodforde at gentlemanly intervals paid his tradesmen or watched a gaudy parade, the village still conveys more than a hint of the isolation and of the amiable melancholy that pervaded his life. His church, large and light, is not much changed; its calm proportions accord well with the unmystical common sense of his belief in the divine. With forgivable vulgarity the pub close at hand now bears his name. His rectory is no more, demolished forty years after his death, but a subsequent house built on a similar plan stands in gloomily impressive grounds on the same spot a spacious quarter of a mile from the church. In a district that undulates only here and there, covered with huge skies of ever-shifting weather, haunted by coverts thick with game, criss-crossed by aimless lanes off which great churches loom at immense distances, it is not difficult for us to coincide in spirit with a compulsively ordinary man who lived two centuries ago in a period that had more in common with the mediaeval than with the modern. He remains intimately at a remove. 'His diary', as Virginia Woolf said, 'is the only mystery about him.'

Woodforde's was a quiet life on the surface. A glance at the only portrait, which now hangs on the west wall of his church at Weston, suggests that he preferred at any cost to be regarded as a quiet man. It is a reserve and inwardly troubled face, the face of a decent man whose conscience and temper stir him against his will, a law-abiding face that is aware of right and wary of wrong. Though a good deal of kindness shows in its innocence and its irony, he looks almost smugly unhappy. On the other hand, though painted by his nephew Samuel, later a Royal Academician, this is a posthumous version of the pastor based on a sketch. The portrait might be fibbing. His real face is on the page.

Of some of the chief characters in the diary paintings do exist. Yet in Woodforde's account they are so alive that with or without the help of art they force their looks on the mind's eye. As in a novel, but with how much more relish, we are at liberty to imagine them physically. Again we base our impression, fortified by the faces and figures of people we might ourselves know, on the diary's vaguest description of their appearance or sharper account of their conduct. Woodforde is an unwitting example of the superior effect of few words over many, provided they are decisively chosen. He thumb-nails people with aplomb. On a very hot day in May when he was forty-six he met and casually immortalised the three Miss Thomases at Dereham. 'We spent a tolerable agreeable Day there,' he wrote a little after nine o'clock. 'Miss Thomas is very reserved and not handsome—Miss Betsy is very agreeable and pretty—Miss Anne very stiff and coarse.' We need not a word more for the three sisters to take shape before our eyes.

It is tempting when reading the diaries to think of Woodforde as lonely in his solitude. Indeed, nobody in that century better expressed, often between the lines but now and then directly, the extremes of tedium that afflict the human spirit. 'Very dull and sleepy in the Mornings between breakfast and dinner,' he records on 16 January 1792, when suffering only from a cold. A couple of years earlier, in good health, he was muttering, 'I was but poorly all day being low spirited had but an indifferent night of rest—I think it is some gouty humour lurking in the Constitution.' Perhaps he chose the drug of daily record as a means of vitalising a boredom otherwise unconscionable; the diary enabled him to digest what today we see as accidie. It certainly enabled him to deal with Nancy, the servants, the daily tribulations. For Nancy too was a bother to him with her moods, her demands for a livelier social calendar.

Yet, the paucity of his parish duties apart, he made sure that he himself had plenty to do. Proud of the immediate garden that surrounded him, careful of the production of his glebe, he regularly recorded the vegetables he grew, the fruit, the beer he brewed, the pond he developed. In the autumn of 1780 we find him ordering from a Norwich nurseryman a selection of plants rich in both number and variety, from twenty poplars and ten acacias to a couple of vines, half a dozen guelder roses, and a nectarine. Apart from plantings he also liked to plan outings, when in danger of boredom, to Norwich or at a sudden venture to one or other of his fellow parsons, Mr Du Quesne at Honingham, Mr Bodham at Mattishall, living in the vicinity. While quite often haunting the open air by day, coursing hares, fishing for pike in the Wensum, he must have spent many days immured in the parsonage awaiting the chance of a passing visit while enduring the pauses between meals.

Yet to think of him as depressed in the modern way is to misunderstand the feel of the era. Patience was more a necessity than a virtue because of the amount of pain about: not just the pain of having a tooth dragged out by a clumsy local—Woodforde's accounts of extraction and its aftermath are sheer agony —or suffering the mystery of a bodily ill that Dr Thorne lacked the capacity of diagnose, but the discomfort of spirit which Woodforde with due philosophy associated with the idea of being alive at all. In the background God was vaguely there to help, but more as a slightly elevated member of the family than as any too numinous a presence. Among many prayers for the recently dead which Woodforde commits to the diary, let his sincere farewell to his friend Mr Du Quesne stand as an example. 'It is a very great Loss to us, but I hope to him, Gain. Pray God he may be eternally happy. Dinner today boiled Leg of Mutton & a rosted Rabbit.'

But for much of the time it was enough for Woodforde to know that he was surrounded throughout England by the like-minded. His superiors, his servants, all were agreed that the status quo was unlikely to be bettered this side of the millennium. The only regret now and then was the inevitable misery in which quite large numbers lived, and Woodforde was far from slow in trying to remedy that condition by personal charity; he is always dispensing pennies or even sixpences to vagrants, beggars, children by the wayside. Although Woodforde's world is only four short lifetimes away from a fifty-year-old alive in the 1990s, it is a long way off in psychic terms. The far-removed rusticity of that world is so different from our own, in every respect but its basic humanity, that it can no longer be readily reconstituted either in the reaches of the imagination or from the history books. Only a diary like the pages that follow can reshape it with the required finesse.

There is no cheating in Woodforde, no posturing; he lives with a guarded honesty in his sphere of prose. His faith in the eternal life is not only absolute but humorous; at a further level it is possibly non-existent. He never noticed his contradictions. With daily truth he stated his life as it came. His close-written pages profess no trace of ulterior motive. He never knew whether he was being interesting or a bore: an unconscious mirror, in fact, is what he stared into. Without artifice or reflection Woodforde held up the looking-glass of his journal to offer, to a posterity he never considered, a reliable, impartial, altruistic image of one of the more mysterious periods in relatively recent history. He hardly noticed—or only just—the more potent of events, an attempt on the King's life, a mobilisation in Norwich, a war in America. Yet up there in the flats of Norfolk he lived through the French Revolution.

Despite typifying England in his own clerical way, Woodforde like everyone else had little idea of the kind of England he inhabited. News—hardly news, for it was always late—resounded like rumour round the few people in a village who vaguely heard of it from gossip or broadsheet. He knew who Pitt was, of course, indeed he memorably glimpsed the great man once in an inn when changing horses, but he had little contact with the realities of politics or war; history in the making stood at a remove from that parsonage. Nonetheless, Woodforde lived in an England which for the first time had come to be governed more or less as it is nowadays. First Walpole, then Lord Chatham and his son William Pitt, had engineered a system of which this informal country could be casually proud. It might appear, if you were to any extent in the know, that seventy families amply represented in the House of Lords were in a petulant or despotic manner running the country under the king — in the diarist's lifetime the monarchs were the second and third Georges — but the powers, not to mention the whims, of this aristocracy were sharply limited by laws that had somehow or another dithered their way through the Commons. The key to the functioning of this newly evolving scheme was, in the eyes of the Government, the local gentry: thus, in Weston Longville, the Custances. In a political understanding that was unspoken, it was expected of a squire that he would act as a voluntary agent of law and order. So loose were these arrangements that they did nothing to stem the abuses that riddled the Court, Whitehall, the Universities and the Church — indeed every institution. But at least, thanks to the broadly liberal character of the men who now led it, this was a country revelling in freedom. Except in times of national emergency, you could say more or less what you liked, you could read in the press to your heart's content all sorts of libel of the high and mighty, you could go wherever you wished without question. Here was a version of Utopia. All Europe gaped in envy at the stability of life across the Channel.

James Woodforde shares these liberties of thought, word and deed, even if he seems to allow the comforts of life to take precedence over the intellect. Up to a point he thought nothing of noting a day's dinner as some salt fish, a couple of boiled rabbits and onions, a boiled leg of mutton, boiled beef and roast beef and plum puddings — a challenging parade of meats not even intended for Christmas, but for the day the local farmers paid their annual tithes to this supposedly greedy rector. Yet there is little evidence to suggest Woodforde overdid it, except now and then with the bottle, or that he took any of his habits too far. Indeed, as the existence of the diary itself proves, his habits, even habits of mind, were slow of change. At one point he tried to cure himself of beginning every entry in the same old manner — 'I breakfasted, dined, &c. again at home' — but his resolution did not last; perhaps he needed that formula to concentrate his mind or prime his pen. If his pleasure in food was a constant support of his days, it was not until May 1791 that in these pages he made a daily meal, as it were, of the contents of his table. Thitherto, as we have suggested, he had taken note only of feasts he provided for guests or had consumed at other tables. Puritanical opinion has sometimes branded him a dreary glutton, but the fact that red meat rather than green vegetables or white bread was at the heart of eighteenth-century diet tends to distort the picture of life at the parsonage into an orgiastic unreality. Besides, Woodforde strikes one as far too fastidious a figure to be branded the kind of rollicking trencherman of a cleric cartooned in a Rowlandson print. Properly, he viewed dinner as no mere punctuation, but the social high point of the day, and thus worthy of honourable record.

His drinking is less frequently mentioned in the later years than at Oxford, where on some of the earlier days he saw fit to write of nothing but the bottle of wine he had consumed: unexceptionable perhaps, until you realise it was port wine, chased during the college day by ample other refreshment. In Norfolk it is not until August 1790 that he estimates his intake—'near a pint of port wine every day'—failing, of course, to take into account the tubs of gin and rum deposited at irregular intervals on his doorstep by smugglers, not to mention the small beer often brewed at the parsonage. The impression is that after Oxford's distinct insobriety Woodforde was wise enough to do nothing to very great excess—he is sharp about tipsiness in his brothers, nicely choosing the word merry, no less than in his servants—but neither he nor his careful doctor related his painful illnesses to dietary or alcoholic practices.

One or two points may be borne in mind while reading. The first (not intended as an excuse) is the absurdity of any attempt to select him; an editor is bound to fail him gloriously. For Woodforde is the most uncuttable of diarists because of the way the clock ticks on and on in the very plod of his words. The effect of his companionable voice is dependent not on drama, event, revelation, but on the daily inexorability of the passage of time in a not unpleasant place where little of ultimate moment was occurring. 'Something very agreeable and with which I was greatly pleased', he wrote on 19 May 1770, 'happened this evening. It gave me much secret Pleasure and satisfaction.' Though we are at no point told what, it is never an annoyance when Woodforde thus sidesteps or suppresses a confidence; he himself knows the answer, after all, and we were not meant to be there in the first place. Rarely, therefore, do we feel we are prying. On the whole, with an exercise of sympathy, we are simply becoming Woodforde as we read, sitting in his chair as he feels for the next word, tasting that word as a due and accurate reflection of the day's often crass reality. Entering into the person of James—few but his family would have dared such name-dropping familiarity—is a way of seeing his century in fresh-minted terms. No amount of history written with hindsight can be anything like as good as a document never meant to be read.

It is sufficiently odd for comment that over the years many Woodfordes, both before and after our engaging friend in Norfolk, have written diaries, the first by a Steward of Northampton, Robert Woodforde (1606–54). Another later in the same century enjoyed a dramatic end, posthumously destroyed in the Great Fire of London. From Mary in the elegant 1680s to Julia in the romantic 1820s and long beyond, the Woodfordes persisted in documenting a private view of their times. Evidently by tradition these efforts were not left to moulder in attics but handed down, give or take an accident, from one generation of Woodfordes to the next. It was Dr R. E. H. Woodforde who passed to his patient J. D. Beresford the sixty-eight little black-bound notebooks of his ancestor's diary with the suggestion that Beresford, to relieve a current illness, might find the leisure to form an opinion of their worth.

The result of this convalescence was an unparalleled window into the eighteenth century. Beresford's five-volume selection from the diaries, missing a great deal of Woodforde's earlier years at Oxford and in Somerset, indeed concentrating almost entirely on Weston Longville, was published by his subject's own university press between 1924 and 1931. Five years later he shortened it to a single volume. Beresford, killed in London by enemy action in 1940, cast himself as an avuncular go-between linking to our own more flighty times the little serious world of that more antique England which in his view Woodforde reflected. By setting the heavily cut text within a liberal commentary of his own, he put himself in front of his material—but, to his credit, only to prevent people from misunderstanding its quaintness. He had little idea how deeply it would appeal to inter-war readers starved of a gentle past. An editor more lucid and meticulous by far, however, is R. L. Winstanley, who for the Parson Woodforde Society since 1979 has been transcribing from its home in the Bodleian and supplying with detailed notes the full text of the diary, so far complete to 1781. My own selection has enjoyed the advantage of Winstanley's monumental valour and application in preparing these privately printed typescripts. Though with his permission I have also plundered his punctilious notes, I have chosen in this edition to keep apparatus to an essential minimum, allowing the text to speak for itself in the interest of uninterrupted readability. Meanwhile I recommend anyone who becomes properly besotted by the implacable daily dose of James Woodforde's domestically panoramic view of his period to enquire of the Parson Woodforde Society (which would be delighted to welcome new members) whether copies of these volumes are still available at so unusually modest a cost.

I have tried in these pages, a fraction of the whole, to catch the steady throb of life that courses unchecked through the diary, by rarely letting a month pass without an entry, by keeping an eye on the serial stories that now and then, to Woodforde's consternation or amusement, disconcert the composure of his life, and by allowing plenty of appearances to the characters

xvii

who over long periods haunt his days whether he liked them or not. Among these are the Custances who favoured him and sent him grapes, Nancy who succoured him while aching for a life of her own, his maid Sukey who saddened him so by her dalliance, a whole pack of familiars who depended on his income and patronage, the fellow priests who met at intervals for blow-outs, the blacksmith who dropped off illegal gin on his doorstep at night—and an endless list of others for whom we fall, who entrance us, whom the pages body forth, who fashion the eighteenth century all over again for us. These people, not least of them the dear James Woodforde himself, are not so much a living past as an instant present.

EDITORIAL NOTE

In this abridged version of the diaries, the text follows James Woodforde's idiosyncratic use of capitals, his spelling and punctuation. Where lines or words in the original manuscript are illegible, the omission is marked by a —— dash in the text.

This edition presents a great quantity of material never before published except in the typescript transcription available only to the members of the Parson Woodforde Society.

1759

July *21st*. Made a Scholar of New-College.

August *19th*. Went to Bristol to see my Brother Jack.

28th. We went & saw Milbury House (belonging to Lord Ilchester) all over, which I think is the best furnish'd House I ever saw.

28th. We lodged at the Kings Arms at Evershot, where we had exceeding good Port Wine.

29th. Went with a Posse at Abbotsbury to see the Sea, which being very rough, and very hazy Wether, disapointed me.

30th. Came back to Ansford.

31st. I went to Sanford to see my Estate.

September *1st*. I had a pr of New Shoes of Dunford.

3rd. Another pr of New Shoes of Dunford. Went & saw the Bear Baiting at Avord.

4th. Sister Jenny and I went & saw Mrs Melliar at Gallhampton The Counsellor being at Plymouth.

4th. Jenny finished my Surplice.

8th. I began to learn French.

13th. Miss Paine of Shepton-Mallett came here. N.B. We made Cyder, being very soon.

16th. Mr Rook called (after Dinner) at our House (with him was a Gentleman whose name was Vyvyan) going in a Post-Chaise to Winton, but unluckily we were all at Church. So after Service I went up but Papa could not, being bad with the Gout. N.B. One Mr Russ of Shepton-Mallet who brought Miss Payne, came after her again but he being so very drunk, and very late, we would not let her go.

I

19th. Mr Humphrey of Bristol & Captain Lorrain of the Milford (a Merchant-Man carrying a Letter of Marque which sails in about three weeks for Jamaica) dined with us.

21st. Papa had but a very bad night, his legs a little easier. William carried home Miss Payne before I was up.

23rd. Papa a great deal worse then ever, not able to get out of his chair; so there were no Prayers at Ansford. Mr Rook & Mr Vyvyan in their return from Winton breakfasted here this Morning, and afterwards they went home. Papa so bad that he could not see them.

24th. Papa somewhat better (I thank God) than he was. Went to Bruton feast and came home very late at night about 11 oclock —all Painter Clarkes fault.

27th. Went & saw my Uncle at Wells, who was extremely well; I saw the Dean at my Uncles, after Dinner I went & saw Young Holliway who brought me going about five miles. Papa near the same as he was Yesterday.

30th. Papa brave (I thank God) but don't venture out yet. Mr Penny was so kind as to serve for him this Afternoon. Mr Penny desired me to carry his Gold-Watch to Oxon to be mended, which accordingly I accepted it.

OCTOBER *1st*. Set out this Morning for Oxford from Ansforde, dined at Mrs Warren at the Black Lyon in Deptford. Thence by Yearnbury Castle, & through some Part of Maddington, which is 5 Miles from Deptford Batch. Thence to Netheravon which is 5 Miles from Maddington, thence to Everly, which is 5 Miles from Netheravon, and lodged (at the Rose & Crown kept by Mr Day) that night.

2nd. Set out from Everly that Morning & came to Sharvord, which is 7 miles from Everly, thence to Winterburn, which is 4 Miles from Shavord, thence to Hungerford, which is 4 Miles from Winterburn, thence to Newtown, which is 3 Miles from Hungerford, thence to Shapwick, which is 4 miles from Newtown, thence to Farnborough, which is 6 Miles from Shapwick, where we din'd at the Hare & hounds kept by Mr Warner. Thence to Abby Milton, which is 8 Miles from Farnborough, then to Abbingdon, which is 4 Miles from Abby Milton, thence to Oxon which is 6 Miles from Abingdon, where we lodged, I at Nicolls Room New. Coll. & my Man at the Blue Boar in fish Street. I sup'd at the Com. Room & then to bed.

5th. Doctor Brown chosen Vice-Chancellor, & Dr Randolph's time being out, very high words between the Senior Proctor & Doctor Randolph.

6th. Geree, Peckham and myself had a Hogshead of Port from Mr Cropp of Southampton.

8th. Had, of Mr Prince the Bookseller in New-Coll. Lane, a Standish with Sand, Ink, Wafers, & Half a Hundred of Pens.

9th. Had Mother Stockly for my Laundress at 15 a Quarter. Tahourdin supp'd with me at Mr Nicolls Rooms who lent them to me for the present. Had a bottle of my Wine that I bought of Hadley.

10th. Had another Bottle of Hadley's Wine.

14th. Mr Turner Junr of this Coll. died this Afternoon, about 3 o clock, in a deep consumption. Age 35. Spent the Evening with Mr Simpkinson, Mr Geree, and a stranger, at Mr Baldwins Rooms. Had another Bottle of Hadlys Wine.

15th. I breakfasted at Kinnersly's Coffee House in New-Coll. Lane, with Geree. Had a Quarter Hundred of faggots & a sack of Coal of Mrs Griffiths. Mr Carne of Oriel Coll. dined with me in Hall. Had another Bottle of Hadly's Wine.

17th. Mr Henry Turner buried, at 10 o clock at night by Mr Gebal one of our Chaplains, in the Cloisters in a very plain & decent manner.

18th. Had of Mr Prince an unbound Wallis's Logick. Very great rejoyceings this night on the taking of Quebec.

20th. Mr Geree & Mr Haynes Junr of Oriel Coll. spent the Evening with me in Mr Sanderson's Rooms. Had another Bottle of Hadly's Wine. Mr Lucas C.F. made a Fellow of New-Coll. by the death of Mr Turner Junr.

3

26th. I declaimed in Chapel, upon, Pompeius adhuc imberbis triumpho potitus est: Affirmatur.*

28th. Breakfasted at Mr Woodhull's of Braze-Nose Coll. with Hobhouse, Simpkins, Heath, & Peckham. Laid in Mr Greens Rooms one night for Funn.

30th. Went with Masters a shooting to Stanton Woods.

DECEMBER *22nd.* Statute reading in Chapel. Had my Study paper'd by Ward the Upholsterer. Had 2 Locks clear'd by Bozwell the Smith. Had a Letter from my Father. My great Aunt Ann Woodforde died of the smallpox at Bicester this morning.

24th. Had the 6 Lecture of Phill Hays. Had a bottle of my Wine.

25th. I received the Sacrament being Xmas Day. The Warden dined in Hall with us. The Bussars gives us Scholars 8 Bottles of Wine, to drink at Dinner Time. they likewise give us a Qtr of a Cheshire Cheese. We have 2 large Grace Cups between Courses. We have Rabbits for Supper, 1 Rabbit between three, at the expence of the Domus. Sent a Letter to my Father.

26th. Had a Bookcase put up in my Study by Bozwell. Had a Bottle of my Wine.

27th. Had 2 Bottles of my Wine.

28th. Had the 7 Lecture of Phill Hays. Had 2 Bottles of my Wine.

29th. Had 2 Bottles of my Wine.

31st. Had 3 Bottles of my Wine.

* 'Pompey, while still beardless, obtained a triumph: affirmed.'

1760

JANUARY *2nd*. Had a tooth drawed by one Webb. Had a Bottle of my Wine. Had the 8 Lecture of Phill Hays.

3rd. Had a Bottle of my Wine. Had a Pencil of Prince the Bookseller.

4th. My Uncle Thomas came here in his way to Bicester, before going to act as Executor for my Uncle at Wells, my Aunt leaving my Uncle at Wells her sole Executor. I dined with my Uncle at the Kings Arms. I supp'd & spent the Evening with my Uncle & Mr Prince the Bookseller.

5th. My Uncle breakfasted with me at my Rooms in New-Coll. & then he sett out immediately for Bicester with Mr Prince, who went with him. I sent an Oxford Almanack to my Father by my Uncle Thomas.

6th. Had a Bottle of my Wine.

8th. Had the 9 Lecture of Phill Hays. Phill Hays dined with me in Hall. Had a Bottle of my Wine.

FEBRUARY *16th*. Ridly took his Batchelor's Degree, & treated the B.C.R.* with Wine all the Afternoon & Night. I cutt my Hand very much with a Glass Bottle.

17th. Had a Bottle of my Wine. Supp'd and spent the Evening with Macock Junr of Lincoln Coll. Commoner. Had a Bottle of Friers Balsome of Mrs Macock.

18th. Had a Bottle of my Wine.

MARCH *7th*. Was up in the Hall from 7 in the Morning till 12, at the Crown Barr with Judge Adams. Caswall and I had a

* Bachelors' Common Room.

Hogshead of Cropp's best Port. Spent the Evening with Edgar of Oriel Coll. at his Lodgings in the Lane.

8th. Had a Pr of Doe Leather Gloves of the Woodstock Man.

9th. Had a Bottle of my Wine.

10th. Sent a Letter to my Father by Mr Penny who goes out of Town very betimes to Morrow Morning.

12th. Had a Lecture of Phill Hays. Had a Bottle of my Wine.

APRIL *29th.* Went & play'd Crickett being the first time of our Clubb's playing. N.B. we play'd in Port Meadow.

MAY *14th.* Plaid at Crikett in Port-Meadow, The Winchester against the Eaton, and we Winton: beat them.

15th. Supp'd & spent the Evening at the Coffea House.

16th. Lent Green half a Dozen of my Wine. Had a Lecture of Phill Hays.

JUNE *2nd.* Had a Lecture of Orthman. Play'd at Crickett in Port Meadow, with Hooke & gave him tea, for half a dozen of Port, & was beat. Dined upon the Rump of Beef that I won of Green, with Hooke, Hearst, &c. Pd my half dozen of Wine. Supp'd & spent the Evening in Greens Rooms with Hooke, & a Stranger.

3rd. Hired a harpsichord of Cross & sent his Spinnet off. Supp'd, spent the Evening in Hooks Room's, with Hearst, & Green & a Stranger. Laid there all night.

JULY *18th.* Hired a Horse of Castel to go into the Country for Half a Crown the first day & last, & one Shilling for all the days between. Set out for the Country this very morning. Breakfasted & dined at the Hare & Hounds in Farnborough. Laid at the Rose Crown at Everly where I danced.

30th. Went to Allhampton with Sister Jenny to see Brother & his Wife & Children. Brother & I walked to Wraxhall to speak with Mr Willmotts Second Son the Organist, but he was not

6

come back from Bristol Fair. We drank one Bottle of Cyder with the Old Man, & then marched back again. Jenny & I supped at Brothers. Sent my Oxford Hack by William to Mr Plucknetts, because his Man sets out for Oxon at ten o'clock this very night.

AUGUST *27th*. Mr Malock, & Mr Spry his Steward called here this Morning, but did not stay, Papa being not at Home. Papa came back from Bristol this Afternoon leaving Tom behind at Mr Patty's upon Tryall. Brother Jack sent his Sister Jenny by Papa a very great Curiosity, being the crucifixion of our Saviour put in a little Vial. Papa gave me a Pr of Silver Buckles, which he brought from Bristol wch cost him 0.15.0. Mrs White supp'd here. Jemmy & Dickey Clarke supp'd & spent the Evening here.

SEPTEMBER *15th*. Went a Coursing this Morning with Mr Coleman and some Raff—caught one Hare which Papa had.

OCTOBER *6th*. Went to Wells with my uncle Tom to Treasurers. Turnpikes—pd 0.0.1. We dined at the Treasurers. Gave my Uncles Man Robin 0.1.0. My Uncle gave me 1.1.0. I gave my Uncle a List of the Fellows of New-College, with the Livings belonging thereto. At the Fountain for my Horse pd 0.0.5. Gave the Hostler 0.0.1. We came Home after Dinner. At Cards this Evening lost 0.0.2.

9th. Mama gave me four Yards of 4s 3 penny Cloth, 0.17.0. For Snuff being an Ounce 0.0.1½. Mr Clarke the Doctor supp'd & spent the Evening here.

Oxford

25th. Had of Mr Clarke of Oriel for the draught that I had of Mr Penny the 7th of this Month 20.0.0. Had a Bottle of my Wine. At Cards with Brewer, Peckham, & Reynell lost 1.6. Had the Cloth that Mama gave me, made up, and brought Home this night, with a Pr of Worsted Breeches, and a Worsted

Waitscoat. N.B. King George the 2nd died this morning at nine o'clock, there being an Express just arrived from London here this Evening at five o'clock.

NOVEMBER *27th*. Sent a Letter to my Father. Gave Dods Boy 0.0.1. Fruit Shop 0.0.2. Had a Lecture of Orthman &c. I changed the draught of £20 with Mr Mallachip. Gave away 0.0.1. For Porter 0.0.1. Haynes Junr supp'd and spent the Evening with me in the Batchelors Common Room, viz, ours.

DECEMBER *9th*. At Billiards with Cotton 0.0.6. At Hazards with Cotton & Williams 0.1.0. Cotton owes me for Hazards 0.0.6. Went with Tom Robinson to Mr Tole's Dancing School, where we staid till ten at night. Supp'd with Tom Robinson at the Kings Head upon Sausages where I pd 0.0.6 and for Porter 0.0.3. At Mr Toles for the Fidler &c. 0.1.0. N.B. at Mr Toles there were 1.6 over for which we all cast lots & which I won being 0.1.6.

25th. I received the Holy Sacrament being Christmas-Day. At the Communion gave 0.1.0. We had Wine, Cake, & Cheese given us being Christmas Day, & Rabbits for Supper. Peckham sent back my Great Coat. Lent Reynell my Great Coat. Took a Walk with Nancy Bignell & her sister this Evening.

26th. Had a Bottle of my Wine. For a Silver Thimble 0.1.6. Had a Letter from Burland. Gave Betsy Bignell a Silver Thimble. Lent Hook two Bottles of my Wine. Supp'd, & spent the Evening at the Kings Head with Cotton where I paid 0.2.0.

1761

JANUARY *7th*. Peckham, Loggin, & Webber went with me to Halse's the Sadler, where I threshed his apprentice Crosier for making Verses on me. For Fruit 0.0.2. At Cards with Brewer, Williams, & Peckham lost 0.5.0. At Piquet with Peckham afterwards lost 0.0.6. A Betting with Williams lost 0.0.6. Sat up all night with Hook in the B.C.R. and then went with Hook to the New-Inn and there I saw him set of in the Glocester Coach. Had two Bottles of my Wine in the B.C.R.

28th. Peckham walked round the Parks for a Wager, this Morning; he walked round the Parks three Times in 26 Minutes, being 2 Mile & a Quarter. Williams & myself laid him a Crown, that he did not do it in 30 Minutes, and we lost our Crown by four minutes. I owe Peckham for Walking 0.2.6. For Fruit 0.0.1. For Porter for Boteler & myself 0.0.2.

FEBRUARY *13th*. A Public Fast for our Fleets & Armies. At Cards in my Room with Dyer, won a Pr of stockings, 3 stocks, & 5 Bands. Valued at 0.7.0. Had my dinner carried to Geree's Room at two o'clock, where I dined with Geree, Berkely Junr, & Dyer.

MARCH *18th*. Paid Mr Badcock for an Norway Oak Beaurou, about a year ago had of him 2.5.0. My Quarter is up with Parsons my Barber, & henceforth for a Barbers coming to me twice a Week, I am to give four shillings Per Quarter from this day. N.B. He charged me ten Shillings for my last Quarter, and coming but three in a Week, so I think I have order'd it much better this very day. I owe Parsons for that Quarter 0.10.0. For Fruit 0.0.6. Gave a Poor Woman 0.0.1. Mr Fisher the

9

University Registrar died this Afternoon of an Apoplexy. Had a Bottle of Wine from the Coffee House in the B.C.R.

APRIL *20th*. For Fruit 0.0.1½. For Porter 0.0.1. Laid again in Geree's Rooms. I had my name taken out of the Crickett Clubb, because I could not go either Mondays, or Thursdays, being Dancing Days.

MAY *21st*. Mundy a Gent Comm. of this House took a Master of Arts Degree by honour, being only 3 Years & half standing. Had a Letter from my father with a draught of Ten pound, eight Shilling. For Fruit 0.0.5. Mundy treated the B.C.R. all the Evening with Punch & Port. I went to bed soon, and about 4 o'clock in the morning, Mundy, & Williams, Ballard, Pitters, & Reynell, Webber broke open my outward Door, and then broke my Bedchamber Door, all to shatters for Funn. N.B. They were all as drunk as Pipers.

JUNE *14th*. Had a Bottle of Geree's Wine in the B.C.R. For Porter 0.0.2. For strong Beer at a Place in Holliwell, with Hearst, Loggin, Bell, Russell, & Ballard where we spent the Evening, and I paid there 0.1.0. Hearst, Bell, & myself, being in Beer, went under Whitmore's Window, and abused him very much, as being dean, he came down, and sent us to our Proper Rooms, and then we Huzza'd him again, & again. We are to wait on him to Morrow.

JULY *21st*. I was made, (together with Webber, Peckham, & Reynell) a Fellow of N. College. We were examined by Mr Whitmore. Paid Pope Beever the publick Notary, for swearing me 0.3.6. Mr Simmonds the Sub-Warden admitted us, the Warden being out. For subscribing to the declaration at the Vice-Chancellors (Doctor Brown of Queens Coll.) gave his Servant 0.1.0. Gave the Choristers 0.1.0. Gave George the Porter 0.1.0. For Fruit 0.0.3. For Porter 0.0.1. Gave a Poor

Man 0.0.1. Peckham paid me 0.6.6. Peckham, Webber, myself & Reynell treated the B.C.R. all the Evening with Wine and Punch. Hayward, George Prince, and Whitmore come into the B.C.R. and spent the evening with us. Had from the C. House this Evening a Bottle of Rum in the B.C.R. Had 2 Bottles of Geree's Wine this evening in the B.C.R. For Lemons, Sugar &c I owe Dod 0.1.3 which is all that we had a piece for our Treat.

AUGUST *17th*. I took a Ride this morning upon The Grey. Had a new Saddle Cloth for my Horse for which I am to give 0.3.6. For a Ribband for the Front of the Bridle I am to give——. For Circingle I am to give——. Gave Pudsy the Boy at Jackson to take great Care of my Horse 0.0.6. Gave the Grey Horse 2 feeds of Oats for which I am to give 0.0.4. To a Ride into Port Meadow this afternoon where I saw some of the Race Horses exercise. For Fruit 0.0.6½. Gave a Boy 0.0.1. Gave a little Boy in Holliwell 0.0.1. Gave a Poor Man of Shottiver Hill 0.1. For Porter 0.0.1. Had a Bottle of my Wine in the B.C.R. At Bowles in our Green with Berkeley sec'dus, Bathurst, & Mr Baldwin— neither won or lost.

18th. At Bowles in our Green with Mr Baldwin, Bathurst, & Berkeley Sec'dus—Paid to the Gardner & lost in all 0.2.0. Rode down to Port Meadow upon my Grey Horse—where I saw the Freemens Horses* for five Pounds run and one— Williams by Carfax won the Five Pounds, and one Cox won the Stakes.

19th. For Fruit 0.0.4. Rode down the Grey Horse into Port Meadow with Hearst, & Bell—no sport this Day, there being but one Horse enter'd to run this day, so that Horse (named Molly Long Legs, belonging to Ld Bolingbroke) had ten Guineas and sent of. For a List of the Horses 0.0.1. At the Coach & Horse Booth, with Hearst, Bell, Stockwell, and one

* An ancient right enjoyed by the Freemen of Oxford is to turn their horses loose to graze on Port Meadow.

John Simpson a Rider to Mr Churchill, who rides Ill bred
o.2.o. Gave my Horse two feeds more this Day for which I owe
o.o.4. There was a shabby Race between Rigby, Williams, &
another man, for half a Guinea each the last won.

20th. For Fruit o.o.2. For a second-hand bristol stone* Stock
Buckle of Lock o.6.o. For a Pr of second-hand bristol stone
Knee Buckles there o.5.o. Had a Bottle of my Wine in the
B.C.R. Rode down to Port Meadow upon my little grey Horse,
with Nicholls, and Bell, where we saw nine Horses start for fifty
Pound, and won by Mr Stevens's Leopard, the Stakes was won
by Lord Bolingbroke's Bounce. At the Coach & Horse Booth
with Bell, Hearst, John Simpson rider, Stockwell, & Middleton
for Punch o.1.o. For Porter for Bell and me o.o.2.

21st. Our Manciple presented me this morning with a very
handsome Plate of Apricots. Gave Dod my old Suit of Blue
Cloaths. Gave Joe Cook an old College Scout, a pr of old
Leather Breeches. Gave Jack that waits on me o.1.o. Rode
down to Port Mead with Hearst, Bell, and Russell. I back up
three to two with Hayward of All-Souls Coll. that after Wild-
mans Horse Leeds, had won the first Heat, he did not win the
Plate — but he did, and therefore I lost with Hayward to the
value of o.2.o. At the Coach & Horse Booth with Hayward and
Hearst o.2.o. Hearst laid me four to one that Madam got the
stakes, and I took him up twice. N.B. There were only two
started for stakes, Madam, & Moscow — Madam won the stakes
and I lost with Hearst o.2.o. We had a Neck and breast of
Venison for Dinner, and we dined at the High Table only the
Junr Fellows, Chaplains, and organist. After we went into the
B.C.R. afterwards, with the Chaplains and Organist, 'till Race
Time. N.B. The Venison comes out of Walton Chase, a Present
of the Gentleman named Mr Smith.

22nd. For a Jackson's Paper o.o.2½. Gave young Piddington
the Chorister o.o.1½. For Fruit o.o.2. For Porter o.o.1. Went

* A transparent rock-crystal found in the Clifton limestone near
Bristol.

into the Senr Comm. Room after dinner with George Prince and spent the Afternoon there with Whitmore, Baldwin, & Boteler.

23rd. Paid Jackson (where I keep my Horse). For eight Nights Grass 0.4.0. For Corn for right Day 0.2.6. Gave John Boteler for a burning glass* 0.1.0. At the Coffea House for Tea this afternoon 0.0.5. Spent the Afternoon in the Temple† in the Bowling Green with Whitmore, and two strangers of his from Cambridge and George Prince, Nicholls, Captain Hall, a Guest of Mr Prince's and Boteler.

24th. Set out for Ansforde this Morning at 5 o'clock. Gave Jackson's Boy Ridey 0.1.0. Turnpikes, pd 0.0.4. Between Milton and Farnborough I overtook one Wills of Wadham Coll. as he was going so far as Wincaunton. We breakfasted at Farnborough and there each pd 0.1.2. I gave the Hostler there 0.0.2. We got to Everly by one o'clock where we dined and each paid 0.2.0. One gave the Girl & the other gave the Hostler each 0.0.6. We baited our Horses again at Chicklade this Afternoon, each pd 0.1.0. We came to the Bear in Wincaunton at eleven o'clock this Night, and being so much fatigued; we took our Lodgings here this Night, and very good they were.

25th. Mr Wills went away this Morning before I got up some time. For Breakfast, Horses &c. at the Bear in Wincaunton pd 0.2.5. Gave the Hostler 0.0.6. Gave the Chambermaid 0.0.6. Came Home this Morning to Ansforde, where I dined with Papa and Mama, and Jenny. Supp'd, & laid at Home this Evening.

26th. Went up street this Morning and saw Sister White & Sister Clarke. Little Molly (Poor Girl) is on the Point of Death. Clarke Coleman dined with us to Day. Sent a Letter to Young Rooke of Somerton to desire him to come over. I gave Jenny 3 Yards of Ribband. I gave an Ivory Thimble to her. I gave

* Used, when there was enough sun, for kindling.
† An artificial temple beloved of eighteenth-century landscape gardeners and used as a summer-house.

her some Court Plaister.* Dined, Supp'd, & laid at Home.

27th. Little Molly White grows worse & worse. Din'd at Home with Papa, Mama & Jenny. Spent the Evening, & supp'd at Mr Whites, with Mrs Fookes, Mrs White, & Jenny.

28th. Little Molly White died last night about 12 o'clock. Young Mr Thomas Rooke called upon me this Morning, but would not dine with us. Supp'd & spent the Evening at Home. Went down this afternoon and saw my Uncle & Aunt Tom with Jenny from our House.

29th. Breakfasted, dined, supp'd & spent the Evening at Home. Went this Afternoon with Jenny and saw little Molly White lie dead in ye Upper Room. Went & read the News (the London Chronicle) with Brother Heighes. For Beer &c. at Ansforde Inn, For reading the News-Paper, each pd 0.0.3. I paid for reading the News only 0.0.0½. Mrs White supp'd & spent the Evening here. I gave Mama a little Pencill & Case.

30th. Went to Castle-Cary this morning, where I heard Mr Robin Penny preach. Dined, supp'd, & spent the Evening at Home. Went this Afternoon to Ansforde Church where I heard Papa preach. Went & saw little Molly White in her Coffin.

31st. Dined at Home. Went afterwards with Papa to little Molly Whites funeral, where I met at Mr Whites, His Brother Lawyer White, Mr Fookes, Mr Pouncett, Brother Heighes, my Uncle Tom, Mr Clarke, & Mr Penny; which is to bury her (we as Mourners). We all had a White Hat-Band and a Pr of White Gloves, but Papa and Mr White the Chief Mourner. We went to church about half an hour after five—where little Molly White was interr'd, & ye Service performed by ye Rev. Mr Penny. Young Mr Rooke of Somerton, in his Way to London for his Ensign's Commission supp'd, spent the Evening and laid here, not with me—but in the Blue Room at the other End of the House.

* A sticking plaster made of silk coated with isinglass, so called from the black patches formerly worn by ladies at Court.

SEPTEMBER *3rd*. I rode the Grey Horse to Wells, to see my great uncle Robert Woodforde whom I found hearty and well. I dined there with my uncle only. I put my Grey Horse up at the Fountain, kept by one of Moore's Daughters. For Hay & Corn for my Horse pd 0.0.5. Gave the Hostler 0.0.2. For One Turnpike pd 0.0.1. Came home this Afternoon, & suppd & spent the Evening, & laid at Home. N.B. it rained almost all the way to Wells, and almost back from Wells. Papa gave me this Morning 0.10.6.

6th. Went to Ansforde Church this Morning. Dined at Home. Went to Cary-Church this Afternoon and afterwards to see Mr Robin Penny, where I spent the Afternoon with Old Mr Penny, Mr John Penny, Mr Caleb Penny, One Mr Stroud and one Mr Brian, both strangers to me, and Mr Thomas Burge of South town. Mr Thomas Burge, Mr Robin and Mr John Penny, and myself went into Mr Pennys Pantry, and there eat (about six o'clock) some Venison Pasty. Supp'd at Home & spent the Evening. Mr and Mrs White supp'd and spent the Evening at our House.

7th. Had a Letter from Whitmore of N. College which informed me of my sending my Verses on the Kings Marriage to him and for which Letter Papa pd 0.0.6. At Ansforde Inn for reading the News and for some Cyder pd 0.0.6.

Oxford

OCTOBER *9th*. My Man Robin Emett, set out this Morning for Ansforde. I was very bad all last night and all this day, having got a bad boil upon my Posteriors. Dined in the B.C.R. Went to bed this Evening very soon, being worse a good deal.

10th. Had but little rest all night last. Had a violent breaking out, all over my body in the night. Had some Water gruel from the C. House which was all my Supper last night. Very bad again I was today, Morning, Evening, and Night. Had some tea & bread & Butter this afternoon from the C. House in the B.C.R. Had two Eggs put on a butter'd Toast, from the C.

House, which was my Supper. Had some Sack Whey from the C. House, this Evening, to take going to bed.

31st. Sent a Letter to my Father. At Quadrille in the B.C.R., with Ballard, Williams, & Peckham won 0.0.6. Had 2 Pr of Shoes heel-pieced & forepieced for which I owe Clements. I shall pay Clements very soon & dismiss him for his bringing in my Bill, without my sending for it. N.B. it is but 0.14.0. I lent Berkeley Senr for the Sacrament to Morrow Morn:—0. 1s 0d.

NOVEMBER *19th.* Had a Lecture of Orthman. Gave a Poor Woman 0.0.1. For Porter 0.0.1. Went this Evening to Haw's (a famous Methodist) Lecture in St Giles's Church. A very stupid, low, and bad stuff. At Quadrille this Evening in the B.C.R., with Peckham, Ballard, and Williams in all lost 0.0.6. For having my Name scratched upon my Tobacco Box by Cole 0.0.6.

DECEMBER *17th.* I have got Hearst's Room that was having a Junior Right under Bell and he will not live in it. Webber turned me out of a Senr Right in Hookes Room that was, and I think he has used me very ill, because he will not live there himself. At Cribbage this afternoon with Pitters, in his Room lost 1.0.0 that is between Russell & me, so that they owe us now but 6.0.0. Pitters pd me 0.1.0. At Cap's Billiard Table a betting won this evening 0.1.0. For Porter 0.0.2. Gave to Dods Nephew Hamstrung 0.0.1. For some soap 0.0.1.

1762

JANUARY *26th*. Reynells pd me 0.0.6. At Billiards with Reynells won 0.1.6. For one Game only 0.0.2. For Porter for Hooke & myself 0.0.4. Had a Bottle of my Wine this evening in the B.C.R., being sconced for breaking Wind, while I was making Water in the Looking Glass, in the B.C.R.; by one Reynells. At Putt with Master won 0.0.1. The Frost is gone of, so it is all over with Skating.

APRIL *11th*. I received the H. Sacrament this Morning being Easter-Day—and gave 0.1.0. Layng died this Morning while we were at Prayers, of a Consumption and of an Inflammation in his Bowels. Had a Bottle of my Wine in the B.C.R. this afternoon.

12th. For Fruit 0.0.1. Gave Dod's Son Thomas 0.0.1. Gave him half a dozen Bunns. For Porter for Weller of C.C.C. and for myself 0.0.3.

13th. For Fruit 0.0.2. Had a Bottle of my Wine in the B.C.R. For Beer at Mr Dentons up the Hill where I spent the evening 0.1.6. Gave the Maid that brought it 0.0.6. Had a Letter from my Sister Jenny by John Atwell who is come up after me.

14th. For two Shuttle-Cocks 0.0.1. For a Baskett 0.0.4. Mr Denton brought me this Morning 5 Steel Bars—for wch I am to give 0.25.0. For Porter in the B.C.R. 0.0.6. For Porter at the Porter House 0.0.1. For Oysters 0.1.0. Mr Layng was buried this evening at nine o'clock in the Cloysters, by Mr Hawkins the Sacrist, being the Senr Chaplain. My William of Wykham that I sent to be framed about a Week ago is not begun nor likely to be, therefore I have taken it away from Williams's.

* Corpus Christi College.

17

N.B. They told me a Number of Lyes concerning the Picture.

15th. Had 2 Bottles of my Wine in my Room this morning. For Pinns 0.0.2. John Atwell and Mr Penny's Man drank a Bottle of my Wine this morning in my Room. Had of Mr Fortman the Hatter a Hat for which I am to give him 0.18.0. Had 1 Dozen of Pinns out of our Butry, and have sent them home. N.B. Had a meeting of the House in the Hall. Had a Bottle of my Wine in the B.C.R.

16th. Hook overtook me at the Pack Horse as I was going into the Country, and I went and dined with him at Peasmore and he went afterwards with me to Everly where we laid. I had my Dog Pero in the Country. For 2 Turnpikes pd 0.0.2. I sent John Attwill on before. Gave Hookes Man at Peasmore 0.0.6. I lent Hook as he went with me 0.4.0. I laid at Everly at the Rose & Crown, Pero my Dog went with me.

17th. I had not Mony sufficient for a Man & 2 Horses at Everly for to pay the charge that Evening and therefore I owe 0.8.0. And out of which John Attwill is to pay as he was hired &c. 0.4.6. N.B. John Attwill and his Horses to bring me down and to pay his and his Horses expenses. For Turnpikes this Day pd 0.0.3. For my Dinner at Deptford pd 0.2.0. Gave the Waiter 0.0.4. Gave the Hostler 0.0.2. Laid at Home this Night. N.B. John Attwill & his 2 Horses was hired 5 Days for 2.2.0 but upon the Account of our Meeting being Yesterday he was obliged to stay 6 Days, and therefore I am to pay the Expences of the 6th Day, and that will make it even with him & me.

18th. Went to Cary Church this Morning and heard Jerry Houlton read Prayers and preach for Mr Penny. Was at Ansford Church this Afternoon and heard my Father. Mr William Melliar, his Brother the Counsellor, and Mr William Burge and my Uncle Tom, & Aunt and Mrs Clarke, and Frank Woodforde and the Counsellor's Eldest Son, spent the Afternoon here. Made Mama a Present of the Jarr of Pickled ——.

19th. I received my Rents from Sanford by the Hands of Robin Speer being 4.10.0. John Bowden for an Orchard pays

0.18.0. Robin Speer for a House & Orchard pays 1.10.0. George Snooke, for another House and Orchard, pays me 2.2.0. Gave Robin Speer for collecting the Rents and bringing of them over, and because he was over twice 0.2.0. Mrs White supped and spent the Evening at our House. Gave Papa a leather Snuff Box.

20th, I begun the Epistles of the G. Testament to learn and read for Orders. Gave a Poor Man 0.0.2.

JUNE *12th.* I have been studying in my Tent all the Day long the G. Testament. Sister Jenny and myself were invited this Evening to Mr White's Sheep-Shearing, but we could not go being Saturday Night, which is a very improper time to spend the Evening out any where. Papa gave me a Bottle of his bottled Porter this Evening. Mama gave me Yesterday two very good Books.

18th. Went this Morning with Mrs White, and Jenny to Shepton-Mallet. We Put our Horses up at the Hare & Hounds. Went afterwards to Mrs Payne's a distant Relation of ours, where we saw Mrs Payne (a Mantua-Maker) and her Daughter Miss Payne, who has lately been out of her Mind. Went with Miss Payne, Jenny, and Mrs White to the George Inn, where we saw the Microcosm*, a thing very well worth seeing indeed, and there I paid for all 0.4.0. For a Book of the Description of it I pd 0.0.6. We all dined at Mrs Paynes. Went this afternoon with Mrs Payne, Miss Payne, Mrs White, and Jenny, to Lawyer Whites at Shepton. & a Brother in Law to Mrs White, where we went into the Garden, and eat vast Quantities of Fruit. We drank Tea at Mrs Payne's, with Mrs Payne, Miss Payne, and little Miss Betsy White, a Daughter of Lawyer Whites. Miss Payne went with us and showed me the Presbyterian Meeting House. Went afterwards this Morning, and saw Young Mr Proviss's Garden, where Miss Proviss, a Sister to this young Mr

* Some form of spectacle, presumably a panoramic painting representing the world in miniature.

19

Proviss, and Miss Coward, were so kind as to go with us. Went and saw Shepton Church, with Mrs Payne, Miss Payne, Mrs White, and Jenny, and little Miss White, where I play'd upon the Organ some Time, as it is now altering and cleaning, by Mr Young, whom I am acquainted with.

28th. Went upon the Grey-Horse this Morning to Oxford by myself. Dined at Deptford-Batch at the Lyon upon Eggs & Bacon. Paid at Deptford for my Horse &c. o . 2 . o. Gave the Maid that waited upon me o . o . 3. For 3 Turnpikes to Deptford pd o . o . 3. Supp'd this Evening and laid at Everly at the Rose & Crown: there were a great many Gentlemen there, who met there concerning Turnpike Roads, therefore I was not waited on as I used to be. Carried a Pr of Saddle-Bags with me.

Ansford

AUGUST *2nd.* Supp'd and spent the Evening at Mr Whites with Mrs White. Jenny drank Tea at Mrs Chicke's. Archdeacon Potter of Wells, and Brother in Law to Daniel Prince my Bookseller in Oxford, called here this Afternoon (but Papa was gone down to the Lower House, and Mama was walking in the Garden, and Jenny was gone to Castle Cary, and I was up in my room reading—so he did not stay long here.)

OCTOBER *9th.* I packed up my things for Oxford, this Afternoon and they were these: 9 Shirts, 9 Stocks, 2 Cravats, 7 Pr of Stockings, 2 White Handkerchiefs, 5 Coloured Handkerchiefs, 2 Night Caps, 1 Towel, 2 Pr of Breeches—besides the things that I wear to use, 1 Pr of Leather Breeches, 1 White Coat, 1 Buff Waistcoat, 1 Great Coat.

DECEMBER *3rd.* For a Hundred of Pens of a Jew that went about selling of them in the street I gave him o . 1 . o. He asked for them at first o . 4 . o. N.B. They are what he called Office Pens, viz, the best of any. I sat over Dyer this Afternoon in the Schools, whilst he did Generals; Dyer was Respondent and Swainson of

Worcester-Coll. was the Opponent. They were not set over by any one. Dined at Dyers Rooms with Swainson, and spent the afternoon there. Had a Black Sermon-Case From Princes, for which I owe 0.1.3. For six Paper books to write Sermons in I owe him 0.1.6. My Stewardship being over for the last Week, I cast up the Stewards Books this Morning, and this Afternoon sent them to the Bursars, for they to inspect them. N.B. I am to receive of the Manciple for being Steward this last Week 0.6.6. Supp'd and spent the Evening at the Kings Head in High-Street, with Cooke, Russell, Dyer, Williams Junior; and I paid there for eating and drinking 0.1.6. N.B. We went on Purpose to drink Porter there.

1763

JANUARY *4th*. Went a skating this Morning upon the River Thames; and I skated from Folly Bridge quite to Elfly, and back again. For some Ale at Elfly, I paid o.o.2. For putting on my Skates gave a Man at a Booth there upon the River, by Folly Bridge o.o.2. For breaking a Glass last Night in the B.C.R. I pd this Afternoon o.o.6. For breaking a Pint Cup likewise o.o.4. For breaking 4 Pipes likewise o.o.2. For Wine this Afternoon in B.C.R. o.o.6. For Porter this evening in the B.C.R. for Taunton and Oglander Junr, and myself I paid o.o.6. They are to treat me another night. For Fruit o.o.1.

24th. Went with Nicholls this Morning a skating, and we skated down to Abingdon where we dined, and for our dinners there &c. each of us pd o.2.6. We were going down about one Hour and Half; N.B. We walked above two Miles out of it. It is about 10 Miles by Water. Gave a Fellow for putting on my Skates o.o.2. For Porter for Nicholls & myself o.4. Supp'd and spent the Evening at Home in the B.C.R. Had a Letter from Captain Rooke this evening. Had a Letter from Burland this evening, and he informs me that there will be no Ordination there this Lent.

FEBRUARY *17th*. I dined at the Chaplains Table with Pickering and Waring, upon a roasted Tongue and Udder, and we went on each of us for it o.1.9. N.B. I shall not dine on a roasted Tongue & Udder again very soon. For Wine this afternoon o.o.6. For Porter for Geree & myself o.o.3. Sent a Letter to Fisher at Hilmersdon near Bath, and with it paid (it being put into the Box after one o'clock) o.o.1. For a Paper, concerning the Days & Hours the Oxford Post sets out, at the Post Office o.o.1. For Fruit o.o.3. Caldecot was admitted this Afternoon, a Scholar of New Coll. vacated by John Boteler, who has got a good Living of his Grandfather's giving. I let Caldecot this Morning Mr Burlands Rooms, for which he is to pay per Annum £4 os od from this day.

28th. Breakfasted with Geree again. Went with Dyer, Russell, and Master, after Dinner; down to the Castle to see the Prisoners; where we drank two Bottles of Port, and for Wine, &c. I pd o.1.6. William Cartwright, a young good-looking Fellow; who is in the Castle for a High Way Robbery; drank with us the last Bottle, and smoaked a Pipe with us, and seemed very sorry for what he had committed. We gave him between us o.2.0. For Porter o.o.2. A Betting in our Lane at the Billiard Table this Evening, won o.6.6. Of Master won o.2.0. And of Williams Junr won o.4.6. Spent the Evening at Hays's Rooms, (the Chaplain) with Dyer, Geree, Cooke, Pickering, and Waring. We sat up rather too late. Dyer was very drunk, and very quarrelsome with one and all of us.

MARCH *30th*. Geree breakfasted out this Morning, or else he would have breakfasted in my Room, as I make breakfast this Week. I have got a bad sore throat, and I mixed up some Rum, Hony, & Oil, to take this evening going to bed. For Oil at Langfords o.o.2. For Hony there o.o.1. I have got Rum of my

Own. For Wine this afternoon 0.0.6. For Porter this evening 0.0.2. For an enamelled Pen-Case, and Ink-Vessel of Goldwire I owe him 0.6.0. N.B. Goldwire owed me 1.6 that being deducted, I owe him for the Pen-Case &c. 6.0 so that I gave in all for the Pen-Case &c. 7.6.

APRIL *10th*. Breakfasted at Geree's again. Dyer had Company to his Room to Breakfast, therefore he did not breakfast with us at Geree's. For Wine this afternoon 0.0.6. Took a Walk this Evening with Caldecott towards Godstow. For Punch this evening 0.0.6. I sent a Baskett with two Dozen of Bunns, and a Letter to my Cousin Frank Woodforde, at Winchester College, by Croton the Winchester Carrier; for the Carriage of them I pd 0.1.0. Our Butler packed them up as it is customary for him. We give Per Dozen for Bunns in our Buttery 0.2.0. Had a dozen of Buns to my Rooms. Gave Dod's little Boy Jim, half a dozen of Bunns out of Buttery.

MAY *2nd*. Breakfasted at Geree's. Webber breakfasted with us. For an Ounce of 10s Tea 0.0.7½. Our Warden was taken very ill last Friday Night; but now he is brave again. We went the Home–Progress this afternoon. Mr Whitmore acted as Sub-Warden; the Sub-Warden being gone the out–Progress. For Wine at the Blue Boar on the Progress 0.0.6. Supp'd in the Chequer with the Senr People upon a very good Supper, as is customary on this Evening for the Junr Fellows, and Scholars, to sup there; we all spent the evening in the Senr Common Room, where we each of us (except the Scholars) send a Bottle of Wine. The Scholars are treated always on this evening by the Sub-Warden with Punch in the Senr Common Room. Sale spoke to me this Morning concerning the Curacy of Newton-Purcell,* which I have now promised him to take and serve the Sunday after Trinity Sunday; it is about 20 Miles from Oxford;

* A village on the Oxfordshire border about four miles from Buckingham, where JW agrees to serve the parish during the period of the

and I am to receive Per annum for serving it, besides Surplice Fees 28.0.0. I am only to serve it during Mr Sale's Proctorship. I have got another Wist upon my right Eye again, and it is very much inflamed, by my going out in the Wind to day. N.B. The Supper that we had this Evening in the Chequer is put upon all our Names, whether present or absent. I played the Organ in our Chapel this Morning, at eleven o'clock Prayers.

5th. Dyer dined in my Room and spent the Afternoon with me. My Eye is quite brave and well. I have been out all day to day. Went to St Mary's this Morning, & heard Jeffrison of Queens-Coll. preach; and after it heard the Coronation Anthem sung there. This is the Thanksgiving day for the late Peace between France, Spain, and England.* Dyer and Berkeley Sec'dus drank Tea with me this afternoon. At Billiards with Dyer for Games 0.6. Bedford supped with me this evening, and afterwards we went (being nine o'clock) to see the Fire Works near Folly Bridge, which were very good, it last 'till half an Hour after ten o'clock; Bedford afterwards spent the remaining part of the Evening with me. Mr Mawbourne sent me this Evening a gally Pot of Electory, and a Quart Bottle of the Decoction of Sasafras, with carraway seeds in it &c. to be taken night and morning. N.B. There were vast Numbers of People to hear the Coronation Anthem at S. Marys and likewise more to see the Fire Works.

9th. Breakfasted at Dyers again with Geree. I did Juraments in the Schools between one and two o'clock this Afternoon under some strangers that were doing Generals. Dined and spent the afternoon at Dyers. I played the Magnificat, and nunc dimittis upon our Organ this Afternoon in Chapel. I have got a Wisp come upon my Eye again, attended with a kind of a Boyle over

incumbent Mr Sale's proctorship of the University (1763–4). In fact JW gives it up after only eight weeks (see 24 July).

* At the Peace of Paris which ended the Seven Years War on 10 February Canada was ceded to England after the capture of Quebec in 1759.

it. Supp'd in the B.C.R. this Evening. Spent the Evening in my own Room by myself.

11th. Dyer and Geree breakfasted at my Room this Morning it being my Week. Webber breakfasted with us at my Room. The Harpsichord that I had of Cross, was carried away this Morning by Cross, and a Spinnet brought in his Place. I owe Cross for the Harpsichord for half a Year, at half a Guinea a Qtr 1.1.0. I am to give Cross per Qtr for the Spinnett, that I have got 0.6.0. My Eye is near the same as Yesterday. Dyer dined and and spent the afternoon with me in my Room, as I keep in. For a Pr of Candles paid Frank 0.0.6½. I was offer'd this afternoon by Fitch of Queens Coll. a Curacy worth £40 Per annum, and to be enterd upon at Michaelmas. It is in Somersett, near Taunton, the name of the Place is Thurloxton, in the Gift of Fitch's Father. I shall write to my Father concerning it to Morrow Morning; I have got to the 20th of this Month to consider of it. Fitch supp'd and spent the Evening with me at my Room, and so did Dyer. For Pipes & Tobacco of Dod this evening I paid 2. Pipes are 3 a penny 0.0.2.

20th. Took a ride this Morning early with Russell, & Fitch to Farnborough; Russell and myself went to bring Fitch going to Hungerford. We all stopt at the Hare and Hounds in Farnborough, where we all eat, & gave our Horses some Corn, we each of us paid for our eating, servants &c. 0.1.6. Fitch afterwards went for Hungerford, and we went and saw Hooke of our Coll. at Hill Green, about 3 Miles beyond Farnborough, where we stopt about four Hours, and there was one Lattin of Wad. Coll. there, and Hook's Wife. Hook keeps House there, never was there such House-keeping to be sure; It gives me a pretty Idea of a Curate's keeping House. We set out for Oxford from Hooke's, about five o'clock this Afternoon; we called at Farnborough at the Hare & Hounds, as we came along, and had a Pint of Port, and some Cake, and gave our Horses some Hay, and there we each pd 0.1.0. We were at New Coll. a little before nine. For Punch in the B.C.R. this Evening from the C.

House 0.0.6. Russell & myself breakfasted at Fitch's this Morning upon doctor.*

23rd. Breakfasted in my own Room by myself. Our Sasafras Clubb is (I am afraid) almost at an End, since Waring has been admitted. For Wine in the Bowling Green 0.0.6. For Fruit there 0.0.6. At Bowles with Fanshawe, Williams Senr, Masters, and Reynels, neither won or lost. I went this Afternoon at five o'clock, to C.C.C. to Mr Hewish the Bishop of Oxford's Chaplain, before whom I was examined for Deacon's Orders, and I came off very well. I was set over in the middle of the fifth Chapter of St Paul to the Romans, and construed that Chapter quite to the End. I was quite half an Hour examining. He asked a good many hard & deep Quaestions, I had not one Quaestion that yes, or no, would answer. I gave Hewish's Man as is customary 0.1.0. Geree and Nicholls of Our Coll. were examined this afternoon for D. Orders and came off very well. Mr Hewish is a very fair Examiner, and will see whether a Man be read or not soon. Spent the Evening with Berkely Sec'dus at Bedfords Rooms.

24th. Breakfasted in my own Rooms again. Took a ride this Morning towards Elsfield and round by Staunton upon the grey. For half a Pint of ale at Bays Water 0.0.1. Gave Jackson's other Man for taking care of the grey, and Saddle &c. 0.0.6. For Fruit 0.0.1. For Wine in the Green 0.2.0. The reason of my paying so much was the Impudence of two Gentlemen like Persons (whose names were Messrs Mercer and Loyd) pushed themselves into the Temple in our Garden, while Hooke and myself were drinking there, and drank two Bottles of Wine with us. Mercer's Wife and 2 more Ladies were with us. Mercer (who wore a gold-laced-Hat) was very drunk and very abusive to us, and Mr Loyd; Loyd is a schoolmaster at Abingdon, and Mercer's Son went to School to him. Mercer's Son was with us. Mercer went away about ten o'clock this evening, and made a great

* Either they took no breakfast but dosed themselves or they took nothing at all.

noise going through College. Mr Mercer behaved very much unlike a Gentleman. Loyd came into the B.C.R. afterwards with Hooke and myself; Mr Loyd was drunk. Mercer broke two Glasses in the Temple for which Hooke and myself + pd 0.1.0. I went to bed at eleven and left Mr Loyd in the B.C.R. with Hooke, and some more Gentlemen. At Bowles this afternoon with Loggin, Pitters, Hooke, Masters, Oglander Senr, Berkely Sec'dus, and Reynolds lost 0.11.6.

29th. At nine o'clock this Morning, went to Christ Church with Hooke, & Pitters, to be ordained Deacon; and was ordained Deacon there by Hume Bishop of Oxford. There were 25 ordained Deacons, and 13 Priests—we all received the H. Sacrament. For an Offering at the Sacrament gave 1.0. The Porter carried my Surplice to C. Church, and brought him back, for which I gave him, it being customary 0.1.0. We were in C. Church Cathedral, from nine o'clock this Morning till after twelve. For wine this afternoon in the B.C.R. 0.0.6. Supp'd and spent the evening in the B.C.R.

JUNE *1st.* I took my B.A. Degree this Morning in the Convocation House, with Reynels, Lucas, Peckham and Webber. Nicholls and Pitters, took their B.L. Degree, with us. We had a grand Procession from N. Coll. to the Convocation House. Nicholls and Pitters treated the Coll. in the Senr Common Room, before they went in Procession this Morning, with Sack and bread & Butter. I paid for my Degree to the Beadle 1.4.6. Gave the Proctors Men being customary 0.1.0. Gave the Porter for carrying my Hood 0.1.0. Gave the Choristers 0.1.0. Gave Dean Whitmore for presenting me to the Vice-Chancellor & Proctors 0.10.6. Pitters and Nicholls made a present of a Dozen of Wine between them, to the B.C.R. Reynels, myself, Lucas, Peckham, and Webber treated (as is usual) the B.C.R. after Dinner with Wine, and after supper with Wine and Punch all the Evening. We had 27 People in the B.C.R. this evening. For Fruit this afternoon 0.0.2. For dressing my Hat paid Goddard at the Golden Leg opposite the Kings-Head 0.0.6. At Bowles this afternoon in our Green with Berkely Sec'dus, Ballard, Williams, Cotton and Pitters cost 0.1.6. For Wine in the Green 0.0.6. Ballard owes me for Bowles 0.1.6. Gave Pemberton for the use of a Hood 0.1.0. I sat up in the B.C.R. this Evening 'till after twelve o'clock, and then went to bed, and at three in the Morning, had my outward Doors broken open, my Glass Doors broke, and pulled out of Bed, and brought into the B.C.R., where I was obliged to drink and smoak, but not without a good many Words. Peckham broke my doors, being very drunk, altho' they were open, which I do not relish of Mr Peckham much.

29th. For another Bottle of Cheltenham Water from Truby's in Jesus Lane 0.0.9. For another Sermon Book from Hoods 0.3. Had three Dozen of my Beer bottled and put into my Cellar in my Room this Morning; and Oglander had likewise three Dozen bottled, being Partner with me. Our Beer ran in both Common Rooms all this day being customary; when any one taps a Vessel of Beer, it runs for one day and night. For a Tin Affair to put my Letters of Orders in, at Millachips 0.1.0. For a Pocket Pistol, alias a Dram Bottle, to carry in one's Pocket, it being necessary on a Journey or so—at Nicholl's 0.1.0. Sent a Letter this afternoon to Fitch, desiring him to acquaint his Father that he may depend upon my taking the Curacy of Thurloxton at Old Michaelmas.

AUGUST *25th.* For a dozen of Shrewsbury Cakes 0.0.6. The Wig that I had of Fell, has been new-mounted, and made fit for my Tupee, and brought home this Morning by Fell, and for which I am to give him 0.7.6. Played the organ this Morning in our Chapel, throughout the whole, but the anthem. Mr Hays the Chaplain, went into the B.C.R. with me this afternoon. Had a Bottle of my Wine out of my Room this afternoon in the B.C.R. Had likewise two Bottles of my Beer this afternoon in the B.C.R. For having W.J. engraved upon my Silver-Pencil-Top

0.0.2. For a Pencil for the Silver-Top 0.0.6. Went up the Water this evening with Gauntlett, Thorpe, & Webber; they all went to a Booth in Port-Meadow, which are put up against the Races; I rowed about till they returned, wch was about a Quarter of an Hour, & then I set out for Oxford, and left them a considerable way; and I never saw them after for the whole evening—for my Boat 0.0.6.

SEPTEMBER *6th*. Mr Ward the Upholsterer spent the afternoon with me in my Room. Mr Collins spent Part of the Afternoon with us. Mr Ward came to value some Goods of mine that Mr Collins is to have, in Mr Collins's Presence. The Things that Mr Collins is to have of me, being valued by Mr Ward are these 7 Matted Chairs 1.9.0. One two flapped Oak Table 0.16.0. One Piller Cherry Tree Table 0.8.6. One Mohogany writing Table 1.1.0. A Feather Bed, Bolster, Pillow, Quilt, and three Blankets 3.3.0. Two Pr of Sheets & two Pillow Cases 0.11.0. Shovel, Tongs, Poker, Bellowes & Brush 0.5.0. A Pr of Brass Candlesticks 0.3.6. The whole that Mr Collins is to have amounts by Mr Wards Valuation to 7.17.0. Mr Ward brought me in a Bill of 6.12.10 and in it he charged for valuing the above Goods 0.5.0. For the Hire of an Old Fashioned Glass for three Years at 2s od Per Quarter 1.4.0. For the Hire of a Bedsted & Curtains and likewise for a small broken Glass for two Years at 1/6 Per Quarter 0.12.0. For Papering a Room, and divers others things had of him from 1759 4.12.10. For Porter this evening in the B.C.R. 0.0.2.

16th. I thank God I found all Friends at Ansforde well, especially at the Parsonage. Breakfasted, dined, supped, & spent the Evening (and laid at the Parsonage) with my Father, and Mother, & Sister Jane.

20th. Went this Morning with Papa & Mama and Jenny to Sherborne, where we dined at the Kings Arms at Sam Wises. Papa and Mama & Jenny went in the Post Chaise, which Papa purchased some Time ago at Bristol for 30.0.0. It is as neat and handsome a Post Chaise as ever I saw almost. It rained all the way to Sherborne, & I was almost wet through as I rode a Horse-back—a coming back we had fine Weather this Afternoon. Papa went to order a Monument for my late deceased Uncle* at Wells, who lays by his Wife in Yeovilton Church— we returned from Sherborne safe & well, and got to Ansforde about seven o'clock. Mrs White supped & spent the Evening with us—Mama bore the Journey very well. Whilst I was at Sherborne I sent a Letter to the Rev. Mr Fitch at High Hall near Winborne—Dorsett, to be informed by him later when I am to enter upon his Curacy.

26th. Went out a shooting for about two Hours this Morning, on Purpose to break in my new Dog Ranger, which was given me when a Puppy by my Tenant's Brother at Sanford whose name is Snooke. My Dog Ranger performed very well considering it being the first Time of his being out with a Gun. Mr Syndercombe dined at our House he being invited by me Yesterday—Jemmy Clarke likewise dined and spent the Afternoon with us; and they both drank Tea with us this Afternoon. Supped &c. at Home.

30th. Went this Morning upon the grey Horse immediately after breakfast, to see Mr Hoare the Bankers Gardens at Stourton with Papa and Mama, Jenny, Mr Will Melliar and his Wife, Mrs Chicke and her Niece Molly Chicke, where we spent the Whole Day; we dined at the Sign of Old Merlin at Stourton upon a boiled Round of Beef & 2 Fowls. Thro' Mrs Melliars Interest we went through Lord Ilchesters Park, going & coming back—we returned by 7 in the Evening. The Temple of Hercules in the Gardens must have cost Mr Hoare £10000, it is excessively grand. The Grotto where the sleeping Nymph laid struck me much more than any thing there. Supped and spent the Evening &c. at Home. Mrs White supped and spent the Evening with us. Gave to two poor Children for opening Gate o.o.1. For our Dinner at Stourton & seeing the Gardens, &

* Consult Brief Biographies under Robert Woodforde (1675–1762).

Servants eating and Horses came to 3 Shillings a Head. Papa paid for Mama, Jenny, himself, and me there 0.12.0.

OCTOBER *3rd*. Went to Sherborne this Morning early on Purpose upon ye Grey to get me a Beaurou of one Hoddinett a Cabinet-Maker and to get a Pound of Cocoa for Mrs Melliar of C. Cary, of one Mr Sansom, and to speak to Young Mr Toogood there whose Father keeps a Shop there, about some Mony being remitted to him (when he went to Oxford) from the Bursars of Oriel Coll. due to Mr Robin Penny who desired me to speak to him about it. Breakfasted at Sam Wise's at the Kings Arms in Sherborne upon Tea & Toast. My Dog Ranger went with me. Went to Hoddinett of Sherborne and looked upon several Beaurou's, and fixed upon a Norway Oak Beaurou which he is to send to me to Morrow, and for which he asked for, he sending it Home 3.3.0. I did not pay it there but it is to be paid for to Morrow at the Delivery of it by my Father who gives it me. I got Home by Dinner Time, and there I dined, supped, &c. &c. Mrs White supped, and spent the Evening with us. Doctor Clarke spent the Evening with us. For going thro' one Turnpike this Morning pd 0.0.1. Gave old Alice Stacy this Evening for taking care of my Dog Ranger when he was a Puppy 0.1.0.

8th. I set out a little after Breakfast for Thurloxton, which is about six Miles in the Taunton Road from Bridgewater, and got there by twelve. I put up my Horse at the Green Dragon in Thurloxton kept by one Weetch. For going thro' one Turnpike pd 0.0.1. For my eating, and drinking in Bridgewater at the Globe, and for my Horse pd 0.3.9. Gave the Chamber Maid there 0.0.6. Gave the Hostler there 0.0.6. Dined at the Green Dragon in Thurloxton, and for my Dinner, Horse, and Beer pd 0.1.6. Gave the Servant Maid there 0.0.6. Went after Dinner and enquired for one Widow Nowel, whom Mr Fitch recommended me to Board, but found upon my Enquiry that she has been dead this Year. I then desired Mr and Mrs Nowel (her Son & Daughter) to take me in, but they could not engage to take me these two Months. I then sent Mr Weetch the Landlord of the Green Dragon to one Farmer Harrison upon his recommendation, but his Wife being not at home, he could not engage. I afterwards went myself to the Esquire of the Parish whose name is Cross, and he took me at the very first Word, and likewise my Horse; which I ordered down immediately to his House, and there I supped, spent the Evening and laid in the Best Room. Mr Cross and myself agreed together concerning the Terms on which he is to take me. The Terms we agreed upon this Evening were these: That I should live as he does, (which is very well I am sure) that I should have my Linnen washed by him, and that he should keep my Horse (Corn excepted) 21.0.0, and that for every Day that I was absent, I should be allowed for each Day 0.1.1½, which per Year is 21.0.0. Mr Cross is married and has three Children all young and has another coming; Mrs Cross is a very good natured Woman, and very much like Mrs Clarke my Sister.

20th. Breakfasted, dined, supped, &c. at Mr Cross's. I took a Walk this Morning upon Kings Clift about a Mile from Mr Cross's, where there is a most noble Prospect; having a fine View of the Bristol Channel, and the Holmes's, and many Miles in Land.

27th. Breakfasted, dined, supped &c. at Mr Cross's. A Hare being found near here, Mr Cross and myself went out and coursed it before Breakfast and killed it with Mr Cross's Dogs, and a good course it was. Gave to the Man that found her 0.0.6, As it is always customary.

NOVEMBER *11th.* Breakfasted and laid at Home. After Breakfast I took a ride to Babcary to one Farmer Bowers to enquire about the Curacy of Babcary, which I hope I shall be able to undertake; it is but six Miles from my Fathers, and at present unsupplied. Farmer Bower is gone to Yeovil Market, and therefore I did not see him, but I heard there that it was not disposed of yet, and in my Return, Monday, from Thurloxton to

Ansforde, I promised to call upon Mr Bower, and to talk with him about Babcary.

24th. Breakfasted, dined and laid at Home. For half a Hundred of Oysters this Morning of an Oyster Man that I met in Mead pd 0.0.6. I pickled the Oysters myself this Morning according to the Receipt I had of Sourby.

29th. For my Horse and myself at the Globe Inn this Morning paid Mr Poles 0.3.10. Gave the Hostler there 0.0.6. Breakfasted this Morning at Padnoller—at Mr Blakes, with his Wife & Mr Hite. After Breakfast Mr Hite and me settled the Conditions upon which I was to undertake the Curacy of Babcary, Mr Hite being the Rector. The Terms that we agreed on were these—That I should be paid Quarterly 5.0.0, That I should have all the Surplice Fees, That I should have the Easter Offerings, the free Use of the Parsonage House, & Gardens & Stable, and likewise to have the Use of Mr Hites Furniture in the Parsonage House, 'till disposed of. All which we both agreed on, and from this Time I am to be the Curate. I dined, supped, and laid at Mr Cross's. For going two Turnpikes at Bridgewater pd 0.0.2. Padnoller is just six Miles from Bridgewater, and about two from Stowey.

30th. Breakfasted, dined, supped, & laid at Mr Cross's. Sent a Letter this Morning to Mr Fitch at High Hall near Winborne Dorsett, to let him know that I shall give up the Curacy of Thurloxton the ninth of January next, together with the Chapel of Newton; having got a Curacy near my Father's. I sent it by Mr Cross's Maid, as she was going to Bridgewater, desiring her to put it in the Post-Office for me. One Butcher Parsons spent part of the Afternoon with us. He lives at N. Petherton.

DECEMBER *2nd*. The wind was excessively high in the Night and continued so 'till the Morning & after. It blew many Times from Mr Cross's House. It shook my Bed like a Cradle, and it made Mr & Mrs Cross get up at two o'clock this Morning, fearful of the Roof of the House being blown in. I do not think I ever knew the Wind so high before. Breakfasted, dined, supped, &c. at Mr Cross's.

26th. Breakfasted, supped, &c. at Mr Cross's. After Breakfast we went upon Cream to Taunton, to speak with Mr Boon, where I dined, smoaked a Pipe of African Tobacco; and spent part of the Afternoon, with Cousin Tom Woodforde, at Mr Boon's Father's, with Old Mr Boon and his Wife, and his Son the Clergyman, and his Daughter; I talked with Mr Boon the Clergyman about the Curacy of Thurloxton, and likewise the Chapel of Newton; both which he promised to take care of and enter upon the 15th of next Month and 'till then I should officiate at them. I took my Leave of Mr Boon's Family, and afterwards went to the New-Inn where my Horse is, and then I wrote two Letters, one to Mr Fitch, and one to Mr Abraham, to let them know, that I had got a Clergyman to undertake both Places, at the Expiration of my Quarter, which will be the ninth of next Month, & there I drank, with Cousin Tom, one Pint of Port, and afterwards went home to Thurloxton. For the Pint of Port and my Horse pd 0.1.2. For having two Straps to my Boots to pull them up at Taunton pd 0.0.6. Gave the Hostler there 0.0.2. Mr Boon the Clergyman who is to succeed me in my Curacy, is but very lately arrived from Senegal in Africa, where he was Chaplain to the 86 Regiment, which was there and is now broke, so that he is now upon half Pay, for wch he receives per annum clear, for doing nothing 56.0.0. While he was at Senegal he lost his left Arm, in shooting of an Eagle, the Gun bursting in his Hand, which carried away all but his little Finger. It was very agreeable to hear him give an Account of that Island. He brought some very curious things from Africa, among which was some African tobacco, and two gold Rings which he gave to his Father & Mother. Two of Mr Cross's Tenants (one a Farmer and the other a Taylor & Miller) from Ash-Priors about 8 Mile from here, supped, & spent the Evening with us — they lay at Mr Cross's this Night. Old Mr Boon is a Coroner, and lives near the New-Inn in Taunton.

1764

JANUARY *3rd*. Breakfasted at Mr Cross's, after Breakfast I went upon Cream for Ansforde. Sent a Letter this Morning to Mr Hite at Mr Blakes of Padnoller near Bridgewater to let him know that as the Church of Babcary must be served twice of a Sunday by express Order of the Bishop, he must make an annual Addition to my present Salary of 10.0.0. My sore Throat is very bad still. Dined at Pipers Inn, & for my Dinner &c., pd 0.1.9. For going through Three Turnpikes pd 0.0.3. Gave the Maid Servant at Piper's Inn 0.0.3. Gave the Hostler there 0.0.2. Supped, spent the Evening, and laid at Home. Mrs Clarke, Mrs White, Cousin Jenny Clarke & Cousin Richard Clarke, supped & spent ye Evening here. At Cards this Evening (Commerce) with Mama, Jenny, Mrs Clarke, Mrs White, Cousin Jemmy & Dickey, two Pools lost 0.0.2½. I have eat no Meat to Day.

12th. Breakfasted, supped &c. at Home. After Breakfast I rode upon Cream to my Curacy at Babcary about six Miles from hence, where I dined upon a Sheeps Heart that I carried there in my Pocket, at the Parsonage House, where I am to be when I go to Babcary upon any occasion. One Old Woman (whose name is Mary Creech) and her daughter live there. I returned this Afternoon, and for going through Avord Turnpike pd 0.0.1. I am to preach at Babcary next Sunday. For six long Pipes at Babcary pd 0.0.1. For some Tobacco there pd 0.1.

15th. Breakfasted, supped &c. at Home. After Breakfast I went upon Cream to my Curacy at Babcary, where I read Prayers and Preached, read Prayers in the Morning and Preached in the Afternoon. This is the first Sunday I ever officiated at Babcary Church; and I like it very well. Dined at my House there upon Bacon & Eggs. I went back to Ansford in the Afternoon. I was rung into the Parish, by Mr John Bowers Order, who gave the Ringers a Pail of Cyder on Purpose to ring me into the Parish. They gave me another Peal this Afternoon after Service, and for which I gave them 2.6.

21st. After Dinner I set forth for Babcary, where I supped and laid in the Parsonage House. I hired Ned Dyke and his Horse this Morning to carry some Cyder &c. to Babcary for me. I carried three Dozen and nine Bottles of Cyder, and eight Bottles of strong Beer, with a little jar of pickled Oysters, some Cheese, and smoked Tongue to Babcary, all which were given by my Father. I paid Ned Dyke for carrying the above 0.2.0. For Ned Dykes and my Horse going thro' 1 Turnpike pd 0.0.2. Paid old Mary Creech this Afternoon who lives in the Parsonage House, for things she bought and laid out for me, last Week 0.8.10. The things she paid for me were these, viz,

For one Hundred of Hay 0.1.6.
For a Gridiron 0.1.0.
For mending the stable Door &c. 0.1.2.
For two Pound of Bacon 0.1.0.
For a Pound of Candles 0.0.6½.
For Soap 0.0.2.
For a Sack of Coal 0.1.6.
For a Peck of Beans 0.1.3.
For Eggs, butter, and Bran 0.0.8½.

FEBRUARY *20th.* Breakfasted, dined, supped, & laid again at my House at Babcary. I have been very busy all this Day in planting my Peas and Beans & Radishes, and Spanish Onions, in my Garden at Babcary. Papa and Mama called upon me this Morning at Babcary, in their Post Chaise, but they did not stop above 10 Minutes ... For two more Sacks of Coal pd 0.4.4. N.B. These two Sacks of Coal are lasting, much longer, and better burning than ye last. I was sent for this Afternoon to a Poor Woman that lives by the Church, to come and pray by her —which I did.

APRIL *1st*. Went this Morning early with Jenny to my Curacy at Babcary—where we breakfasted, dined, and spent the Afternoon. Captain Rooke and Sister Nanny dined & spent the Afternoon with us at Babcary. We had nothing but Bacon & Eggs for Dinner. There was an Eclipse of the Sun this Morning about nine o'clock, but it was nothing to what was expected by most People. Read Prayers this Morning, read Prayers & preached this Afternoon at Babcary.

16th. Breakfasted, dined, & spent the Afternoon at Babcary. I brewed a Quarter-Barrel of Ale to Day. Mary Creech (out of the Mony I left her) paid for six Pd of Malt ready ground 0.9.0. For Butter & Cream she paid 0.0.9. And afterwards she returned me 0.1.0. I gave Mary Creech's Daughter Betty for washing, and ironing a Shirt, Band, Cravet &c. 0.0.6. I gave Mary Creech & her Daughter a Pair of Garters each, which I bought of an Irish Traveller that came to the Door, & for them I pd 0.0.6. After my Ale was tunned this Evening, I set forth upon my little Horse for Ansford—where I supped, spent the Evening, & laid.

30th. I got up this Morning at two o'clock, to get or make a Sermon for Farmer John Bartelot's Funeral this afternoon, and by twelve o'clock I had finished almost all of it. I breakfasted, and dined at Home. For fifteen more Numbers of the History of Religion, brought by the Sherborne News Man, who brought them from Sherborne, from Goodby the Printers there, by my order, I paid 0.7.6. I gave the News Man for bringing them 0.0.6. Went this Afternoon to bury Farmer John Bartelot, and likewise to see the half-Hogshead of Cyder, that my Father gave me, carried to Babcary which was carried in Farmer Speeds Cart by Ned Dyke. I paid at Avord Turnpike for the Cart 0.0.9. I gave Ned Dyke for going with the Cart 0.1.0. I buried Farmer John Bartelot this Evening at six o'clock and preached a Funeral Sermon, the Church was exceedingly throned with People. Supped, spent the Evening and laid at Babcary.

MAY *6th*. Mrs Bartelot (Widow to the late Farmer Bartelot) called upon me this Afternoon to pay me for the Funeral Sermon that I preached at her Husband's Funeral and she gave me for it 0.10.6. She desired me to give her little Boy (which was with her) something out of it, and I gave him 0.1.0. Samuel Hutchins my Clark at Babcary, according to my Order has been collecting my Easter Offerings (which Mr Hite gave me) this last Week, & he has collected for me at two Pence a Head, and no one gave more 0.8.4. I gave him for collecting them 0.2.0. N.B. All have not paid their Easter Offerings yet — the Shilling that I left with my Old Woman last Week to lay out for me, has been spent in the following Manner — For a Loaf 0.0.6. For Eggs of Dame Clothier, 15, 0.0.3. For Half a Pound of Butter 0.0.3. Mr and Mrs White supped, & spent the Evening here.

JUNE *17th*. Breakfasted, and laid at Home. After Breakfast I went to Babcary upon Tom (my Horse) where dined, spent the Afternoon, and did the Duty of a Sunday. I churched Mary Eeds this Afternoon at Babcary one of my Parishioners, for which she paid me 0.0.6 and which I sent to her again. Spent the Afternoon at Mr John Bowers with Miss Hill a very agreeable Lady, Mr John Bower and his Brother Lewis, Miss Bower their Sister, and one Master Hill, Cousin to Miss Hill. Mr John Bower is very ill in the Gout. For half a Pound of Butter that Mary bought me at Babcary pd 0.0.2½. For a Quarter of a Pd of Tobacco pd 0.0.4. For Pipes pd 0.0.1. Gave Mary Creed my Old Woman 0.0.4½. Supped, & spent the Evening at Mr John Penny's at Clanville, with Mr John Penny, his Brother Caleb, Mr Will Melliar, Painter Clarke, and Mr Terrill of C. Cary. For going thro' Avord Turnpike pd 0.0.1. Had some Peas for Dinner which I planted myself in my Garden at Babcary. Mr Melliar, Mr John Penny, his Brother Caleb, Painter Clarke, and Mr Terrill promised to dine with me upon Peas at Babcary next Friday. As I returned this Afternoon from Mr John Bowers at Babcary, I overtook one William Wettle, who offered me for an Easter Offering 0.0.2. But as he is very Poor I gave it him.

22nd. Breakfasted, and laid at Home. I went to Babcary after Breakfast, where I dined, supped, and spent the Evening; and returned home afterwards. Mr Will Melliar, Doctor Clarke, his two Sons James, and Richard, Mr Terrill, Painter Clarke & Parson Penny, all dined, supped, & spent the Evening with me at Babcary. Young Mr Caleb Penny and Mr Lewis Bower supped, and spent the Evening with me. For half a Bushell of green Peas pd 0.1.0. For a Pound of Bacon pd 0.0.7. For a Breast of Veal (as I could have no other Butcher's Meat) being disappointed pd 0.1.9. For some Carrots with it pd 0.0.2. The whole cost me, which Mary Creech my Old Woman paid out of the five Shillings I gave her last Wednesday to pay for Provision 0.3.6. I gave Mary Creech for her trouble 0.1.6. I gave Samuel Hutchins my Clarke, for looking after my Horse, and going after the Veal to Camel 0.0.6. Mr Caleb Penny, Mr Terrill, Mr James and Richard Clark, played at Five's in Babcary Churchyard this Evening, and I lost there with Mr Lewis Bower at Betting with him 0.1.6. The Gentlemen pleased me very much by seeing them so well pleased with the homely Entertainment. For going through Avord Turnpike to Day pd 0.1.

23rd. Breakfasted, dined, supped, and laid at Home. Cousin Frank Woodforde spent part of the Afternoon here. One Prince a Shoemaker at Bruton came here this Afternoon to measure me for a Pair of Shoes for which I am to pay him when he brings them home 0.5.0. This Prince being a musical Man, I desired him to tune my Spinnett for me, which he did and pretty well, but would have nothing for it. N.B. My chief Intent for sending for him was to tune my Spinnett for I have at present Shoes sufficient.

JULY *22nd*. After Breakfast I went to Babcary, where I did the Duty of a Clergyman of a Sunday. I dined and spent the Afternoon at my House there. Miss Bower, her Brother Lewis, and Miss Hill drank Tea with me at my House there; Mr John Bower spent Part of the Afternoon there. I gave my old Woman (Mary Chrich) to Day 0.1.0. My old Woman has told me that she had heard that the Living of Babcary was given to Mr Hopkins, but I hope not as he will make the Parish miserable.

SEPTEMBER *19th*. Breakfasted at Home. After Breakfast I went to Wells. Ned Dyke went with me, to bring back my Horse and carry a Portmanteau for me there. We got to Wells about ten this Morning. I put up my Horses at the George, kept by John Canning whose Son I went to School with at Urchfont. Immediately as I got to Town I waited on the Arch-Deacon, and he told me that he had appointed me to preach next Sunday at the Cathedral in the afternoon, which I agreed to do as I brought a Sermon with me for fear. I went to Mr Nash's at Wells, the Mercer and paid him for the Pieces of Worsted he sent 0.19.0. I paid Ned Dyke for himself and horse for going with me to Wells 0.2.0. For a Pr of Gloves at Wells this Morning pd 1.4. I gave the Chamber Maid at the George to get me a good Bed Room &c. 0.1.0. Dined, supped, and laid at the George Inn. Mr Price a Candidate for Deacon, a strange Captain, and the Landlord Mr Canning dined with me. For my Dinner, and Servants Dinner and Horses and for my Supper pd 0.6.0. I went to Prayers this Afternoon at the Cathedral.

23rd. Breakfasted and laid at the George again. For my Breakfast there pd 0.0.8. Immediately after Breakfast we all went to the Bishops Palace, and were ordained in his Chapel—six made Deacons and four Priests there. We all received the Sacrament after we were ordained, and for an Offering there gave 0.1.0. Arch-Deacon Potter presented us to the Bishop, and Arch-Deacon Wills assisted in the Sacrament &c. For a Surplice to day, to appear in the Bishops Chapel we each paid one of the Virgers 0.2.0. Dyer preached at the Cathedral this Morning. We all dined with the Bishop, with his Lordship, his Daughter that is not married, and his Son the Arch-Deacon of Taunton, & Mr Parfitt.

For Fees to the Bishops Servants pd 0.4.6.

viz., for the Butlers Attendance 0.2.6.

To the Bishops Footman 0.1.0.

To the Bishops Porter 0.1.0.

I preached this Afternoon at the Cathedral, for Mr Forster, one of the Priest-Vicars there. I drank Tea this Afternoon at Mr Slades the Justice's with the Justice, his Son, his Daughter, Mr Moss who married one of his Daughters, and two Miss Coles of Bridgewater, who are on a Visit there. Supped with all the Candidates at the Christopher. For our Supper &c. we each paid there 0.4.6. Mr Edward Holloway, and Mr Parfitt supped with us. Poor Holloway was sadly overtaken with Liquor.

OCTOBER *30th*. Breakfasted, dined, and laid at home. Papa and Mama, and our Maid Elizabeth Clothier, went this Morning early for London in Ansford Inn Post-Chaise. The Lord send them a good, prosperous, and safe Journey to London. Papa and Mama have left me the whole care of his House, with all the Keys, and I will take great care to be faithful in the Trust committed to me. Papa left me for housekeeping &c. 7.7.0. Alice Stacy a very honest and faithful Woman a Neighbour, is to be with me till they return. William Corp our Man is left here with me. Supped, and spent the Evening at Mr White's, with him, his Wife, and their Son John, and Mr Sam White.

DECEMBER *4th*. Breakfasted, supped, and laid at home. Clark Coleman breakfasted with me upon Peas Soup. Farmer John Jukes of Meer, aged about 80 was married this Morning at Ansford Church to Mrs Simpson of this Parish aged about 70 by me Js Woodforde. Mem; This is the first Couple I ever married. I recd for marrying the above Couple 0.5.0. Dined, and spent the Afternoon at Uncle Tom's with him and his Wife. Drank Tea this Afternoon at Aunt Parr's.

1765

JANUARY *16th*. Breakfasted, dined, supped, & laid at home. Papa and Mama returned this Afternoon with their Maid Elizabeth Clothier, from London, perfectly well and easy! Blessed be God for all great mercies bestowed upon me a miserable & sinful creature. They had not dined, therefore they dined upon some Veal, spent the Afternoon, supped & laid in their old House. Doctor Clarke, & his Wife, Mr White and his Wife, supped & spent the Evening here. Uncle Tom spent the latter part of the Afternoon with us.

MARCH *4th*. Breakfasted and dined at Babcary. One Edward Ganfield called upon me this Morning at Babcary to let me know that he will not take the Glebe at 25 Pounds Per Annum as he promised me before both the Mr Bowers, which is behaving very shabby, he will give but 20.0.0.
Paid William Cooling for a Hundred of Hay 0.2.0.
For things my Old Woman has bought me pd 0.0.9.
viz, for two Pound of Pork 0.0.8.
For Cream and Eggs 0.0.1.
For Pipes 0.0.2.
Gave my Old Woman 0.0.4½.
After Dinner I returned to Ansford where I supped, spent the Evening and laid. In my Return here I called upon Mr Andrew Russ at Clanville and spent the remaining part of the Afternoon with him, Mr Dod a Baker & a Roman Catholick, Mr Thomas and Seth Burge. Mr Dod and myself touched a little on Religion which I own was not right at all. For going thro' Avord Turnpike pd 0.0.1. Gave a Poor old Soldier 0.0.1 coming from Babcary this afternoon.

11th. Breakfasted, dined, supped, and laid at Babcary. Farmer William Baker Snr of Babcary, an honest industrious and wealthy Man applied to me to have the Glebe Lands &c. and I let it to him for twenty-six Pounds Per annum, and he signed an Agreement that I drew up. The Farmer supped and spent the Evening with me.

APRIL *18th*. Breakfasted, dined, supped, & laid at home again. Parson Penny called upon me this Morning and desired me to bury poor Mrs Lucas this Afternoon for him. Mr Penny is presented to the Living of Evercreech, to hold it for a Minor (Justice Rodbard's Son of 12 Years old) and therefore is going to quit my Father's Curacy at C. Cary, which I am to undertake for him, & Babcary too, but I cannot serve Babcary but once of a Sunday. Spent the Afternoon at Dr Clarke's with him, his Wife, Mr Richard Clarke & Brother Heighes Woodforde. I buried poor Mrs Lucas this Evening for Mr Penny.

JUNE *18th*. I have been very busy all Day with Brother Jack in enlarging my Tent in our Garden, we got up this Morning at 4 o'clock. Aunt Parr and Mrs Clarke spent the Afternoon here. Mr James Clarke and Mrs White spent the Evening here. For having my Pladd Morning Gown turned by Isaac Worme, paid him this Evening 0.2.6. Upping with Jack this Afternoon, lost 0.0.2.

JULY *8th*. Brother John is very indifferent, by his being too busy with Girls. Gave Mary Coleman's Son Will for going to many Places this Afternoon for me to invite People to Babcary next Thursday to dine with me there 0.0.2.

11th. Went to Babcary this Morning after breakfast to prepare things for Dinner, as I have many C. Cary Gentlemen to dine with me to Day—at my House there. Our Man William went to wait at Table there and he carried with him a fine Piece of Beef of mine. For William's and mine Horse going thro. Avord

Gate pd o.2. We all spent the greatest Part of the Afternoon in the Church-Yard at Babcary, where we were diverted by some of the Gentlemen playing at Ball, At which I won a betting o.2.9. The Gentlemen seemed well pleased at the Entertainment, which gave me infinite Satisfaction. A terrible Accident happend while we were at dinner, which many of us went to see the Body—viz, a poor Boy was dragged and killed by a Horse about half a Mile from us on the Ilchester Road. The boy was about 14 Years old—I hope to God the Poor Boy is happy. There was no bone broken neither was his Skull fractured—but he is dead. We all came home singing, and I thank God well. My Brother John was indisposed, therefore he cd not go. For six Cucumbers at Avord Gate to day pd o.o.6. A Strange Farmer came after William to Babcary before Dinner to desire him to come back to Ansford to dress a Horse for him, but I could not let him go till after Dinner.

45

SEPTEMBER *9th.* I received this Morning of Papa for serving the Cure of C. Cary one Quarter due August 25, 5.0.0. For a Pr of second-hand Gloves of Brother John pd 0.1.0. For having five Chimneys swept at the lower House this Afternoon where I am going to live partly soon paid Thomas Clements 0.2.0. I gave Toms two Poor little Boys 0.0.6.

OCTOBER *6th.* Breakfasted, dined, supped, and laid at home again. After breakfast I went to Babcary for the last Time, where I read Prayers, Preached and administered the H.S. Mr and Mrs Colmer & Family are come to Babcary. I returned to Ansford afterwards and dined at Home and after Dinner I read Prayers and Preached at C. Cary, and after Prayers I buried the Child that I privately baptized last Friday. It rained all the way going and coming back from Babcary.

NOVEMBER *2nd.* Breakfasted and laid again at the lower House —I bought a second hand eight Day Clock a very handsome and almost new lately Dr Upcots, of Clark Coleman this morning for which I paid him 6.0.0. I had him put up this morning in the Parlour at the lower House of Edward Creed for which I pd him 0.1.0. Dined, supped and spent the Evening at Parsonage. Spent the Afternoon at the lower House with Jenny, Jack, Doctor Clarke and his Son Mr Richard Clarke. For three Pound of Candles for the lower House pd 0.1.8½. For half a Pound of Nails pd 0.0.4. Roger Coles and Boy have been at work again all Day. I paid Roger Coles this Evening for him and his Boys Work for these last three Days to make out the Week 0.5.6. I have now done at present with my Carpenters.

4th. Dined, supped, and spent the Evening at Parsonage. One Mr Fry a Distiller in Bristol, and Acquaintance of Jacks, dined and spent the Afternoon at Parsonage. I went down this afternoon to Horn-blotton, to Parson Dymocks Funeral, who was buried this Afternoon by me at Horn-blotton Church in the Chancel. He was buried handsomely there, there being six

Parsons all Pall-bearers, we had all of us Hat-Bands & Gloves. The Clergymen were the undermentioned, Mr Hopkins, Mr Brice, Mr Tuckher, Mr Leach, Mr Marsh & myself. Painter Clarke was the Undertaker at the Funeral. Our Man William went with me and carried my Gown. For going thro' two Turnpikes with two Horses pd 0.0.4. We did not return till nine o'clock this Evening. I came back with Painter Clarke and his Son Charles, and as we returned we stopped a Quarter of an Hour at Lovington at Mr Rush's, I went down with Dr Clarke another way and very bad that way was; Dr Clarke did not go to Church on account of some people not having the small-Pox. Horn-blotton is a very dismal and dirty Place and the Parsonage House is near a mile from the Church. Parson Dymock was carried to Church in a Hearse.

DECEMBER *1st*. Breakfasted and laid again at the lower House. I read Prayers & Preached this Morning at Ansford C. Dined, supped and spent the Evening at Parsonage. Mr White, Mr Sam White, Mr Andrew Russ, Mr James and Richard Clarke, and Brother Heighes, supped & spent the Evening with us at Parsonage. My Father did not come down stairs all the Evening on account of the Company & Mama being ill. It vexed my Father & Mother greatly to have Company brought to the House by Jack on a Sunday, and especially as Mama is so bad.

26th. I read Prayers this morning at C. Cary C. being St Stephen. After Prayers I christened two Children Publickly in the Church, I had previously baptized them before. Dined, supped and spent the Evening at Parsonage. Mrs White dined and spent the Evening at Parsonage. Poor Mama came Down Stairs this Afternoon for the first time for the last six Weeks — I hope she will continue better & better daily. Jack was at John Coleman's Christening this Evening and staid out very late there being a deal of Company. We had Ansford Mummers this Evening at Parsonage.

47

1766

JANUARY *23rd*. Breakfasted, and laid again at the lower House. Jack breakfasted, and laid again at the lower House. I dined, supped and spent the Evening at Parsonage. Mrs White supped and spent the Evening with us. Mama still better to day—She acquainted us with some secret Affairs this Afternoon.

26th. I read Prayers and Preached this morning at C. Cary Church. I read Prayers and Preached this Afternoon at Ansford Church. I prayed for Mama again this Afternoon at Ansford Church—Poor Mama is worse than she was considerably. I dined, supped, and spent the Evening at Parsonage. Mr & Mrs White, and Mr Pitt from Poole supped & spent the Evening.

FEBRUARY *6th*. Breakfasted, and laid again at the lower House. Jack breakfasted, and laid again at the lower House. I lent Brother John this morning 0.11.6. I dined, supped, and spent the Evening at Parsonage. Mrs White supped, and spent the Evening with us at Parsonage. Poor Mama grows weaker and worse daily—The Parsonage is a very melancholy House now indeed.

7th. Poor Mama sent for me and Jack this Afternoon up into her Room and very solemnly took her Leave of us: therefore I do not believe she can exist very long in this World. Uncle Tom, Mrs White & Mr White & Mrs Clarke supped and spent the Evening with us at Parsonage.

8th. It pleased Almighty God of his great goodness to take unto himself my Dear good Mother this morning about 9 o'clock out of this sinful World, and to deliver her out of her miseries. She went out of this World as easy as it was possible for any one. I hope she is now eternally happy in everlasting Glory. I breakfasted, dined, supped and spent the Evening at Parsonage. O Lord God Almighty send help from thy Holy Place to my Dear Father, and to all my Dear Mother's Relatives, to withstand so great a Shock, and to live, and dye so easy as she did. I laid at the lower House again, as did my Brother John.

9th. There were no Prayers this Morning at Castle Cary by my Orders. One Parson Cooke of Exeter who is at Ansford Inn, was so kind as to send to me this morning and offered to serve Ansford C. this Afternoon for me, hearing I was in great Distress—and he performed the Afternoon Service there for me. Parson Cooke's Nephew who came with him has got the Living of Hornblotton vacant by Mr Dimmock's Death.

12th. My poor dear Mother was interred this afternoon about 4 o'clock in a Vault in the Chancel at Ansford Church by Mr Penny made for her & Papa. The Procession was thus: Mr Penny who buried the Corpse went immediately before the Corpse, then followed the Corpse borne on six Men's Shoulders, with six chosen Gentlemen to support the Pall—then followed the Mourners &c. &c. The under Bearers were these, Farmer Gore, Old Roger Coles, Mr Clark's Man William, Mr Whites Man Edmund, Uncle Tom's Man Richard, & my Fathers Man William. They had each a Pr of Gloves and each 0.2.6. The six Pall Bearers were old Mr Creed, Old Mr Penny, Old Mr Pew, Mr Will Melliar, Mr Serrill in Room of Mr Thomas Burge who was out of Town, and Mr Seth Burge. They had all silk Hatbands & a Pr of black Gloves. The Mourners were Brother Heighes and myself, Brother John and Dr Clarke, Mr White and Uncle Tom, Mr James and Richard Clarke, we had all Crape Hatbands & Cloaks, The Pall Bearers had all Cloaks likewise. Painter Clarke was the Undertaker to the Funeral. It has been a very windy and rainy all Day long. Mr Poor dear Mother was buried very decently & well—Her Coffin was covered with Superfine Black Cloth & black Nails. Mama has given to me, Sister Jane, & Brother John jointly between us all her whole Estate below by an appointment in Fee.

14th. I had a Suit of mourning for my poor dear Mother, brought home this Morning by Isaac Oram given me by my Father. I lent Brother Jack this Evening for a Letter 0.0.6. Papa gave me this Afternoon my mony Box that poor Mama kept for me from a Boy, in which were half a Guinea, two half crown Pieces, a sixpence, two small Silver Coins and 0½.

AUGUST *22nd*. I supped, & spent the Evening at Parsonage. I read Prayers this morning at C. Cary being the Bishops Triennial Visitation, Archdeacon Potter officiated for the Bishop, the Bishop not coming being very old. Parson Paggett of Doulton Preached the Visitation Sermon. We dined as usual at Ansford Inn. The Arch-Deacon treated me, being the Reader, for my Dinner and for Liquor as long as he stopped. I paid myself afterwards for Wine &c. 0.1.0. Mr Parfit, the Bishops Registrar dined with us.

I paid Mr Parfit my Father's Visitation Fee being 0.7.2.

I paid Ditto for Mr Ragg of N. Cadbury 0.6.0.

I paid Mr Hunt for my Father's dues to the C. Widows 0.10.0.

I paid Ditto for myself for the Clergymen's Widows 0.5.0.

I buried a little Boy, this Evening at C. Cary in the Small-Pox. I paid to the Apple-Man at Ansford Inn 0.0.6. Mr Sansom paid me for my Father the sum of 4.10.0 being a Years Interest for one hundred Pound, which my Father had lent him some time ago.

OCTOBER *15th*. For sweeping the Hall Chimney this morning pd 0.0.6. I gave the Poor Chimney Sweepers Boy 0.0.6. John Gardener brought me some Fruit Trees and planted them this morning in our Garden—I pd him for them 0.10.6 viz, for twelve Espalia Apple Trees at 0.6 each—0.6.0. For a Peach and Nectara Tree each 1/6—0.3.0. For a Cherry-Tree 1.0. Grape Ditto 0.6.—0.1.6. I had a Sweet Brier given into the bargain. I dined, supped and spent the Evening at Parsonage. Mrs Grant of Henbridge spent the Afternoon at Parsonage, she came to talk with my Father about Jack & her Daughter Nancy which I hope now will soon be settled to their satisfaction. I gave Mary Chrich this Evening for a Pig's Kidney £0 1s 0d.

NOVEMBER *14th*. After breakfast I went to Mr Gappers of Yarlington and just going into the Parish I met him, & he informed me that he could not serve me, as he preaches three Times every Sunday; but he told me of a Person (whose Name is Hopkins and lives at Mr Croft's at Charlton Musgrove) where from him I went and spoke with him but he could not promise me by any means—from him I went to young Mr Leir's at the same Place where I dined & spent the Afternoon with him, & he has promised to assist me one Sunday if Hopkins cannot yet. For going through three Turnpikes pd 0.0.3. I returned in the Evening to Parsonage where I supped & spent the Evening.

DECEMBER *31st*. I did not go to bed till after one o'clock this morning, but during the time I was in bed I slept very well & my Cold is brave this morning, blessed be Almighty God for it. I dined, supped and spent the Evening at Parsonage. Mrs Parr and Mrs White dined & spent the afternoon at Parsonage. Mary Chrich's Son James of Wedmore & Wife & Daughter came to see his mother, and they dined, supped and laid at the lower House—He is a very industrious little Farmer—Miss Molly Pew, her Sister Hannah and Miss Hyat of Shepton Mallet an Acquaintance of the Pews supped & spent the Evening at Parsonage. At Cards this Evening at Parsonage I lost 0.1.0. We kept tolerable good hours this Evening. The Miss Watsons were inoculated at home yesterday by Dr Clarke. We dined upon a fine goose to day—A Present of Mrs Grants. I privately baptized a Child of Giles Francis's by name Jonas at the lower House.

51

1767

FEBRUARY *3rd*. Mr Richard Clarke breakfasted with us at the lower House. I dined and spent the afternoon at Parsonage. I spent the Evening & Supped at Ansford Inn, there being a Masquerade Ball there this Evening, and very elegant it was, much beyond my expectation in all respects—We did not break up till five o'clock in the morning. It cost me in the whole the Sum of 0.7.0 (with my Ticket—without only 4s od). Parson Penny, Gapper, Witwick & Overton & myself were the Clergymen that were there. Mr Will Melliar was in the Character of a Cardinal, his Wife, Queen Elizabeth, his Daughter a Haymaker, Counsellor Melliar Lord Leicester, James Clarke a Harlequin, Richard Clarke in a Dominee. Brother John a Counsellor, Brother Heighes King Richard the Third, John Burge Othello, Sister Jane a Shepherdess, Sally Chicke a Pilgrim, Miss Jordan a Princess, Uncle Tom Nothing Aunt an old Woman, Nancy Clarke a Milkmaid, Agatha Clarke a Quaker, Sally Clarke Diana Trapes, Painter Clarke a Beef-eater, Captain Stroude a Hunter, Caleb Penny a Sailor, Dr Samson, Young Golsborough, & Captain Dampier in Dominees, Andrew Russ a Turkish Prince, Frank Woodforde a running Footman, Tom Francis a Jockey, little Jem Melliar a Skeleton, Mrs Clarke Miss Gatehouse & Sister, Miss Ford, Miss Barber, Miss Pew, Mr & Mrs Pew, George & William Pew cum multis aliis, all in very rich Dress but in no particular Characters. Admiral Hunt was Beau Nash & Master of the Ceremonies. I played at Cards part of the Time & won 0.1.0. I did not dance the whole Evening. We had good Musick viz, four Violins, a Base Viol, a Taber & Pipe, a Hautboy and a French Horn played by Mr Ford.

MARCH *18th*. I read Prayers & Catechized Mr Titcombs Boys this morning at C. Cary. Coming from Church I walked home with Uncle Tom whom I overtook in C. Cary street, and with whom I had some private Confabulation concerning the Livings of C. Cary & Ansford & I asked him whether he did not (When at Mrs Powels) ask her for them, he told me he did; which therefore is I think very ungenerous Treatment to me & my Father, especially because my Father desired him not (as he intended to get C. Cary) not above three days before he went, and Uncle moreover said in answer to it that he should not see Mrs Powel, and would not try for it. N.B. Our Family have been always flung by my Uncles, by dishonourable & dishonest actions. I dined, supped, & spent the Evening at Parsonage. Uncle Tom came to Parsonage this afternoon and wanted to set matters right which he could not do to me I'm sure.

APRIL *9th*. Mrs Grant of Hambridge came early this morning on Horse back to the L. House and gave it to Jack, for breaking of the Love Affair with her Daughter. Mrs Grant is too selfish. Mr Thos Leir Junr of Charlton called at my Father's this morning and sent for me, to inform me that he would serve me and that if he did not Mr Sollers of Wincaunton would as often as required, & he said it would be Charity to employ him.

10th. I read Prayers this morning at C. Cary Church. I dined, supped and spent the Evening at Parsonage. I called upon an old School-Fellow of mine (one Haynes of Southampton who was Jnr under me in Fourth Chamber at Winton College) he is married to a fine Woman and is in the Militia, and is now under inoculation at Dr Clarkes. Justice Creed spent part of the Afternoon at Parsonage. Brother John returned home this Evening from a very mad chase. I sent Luke this morning on Foot to Gannard's Grave to hire two Horses for my Oxford Journey & am promised. Jack did not please at Parsonage this evening being very much disguised in Beer, but it is but seldom and I hope will be more seldom, the more so the better.

53

MAY *17th*. I went this morning upon a Hack to Wooton, where I read Prayers & Preached in the morning & read Prayers in ye Afternoon. Oglander Junr was to have went for Whitmore, but Oglander's Father being just now dead, he desired me to serve it. It rained all the way there, with the Wind directly in my Face. Wooton is about ten miles North of Oxford. I dined at Mr Banks's the Rector's House on seven or eight dishes, with him, his Uncle and one Parson Hinds of Hampton a Clergyman of about five hundred pounds Per Annum. Parson Hinds came great part of the way back with me, as he lives in the Road almost to Oxford. It rained very hard when we set out from John Banks—I gave his Man 0.1.0. Going through two Turn-pikes this morning pd 0.0.2½. John Banks has got a charming pretty House & Gardens. The Living belongs to us—worth 300 Per Annum or more. I thank God I got safe back to N. Coll. about eight o'clock. I supped in the Chequer and spent the Evening in the M.C.R.* by myself, And for Punch this Evening from the C.H. pd 0.0.6. I breakfasted and slept again in Reynels Rooms. I sent a Letter this morning to my Father at Ansford.

23rd. I breakfasted in Bedfords Rooms & slept in Oglander Senrs Rooms, Bedfords Matrass being very disagreeable to lay upon. After breakfast I went to the Schools with Whitmore and had a Masters Degree conferred on me by the V. Chancellor &c. &c. The Fees, and dispensations &c. amounted to & which I pd 3.0.6.

I gave the Proctors Man as usual & customary 0.1.0.

I gave Mr Whitmore for presenting me as usual 0.10.0.

I gave our Porter for carrying my Hood & Gown 0.1.0.

I gave the Choristers of our Coll. as usual 0.1.0.

I gave the Masters C. Room Man as usual 0.2.6.

I treated the M.C.R. this Afternoon with Port Wine; and with Rum Punch and Port Wine the whole Evening. I sent as usual to the B.C.R. or Batchelors C. Room one Dozen of Port Wine

* Masters' Common Room.

—there was but little drank all Day in the M.C.R. For Porter this Evening at the Kings Head pd 0.0.2. For Fruit this Afternoon in the M.C.R. pd 0.1.0. I dined and supped in the Chequer and spent the Afternoon and Evening in the M.C.R. Very few People in the M.C.R. this Evening.

Ansford

JUNE *12th*. I have been very busy in the morning, bottling of Port Wine which I had from Dr Clarkes being concerned in a Pipe which was brought to the Drs from Dorchester by Mr Morgan Yeatman. I had fifteen Gallons of it for which I paid this Afternoon at Dr Clarkes to Mr Wm Melliar at 5s 6½d Per Gallon—4.3.10. I had one Gallon, one Quart, and one Pint above measure as it ran very well. The whole Pipe came to upwards of 130 Gallons. I dined at the Lower House & spent the Afternoon at Dr Clarke's. I presented Edward Speeds Child into the Church this Evening and likewise buried his Wife immediately after at Ansford.

JULY *7th*. I have been very busy all Day in brewing. I dined and spent the Afternoon at the lower House. Jack dined with me at the lower House being displeased above. I refused to bury 2 Corpses this afternoon at C. Cary, one that died Yesterday a Woman by name Cooper, and another Woman Peter Longman's Wife the Blacksmith, who died Sunday. The reason of my refusing them, was their not giving me proper notice of interring them. It has occasioned a good deal of talk about me, which I am sorry for, as I only did it, to make them more careful for the future, for the People of C. Cary have been very remiss in respect to that and have gave me a great deal of trouble always.

AUGUST *1st*. I dined, supped and spent the Evening at Parsonage. I recd a Letter by David Maby this Evening from Edward Bishop of Bath and Wells to desire me to transmit to him a correct List of Papists or reputed Papists with an Account of their Ages, Sex, Occupation and Time of Residence in the Parish of Castle Cary with all convenient Expedition to Wells in order to its being laid before the House of Lords next Session.*

SEPTEMBER *11th*. I got home this morning about 8 o'clock & after eating some Toast & Butter & drinking some Tea I went to Bed & slept till 2 in the Afternoon, & was then brave. I dined and spent the Afternoon at Justice Creeds with him, his Father, Mr Hindly, Parson Gapper of Yarlington, & Parson Brinsted of Sherborne Schoolmaster, a very deserving young Man, & very sensible. We had a noble Pine Apple after Dinner. I supped and spent the Evening at Parsonage. I gave Mr Creeds Servant Maid Sarah 0.1.0. Mrs White & Son John spent the Evening at Parsonage. My Brothers Dog, Dashwood, was found dead supposed to be killed by some Rascal or other & if so Hope he will be found out.

OCTOBER *11th*. Brother John went for Taunton this morning early, I lent him my Man Luke to carry his Portmanteau there. He is gone to join the Somersett Militia being an Ensign — I read Prayers, Preached and administred the Holy Sacrament this morning at C. Cary Church, and for an Offering there I gave 0.1.0. I dined, supped & spent the Evening at Parsonage. Aunt Parr dined, & spent the Afternoon at Parsonage. Mrs White & Son John supped & spent the Evening at Parsonage. Mr Will Melliar sent me a Note this morning to desire me to be at the meeting of the Gentlemen &c. of this County at Bridgewater to Morrow to put in nomination two proper Persons to represent this county in Parliament the ensueing Parliament; and it was so civil a note that I could not refuse him. Miss Rooke dined, supped and slept at Parsonage. I borrowed of Sister Jane this Evening 5.5.0 to defray my expences to Morrow &c.

* Although no Catholics had been prosecuted under the Recusancy Laws for a long time, they were still in force and the Government considered it desirable to know the numbers involved.

12th. After breakfasting at Catcott, I went to Bridgewater in Pipers Inn Chaise, Mr Wm Melliar & his Brother went with me in Counsellor Melliars Chaise. At Bridgewater for a Turnpike pd 0.0.6. There was scarce ever seen so numerous an Assembly on such an Occasion. We put up our Horses at the Globe-Inn in Bridgewater. We dined at the Swan with near fourscore Gentlemen of the first rank in the County. For our Ordinary, we each paid 0.3.0. For Wine, Fruit, and Servants pd 0.1.6. At 2 o'clock we all went to the Town Hall and Sir Charles Tynte and Mr Cox, Lieutenant Colonel of the Somerset Militia, were the two Persons put in nomination, they having by much the majority. Mr Trivilian opposed them, and is determined to stand the Poll at the Election, though desired by his Friends to relinquish it there. Mr Mildmay, Sergeant Burland, Sir Abraham Elton the Sheriff, Mr Proviss, Junr of Shepton Mallett, & Peter Taylor spoke in the Hall for Sir Charles & Mr Cox— Sir Wm Hough (a very mean Fellow) and Major Putt, and Mr Allen, both very cleaver men, for Trivilian. We were all handsomely squeezed in the Hall. Sir Charles Tynte spoke & cleared himself from the imputation he laid under, concerning Cyder Tax. Mr Cox spoke and most elegantly and genteelly. Old Mr Cox spoke and very well with regard to his Son. At the Globe Inn in Bridgewater, Baker &c. pd 0.2.6. I returned in the Evening in Pipers Inn Post Chaise which I kept there, with Mr Melliar & his Brother to Catcott, where I supped and slept at Mr Melliars. I gave Pipers Inn Post Chaise Man 0.2.6. At Whist this Evening at Catcott with Counsellor Melliar against his Brother & his Wife won 0.2.6. Mr Trutch a very civil Man keeps the Inn, called Pipers Inn—10 Miles from Bridgewater.

NOVEMBER *16th*. I married Joseph Sweetman and Elizabeth Kingstone this morning at Castle-Cary for which I recd 0.5.0. I paid Mary Chrich this morning 0.3.11. Our Visitation was held this Day at Ansford Inn. I read Prayers at C. Cary this morning on the above account. I was the Arch-Deacon's Representative, He (Mr Potter) being lately dead, the Fees belong to his Executors. I was treated at Ansford Inn, ordinary & extraordinary, by Mr Parfitt, the late Arch-Deacons Secretary. We had but few Clergy at the Visitation. Mr Grove and Mr Golsberry supped and spent the Evening with me, my Brother, Mr James & Richard Clarke at the lower House—they quite knocked me up, and kept me up till after 2 o'clock in the morning. We played at Cards in the Evening and very high, but I believe I neither won or lost, anything great.

17th. I was very much out of order this morning, and was the major Part of the Day on the Bed—The Liquor was too much for my weak Head yesterday. I eat very little all the Day, but was very ill. I supped & spent the Evening at Parsonage. Jack supped & spent the Evening at Farmer Cocks at Hatspen and kept very late Hours again, with James & Richd Clarke.

DECEMBER *3rd.* My Man Luke Barnard acquainted me this morning that he did not like his Wages, and unless I would raise them, he must leave me, which he is to do at Lady Day next, and his Year being up Yesterday, I am to give him at the Rate of five Pounds a Year till Lady Day without any new Cloaths &c. I am not very sorry, He is a willing Fellow, but indolent & too fond of Cyder. He is going to farm, that is the reason of his leaving me. For 2 Pr of blue Buttons of a poor old Soldier pd 0.0.8. For a Leaden Spoon also of him, at my Door 0.0.4. I dined & spent the Afternoon at Parsonage.

11th. I dined, supped and spent the Evening at Justice Creeds, with him, his Father, Mrs Betty Baker, her three Nieces of Bridgewater, that is, Miss Baker rather ordinary, Miss Betsy very pretty, and Miss Sukey very middling rather pretty than otherwise, all very sensible & agreeable, and quite fine Ladies, both in Behaviour & dress, & Fortunes. At Quadrille this Evening at the Justices lost 0.1.6. I gave the Justices Servant Jacob 0.1.0. Jack went from home this morning & was out all night.

1768

JANUARY *1st*. I should have read Prayers this morning at C. Cary but there being a great Fall of Snow last Night and continued snowing till Dinner Time prevented me as I thought of having no Congregation, but there were 2 Children to be christened which I was ignorant of, till too late for Prayers. However I went to C. Cary in the Afternoon & christened them, by Names, Mary and Ann Bartelot—Mr Titcombs & Mr Hadleys Children. I dined, supped &c. at the lower House with Jack. Jenny, myself, & Jack were to have dined to day by promise at Mr Creeds, but the Snow prevented us. I sent a Note to the Justice of it. I gave my Barbers Boy a Xmas Box 0.0.6. I gave him also for going to C. Cary to the Clerk to let him know there would be no Prayers 0.0.6.

FEBRUARY *3rd*. I dined, supped &c. at the lower House. Dr Clarke, his two Sons, James & Richard, Cousin Frank Woodforde, and Brother Heighes and John dined, supped & spent the Evening at lower House with me. I gave them some roast Beef, boiled Neck of Pork, a plumb Pudding &c. Veal Cutlets for Supper &c. &c. Mr White supped & spent the Evening with me, at Cribbage with Cousin Frank this Evening lost 0.0.6. Paid Mr Younge this morning for tuning my Spinnett the last half Year in full of all demands 0.10.6. He is not to tune him any more, as I have made little use of him now.

MARCH *1st*. For an Iron Fender to roast with—30 Pound Weight—pd 0.6.6. For an Iron sliding Crook of Peter Longman also and a Pr of Jointed Pot Hooks at 6 Per Pound, Weight 13 Pound—pd 0.6.6. I recd for 8 Pound of Iron left out of a

Barr — 7/6 at 2½ Per Pound. I paid Mr Francis this morning for the Barr of Iron 0.7.6. I dined, supped and spent the Evening at Justice Creeds with him & Father. Mr Vigor dined & spent part of the Afternoon there. Great Dinners &c. given to day at the George Inn and the Angel by Sir Charles Tynte's & Mr Cox's Friends, viz, by Lord Ilchester Lord Berkely of Bruton and Mr Mildmay, but neither were there. There were a great multitude of all Sorts, gentle and simple Mr Cox himself was there, Bells ringing &c. and a great Procession through Town with Musick playing & guns firing. They all came up in the Afternoon as far as Justice Creeds, and Mr Cox himself being there, we both went out and spoke to him, and we both went back with him with the Procession down to the George Inn, where we drank success to him and was there for an Hour in the large Room with the multitude, till Mr Cox made a very handsome, sensible and genteel Speech, and then he withdrew, as did we immediately. Brother John dined, & spent the Evening with the Multitude.

17th. Paid George Davidge this morning for two hndrd and half of Wood brought here at 1.6.0 Per Hndrd, before Mary Chrich & Betty Chrich — 3.3.0. It was extravagantly dear and too much by five Shillings per Hndrd. He is a dear Fellow. I dined, supped and spent the Evening at Justice Creeds with him his Father and Parson Penny. Great rejoicings this day at C. Cary on Account of Mr Trevylyans declining the Poll for the County of Somersett after so much Hurry and disturbance, So that Sir Charles Tynte and Mr Cox are to be our Members. May they make great and worthy Representatives. I had a Letter this Evening from Williams Senr of New-College to inform me that March 23 is the Day for the University Election*

* The purpose of the 1 March festivities was to persuade the electorate that the two Parliamentary candidates, Tynte and Cox, had the backing of the local magnates. By the 17th their opponent Trevelyan, his position hopeless, had withdrawn. JW, however, still had an interest in the election for the University seat.

and that I must be there next Tuesday night which (please God) I design to be. Mr Francis of C. Cary has offered me an Horse which I take very kind of him and intend to embrace.

29th. I read Prayers again to day at C. Cary Church. I dined, supped & spent the Evening at Parsonage. I went to see Mr Creed this afternoon and just by his House I met him coming over to Parsonage, & he would make me go back & drink a Dish of Coffea which I did, and then I took a Walk with him to Parsonage, where he spent part of the Evening. My Father would not play Cards, it being Passion Week, and the Justice was not very well pleased. N.B. No Cards &c. this Week at Parsonage which I think is not amiss though there might be no Harm.

APRIL *6th.* This morning I discharged Luke and paid him his Wages to the full, viz, remaining from last Year—0.18.0. For 1 Quarter 1 Month & 3 Days besides at 5d Per Day: 1.13.6. For the Coat & Waistcoat being my Livery he gave me 0.13.0. I paid Luke Barnard the Ballance this morning—3.4.6. My New Boy with his Father came to me this morning, his Name is George Hutchins as well as his Fathers and they come from Lidford. I settled as underneath with his Father for Wages, To give him Per Annum 2.2.0. To let him have (that is only to lend it him during the Time, he lives with me) a Coat and Waistcoat & Hat &c. He is to find himself in Shoes, Stockings, Breeches & Shirts, or if I buy them for him to deduct it out of his Wages. He is a likely Boy and bears a good Character. I dined, supped & spent the Evening at Parsonage. I buried Eliz. Yonge this Afternoon at C. Cary, aged 27.

14th. I made a Visit this morning to old Mr Creed in South-Cary. I made two Dinners this Day one at the L. House by myself to teach my new Boy to wait at Table, and another at Parsonage where I supped and spent the Evening. I went over to C. Cary this Night after eleven o'clock and privately baptized a Child born this day and very dangrously ill in Convulsions by name George of Perry's, a Mason and a poor Man in South Cary. Mem: Never did I an ecclesiastical Duty with more Pleasure, as it gave such great Satisfaction to its Parents, & that they were so good & charitably disposed to have it done. The poor Innocent Babe was taken with a violent Fit immediately after I had named it, and I really thought was dead, but it pleased God to restore it again, which was undoubtedly a blessing from Heaven for their goodness. Blessed is the man whose strength is in thee, in whose heart are thy ways! Great is thy mercy O Lord God of Hosts.

15th. The poor little Infant which I privately baptized last night, departed this World this Afternoon.

MAY *22nd.* I dined, supped & spent the Evening at Parsonage. I read Prayers, Preached and administred the Holy Sacrament this morning at Ansford Church being Whitsunday. For an Offering gave 0.1.0. I read Prayers & Preached this Afternoon at C. Cary. Aunt Anne, Aunt Parr dined and spent the afternoon at Parsonage, Clerk Maby dined at Parsonage. My Poor Father & Jack had a dispute this Evening. O that Jack was well settled in Life what Pleasure would it give to us all. Mrs White spent part of the Evening at Parsonage. Brother Jack did not come to Parsonage till late & kept up my Father late by his talking to him.

23rd. I recd a Note from my Father this morning by Sister Jane, wherein he insists on Jacks not coming to his house again for some Time, as he disturbed him so much last night that he could not sleep. I read Prayers being Whitmonday at Cary. I dined, supped and spent the Evening at Parsonage. Jack dined &c. I believe at Ansford Inn. Brother Heighes was dismissed, that is, resigned his Clerkship to Justice Creed—N.B. The Justice never behaved handsome towards him. Lord make us all more diligent in our Duty to thee & then we shall have more Peace. Dr Clarke & Brother Heighes spent the former part of the Evening with me at lower House.

JUNE *7th*. I dined, supped & spent the Evening at Lower House — Mrs White, Mr Perham, Cousin Lewis, Brother Heighes & Son Willm a very cross, ill tempered little Boy dined, supped, & spent the Evening with me & Jack at L.H. Jack is something better to day in his way. I gave the above People for Dinner a boiled Leg of Mutton, a round Neck of Pork & a Gooseberry Pudding. Sister Jane & James Clarke supped &c. with us. Dr Clarke spent part of the Afternoon at Lower House. Cousin Lewis breakfasted with us this morning, I gave to Cousin this Evening as he sets forth to morrow for the North 0.10.6. Violent Thunder & Lightning this morning till after 12. My Father made us a Visit this morning at Lower H.

AUGUST *9th*. I went to Mrs Melliars publick Breakfast in the Vicarage Garden, where was Coffea, Tea & Chocolate & all kinds of Cakes &c. proper for the above (a very large Company there, a very good Band of Musick, Bells ringing, 80 Loaves given to the Poor of Cary, every thing very elegant and handsome) all done in honour of Lord Stavordale being this day of Age. His Lordship is on his Travels abroad. There was dancing after breakfast in the Garden till three in the afternoon. I danced one Minuet in the Garden with Miss Martin, but would not dance Country Dances. I dined & spent the Afternoon at Justice Creeds, with him, his Father & Dr Vigor, to his Servants gave 3.0. There was a genteel Ball in the Evening at Ansford Inn, at which I was present till 12 o'clock. Most of the breakfast Company was present, I did not dance at all this Evening. At Quadrille this Evening with Mrs Melliar, Mrs Gapper and Mr Scroggs lost 0.0.6. Brother John Staid up all the night. At the Ball, I paid as there was no Supper 0.2.0. Painter Clarke was with us in the Evening. Justice Creed was not invited to the breakfast as there is a misunderstanding between the Houses. He was not at the Ball this Evening neither.* Both Aunts dined, supped &c. again at Parsonage.

14th. I gave Mary Chrich leave to go to Babcary to Day. I read Prayers & Preached this morning at Ansford C. I read Prayers & Preached this Afternoon at C. Cary C. There was a kind of Riot this Afternoon in the Gallery at Cary Church, between James Clarke and Hoskins about sitting in the Gallery, but it was just before I came into Church, all quiet afterwards.

SEPTEMBER *11th.* I read Prayers & Preached this morning at Ansford C. I read Prayers & Preached this Afternoon at C. Cary C. I dined at Parsonage; and spent the Afternoon, supped & spent the Evening at Dr Clarkes with him, his Wife, James & Richard, Old Mr Burge & Son William. Mr Hindley & Mr Creed drank Coffea this Afternoon at Dr Clarkes, as did Sister Jane Woodforde. The Singers in C. Cary Church kept out Mr Creeds Man again from coming into the Gallery — Mr Creed therefore is determined to seek for redress — Mr Creed & Mr Hindley made a Visit to the Parsonage this morning, & was very wet going home to C. Cary. Aunt Anne dined with us at Parsonage to day. We had a Shoulder of Venison to day for Dinner roasted. It was bought of Lord Ilchester's Game-Keeper (Dick Cox) for the Sum of 0.2.6.

13th. I caught a Brace of Tench very fine ones out of our Pond in Pond-Close this morning in less than an Hour, by my Fathers Drag-Net, that I borrowed. Mr Hindley, Justice Creed and Sister Jane dined, supped & spent the Evening with me at Lower House. I gave them for Dinner, a Dish of Tench, Ham & Fowls, roast Leg of Mutton & an Apple Pudding.

14th. Mr Hindley & Justice Creed called at Parsonage this

* A first mention of the quarrel between Mr Creed and Mr Melliar which was to last on and off for two years (see 12 February 1770). The west gallery in parish churches was traditionally reserved for the choir. Creed wanted his servant to sit in the gallery and was prepared to have the door broken down if it were locked against the man.

Evening in their Chair to ask me to dinner to Morrow to talk about going to Wells with them Friday concerning the Gallery Work to wait on the Bishop, but I shall not go (I believe) nor interfere at all concerning it but to live peacably with all men. It is a little unreasonable to desire it, as I must then fly in the face of allmost all my Parishioners. Great & many are the Divisions in C. Cary almost irreconcilable. Send us Peace O Lord. With thee all things are possible.

OCTOBER *26th.* I had a poor little Cat, that had one of her ribs broke & that laid across her Belly and we could not tell what it was, and she was in great pain. I therefore with a small Penknife this morning opened one Side of her and took it out, and performed the operation very well and afterwards sewed it up and put Friars Balsam to it and she was much better after, the incision was half an inch. It grieved me much to see the poor creature in such pain before, and therefore made me undertake the above, which I hope will preserve the Life of the poor Creature. I dined, supped & spent the Evening at Parsonage.

NOVEMBER *1st.* Justice Creed has put Mr Seth Burge and Davd Maby Churchwardens of C. Cary into the Court of Wells, and they are cited to appear the 9 Instant, for not presenting the last Visitation, some particular People for making disturbances in C. Cary Church &c. I am really sorry that there is so much Likelihood of Endless Quarrells in the Town of C. Cary.

5th. I read Prayers this morning at Cary being the 5 of Novem. the Day on which the Papists had contrived an hellish Plot in the Reign of K. James the First, but by the divine Hand of Providence was fortunately discovered. I dined, supped & spent the Evening at Parsonage. The Effigy of Justice Creed was had through the Streets of C. Cary this Evening upon the Engine and then had into the Park and burnt in a Bonfire immediately before the Justice's House for his putting the Church-Wardens of Cary into Wells Court, for not presenting James Clarke for making a Riot in the Gallery at Cary Church some few Sundays back. The whole Parish are against the Justice, and they intend to assist the Church Wardens in carrying on the Cause at Wells. The Justice is now at Lord Pawletts at Hinton.

28th. I paid Mary Chrich this morning 0.17.10¼. N.B. She owes me 1¾. I dined, supped & spent the Evening at Lower House, being busy making up my Cyder at Farmer Gores. My Fathers Man Willm Corp assisted till the Afternoon, when he met with a bad accident in the Wring-House. The Lever flying back & gave him a most violent blow in his Side and Dr Clarke being at Lower House bled him soon after, and then he went home & went to bed. I hope it will not be attended, if it pleases God, with any very bad Circumstances, but he is at present very bad.

DECEMBER *11th.* I read Prayers & Preached this morning at C. Cary C. N.B. Justice Creed was at Church & behaved very shy to me. I went to Cary in our Chaise, William being brave, thank God. I read Prayers & Preached this Afternoon at Ansford C. I dined, supped & spent the Evening at Parsonage.

1769

JANUARY *11th*. Brother Heighes breakfasted with me at Lower House. I dined and spent the Afternoon at Parsonage. I supped & spent the Evening at Mr White's with him, his Wife, Mr Willm Mellior, his Wife and Daughter, Dr Clarke, his Wife, his two Sons James & Richard, his Daughter Jane. We made it late again—I am heartily weary of visiting so much as I have, but if I did not it would be taken amiss in some. I gave Mr Whites Servant Maids o.2.o. At Cribbage this Evening at Mr Whites with Miss Melliar against Sister Clarke & Sister Jane won o.o.6.

13th. The Estate at Almsford late my dear Mothers, which she left between Sister Jane, Brother John and myself, was this day divided between us, by Dr Clarke Senior, Mr Robin White and Painter Clarke of Cary, who went over all the Estate this morning with me, and Afterwards put it into the three undermentioned Lots

First Lot
The Mansion House, Garden & Walk & Barton. The Great old Orchard, the Pear Orchard, the Milking Barton, Druids and Pond Close.

Second Lot
Newports and Shearandgo, Eyles's Paddock, Upper Longlands and Lower Longlands.

Third Lot
The Farm House, Garden, Barton & outhouses, and the Orchard behind the Farm House—All the Poor Houses—Worthies, Little Field and West Field.

The above were put into a Hat after Dinner and were drawn as underwritten. Sister Jane drew first, and she took the 2nd Lot, I drew next and took the 3rd Lot, Brother John drew last and took the 1st Lot. These were present when we drew the Lots Dr Clarke Senr, and Mr Robin White, Painter Clarke, Mr James and Richard Clarke, & Brother Heighes. It was done very fair and honest on all Sides. Dr Clarke, Mr White, Painter Clarke, & Brother Heighes, & Son Willm, Mr James Clarke, Sister Jane and Brother John, all dined with me at Lower House. I gave them for a Dinner, a Surloin of Beef rosted, a boiled Chop & Greens & a plumb Pudding. Brother Heighes, & his Son, and Sister Jane supped and spent the Evening with me, the others went away in the Evening about six, being Clubb Night at Cary. Mr Janes of Allhampton was with me in the Afternoon to offer me some more Wood, but it is very small Stuff, therefore would have but what I ordered before.

FEBRUARY *7th.* I dined & spent the Afternoon at Parsonage. Dr Clarke spent part of the Afternoon at Parsonage, he came to the Parsonage to desire my Father or me to meet some Gentlemen at the George Inn at Cary this Evening to endeavour to compromise matters with regard to a Law-Suit that is now carry-on between Justice Creed on the one Part and the Church-Wardens of Cary on the other; accordingly I went with the Dr down to the George as my Father would not & there I supped &c. Dr Clarke, Mr Pew, Mr Tom Burge, Uncle Tom, Mr White, Painter Clarke and the two Church-Wardens Seth Burge and David Maby were all present. It was proposed that as the Gallery at Cary Church was large enough to contain between 3 and 4 Score People and the Singers being not above 30 in Number, that there should be a Partition made in the Gallery for the Singers, and the other Part open to any Body, and also for Mr Creed to pay his own costs & the Parish the other but the Church-Wardens would not come into it, therefore Hostilities are likely to be very great indeed.

19th. I read Prayers, preached; buried 2 Infants that I so lately christned, aged 10 Days this morning at C. Cary. I read Prayers & Preached this afternoon at Ansford. No singing at Cary this morning on Old Mr Burges Account as reported he sending Persons up into the Singing Part of the Gallery, which was lately agreed on the contrary. I dined, supped & spent the Evening at Parsonage. My Father continues brave I thank God, but in little Pain. Jack supped & spent the Evening at Dr Clarkes. Jacks Stomach is not come down yet to breakfast at L.H. He breakfasts now at Parsonage.

MARCH *12th*. I read Prayers & Preached this Morning at Ansford Church. I read Prayers & Preached this Afternoon at C. Cary Church. Mem: as I was going to shave myself this morning as usual on Sundays, my Razor broke in my Hand as I was setting it on the Strap without any violence. May it be always a warning to me not to shave on the Lord's Day or do any other work to profane it pro futuro. I dined, supped & spent the Evening at Parsonage.

APRIL *18th*. Some high Words between my Father & Jack this Evening—at Parsonage, and on mere Trifles: both passionate.

MAY *29th*. Paid Mary Chrich this morning 0.7.0. I read Prayers this morning at C. Cary being 29 of May, the Restoration of King Charles 2 from Popish Tyranny. I dined & spent the Afternoon with Jack at Lower House. Jack expects the Hatspen People to spend the Evening with him therefore he bought a Leg of Mutton which we dined on. I supped & spent the Evening at Parsonage. Great Cock-fighting at Ansford Inn to day. Jack brought home with him from Ansford Inn after ten o'clock this Evening, instead of the Hatspen People Dr John Graunt, and James Graunt, Joseph Wilmot and Hines all of Ditchet, which supped & stayed till 3 in the Morning, quite low life People much beneath Jack—I really wonder Jack keeps such mean Company. George Green our Man very bad in a Fever.

69

JUNE *3rd.* To Sister Whites Son John who brought me a Present of a Couple of Ducks sent to me by Sister White, gave 0.1.0. I dined & spent the Afternoon at Mr Whites with him, his Wife, Mr Harry Yeatman, Mr James Clarke & Sister Jane. The transit of Venus over the Face of the Sun I saw this Evening between seven & eight o'clock at Dr Clarkes. It appeared as a black-Patch upon a fair Lady's Face. It will not appear again they say till in the Year 1874. We should have seen it much plainer had not little Sam Clarke broke the window Glass of the Telescope Yesterday, I could however perceive it with my naked Eye but very little. During the transit it was remarkable cold indeed. I supped & spent the Evening at Parsonage.

10th. Had a most violent Raish in my Face, Hands &c. but very bad and much worse in my Face than any where else. I sent for Doctor Clarke or his Son James to come to me directly, and accordingly Mr James Clarke came and he advised me to keep myself very warm, and not go out and also not to live low, but encourage the Raish; I therefore kept in all Day & eat and drank hearty as I could. Small Rum & Water allowed to be drank hot.

17th. I dined, supped & spent the Evening at Parsonage. Dr Clarke & Brother Heighes spent part of the Afternoon at L.H. Dr Clarke supped & spent the Evening at Parsonage. Jack dined at Mr Melliars and went with him in the Afternoon to Bruton and returned & supped at Parsonage and was quite merry & talked very pertly to his Father. Jack made a terrible Noise at Lower House with all the Folks there. I got up out of my Bed & came down at twelve at Night, & found the House quite in an Uproar Jack abusing of them all in a terrible manner. Very bad Work indeed of a Saturday Night in a Parson's House—it disturbed me all night. N.B. we must part.

19th. Paid Mary Chrich this morning 0.5.6. I dined, supped & spent the Evening at Parsonage. Sister White dined & spent the Afternoon at Parsonage. Jack dined &c. at Dr Clarkes. He spent the Evening at Parsonage & made a Riot there being in want of mony. Jack had a new Mohogany Beaurou brought him this Afternoon to the L. House from one Smart of Glastonbury and a very neat one it is, but dearish, he asking for it 5.0.0. Whenever Jack wants mony, he disturbs both Houses. Old Justice Dawe of Ditchet died last Saturday by drinking.

26th. I spent part of the Afternoon at Uncle Toms & at Dr Clarkes, drank Coffea this Afternoon, with Sister Clarke her Daughter Jane & Justice Creed. The Justice and myself had a great deal of Talk together about past affairs. And he told me that he intended claiming Sandford Estate which at present I hold. It is all owing to Brother Heighes's sending for a Copy of my late Aunt Collins's Will & publishing it. The Justice is very angry indeed with our Family. Mr Frank Woodforde spent part of the Aft. at Parsonage. Mr Richard Clark supped & spent the Evening at Parsonage. Sister Jane dined at Sister White's & spent the Afternoon at young Mrs William Burge's at Castle-Cary. It was merely by accident that I met the Justice.

JULY *6th.* I dined, supped & spent the Evening at Justice Creed's with him and his Father — & they were very Civil.

AUGUST *10th.* For a Pound & half of Coffea of Marshall pd 0.6.0. I dined, supped & spent the Evening at Lower House. Miss Rooke, Sister Clarke, Sister Jane, Mr James & Richd Clarke Brother Heighes & Brother John dined, supped &c. with me. I gave them for Dinner, a Batter Pudding, a Couple of Ducks rosted and a Codlin Tart. Jenny Clarke & Mr John Burge supped &c. with us at Lower House. Brother Heighes slept there. For a Letter from Bob Master this Evening pd 0.0.8. N.B. I invited Dr Clarke & Mr White, and neither came either to Dinner or Supper. I think to return the Compt to Dr Clarke, as for Mr White he was detained involuntarily.

SEPTEMBER *22nd.* I dined, supped & spent the Evening at Justice Creed's with him, his Father, Mr Hindley, Mr Potts, Mr

Duck, Old Mr Willm Burge, his Son William, Mr Pew and one Farmer Neate. We had a fine Haunch of Venison for Dinner. Great Rejoicings at Cary to Day, being the Coronation Day— Bells ringing all Day, Cudgell Playing at Crokers, a very large Bonfire on the Top of the Hill, & very great Fireworks in the Evening with fireing of many Gunns—All at Mr Creeds, Mr Hindley & Mr Ducks expence. I was at all—at the Cudgell Playing I gave 0.4.6. The Fireworks were sent from London,

and were Sky-Rocketts, Mines, Trees, Crackers, Wheels & various Indian Fireworks. Old Mrs Burge & Daughter, Mrs Pew & Daughter Polly, Sister Clarke and Sister Jane, & young Mrs Willm Burge, drank Tea & Coffea. Supped & spent the Evening at Justice Creeds. George Pew & Mr John & Saml Burge supped &c. there. We did not break up till near two in the morning. Every thing extremely handsome and polite indeed. To Mr Creeds Servants gave 0.3.0.

OCTOBER *18th*. After breakfast went with Mr Creed in his Chair to Wells with a great Possy from Cary to attend at the County Meeting to consider of a proper Petition to his Majesty in the present Crisis of Affairs.* We went to the Swan where we dined with upwards of a hundred Gentlemen of the first rank in the County. We had a very respectable meeting on the Occasion. Mr Coxe, Mr Smith Member for Bath, Mr Allen Member for Bridgewater, Mr Seymour, Mr Creed, Revd Mr Sansom & Revd Mr Gatehouse spoke on the Occasion upon the Petitions that were presented to the Publick. Mr Coxe's Petition with some alteration was approved of most, and agreed in the Town Hall to be presented to his Majesty by proper Persons. To my Dinner only at the Swan paid 0.3.6. To the Waiters and Music gave there 0.1.0. Britons never will be slaves was played during Dinner. I returned with Mr Creed After we had signed the Petition and got home by eight o'clock this Evening.

NOVEMBER *20th*. Brother Heighes & John dined &c. at Lower House again, and they kept me up till 2 in the morning being very quarrelsome especially my Brother John. N.B. It is too much indeed for me.

22nd. Our Man George Greene was this morning turned away by my Brother John for being a little saucy last Night— he pd him—after 6. Jack I am afraid will never keep any Servant long.

DECEMBER *5th.* I dined & spent the Afternoon at Ansford Inn upon an Haunch of Doe Venison given to Mr Willm Burge Junr by Sir Joseph Mawbey in London as he says, to which I was invited. A strange Man was found this Evening in my Fathers little House. N.B. A Farmer's Daughter near Bristol who was to sleep at my Fathers to night had occasion to go to

* For a short time almost the whole country saw the refusal of Parliament to admit John Wilkes (twice elected for Middlesex fairly and with a large majority) as an Absolutist plot, and it was with this concern that the freeholders of Somerset met to petition the King to dissolve Parliament.

the necessary House & there was a man there, but he got clear of. He was upon no good there.

17th. I read Prayers & Preached this morning at Ansford Church. I read Prayers & Preached this Afternoon at Cary Church. The Singers at Cary did not please me this Afternoon by singing the 12 Psalm—New Version—reflecting upon some People. I dined, supped & spent the Evening at Parsonage. Aunt Anne dined &c. at Parsonage. Jack dined I believe at Mr Whites —our Dinner not being the best. Mr & Mrs White & Son John supped &c. at Parsonage. Brother Heighes I believe dined at Allhampton to day. Some People have been about my Fathers House again this Evening about 8 o'clock—Jenny & the Maid being at the little House some Person or another came to the Door of it & rapped against it three Times with a Stick. What it means I know not. Brother Heighes, Jack & myself all armed, took a Walk at twelve this Evening round the Parish to see if we could meet any idle Fellows but we did not, & therefore came home about two. We waited at my Fathers some considerable Time, till Brother Heighes was very uneasy, being very cold in his Feet.

1770

JANUARY *23rd*. I dined, supped & spent the Evening at Parsonage. Sister White, Betsy White of Shepton Mallett a very fine Girl, Jenny Clarke & Jenny White & John White dined &c. at Parsonage. Betsy White, Jenny Clarke, Mrs White, & Brother John who dined with us, supped & spent the Evening at Parsonage. At Back-Gammon this Evening at Parsonage lost 0.0.6.

FEBRUARY *12th*. I married Samuel Bangor of Linnington in Dorsett, and Anne Oram this morning at Cary by Banns recd 0.5.0. Paid Mary Chrich this morning 0.11.11½. I read Prayers by poor Rose Gristock who is worse & worse. After marrying the above Couple I went to Mr Willm Melliars and Mr Creeds & to Dr Clarkes, to desire all three of them to drink a Dish of Coffea with me this Afternoon at Lower House and if possible to reconcile all animosities in Cary and to stop & put an end to all Law Suits now subsisting. It was agreeable to all Parties for Mr Creed & Mr Melliar to settle all matters & to make Peace. Mr Creed & Mr Melliar agreed to meet each other this Afternoon at my House. I dined & spent part of the Afternoon at Mr Creeds with him and his Father—And after the Justice took a walk to my House and drank a Dish of Coffea with me. Mr Willm Melliar & Dr Clarke also drank a Dish of Coffea with me & after Coffea we talked over the Parish affairs. After much altercation it was settled for Peace. After the above was agreed to by us all Four and Mr Melliar had made a memorandum of it in writing, Mr Creed & Mr Melliar hobbed & nobbed in a Glass of Wine and drank Success to Peace. Mr Creed & Mr Melliar then walked away together for their respective homes—and it was about five o'clock. Dr Clarke afterwards supped & spent the remaining Part of the Evening with us. Jack came home a little merry this Evening and he laid a Wager of one Guinea that he would not from this Night get drunk all the Year 1770—that is, as not to be able to tread a Scratch.

MAY *19th*. I had a new dark-grey Coat and Waistcoat brought home this morning by my Taylor Isaac Oram for making pd 0.9.0. I dined, supped & spent the Evening at Parsonage. I played at Back-Gammon again this Evening for the first Time this Fortnight with my Father & we neither won or lost. Gay and Benson two of the Players at Cary spent the Afternoon, supped & got themselves quite merry at the L. House with my Brothers. They were gone away and my Brothers with them before I got home at Night—And my Brothers stayed out till near 12, something very agreeable & with which I was greatly pleased happened this Evening. It gave me much secret Pleasure & satisfaction. Brother Heighes was quite merry this Evening.

JUNE *26th*. I supped & spent the Evening at Parsonage and stayed there till 11 o'clock, my Father being taken seriously ill soon after Supper with a Violent Pain in his Stomach and a giddiness in his head. I am afraid my poor Father is in a bad way—Pray God send him better health if it be thy good pleasure of if thou hast otherwise ordered it, give him Grace so to take thy visitation that after this Life ended, he may dwell with thee in Eternity thro' Jesus Christ our Lord. Mr & Mrs White spent the Evening at Parsonage, Mrs White supped there. My Poor dear Father was something better when I came away. N.B. When my Father was at Bath a Mole or Want was run & killed in our House at Parsonage. Some say it is a sure sign of Death.

27th. This very Day I am thirty Years of Age—God make me truly thankful for thy great goodness as on this Day shewed me by bringing me into the World and for preserving me to this

Day from the many & great Dangers which frail mortality is every day exposed to, grant me O Lord the continuance of thy divine goodness to me, that thy Holy Spirit may direct me in all my ways and that the remaining part of my Days may be more spent to thy honour and Glory than those already past.

JULY *4th*. After breakfast walked up to Justice Creeds, and about 8 o'clock went with the Justice in his Chaise to Horsington and made Mr & Mrs Spencer there a morning Visit who were both at home with their two Sons & five Daughters, the two eldest Miss Spencers are very fine young Ladies about 15 Years old. The eldest entertained us upon the Guitar & sung charmingly with it. Mr Spencer has a noble House & every thing in the neatest manner. They pressed us much to dine with them but we did not—I drove the Justice there and he drove me back, coming back we called upon Parson Plucknett at Cheriton and stayed with him about 20 Minutes. We got home by 2.

17th. Miss Tucker, Sister Jane & Mr Richard Clarke with both my Brothers dined & spent the Afternoon with me. I gave them a Leg Mutton rosted & a Gooseberry Pudding. They all went to see the Mountebank at Cary after. To Stephen Bennett Senr & Junr for making me two Garden Chairs, Timber & Labour, pd him 0.10.6. To Peter Longman making a Grate for my Bedroom & other little Jobbs, paid him this morning 0.6.5. I went up in the Evening to see the Masons that are building up one End of the Poor Houses for me and there I met the Justice and we had some Words concerning the Masons (as he said) having gone upon his Ground—but I think they have not—however I stopped the Masons till they heard further from me. I cannot think it at all the Act of a Friend in Mr Creed, as it is not more than six Inches in dispute.

AUGUST *28th*. For Popes Works 10 Volumes, of Brother Heighes this morning I gave him and they were second Hand & third

1.1.0. I dined & spent the Afternoon at Lower House. I had a Shoulder of Mutton rosted and French Beans for Dinner. I supped & spent the Evening at Parsonage. Jenny supped & spent the Evening at Sister Whites. Brother John went to Wells Races this morning & did not return all night.

SEPTEMBER *26th*. Exceeding windy & very wet and tempestuous nevertheless as I promised to dine at Mr Farr's in Dorsetshire this day after Breakfast set forth in Ansford Inn Chaise for that Place. I called upon my Niece Jenny Clarke & she went with me as promised. The Waters were out very high. At Henstridge we called & wanted a fresh Chaise there of Mr Baker who keeps the Inn but both his Chaises were out, therefore I had the same Chaise & Horses to Stocke after baiting them. We got to Stocke I thank God safe & well by a little after two in the Afternoon & found Mr Farr's People at dinner. For Wine &c. at Henstridge pd 0.1.6. We had a Guide with us from Henstridge to Stocke as the Waters were out & our Driver never was there. He was an old Man & rode behind the Chaise, but was very serviceable. Gave him for going with us 0.1.0. Going through one Turnpike pd 0.0.6. I gave Peace who drove us to Stocke from Ansford 0.2.6. I dined, supped & slept at Stocke at Mr Farr's. We found Mr Farr better than he has been tho' now very bad. Mrs Farr & Miss & Jenny White very well, as were Sister White & Sister Jane. Mrs Ford & one Captain Ford Relations of Mrs Farrs dined at Stocke. At Cards this Evening at Stocke lost 0.1.0. Exceeding tempestuous all night. I slept but indifferent.

27th. I breakfasted, dined, supped & slept again at Stocke. Sister White, Sister Jane & Jenny Clarke did the same. We had as fine a Pine Apple after Dinner as ever I saw. Every thing in the genteelest Manner we had at Stock & very fine. As for Miss Farr she is without exception the best and most accomplished Young Lady I ever saw and very good.

OCTOBER *23rd*. I dined and spent the Afternoon at Lower House. Cousin Harry Yeatman, Sister White, Sister Jane, Cousin Frank Woodforde, Sister White's Son John, and both my Brothers dined & spent the Afternoon with me at L. House. I gave them for Dinner a Surloin of Beef rosted, & a plumb Pudding. We all went in the Evening to Ansford Inn to hear Mr Rice play on the Welsh Harp, where we met my Uncle & Aunt Tom, Sister Clarke, Jenny Clarke, old Mrs Willm Burge, Mr Francis's three eldest Daughters, Molly Pew & her London Cousin, two strange Clergymen that came by chance to Ansford Inn and whose Names were Smith and Bowls & joined us after Tea. I treated the Company with Coffea & Tea this Afternoon at my own expence at Ansford Inn for which I pd 0.11.4. We each gave the Harper one Shilling apiece but myself as I gave him two & collected for him 1.1.0. For myself, Jenny Clarke & Jacky White I paid 0.4.0. After Tea we had a Hopp till 10 then went to Supper below Stairs on a cold Collation and danced after till 1 o'clock. Our Musick was nothing else but Mr Rice's Harp, and we did very well by it. My Partner was the eldest Miss Francis, she dances but poorly & says but little. Agatha and Nancy Clarke the two Painters Daughters joined us before Supper & danced with us. We had the great Room to dance in At Ansford Inn. For Supper, Negus &c. as we did not suffer the Ladies to pay for any thing, and only seven Gentlemen, that is, the 2 strange Clergymen, myself, Cousin Harry Yeatman, Cousin Frank, and both my Brothers, we each pd 0.7.0. I paid my Brother Heighes's 7/0 back again as I intended treating him this afternoon, so that it cost me 0.14.0 besides the above 15/4, which will amount in all 1.9.4. It was near two o'clock before we got home—however we spent a very agreeable Afternoon and Evening. Indeed I think it quite odd that neither James nor Richard Clarke were there, as I asked Richard myself. It is not using Cousin Frank, Jack &c. I think well. We gave the Servants at the Inn between them 0.5.0.

1771

JANUARY *5th*. I dined, supped & spent the Evening at Lower
House. Mrs Farr & Miss Farr, Sister White, Sister Jane, and
both my Brothers dined, supped & spent the Evening with me.
Justice Creed dined & spent the Afternoon and part of the
Evening with me at Lower House. I gave them for Dinner a
Dish of Tench, a Round of Beef boiled, a Neck of veal rosted
and an Apple Pudding. I buried a little Girl of Farmer Biss's of
Pennard this Afternoon at Ansforde, aged about 5 Years. Dr
Clarke, his Wife, Mr James & Richard Clarke, Jenny Clarke
and the two Miss Pynes; Mr White and Mr Andrew Russ &
Cousin Frank supped & spent the Evening with me at Lower
House. I invited Cousin Robert Woodforde to dine &c. with me
but he could not come. To some Well-Sailers this Evening gave
o.1.o. We had a hop this Evening at Lower House & danced
till half an Hour after Eleven & then it ceased. I had a Bass
Viol Mr Hooper, and a Violin one Ryal a very good hand to
play to us. I gave them o.10.o. Red Wine & White, Negace,
Beer & Cyder we had to drink. Mrs Farr & Miss slept again at
Parsonage. The Company seemed very well pleased with their
Entertainment. I treated them also with my large Wax Candle.

10th. Brother John was greatly astonished by a Light this
Evening as he came thro' Orchards, a Field by Ansford Church,
which Light seemed to follow him close behind all the way
through that Field & which he could not account for. I hope it
is no Omen of Death in the Family. N.B. The Reflection of the
snow I apprehend occasioned the Light that my Brother saw.

FEBRUARY *10th*. Brother John & Andrew Russ stayed at Parsonage this Evening till after 12 o'clock, then came to the Lower

House and after Andrew Russ went home. Brother John being very full in Liquor at 2 o'clock in the morning, made such an intolerable noise by swearing in so terrible a manner & so loud that it disturbed me out of sound sleep being gone to bed, and was so shocked at it that I was obliged to get up to desire him to go to bed, but all my arguments & Persuasions were in vain, and he kept me up till five in the morning & then I went to bed & he went on Horseback for Bath. It was an exceeding cold Night & a very hard frost—And at seven o'clock in the morning snowed very hard. O that Jack was in some way of business and that his Life was something better and more religious for in the morning whilst I was in Church, he was shooting.

19th. My Father was brave & in very good Spirits this morning, but in the Evening was as bad as ever and talked very moving to Sister Jane and me about his Funeral—And that he wanted to alter his Will, and mentioned the underwritten to me & Sister Jane, that he desired that his Maid (Eliz. Clothier) should have that House where Grace Stephens lives at present during her Life, and after her Life to go to Sister Jane, as well as all the other Poor Houses & Mrs Parrs House, and the Field called four Acres to her my Sister Jane: That Sister White has one hundred Pounds to make her equal to her Sister Clarke in Fortune: That I have all his Books and Book-Case in his Study: And that he would have no People invited to his Funeral to make a Show, but that he is carried to Ansford Church by six of his Poor Neighbours. Robin Francis & his Brother Thomas were mentioned and that they had half a Crown apiece—to be laid in the Vault where my Mother is by her Side. And that a little Monument be erected in the Side-Wall near the Vault in Memory of him & his Wife. My Poor Father is I think in much the same way as my Poor Mother was. Pray God Bless him & keep him, and give us all strength to bear so sore an Affliction as such a Separation must occasion, if it be thy divine Will to remove him from us. O God whenever such an Event happens take him to thyself, and give us Grace to follow his good Examples, that with him we may deserve to be Partakers of thy Heavenly Kingdom. Grant him O Lord an Easy & happy Exit. Better Parents no Children ever had than we have been blessed with—blessed be God for it—and make us more worthy than we are, for all thy goodness to us. Praise the Lord O my Soul, and forget not all his Benefits. Thou hast not dealt with us after our Sins, nor rewarded us according to our wickednesses. Praise thou the Lord O my Soul. I played at Back-Gammon with my Father in the Evening, it takes him in some degree off from thinking of his Pain I won 0.0.6. He went to bed before I went home being uneasy in his Bowels. Brother Heighes continues weak, but I think better.

MARCH *13th*. I sent a Letter this morning to Mrs Powel at Harding near St Albans, Hertfordshire, to apply to her for the

Livings of Cary & Ansford in case my Father should not recover.

APRIL *9th*. I dined, supped, spent the Evening and sat up all Night till five in the morning—my poor Father being in most racking pain all Night & Day much worse than ever, he groans very loud indeed. Pray God release him from his Pains which are acute. Brother Heighes dined, supped & was up all Night at Parsonage. Aunt Anne spent the Afternoon at Parsonage. Dr Clarke & Wife & Mr James Clarke, Sister White & Brother John supped & spent the Evening at Parsonage. Dr Clarke gave my Poor Father 40 Drops of Tinctura Thebaica or liquid Laudanum this Evening to compose him, wch did not take effect till 3 in the morning & then he slept. Sister White, Brother John & Jenny were up with us till Night. The Parsonage is most melancholy at present.

30th. Cousin Tom Woodforde sent a Baskett to the Parsonage and which came this Afternoon, in which were a Couple of Widgeons, some electuary for Aunt Parr, some spirit of Lavender for Aunt Anne, a Pot of Confectio Cardiaca for my Father and a Letter for me in Answer to mine which came safe. My poor dear Father very bad this Afternoon, almost choked with Phlegm in his Stomach which I am afraid is the Rattle and a foreboding of his near departure hence, which if it is—O God receive his soul into thy everlasting Kingdom.

MAY *16th*. I breakfasted, dined, supped & slept again at Parsonage. I recd of Farmer Corpe this morning half a Years Rent due at Michaelmas last 24.0.0. My Poor Father worse than ever a great deal, & altered greatly after 12 at Night, & in great Agonies all the morning; and it pleased the Almighty Creator to deliver him out of all his Pain & Trouble in this World about $\frac{1}{2}$ an hour after one o'clock at Noon, by taking him to himself —blessed therefore be the Name of the Lord. It is the Lord let him do what seemeth him good, the Lord gave & the Lord hath taken away, blessed be the name of the Lord. Have mercy upon us O Lord miserable Sinners, and send us Comfort from above. My ever dear Father left his whole Effects both real and Personal between me, my Brother John & Sister Jane, and he left me his sole and faithful Executor, his own Words. O Lord support me under these sore Afflictions. I have the management also (for my Father) the Care of my Poor Aunts Affairs & likewise her Funeral. The Visitation also this Day at Bruton, but could not go, my Father being so bad. Sent a Letter however to the Arch-Deacon to excuse myself on the Illness of my Father by Davd Maby my Clerk—And another to Mr Leir Junr concerning the burying of my Aunt Parr. I had Christian Masters to bury this Evening at Ansford but could not do it, therefore sent to Mr Leir Junr at Ditcheat to do it for me—which he accordingly did. Sister White & Brother John dined, supped &c. at Parsonage. Dr Clarke & Mr White spent part of the Afternoon at Parsonage. I was very ill this Evening, being hurried greatly in my Spirits by Brother Heighes, when he heard my Fathers Will to him and before Sister White, Sister Jane & Brother John—my Father not leaving him any thing, but he has the Sussex Estate settled upon him by Marriage & which brings him per Ann. 46.0.0.

22nd. I breakfasted, dined, supped & slept again at Parsonage. Brother John, Sister White, & Brother Heighes, dined, supped and spent the Evening at Parsonage. My poor dear Fathers mortal Remains were deposited this Evening between six and seven o'clock in his Vault in the Chancel of Ansford Church by the side of his dear Wife, whose Coffin is quite entire, tho' dark & gloomy, the breast plate quite plain—just Room for both Coffins & no more. Mr Thos Leir Junr buried my poor dear Father. The Pall Bearers were Mr Wm Melliar, Mr Willm Burge Senr, Mr Willm Pew Senr, Mr John Penny Mr Creed Senr not being able to come, Mr Thos Burge and Mr Seth Burge—they had all black silk Hatbands & Shammy Gloves. Mr Leir had the same. The Under-Bearers were my Father's

Man Willm Corpe, My Uncles Man Thos Hutchins, Mr Clarkes Man Simon Brayne, Willm Biggen, His Substitute Mr Whites Man Willm Butt, Robin Francis & Thos Francis his Brother. They had all black Lamb Gloves and each o.2.6. Willm Corpe had a black crape Hatband, Buckles and a black broad Cloth Coat and Waistcoat given to him by us. Davd Maby the Clerk had a black silk Hatband common, and a Pair of mock Shammy Gloves. Stephen Bennett Senr and the Sextons of Ansford & Cary, Edwd Creed Sexton of Cary & Frank Dawe Sexton of Ansford had Lamb Gloves—The Mourners were Brother Heighes, myself, Brother John, Uncle Tom, Dr Clarke & Mr White. And we all had black Crape Hatbands and black Shammy Gloves. Mr James & Richard Clarke, and Mr Frank Woodforde, second Mourners had black silk Hatbands and black Shammy Gloves. Mr Francis the Undertaker had a black silk Hatband, and black Shammy Gloves. Aunt Anne Woodforde, Aunt Jane Woodforde of Bath, Aunt Tom Woodforde, Sister Clarke, Sister White, Sister Jane & Mrs Heighes Woodforde, though they did not attend the Funeral had or are to have all black Shammy Gloves. My Fathers Maid Eliz. Clothier who attended the Funeral had Mock Shammy Gloves, & a black Gown & Buckles given. Mary Chrich, Eliz. Chrich, Alice Stacy, Mary Coleman, Christian Speed and Anne Stephens who sat up of a Night after my Father was dead with the Corpse called Wakers, they had each a Pr of black Lamb Gloves, and they attended the Corpse to the Church. The six Pall Bearers, Brother Heighes, myself, Brother John, My Uncle Tom, Dr Clarke, Mr White, Mr James and Richd Clarke and Mr Frank Woodforde, all of us had black Cloaks. The Procession to Church was as follows—Mr Maby the Clerk about 2 Yards before Mr Francis the Undertaker who went next, then Mr Leir about 2 Yards from the Undertaker in a black Gown and Band, then the beloved Corpse which was covered with a black Velvet Pall, then Brother Heighes and myself, Brother John & Uncle Tom, Dr Clarke and Mr White, Mr Frank Woodforde

& James & Richard Clarke. The Coffin was covered with black broad-Cloth. My poor Father was 76 Years of Age. Cary Bell as well as Ansford Bell tolled from 12 at Noon till 8 in the Evening. Every thing I hope was done decently, handsome and well — And nothing omitted but want of speaking to the Gentlemen to return to the Parsonage to pull of their Cloaks at the House, which however most of them did — & drank a Glass of Wine & went. Aunt Anne, Sister White & Jenny Clarke spent the Aft. at Parsonage. I gave Mrs White this Aft. for mourning as agreed on, 5.0.0. My Brother John and myself had Weepers on the Occasion. I did not read my Fathers Will as there was no Occasion.

JUNE *4th*. I breakfasted, dined, supped & slept again at Parsonage. Brother John, Sister Jane & myself divided & settled all Eatables, Liquors of all kinds, Wood, Coal, Soap, Candles, Tobacco, Sugar, Tea, Chocolate, Coffea, Hay and Straw, equally amongst us, & late my dear Fathers, this morning amicably settled. For Hay about 6 Tons & Straw near a Load, I took to myself and to each of them for it pd 3.0.0. Brother John, Nancy Woodforde dined, supped &c. at Parsonage. Brother Heighes spent the Aft. supped &c. at Parsonage. I took a Ride this Afternoon upon my Mare, called at Mr Leaches, bought 40 Reed-Sheaves & 3 Bushells of Beans of him, Beans at 5/6, Reed-Sheaves at 7d. Poor Mrs John Penny of Clanville died about noon. It is said that she hurt herself greatly by drinking. After to day I am to keep the Parsonage House.

5th. This morning between James Woodforde, Jane Woodforde and John Woodforde, Housekeeping was settled as follows that I should keep house at Parsonage, Jack at Lower House, and that Sister Jane should board with me for sixteen Pounds per Annum, Tea, Sugar & Wine excepted. I purchased their Parts of all the Eatables, Liquors of all Kinds, Wood &c. &c. this morning, mine below of all kinds included in the Charge, in the whole mine being valued below at the same Rate pd 27.13.10 each Part being valued at 13.19.5. What I had received for Tithe &c. since and before my dear Fathers Decease to this Day, was also settled this morning between us, as was also all disbursements accounted for & settled.

I had received in the whole 82.9.10.

I had paid in the whole 70.2.9.

Balance 6.7.1 which I then paid & discharged.

22nd. Mr Frank Woodforde has declared that he has both the Livings of Castle-Cary and Ansford promised him. Very ungenerous proceedings if true I must confess, as my late good Father has been the making of that Family.

24th. I read Prayers this morning at Cary being Midsummer Day. After Prayers I made a little Visit to Mrs Melliar where I met Mr Frank Woodforde & told him before Mrs Melliar, Miss Melliar & Miss Barton what great obligations I was under to him for not offering me to hold his Livings for him, instead of Mr Dalton & Mr Gatehouse. From such base Actions & dishonest men O Lord deliver me.

JULY *9th.* I inducted Mr Dalton this morning into the Rectory of Ansford. Mr Perry was witness to it of Ansford Inn. Mr Dalton told me before my Sister Jane that we need not be uneasy about being turned out of the House, he would take care of that, as none could turn us out but he himself & he will not. I breakfasted, supped & slept again at Parsonage. I dined & spent the Afternoon at Justice Creeds with him and his Father. The Justice & myself played at Bowls this Afternoon till 8 at Night. I beat him several Games. Mr Dalton went home to Dinner, I asked him to dine with me.

AUGUST *20th.* I breakfasted at Parsonage and Mr James Clarke breakfasted with me. And after breakfast I went with Mr James Clarke & my Brother John to Wokey to see Dr Clarke who is now there. I called at Shepton Mallett & saw Miss Paines Mother there. We got to Wokey (alias Ripple) a little after eleven o'clock. We dined & spent the Afternoon there with the Doctor, his Son Richard Clarke, Jenny Clarke & little Sam Clarke. Dr Clarke was exceeding low & cried very much all Day. Dr Arnold of Wells drank Coffee at Wokey this Afternoon. After Coffee Dr Clarke, myself, Mr James & Richard Clarke, my Brother John, Jenny Clarke & Sam took a ride to see Wokey Hole, we stayed there about ½ an Hour. I gave there 0.1.0. I gave to Mr Clarkes Servants at Wokey 0.2.6. Mr James & myself & little Sam parted with the rest of the Company at Wokey Hole and went for Ansford after 7 o'clock in the Evening and we did not get home till very near 11 o'Clock, poor little Sam being greatly fatigued. Sam rode behind me most part of the Way home. Brother John went back to Wokey with the rest, and he sleeps there, as Priddy Fair is to Morrow, which is near Wokey. The Doctors House at Wokey is really very good it is about 3 Miles below Wells and lays well. We had for Dinner a Leg Mutton boiled and a Couple of Ducks rosted, and an Apple Pye—Wine &c. to drink. We were most cordially & heartily entertained. I was quite fatigued & very sick when I got home to Ansford. Little Willm Coleman my Boy I took with me to day. Miss Paine breakfasted, dined, supped &c. at Parsonage. For a Horse to day recd 0.2.6.

SEPTEMBER *25th*. I breakfasted, supped and slept again at Parsonage. I went this morning to Shepton-Mallet in our Chaise, to dine with Mr Wickham which I did with him, his Wife and one Mr Hughes who is Curate of Shepton. I carried Miss Betsy White and little Jacky White with me and brought them both back with us to Ansford. I had hard Work to prevail on Mrs White of Shepton to let Miss White return with me, but she did at last. She is a sweet tempered Girl indeed and I like her much, and I think would make a good Wife, I do not know but I shall make a bold stroke that way.

OCTOBER *19th*. I dined, supped & spent the Evening at New-

College. For Wine & Fruit this Day pd 0.0.7. The Streets in Oxford are much improved, as the Signs are taken down and put against the Houses, the Streets widened, East-Gate & Bocardo taken down & a new Bridge going to be built where Magdalen Bridge now stands, and temporary Bridges during the building of it now making by Christchurch Broad-Walk, for to go up the Hill &c. I bought a Piece of Holland, 2 Pr of silk Stockings, 9 coloured Handkerchiefs, & 6 white Handkerchiefs of my old Mercer Mr Austin, for which I owe him near 12.0.0. Some Stuff for a Cassock included in the above. I have bought also a new Hat for Fortnam—for it owe 1.1.0

NOVEMBER *21st*. I married James Russ & Rebecca Barns this morning at Cary Church by Licence for which I recd 0.10.6. I breakfasted at Home and about twelve took my Mare & went for Shepton, having promised to dine at Mr Wickhams. My Boy went before to Shepton to have back my Mare. I dined & spent part of the Afternoon at Mr Wickhams with Sister Jane and Miss Paine, with Mr and Mrs Wickham & Mr Hughes. We had a very genteel pretty Dinner indeed, the young Ladies did not dine with us but came in to us after Dinner. We all went in the Afternoon & drank Tea at Mr Hughes's Lodgings at Mr Stones the Barbers—and Miss Hyat, Miss White and Miss Frost drank Tea with us there—from thence we all went to a Play at the George, Henry the 4 and the Citizen the Entertainment performed pretty well. For Seven Tickets of Mr Morris the Player pd 0.10.6. I gave a Ticket to each of the Miss Wickhams, one to Miss Hyat, one to Miss Paine, one to Miss Betsy White, and one to Miss Frost, an acquaintance of Miss Whites. Whilst we were at the Play who should join us but Brother John, Mr Richard Clarke & Jenny Clarke from Woky. I supped & slept at Mrs Paines as did Sister Jane and Jenny Clarke; Brother John & Richard Clarke supped and spent the Evening with us at Mrs Paines. Mrs Paine kept her Bed all Day having the Head-Ache. I caught a bad Cold Yesterday and am but poorly.

DECEMBER *10th*. I bottled of my Rum & Brandy this morning and had of Rum 2 Dozen & 2 Bottles; of Brandy 2 Doz. and 4 Bottles, which I think good Measure. I recd of Robin Francis this morning for Tithe 1.10.0. Paid him a Bill for Port &c. 1.13.0. Betsy White, Jenny Clarke & Brother John supped and spent the Evening at Parsonage & very agreeable. Jacky White, in great Pain, but there is something rising externally on his Side, which might indeed save his life.

12th. I supped and spent the Evening at Mr White's with him, his Wife, Betsy White, James Clarke & Brother John; little Jack Whites Side was opened this afternoon by Mr James Clarke, from whence issued vast quantities of well concocted Matter, which I hope by the blessing of God, will be the means of his Recovery. There appears now some hopes of his doing well.

1772

JANUARY *23rd*. I breakfasted, dined, supped & slept again at Parsonage. Miss Tucker & Brother John dined, supped &c. at Parsonage. Mrs Collins (Fanny Morris that was) dined & spent part of the Afternoon with me at Parsonage. Mrs Tucker could not dine with me having had notice of Mr Tuckers coming home from London this Afternoon. Jenny Clarke supped & spent the Evening with me. I went up to Sister Whites this Evening to desire Betsy White to spend the Evening with us, but she would not. She is highly affronted with me or Sister Jane I believe. At Cards, Whist, this Evening won 0.1.0.

FEBRUARY *21st*. I drank Coffee this Aft. at Mr Creeds with old Mr Creed and Mrs Baker, and we were very agreeable & chatty. I gave old Sam Gibbs this Aft. as I was going to Mr Creeds for cleaning the Pond by Cary Church gave 0.0.6. As I returned from Mr Creeds in the Evening I called at Dr Clarkes, and who should soon come in there, but my old Friend Captain Rooke from Ansford Inn; He is as remarkable as ever, I never met with his equal. He said that he came out of Lincolnshire this morning. He came in a Post-Chaise & Four. He also said that he had got me a Living in Lincolnshire of Col. Owen of 180 Pound Per Annum, that he had now 30 Pounds a Day, that he intended to stand for Somersett the next Election, that he had two Ships, had several fish Carts & near forty Horses coming to Ansford Inn to Morrow, that he intended to buy the Manor of Ansford & every thing unsold hereabouts, that he had more mony that he could spend, with many other such unaccountable things. I went with him to Mr Whites afterwards and there he talked the same and then Perry & he had words. Perry took a Watch of him for a Debt, which he let him have for 2 Guineas, & that he had a Hundred more of them, the Captain behaved very shabby there. He afterwards went with me to the Parsonage and there supped & immediately after Supper at 10 o'clock he went in a Post-Chaise & four of Perrys to his House at Ivythorn. N.B. I was glad he did not stay. My Sister Jane by good luck did not appear in his Company, tho' she was at Mr Whites, when we were there, and there she supped & spent the Evening. I do not know what to make of him, unless he is mad.

29th. This morning after Breakfast I went down to Henbridge, where I saw & spent the Morning with Mrs Grant & her two Daughters, Miss Jenny Wason & Miss Nancy Wason. They all seemed to be very uneasy, particularly Mrs Grant, who said, that my Brother seemed too gay to be able to make a good Husband to her Daughter, kept too much Company for his Circumstances &c. &c. I told her that he had some Failings as other young Men, but I thought his good ones overbalanced them as I never saw any thing tending to any very bad. I staid at Henbridge till after one & then returned & dined, supped and slept again at Parsonage.

MARCH *22nd.* Sister Clarke spent the Afternoon at Parsonage — she and Jenny had some few words. N.B. both touchy. It was about a ring of mine that was found in Sam Clarkes Pocket some time ago that I had lost. Brother Heighes spent part of the Aft. at Parsonage. Brother John & with him Mr Nicholls supped &c. at Parsonage.

31st. Mem: Mr Wickham and myself entered into a written agreement between ourselves, which I have in my Hands concerning my Serving the Curacy of Castle-Cary, as follows agreed. I am to have 30 Pounds Per Annum & all the Surplice Fees, for serving it once on a Sunday — to be paid quarterly — to give Notice in writing 3 Months on leaving it or his taking it the same mutually agreed unto.

APRIL *21st*. I breakfasted, dined, supped & slept again at Parsonage. I read Prayers this morning at Cary being Easter Tuesday. As I was coming from Cary after Prayers I met Mr and Mrs Wickham of Shepton in Cary Street in a one horse Chair going to see Cary Church: I therefore went back to Church with them: I asked them to dine with me, but they would not without giving me notice. They dined at Ansford Inn—and whilst we were at Dinner they came to us to the Parsonage and caught my Sister Jane at Table with her Hair up in Papers, as she is going this Evening to Shepton Assembly, but they excused it very kindly. They drank Coffee & Tea with us, as did Justice Creed.

30th. I breakfasted, dined, supped & slept again at Parsonage. Brother Heighes dined & spent the Afternoon at Parsonage. I was busy most part of the morning in pruning up some old Apple Trees in the old Orchard, Mr Thos Woodforde & his Son went by in the old Orchard whilst I was cutting them, said nothing but I believe thought that I was doing great mischief to the Parsonage. I ordered my Man to pursue his Work before them.

MAY *1st*. I breakfasted, supped & slept again at Parsonage. I dined & spent the Afternoon at Justice Creeds with him and his Father. Counsellor Melliar spent the Afternoon at Mr Creeds. in the Evening Mr Creed, myself & the Counsellor walked down into Cary & saw the Fair it being Cary Fair to day. I saw Miss Hannah Pew in the Fair and I gave her some Sugar Plums half a Pound of them and they cost me 0.1.4. Mr Creed and myself called at Mr Francis's Senr, & Mr Creed bought a silk Handkerchief there of Miss Melliar Francis, & I bought 2 of the same. I pd 0.9.4.

Gave a poor Woman going up to Mr Creeds 0.0.6.

Gave little Sophy Clarke 0.0.6.

Gave little Anna Maria White 0.0.2.

Jenny spent the Afternoon at Dr Clarkes. Brother John supped & spent the Evening at Parsonage was very much in Liquor & behaved like a Madman. N.B. He has received a Letter from Nancy Wason, which I saw & think she has used Jack very ill, she declares of entirely, & will answer no more Letters of his. It is, I believe, her Mothers & Sister's doing all this. For a Horse to day recd 0.5.0.

JUNE 7th. Mr Creed called upon me in the Evening and we took a Walk—after I had buried a Child of Giles Francis by name J. Francis, aged 5 Years. The Child died at Bath owing to a kick in the Groin by another Lad. Giles works at Bath. And he & his Son brought the Child in a Coffin upon their Heads from Bath, they set out from Bath last Night at 12. Sister Jane drank Tea this Afternoon with a Possy at Mr Caleb Penny, Mr Creed & myself met at Mr Clarkes, the Miss Pynes, Jenny Clarke, Sister Clarke & Sister Jane & Dr Clarke & we all went over Cary Hill together & we all stayed at Mr Creeds House in our return from walking some little Time.

18th. I breakfasted and slept again at Parsonage. After breakfast I went to Shepton Mallett to Mr Wickhams, & after staying there some little time I went with Mr Wickham in his Chair to Wells and went immediately to the Deanery to Lord Francis Seymours, where we stayed till after one and after putting on our Gowns, we went to the Palace to see the bishop, and there we dined with his Lordship, Mrs Awbry his Daughter, Mr

Weston, Mr Keetes, and Mr Hughes, Mr Wickhams Curate at Shepton. I mentioned to the Bishop the usage my Uncle has treated me with, & that I was to be turned out of my Curacy at Ansford—Whereupon his Lordship promised me to send Mr Dalton a Letter to continue me if possible. His Lordship vindicated my cause much, and I shewed him Mrs Powels Letter to me concerning the purchasing the Living of Ansford, but it did not amount to Facts. Mr Wickham also mentioned to his Lordship concerning the Parisioners of Cary petitioning his Lordship to have Service twice on a Sunday, which his Lordship will not suffer, as it has not been usual. We all retired from the Palace about an Hour after Dinner, and all went to the Cathedral to hear Prayers. Whilst I was at the Cathedral, who should I cast my Eyes upon, but James Townshend of New-College, who is come to Wells for Institution for a small Living in the Diocese near Bristol. I lent my Gown & Band to him to go to the Bishop this Afternoon, immediately as I came out of the Cathedral. I afterwards went with Mr Wickham to the Deanery where we drank Tea with Lord Francis Seymour & his Lady, his two Daughters, his Son the Lieutenant in the Artillery, Mr Weston, Mr Turner, & Captain Duglass whose Company is at Wells. At Tea Captain Duglass ordered the Band of Music belonging to the Regiment, to play in the Church-Yard opposite the Deans dining-room windows, and they played exceeding well & we were all delighted with it indeed; Lord Francis's whole Family are fond of Music. Lord Francis & Lady & the whole Family behaved exceeding complaisant & civil to me. His Lordship told me that I had now found the way to the Deanery, he would be glad to see me at all times & often. His Lordship would fain have had us dine with him. The Bishop made his Lordship a Visit in the morning whilst we were there, but we did not then see him. Lord Francis behaved with the utmost Affability to us. It is indeed as good a Family as ever I was in. Miss Kitty Seymour talked to me a good deal as did the Lieutenant. His Lordship showed us his Garden &c. The Soldiers in the Town were exercizing in the C. Yard Whilst we drinking Tea. It was really very pretty. I don't know when I ever spent such an Afternoon or Day. At seven o'clock or after, Mr Wickham & myself returned to Shepton in the Chair. I supped at Mr Wickhams & spent the Evening with him, his Wife and Mr Hughes —and at eleven o'clock (tho' much desired to sleep at Mr Wickhams) I set forth for Ansford, where I got by 12 o'clock. My Boy went with me to Shepton & to Wells. I put up my Mare at the George Inn, whilst I went to Wells. I gave the Hostler there 0.0.6. Gave the Porter at the Palace to day 0.1.0.

SEPTEMBER *23rd*. I breakfasted, dined, supped & slept at Parsonage. It rained almost the whole Day, & I did not stir out at all.

OCTOBER *1st*. I breakfasted at Parsonage and at 8 o'clock set forth for my Oxford Journey to vote for a Chancellor. I dined at Wiley at the Bull kept by Locke. At Wiley paid for myself, my Boy & Horses 0.3.3. To Servants at Wiley gave 0.1.0. I supped & slept at Everly at the Rose & Crown kept by Day—The Weather very favourable. To Turnpikes & gave away pd 0.0.7. I bore my Journey to Day without the least fatigue. I got to Everly by five in the Afternoon, I had nothing at Wiley but poached Eggs & strong beer. Day's grandson (a little Boy) at Everly supped with me. I gave the little Boy 0.0.6.

2nd. I breakfasted at Everly & then set forth for Oxford. Going from Hungerford to Farnborough I overtook the four following Gentlemen, Stockwell of C.C. Coll., Maud Chaplain of C.C. Coll., Boys and Bowls both Fellows of Trinity Coll., who were all going to Oxon to the Election.* Stockwell, Maud and myself are for Lord Radnor, Boys & Bowls for Lord North. We all dined together at Farnborough—I pd 0.5.0. In the Afternoon we set forth for Oxford, where we got safe & well (I thank

* For a new Chancellor of the University.

God) about 7 o'clock. I put up my Horses at the blue Boar at Lads. As soon as we came to Oxford, Stockwell, myself, and Maud went to a meeting of my Lord Radnor's Friends in High Street, where I met our Warden who was Chairman, & several more Friends. I stayed at the meeting till near eleven o'clock, and then the meeting broke up, after coming to this determination, to drop all thoughts of L. Radnor as we could raise no more votes than 73 in all, and that the Duke of Beauforts Friends would not come over to us—having sent to them several Times, to their meeting at the Mitre. It is therefore to be an Unanimous Election for Ld North declared to by both meetings, as an opposition to him cannot be anywhere respectable. I paid at our meeting for Wine & Biscuits 0.1.0. After our meeting broke up I went to my Inn, had a welch Rabbit, and a Pint of Porter & went to bed. I had an indifferent Room—the Inn being very full.

31st. I breakfasted, supped & slept again at Parsonage. Nancy made me a Present of a silk purse of her own Netting, for which I gave her 0.3.0. Very much out of Order this morning being terribly flutterd owing I believe to drinking green Tea in a morning. I design to leave it of, & to Morrow take to Sage Tea. I dined & spent the afternoon at Mr Creeds with him & his Father and my Sister Jane—we had a fine Hare.

NOVEMBER *24th.* Paid Mr Owens my Barber his Quarterage. Brother Heighes dined & spent the Aft. at Parsonage. I sent a Card this morning to Mr Guppey at Cole to desire him, Mrs Pouncet & Mr Pouncet to dine with me Thursday next—but recd no answer back yet. I supped & spent the Evening at Dr Clarkes with Sister Clarke, James, Jenny, Sam & Sophy Clarke & Sister Jane. The old Doctor was taken very ill just before I came there, went to bed, vomited only black Matter, and continued very bad when we came away. I am afraid the poor Doctor will not live long indeed.

1773

JANUARY *6th.* I breakfasted, dined & slept again at Parsonage. I read Prayers this morning at Cary being Epiphany. I made a morning visit to Mrs Penny's, Mr Creeds, Mr Clarkes &c. &c. The Justice is still at my Lord Pauletts at Hinton. Brother Heighes dined & spent the Afternoon with me. I supped & spent the Evening at Dr Clarkes. To Mr Clarkes Servants being Xmas gave 0.3.0. For 1 Woodcock & 1 Snipe of Tom Davidge pd 0.1.0. Painter Clarkes Family is under great Distress concerning his Son Charles, who went to London on Xmas Day & have heard nothing of him since and also that a Horse & Bridle were found on Hounslow Heath on Monday Dec: 28—with a Man genteely dressed, booted & spurred was found under a Hedge near the Horse shot thro' the head as mentioned on the Salisbury Paper Monday last. No one knew of his going to London but John Burge, & to whom he promised to write when he got to Town, & he has received no Letter at all from him.

21st. I dined & spent the Afternoon at Mr John Pouncetts of Cole, with him, his Mother, Mr Guppey, Sister White, her Son John, Sister Jane & Brother John. Mr Sam White spent the Afternoon there. Sister White & Son John & Sister Jane went in my Chaise there and back again & were at home by 6 o'clock. Brother John & me were on horseback & stayed till 8. Gave Mr Pouncetts Maid 0.1.0. Brother John got quite merry & coming home was thrown from his Horse—but blessed be God received no great hurt. His Horse run away home. He was thrown just by Mr Tuckers at Honeywicke. I walked with him home & led my Horse in my hand. I was most miserably terrified by his fall, he riding in so disagreeable a manner as to frighten me every Step till he was thrown. It was a great mercy of thine O God that he was not killed, as there was a Waggon not twenty Yards before him when he fell & the Horse full stretch almost. He stayed at my House till he was much soberer. My Man Willm also met with an Accident this Evening at my Door in his return from Cole. Soon as the Chaise stopped the Horse which he rode fell down & bruised his Leg much. The Horses breath was stopped by the Harness. I thank my God most sincerely that neither Accident proved very bad. Ever praised be thy Name. We had a very handsome Dinner & a very hearty welcome. Mr John Pouncet made me a Present of a fine Woodcock & Sister White another. Mr Guppey's Gardens are very pretty indeed. We walked over them & saw his House. He is a very hearty Man indeed.

FEBRUARY *9th.* John Horners little tilted Cart went to Bath for me this morning after the Monument for my Father and Mother, I sent with it a Letter to Mr Ford.

MARCH *1st.* I was busy with Jack this morning taking an Inventory of my Fathers Goods above Stairs. Brother John spent the Evening at Parsonage but was noisy, being merry, & his seeing Nancy Wason ride by our House this Aft. & is reported to be married to Andw Russ this morning.

28th. Mr John Pouncett of Cole spent the Afternoon, supped & spent the Evening at Parsonage. He has an inclination for my Sister Jane—I think it would do well. Dr Clarke & Wife, & Mr White spent the afternoon with us. Nancy Woodforde spent the afternoon with us.

APRIL *22nd.* I went up to Dr Clarkes this morning by the desire of Sister Clarke & James, & desired him to make a Will agreeable to his Family & himself & he agreed so to do which I am very glad of. The poor Doctor cried a little.

27th. Sister Clarke spent part of the morning at Parsonage. She brought me down Mr Clarkes Will for me to keep for them. It was drawn up by Mr Messiter to the Satisfaction of all. Poor old Aunt Anne was so bad this morning that we all thought her dying. She was quite delirious owing I believe to drinking so much Rum, being so very cold. Mr Pouncett spent the Aft. supped &c. at Parsonage.

MAY *3rd*. I breakfasted, dined, supped & slept again at Parsonage. I took Physic this morning & kept within all Day— operated 3 Times. Hard Frost this morning and very cold & Wind NNW. I did not eat any meat all Day to day. Cousin Tom & his Wife breakfasted, dined & slept at Parsonage. Brother Heighes & Son Sam supped &c. at Parsonage. James Clarke dined & spent the Afternoon with us. Cousin Tom & Wife supped & spent the Evening at his Uncles. I went to bed before they came home being very sleepy. Cousin Tom took a ride upon my Mare this Afternoon with James Clarke to Lovington, to try to get some Small-Pox Matter. Sister Jane spent the afternoon at Sister Whites—poor Jack White worse & worse. He cannot hold it long. Pray God release him of his Misery & take him to thyself.

4th. Cousin Tom breakfasted at Parsonage & then set forth for Taunton, leaving his agreeable Wife to spend a few Days here. Mrs Woodforde breakfasted, dined, supped & slept at Parsonage. Mr Pouncett dined, supped & spent the Evening at Parsonage. Sister Clarke spent the Afternoon, supped &c. with us. I thank God I am brave to day & fared sumptuously.

21st. A Grey Owl was found in my Back-Kitchen this morn', he came down the Chimney—I gave him his Liberty again.

JUNE *13th.* I breakfasted, supped & slept again at Parsonage. After breakfast I went to Batcombe by Mr Wickhams appointment & read Prayers, Preached, churched a Woman & buried a Corpse there this morning. I called on Mr Pouncett at Cole & he went with me. We went thro' Bruton—to one Turnpike pd 0.0.2. As soon as I got to Batcombe Church my Man Willm Corpe was come after me to let me know that Mr Wickham was not come to serve my Churches. So after we had dined which was at a Mr Waters, with him, his Wife, a Mr Watley, & Mr Waters Son, we set out about ½ past two o'clock, & we got to Ansford in about half an Hour, we rode very hard & it was exceeding hot moreover, quite sultry. Mr Cowards Family of Spargrove was at Batcombe Church, with many other good Families. N.B. Batcombe must have been unsupplied if I had not been there. Mr Wickham promised me by Letter that he would serve both my Churches if I went to Batcombe to day. It was a very great disappointment to me—and Ansford Church was not served at all this morning by it—many grumbled about it, as there was a great many People at Church. I read Prayers, Preached & christned a Child this Afternoon at Cary Church by name George owing to Mr Wickham disappointing me— and I was quite in a fever being hurried so much when I went to Cary Church this afternoon. Many People were gone from Cary Church before I came, as it so much later than usual.

15th. It pleased Almighty God this morning to relieve my poor old Aunt Anne from the Miseries of this world by taking her to himself, between nine and ten o'clock. She went of quite easy. My Aunt Tom was present with her. I was sent for in a hurry, but she was gone before I could reach the House, tho' I went up immediately. As I have the management of her Affairs, having her Will, read the same to my Aunt Tom and Sister Clarke this morning.

JULY *2nd.* I thank God that he has delivered my poor Nephew John White from his great Misery this day about noon by taking him to himself. Pray God he might be happy. I was at Mr Whites about a Quarter of an Hour after he departed this troublesome Life—Pray God comfort his poor distressed Parents under so sore an Affliction.

8th. Mr Pouncett, myself, & Sister Jane went and drank Tea this Afternoon at Sister Clarkes, with her, Jenny Clarke, Miss Pope of Shepton, James Clarke & Sophy Clarke. We all went from Sister Clarkes up into South-Cary to the Royal Oak to see Nevil's grand Machinery, being the whole of the woollen Manufactory, from one end of it to the other, and all in motion at once. It is very curious indeed & three thousand Movements at once going—composed by Mr Nevil himself, and which took him twenty Years in completing it. I paid for Jenny Clarke & myself seeing it 0.2.0.

19th. Mr Frank Woodforde was this morning inducted into the Living of Ansford, and he immediately sent me a Line that he intends serving Ansford next Sunday himself, which notice of my leaving the Curacy is I think not only unkind but very ungentlemanlike. I must be content. Far be it from me to expect any favour at all from that House. All their Actions towards me are bad. Mr Pouncett went to Frank this morning by my desire, to ask him to let him the Parsonage House which was promised him by Frank. I intend to quit the Parsonage House when my Year is up, which will be at Lady Day next, and to take up my residence once more at New-College. One thing upon another makes me at present very unhappy and I cannot expect to be otherwise whilst at Ansford.

AUGUST *13th.* I had a Note from Frank Woodforde this morning to leave the great Orchard and turn out my Horses, but I sent him a Note back that I would not leave either Orchard or House till Lady Day next.

24th. When I returned from Church I took my Mare and went to Shepton Mallett and dined & spent the Aft. at Mr Figgus's, with him, his Wife and Mrs Paine. We had a Goose for Dinner. Gave the Maid 0.1.0. I put my Horse up at the George—pd & gave 0.0.6. I called at Mrs Whites & stayed with her & her Daughter Betsy till 8 o'clock this Evening. I was at home however at 9 o'clock, but went at a smart Pace. Mr Pouncett supped & spent the Evening at Parsonage. To a Turnpike to day pd 0.0.1. Betsy White came from London only last Saturday. She is greatly improved & handsomer than ever. I did not call at Mr Wickhams, being much engaged.

SEPTEMBER *1st*. Mr Richard Clarke supped & spent the Evenwith us. He came down to let me know what Mr Phillips of Alford told him concerning Bedford School, for he was born and bred at Bedford and his Father still lives there and is one of the Aldermen. He told him that it was the third best thing in the Gift of New-College—a new built House with an exceeding handsome Garden, 50 Guineas paid the Master every Quarter, Fuel, Candles, & all kinds of expences about the House and Gardens paid for the Master & no Taxes whatever. An Usher also found & paid for by the Charity—About 12 Boys to teach, by the Master and Usher. The only bad thing belonging to it, is, being a Borough Town, and there is no such thing as being neuter.* Upon the whole I like it very well and I believe shall accept of it, if it comes to me. O almighty God, how good and kind art thou to me a miserable Sinner—It is more than I can possibly express! Lord make me more deserving thy Favours, and make me for the future to observe & obey thy Laws more than I have hitherto & that I may, may God of his infinite mercy grant thro' Jesus Christ my blessed Lord & Saviour. D.S.G.† Mr Pouncett made us a present of a brace & half of Partridges which he shot this morning. N.B. The first Day of Partridge shooting.

6th. At one o'clock I eat a bit of cold rost Beef for Dinner and

* In this context it means that JW would have had to take political sides, which he was always reluctant to do.
† Deo Sit Gratia.

then I took my Mare and went to Shepton Mallett, put up my Mare at the George Inn, and walked down to Mr Wickhams House, but he and his Wife are at Wells. I left a Note at the House for him, wherein I told him that I must leave the Curacy of Cary at Michaelmas. I then went & spent the whole Afternoon at Mr Whites with Mrs White and my dear Betsy White.

16th. I drank Tea this afternoon at Mr Whites with him, his Wife and my dear Betsy White. Gave Mrs Whites Maid coming away 0.1.0. For my Horse at the George & to the Hostler gave 0.1.0. To a Turnpike to day pd 0.0.1. Had a Letter from Robt Taunton this Evening to let him know whether I shall accept of Bedford School. Mr Pouncett supped & slept at Parsonage. I carried my dear Maid of Shepton some Peaches &c. &c.

OCTOBER *5th.* We got to Oxford I thank God safe & well about 7 o'clock. Supped &c. at New College with Master Senr, Williams Senr, Whitmore & a Friend of his. I heard at College this Evening that Hooke intends taking Bedford School—so far bad. I slept at the Old Boar kept by Mrs Ladds, her husband being lately dead.

14th. I breakfasted, and slept again at the blue Boar. To my Barber to day for setting my Rasors gave 0.0.6. For an exceeding good Microscope with a Stand & all the Apparatus belonging to it of Mr Treadwell pd 0.4.0. He promised to send it me next Week into the Country. At 12 o'clock we had a Meeting of the House in New-Coll. Hall, at which I attended—we had a large Meeting. The Warden, Webber the Subwarden &c. &c. were present. Hooke was nominated to be Master of Bedford School & he is to have a Year of Grace from the Day that he takes Possession of it till that Day twelvemonth. And in case he should relinquish it before, he is to receive what shall become due to him from it. Hooke treated both the Common Rooms with Wine and Rack Punch—Wine after Dinner & Punch after Supper. The Warden dined with us in Hall and spent the Aft. in the Senior Common Room with us. I dined, supped & spent the Evening at New-College. We had a meeting of the thirteen in the Audit House after the Hall Meeting and I was one of the thirteen.

NOVEMBER *7th*. I breakfasted, dined, supped & slept again at Parsonage. Mr Pouncett breakfasted at Parsonage & then went home. I had a very restless Night last night being very feverish. was very heavy all day Yesterday, I took some Brimston & Treakle & Cream of Tartar last night going to bed. I did not go to either Church to day being but indifferent. I eat no Meat all day to day & am the better for it.

8th. I had a very good night & am brave thank God to day. Very busy this morning in making some Horse Medicines. Sister White, Brother Heighes & Nancy dined &c. with us, I had a fine Hare for Dinner given me by Mr Pouncett.

DECEMBER *1st*. Soon after Dinner we all went to Cary and saw some very remarkable Feats of Horsemanship, performed by a Man just come to Town and he performed exceeding well— gave him 0.1.0. He rode full galop upon three Horses, laid down on them & got up on his feet on them with Ease with two Horses also standing upon two Quart Pots, between two Horses, stood on his head one Horse on a full gallop, hanging with his Head downwards & his hands touching the ground full Galop & taking up 4 Handkerchiefs. Another Man rode full Galop standing upon his Feet in the Saddle & a Boy on the Man's Head. Great Numbers of People present near a Thousand. It began at 3 and lasted till five o'clock.

Oxford

24th. I breakfasted in Bowls's Rooms again. Paid this morning to Adam Couldray for China & other things as per Receipt 2.16.6. I dined in the Chequer to day the Hall being cleaning again to Morrow, Christmas Day there. I spent the Afternoon in the Sen. Com. Room. I supped & spent the Evening in the

Chequer. For Wine to day pd 0.1.3. I went to Chapel this Evening being Christmas Eve. I got into my own Rooms this Afternoon and there slept for the first Time — they are very good Rooms in the Lower Court, the second Stair Case next to the Chequer, one Pair of Stairs and the Door on the right Hand. Very wet, windy, and dismal Day. Mem: I dreamt very much of poor old Alice Stacy of Ansford & my Man Willm Corpe last Night, the former that she had a vast discharge of Matter from her Breast, the latter that he was very drunk & almost killed by a Fall from a Horse, both which I thought I saw very plainly.

25th. I breakfasted and slept again in my Rooms. I went to Chapel this morning at 9 o'clock being Christmas Day, and recd the Holy Sacrament from the Hands of our Warden who was present. The Warden was on one Side of the Altar and myself being Sub-Warden on the other Side. I read the Epistle for the Day at the Altar and assisted the Warden in going round with the Wine. For an Offering at the Altar gave 0.1.0. The Dean of Christchurch who is Bishop of Chester preached this morning at Christchurch, but I did not attend it. N.B. The Dean of Christchurch always preaches this Day in the morning at Christchurch Cathedral. I dined in the Hall & 14 Senr Fellows with me. I invited the Warden to dine with us as is usual on this Day, but his Sister being here, could not. We had a very hand-some Dinner, of my ordering as I order Dinner every Day being Sub-Warden. We had for Dinner two fine Codds boiled with Fryed Soals round them & Oyster Sauce, a fine Surloin of Beef rosted, Some Peas Soup & an Orange Pudding for the first Cours, for the Second we had a Lease of Wild Ducks rosted, a fore-Qtr of Lamb & Sallad & Mince Pies. We had a Grace Cup before the second Course brought by the Butler to the Steward of the Hall who was Mr Adams a Senior Fellow, who got out of his Place & came to my Chair and there drank to me out of it, wishing me a merry Xmas. I then took it of him & drank, wishing him the same & then it went round, three standing up all the time. From the high Table the Grace Cup goes to the

106

Batchelors & Scholars. After the second Course there was a fine Plumb Cake brought to the Senr Table as is usual on this Day, which also goes to the Batchelors after. After Grace is said there is another Grace-Cup to drink omnibus Wiccamisis, which is drank as the first, only the Steward of the Hall does not attend the second Grace Cup. We dined at 3 o'clock & were an Hour & $\frac{1}{2}$ at it. We all then went into the Senr Com. Room, where the Warden came to us & sat with us till Prayers. The Wine drank by the Senr Fellows, domus pays for. Prayers this Evening did not begin till 6 o'clock at which I attended as did the Warden. I supped &c. in the Chequer, we had Rabbit for Supper rosted as is usual on this Day. The Sub Warden has one to himself, the Bursars each one apiece, the Senr Fellows $\frac{1}{2}$ a one each. The Junr Fellows a Rabbit between three. N.B. Put on this Day a new Coat and Waistcoat for the first time.

1774

JANUARY *4th*. I breakfasted, and slept again at College. I dined in Hall, spent the Afternoon in M.C.R., supped & spent the Evening in the Chequer. For Wine this Afternoon pd 0.1.0. For Fruit 3d—gave the fruit Boy 3d—0.0.6. At Back-Gammon with Milton & Holmes won 0.2.0. Went to Chapel this Evening—after Prayers I sent for the Sexton Mr Parsons & gave him a Lecture for behaving indecently in Chapel, and not waiting at the High Table to day as I ordered him. He seems to be rather saucy.

11th. I dined in Hall, spent the Afternoon in M.C.R., supped & spent the Evening in the Chequer. For Wine this aft. in M.C.R. pd 0.1.6. For Fruit this Aft., in M.C.R. pd 0.0.3. I sconced Long & Huggins 2 Clerks for not waiting at the High Table to day half a Crown each. At Back-Gammon with Milton this Evening lost 0.10.0. A report went about to day of the Death of my good Friend John Geree, He has been in a very bad way a long Time and his Life despaired of for some Time, being in a Consumption. 'How great is the Loss of a sincere Friend.' Pray God that his Change (if true) might be happy. He was deservedly esteemed by all that knew him, and most universally is his Death lamented. Dr Ballord of our Coll. is expected to succeed him in his Fellowship at Winton College.

14th. I breakfasted, and slept again at New-College. At 10 o'clock this morning went up into the Senior Common Room where the Warden & all the Fellows met. & we had given by the Warden some Sack Wine & some bread and Butter, as he takes his Doctors Degree to day—from the Common Room we went in Procession a Beadle going before to the Convocation House, it being the first Day of Term. Cooke Junr went also to

the Convocation House to take his Masters Degree. I scio'd
for him there.* We all went in our proper Hoods to the
Schools. I took a Walk with Boyce this morning after having
been up into the Schools—up the Hill and for a Shaving
Box of one Darcy up the Hill pd o.1.o. I dined in the Chequer
and the Warden dined with us & treated the Senr Fellows
with a very handsome Dinner, and after Dinner we all went
into the Senr Common Room, where the Warden treated us
with Wine till near 9 o'clock at Night—and then he retired.
The Warden also treated us with a large Dish of Fruit after
Dinner in the M.C.R. Had a new Wigg brought home this
morning, which I put on before I went to Dinner, it is a more
fashionable one than my old ones, a one curled. At Back-
Gammon this Evening with Milton only one Gammon and I
lost to him by bad luck, o.10.6. I supped in the Chequer &
went to bed soon after.

FEBRUARY *1st*. I got to Ansford I thank God safe and well this
Evening about 6 o'clock. It snowed all the Way from old Downe
to Ansford and the Wind blowed very rough & it was very cold
indeed. Gave the old Downe Driver a Dram at Gannards Grave,
another at home, & gave him also o.1.6. I found Mr Pouncett
& my Sister Jane at home by themselves & I supped & slept at
Parsonage. Brother John supped & spent the Evening with us.
All Friends pretty well but poor Dr Clarke who is worse rather
than I left him—his Legs swell and he talks but very little, &
looks very ill indeed. Mr Pouncett supped & slept at Parsonage.

15th. I breakfasted, dined, supped & slept again at Parsonage. Very busy this morning with Jenny & Jack in dividing the
Silver Plate—there was not an Ounce difference in each Share
of the other. Mine was—1 Quart Mugg, 1 Silver Sauce Boat,

* Academic Oxford slang of the period. As the candidate's sponsor
JW was asked whether Cooke was fitted to hold the degree; his
answer was Scio (I know). The alternative responses were Credo (I
think so) or Nescio (I don't know).

1 Chased Cream Mugg, 1 Punch Ladle, 4 Salts with 4 Spoons belonging to them, 2 old Pepper Boxes, 6 large Spoons, 8 Tea Spoons, 1 Pr of old Spurs. Jennys were—1 large Octagon Coffee Pot, 1 large Soup Spoon, 2 Table Spoons, 1 Silver Pint, 1 Cream Pot, 1 Silver Salver, 1 large Candlestick, 1 Punch Ladle, 3 Tea Spoons. Jacks was—1 large Silver Tankard, 1 old Silver Pint, 1 Silver smoking Candlestick, 1 Silver Salver, 1 large Silver Candlestick, 5 Tea Spoons. Brother John & Nancy dined, supped &c. at Parsonage. Brother Heighes dined & spent the Aft. at Parsonage. My Brother John & Sister Jane and my-self agreed to give Brother Heighes an old gold Ring which formerly belonged to the Family of Heighes's in Hampshire & from which my Brother had his name—& which ring was given to him this Afternoon by us. N.B. as the Ring fell to Jacks Share, it was agreed that Jack should have my late Fathers gold Buttons, which by mistake I carried to Oxon.

MARCH *23rd*. I breakfasted at Parsonage this Morning as did Mr Pouncett who after breakfast went home and returned about 12 to take his Leave of me. I got up very early this morning, packed up my Things settled all Accounts with my People, dined at 12 & at one set of in Ansford Inn Chaise with a very heavy Heart for Oxford thro' Bath. I left with Mr Pouncett two Guineas to be given to the Poor of Ansford, as directed by me in writing. I left with him also one Guinea to be given to the Poor of Cary as also directed by me in writing. Mr White called upon me this morning & took his leave. Robin Coleman called upon me this morning on the same. I gave my Man Willm a good deal of my old Cloaths. I gave my Maid Betty Chrich an old Prunella Gown.*

Paid Eliz. Chrich this Morning a Yrs Wages 3.3.0.
Paid her one Years Interest of 20 Pound 1.0.0.

* Prunella was a strong stuff, originally silk, afterwards worsted, used for the gowns of graduates, clergymen and barristers; possibly from the French '*prune*', plum-coloured.

Paid her for her Mother Do. 1.0.0.
Paid Willm for Washing 1 Yr 0.10.6.
Paid Eliz. Chrich for Housekeeping to this Day 0.2.9.
Paid Will & Boy & Poor to this Day 0.3.6.
I gave each of my Servants going away 0.2.6.
I left all my House in Tears & I could not refrain myself from the same. Pray God bless them all. This Day left of all House-keeping to Mr Pouncet. We had some Trout for Dinner to day, but my Heart was so full that I could eat but little.

31st. I breakfasted & slept again at New-College. Master Senr and Boys breakfasted with me. We had a meeting of the thirteen this morning at ten in the Audit House & there is to be another Monday next. The two Hgshds of Cyder that I bought of James Clarke & a Box of my Books came to College this morning about 11 o'clock in a Cart drawn by only two Horses. A Boy of about 15 came with the Cart by himself. It was Mr Pews Cart of Castle-Cary & Horses. It came very safe and well to College & very sound. I received with it three Letters, one from Js Clarke, one from Mr Pouncett & one from Mr Pew—I sent an Answer back to James's and Mr Pouncetts. I gave the Boy out of my own Pocket 0.2.6 and as much Victuals and drink as he would have. The Boy returned in the Afternoon about 4 o'clock. I had my Cyder put in my Cellar this afternoon & properly secured. One of the Hoops of one Hgshd slipt as it was going thro' the lower Court, by which I lost some small Matter of Cyder, but nothing to signify. I gave two Porters for having it into the Cellar 0.2.0. I pegged both Hgshds in the Aft. & it was both very good. I dined in Hall, spent the Aft. in the M.C.R., supped &c. in the Chequer & to bed a little after ten o'clock. At Baggs's Coffee House this Evening pd 0.0.8.

APRIL *6th.* I dined & spent the Afternoon at the Wardens Lodgings. Harry Oglander, Mr Caswall of Swacliffe late Fellow of this College, Webber and Thorpe also dined &c. there. The Warden gave us a very elegant Dinner indeed. I supped & spent the Evening in the Chequer. I eat some Macarony at the Wardens & very disagreeable eating is it. We had for Dinner some Fish, a Chine of Mutton, a plumb Pudding, a Couple of Wigeon, some sweet Breadbreads with force Balls, Oystres & Mushrooms with it, & some Tarts. We had Madeira & Port Wine to drink. We had also for Dinner some hot Cream & Macarony.

15th. Immediately after breakfast, myself & Cooke went with Proctor Webber to Proctor Berkeleys of C. C. Coll. where we met with Morris, and we all took a Walk over the Town to all the Inns, Coffee-Houses, Taverns & Billiard Tables, to give Instructions to them not to entertain Gownsmen after 11 at Night, Billiard Tables not after 9. Selstone joined us in the Town about 12 o'clock. We went to the Vice-Chancellor at Queens Coll. concerning Toms's Coffee-House and an Auction of Books of bad repute now selling at the black Horse in St Clements. The V. Chancellor was hurried. He is an exceeding good kind of a Man, and seems very fearful of doing any thing that is disagreeable. I dined in Hall & spent the afternoon in M.C.R. For Wine this Aft. in M.C.R. pd 0.0.6. I went to Chapel this Evening at 5 o'clock. At 7 o'clock this Evening, Proctor Webber & myself took a Walk into St Clements to the Auction at the black Horse, to turn away all the Gownsmen that we should find there but there had been an Alarm given so that we found none at all at the Place. We then took a Walk over the Town till 8 o'clock. I supped & spent the Evening in the Chequer. For Punch this Evening in the Chqr. pd 0.0.6. I paid my Taylor Wallington this morning 1.7.0. Webber is not a little proud of his Velvet Sleeves. Mem: Had this morning of our Porter one Hndrd Weight of Pit-Coal at 2/6 Per Hndrd. I made this Memorandum to take notice how long the above will last me — having Fires only till 2 in the afternoon.

20th. At 3 o'clock went with Webber to Christchurch — to the Senr Proctors Mr Berkeleys, and there we dined & spent the Afternoon, & at 8 came away. Mr Bowerbank, Mr Shackleford, Mr Mines, Mr Rigby, Mr Selstone, Mr Morris, & Mr Rawbone dined &c. with us there. Mr Nicholls was ill & could not come & Mr Cooke not in Town. We had a very elegant Dinner—the first Course, was part of a large Cod, a Chine of Mutton, some Soup, a Chicken Pye, Pudding & Roots &c. Second Course, Pidgeons & Asparagus, a Fillett of Veal with Mushrooms & high Sauce with it, rosted Sweat-breads, hot Lobster, Apricot Tart, & in the Middle a Pyramid of Syllabubs & Jellies. We had a Desert of Fruit after Dinner and Madeira, White Port & red to drink as Wine. We were all very cheerful and merry. I supped & spent the Evening in the Chequer. N.B. We had at Dinner to Day, some green Cucumbers, the first I have seen this Year.

MAY *12th*. Lent Blisse this morning 8 of my MSS Sermons. Holmes & myself went to Exeter-College about 2 o'clock and dined with Mr Stinton a Senior Fellow of Ex. Coll. We dined in the Publick Hall at Exeter Coll. at the High Table. The Rector Dr Bray &c. dined with us. We had but an indifferent Dinner & served up slovingly. Nothing near so neat or genteel as at New-College. We spent the afternoon in their Senr Com. Room and the Rector did the same & smoked a Pipe with us. We came away before five o'clock. I went to Prayers this Evening at 5 o'clock. I supped & spent the Evening in the Chequer. Whilst I was at Supper I was sent for to quell a Riot in Holliwell. I left my Supper and went with Holmes & Oakeley into Holliwell but it was pretty quiet. However I met with two Genlemen going into a House & I accosted them & I believe they were the same that made the disturbance, I asked them their Names & Colleges & desired them to go to their Colleges directly & wait on me to Morrow Morning at New-College. Their names were Taylor of Worcester Coll. and Duprie of Exeter College. I received a Letter this Evening from my Sister Jane—who acquainted me that my poor old Servant Man William Corpe dropped down in an apoplectic Fit May 2 and expired directly. He was that morning married to his old Sweet-heart, and this happened in the Evening in the Street.

24th. I breakfasted, dined, supped & slept again at Parsonage. Mr Pouncett breakfasted, dined, supped & slept at Parsonage. After breakfast I went down to Ansford Church and married my Sister Jane to Mr Pouncett by Licence. Pray God send thy Blessing upon them both and may they be happy in each other. I would not have any thing for marrying them, but Mr Pouncett gave Mr Frank Woodforde 1.1.0. Mr White was Father & Sister White only present. Mr Pouncett gave the Clerk, Davd Maby 0.10.6. He gave also to Ansford Ringers 0.10.6. He gave also to Cary Ringers 0.10.6.

28th. I supped & spent the Evening at Brother Johns with him, Nancy, Sister White & Betsy White, Sister Jane & Mr Pouncett. Mr Pouncett, Sister White & Betsy dined at Jacks. I went home with Betsy White & had some talk with her concerning my making her mine when an Opportunity offered, and she was not averse to it at all.

Oxford

JUNE *3rd*. Dr Wall, myself, Oakeley, Master Senr and a Mr Townshend of London a Wine & Brandy Merchant Brother of James Townshend of this Coll. who dined with us to day in Hall went this Evening in one of Kemps Post-Coaches to Abingdon to see a Play there. We put up at Powels at the Crown & Thistle, where we had Coffee & Tea—and afterwards we went to the Markett House & saw the Tragedy of Cato, & the Padlock for an Entertainment. It was Woods Company of Players who were some time back at Castle-Cary in Somersetshire. I went up into the Dressing Room, and saw Mr Wood, Miss Wood, Mr and Mrs Morris & Mr Browning, all whom I remembered at Cary. They did not perform very extraordinary, but tolerable enough. It is reported that Trotman of our College pays his Addresses to Miss Wood & is engaged to her. Miss Wood is very pretty but pokes a good deal.* There were two Gownsmen at the Play in the Boxes with two noted Ladies of

* Carries the head thrust forward, stoops (*OED*).

Pleasure, a Miss Allen & a Lady who goes by the Name of Miss Burford. A Mr Brown also of Queens Coll. was very much in Liquor at the Play & exposed himself much.

JULY 5th. Lent Thorpe one of my Proctors Gowns this morning as he is one of the occasional Proctors for this Week, this Week being our grand Gala for this Year. There was a Sermon this morning at St Marys for the Benefit of the Infirmary preached by the Bishop of Lichfield & Coventry, but I could not conveniently go. We dined at 2 to day. For Wine this Aft. pd 0.1.0. A little after 4 this Aft. went to the Theatre and heard the Oratorio of Hercules—for a Ticket pd 0.5.0. There was a good deal of Company present. The Music very fine. A Miss Davies from the Opera House sung most delightfully, Miss Molly Linley sung very well. A Mr Crosdall gave us a fine Solo on the Violencello, as did Mr Fisher on the Hautboy. Miss Davies is to have they say, sixty guineas. Mr Woodhouse a Gent. Com. of University College was very drunk at the Theatre & cascaded in the middle of the Theatre. Mr Highway one of the nominal Proctors for this Week desired him to withdraw very civilly but he was desired by one Mr Peddle a Gent. Com. of St Mary Hall not to mind him, my seeing Highway in that distress I went to them myself & insisted upon Woodhouse going away immediately from the Theatre, and then Peddle behaved very impertinently to me and which I insisted upon his coming to me to Morrow Morning. Mr Woodhouse after some little time retired, but Peddle remained & behaved very impertinently. I therefore intend putting him in the black Book. We did not come out of the Theatre till near 9. For Wine this Evening in M.C.R. pd 0.0.6. Webber, myself & Thorpe took a Walk between 11 and 12 this Evening & returned a little after 12. I met with one Mr Broome this Evening of brase Nose-Coll. very much in Liquor & who talked rather saucily to me—but I saw him to his Coll. & desired his Company to Morrow Morning.

7th. I breakfasted, dined, supped & slept again at College.

115

Mr Broome waited on me this morning with an Epistle & I set him one of Swifts Sermons to translate into Latin for the Offence he was lately guilty of.

AUGUST *15th*. Dr Wall, Holmes, Blisse, & Coker breakfasted with me as did Master Senr also. Gambling with Coker this morning lost 0.14.0. Master Senr lost also to Coker about 2.0.0. Coker & Gratton dined & spent the Afternoon with me. Only Master Senr with us—we drank six Bottles of Wine. Coker went out of Town in the Evening, and Gratton and myself went to the Coffee House & then to the Music Room. We were both merry and were taken notice of.

For Coffee at the Coffee House pd 0.0.6.

At the Music Room pd 0.1.0.

For Wine this Afternoon in M.C.R. pd 0.7.6.

I got to bed pretty soon being rather fatigued.

SEPTEMBER *27th*. I breakfasted, and supped & slept again at Parsonage. Sister Jane, Sister White & Mr Pounsett dined at Cole to day. I took a ride this morning to Shepton Mallett to see my dear Betsy White, but she & her Father are gone to Bristol to day so that I only saw her Mother & that after Dinner. I dined & spent the Afternoon at Mr Figgus's with him, his Wife & old Mrs Paine, who were all glad to see me. I gave Mr Figgus's Maid 0.1.0. For my Mare & Hostler at Shepton, pd & gave 0.1.0. I returned in the Evening about 7 to Parsonage.

OCTOBER *6th*. To Mr Owens my Barber for shaving and dressing my Wiggs for me since I have been in the Country, pd 0.6.0. In the Afternoon I set forth for Bath to Oxford. Mr Pounsett went with me to Bath—we rode and had the Boy with us to carry a Portmanteau. Gave Eliz. Chrich our Servant Maid 0.2.6. Gave Mary Chrich, Alice Stacy & Priscilla Jeffries this morning three poor Neighbours a shilling each 0.3.0. I left my Sister Jane very low indeed. I called at Brother Johns as I went to Bath to take my Leave of him, Brother Heighes was at Jacks. I gave my Brother Heighes going away 1.1.0. Mr Pounsett gave me a Leverett to carry with me.

13th. I breakfasted, dined, supped & slept again at College. Coker, Master Senr & Gratton breakfasted with me this morning upon Cocoa. Very low to day having a great Purging upon me. We had a Meeting of the House in Hall to day at 12 concerning the Signing of Leases this Year. We dined in Hall to day the Hall being finished. I asked the Warden to dine with us, but he could not. For Wine this Afternoon in M.C.R. pd 0.0.6. I went to Chapel this Evening at 5 o'clock. Had a Letter from my Brother Heighes to let me know that my Brother John was married to Miss Clarke of Evercreech Monday last. Pray God they may be happy. At Back-Gammon this Evening with Blisse won 0.5.0. I took some Rhubarb this Evening about 10 & went to bed.

15th. I caught a remarkable large Spider in my Wash Place this morning & put him in a small Glass Decanter & fed him with some Bread, & intend keeping him.

NOVEMBER *5th*. The Warden recd an Account of the Death of Dr Ridley, Rector of one of our Livings in Norfolk by name Weston Longeville—worth it is said 300 Per Annum. I went to bed at 10 o'clock to night.

14th. Master Senr set of this morning for Norfolk to look at the Rectory of Weston Longville—now vacant by the Death of Dr Ridley.

DECEMBER *2nd*. Master Senr returned this Evening from Norfolk, he makes many Objections to Weston-Longville.

6th. I breakfasted, dined, supped & slept again at College. Master Senr & Cooke breakfasted with me again. For a Pr of Gloves, & mending others pd 0.2.6. For 2 Oxford Street Almanacks to Day pd 0.2.2. Master Senr publickly declared this Afternoon in M.C.R. his Intention of not taking the Living of Weston, I therefore immediately being the next Senior in Orders canvassed the Senior Common Room, and then went with Master Senr into the Junior Common Room, and canvassed that. The Junr Common Room pretty full. For Wine this Afternoon in M.C.R. pd 0.0.6. I went to Chapel this Evening at 5 o'clock. Had a long Letter this Evening from my Sister Jane.

11th. Mr Caldecot presented a Petition or rather a Case this Evening to the Senr Com. Room in favour of Mr Hookes Claim to the vacant Living, but it did not answer the Gentlemans Expectation so much as was thought therefore I believe he will not succeed.

15th. I breakfasted, dined, supped & slept again at College. Cooke, Master Senr & Townshend breakfasted with me. Recd of Mr Shirly for Underwoods Tenement 7.0.0. Recd of him my Fee for the same 0.10.0. We had a meeting of the whole-House in the Hall at 12 o'clock, to present a Person to the Living of Weston Longeville & to seal the remaining Leases. The former came on first—Hooke & myself were the two Candidates proposed. Many learned & warm Arguments stated & disputed, And after 2 Hours Debate the House divided, & it was put to the Vote—when there appeared for me 21 Votes for Mr Hooke 15 only, on which I was declared & presented with the Presentation of the Rectory. The chief Speakers for me were the Warden, Mr Holmes, Mr Webber, Mr Gauntlett and Dr Wall. The chief Speakers for Mr Hooke were Mr Caldecot, Mr Coker Senr, Mr Adame, Mr Thorpe & Mr Milton, the latter talked nothing but Nonsense. The Warden dined with the Bursars & spent the Afternoon with us in M.C.R. & spent the Evening there. I treated the Senr Com. Room with Wine & Fruit in the Afternoon & in the Evening with Arack Punch & Wine. I treated the Junior Com. Room with one Dozen of Wine, afternoon and in the Evening with Arrac Punch & Wine. I gave the Chaplains half a Dozen of Wine, the Clerks, 2 Bottles, & the Steward one Bottle. I smoked a Pipe in the afternoon with Cokers Father. A little after 11 o'clock this Evening I went down into the Junr Common Room attended with Master Senr, Cooke, Adams, Townshend & Holmes (& Swanton) to thank them for the Favour conferred on me. We stayed there till after 12 & returned them to the Senr Common Room, & stayed there till near 4 o'clock. We were exceeding merry in the Junr Com. Room, & had many good Songs sung there by Swanton, Williams Junr & Wight, And also a very droll one by Busby, which occasioned great Laughter. The Junr Common Room was exceeding full & so was the Senr both after Dinner & Supper. Hooke dined with the Bursars & spent the Afternoon in M.C.R. In the Evening he and Milton set of in a Post Chaise for Wallingford.

16th. I did not get up to day till near one o'clock. I dined, supped & slept again at College. For Wine this Afternoon in M.C.R. pd 0.0.6. I spent the former Part of the Evening in my own Room, as there was some Arrac left I had a large Bowl in the Chequer this Evening after Supper there.

1775

JANUARY *2nd*. I got up this morning between 6 & 7, breakfasted at my Room upon Cocoa and afterwards went to the Cross Inn in the Corn-Markett, where I got into the Bath Machine to go into the West-Country. Dr Wall breakfasted with me & went with me in the Bath Machine, it being a Frost, as far as Burford. Mr Fisher of University Coll. went with us in the Machine as did one Sally Kirby a Servant Maid for one Mrs Norwood of Holton near Ansford who is now at Bath and bad in the Gout. We stayed at Whitney & made a second breakfast. We treated the Maid at Whitney, I pd o.1.6. Gave the Porter at the Cross Inn Oxford o.1.o. We then went on to Burford where we stayed to change Horses. Dr Wall left us at Burford & went to his Brothers in a Chaise about 13 Miles from Burford. We took up another Servant Maid at Whitney who went with us to Cirencester. Mr Fisher, myself & Mrs Norwoods Maid all go Bath together. We dined at Bibury & we treated the two Maids. Fisher & myself pd at Bibury o.4.6. We got to Cirencester about 6 o'clock where we supped & slept at the Bull there. The two Maids supped & spent the Evening with us. Fisher & myself went to an Auction of Books this Evening at Cirencester, the Auctioneer very saucy. I met with Brother Small at the Auction. Fisher & myself treated the two Maids, pd o.6.o apiece this Evening as we might not be hindred to Morrow.

18th. I breakfasted, dined, supped & slept again at Parsonage. Gave old Mary Chrich this morning o.1.o. To the Taylor Inglefield for making a Coat &c. o.8.o. Gave him besides o.1.o. Mrs Pounsett from Cole came to Parsonage this morning & she dined, supped & slept at Parsonage. Brother John & Wife

& Sister, Brother Heighes, Sister White dined, supped & spent the Evening at Parsonage. Mr Creed was brought this Afternoon in a Hearse from Bristol this Afternoon to be buried. Mr Creed was buried in the Church about 5 o'clock by Mr Thomas the Curate of Cary. It was a handsome Funeral & Church full. Mr Creed was 67 Years of Age. After he was buried we all went to our Houses. At Cards (Commerce) this Evening at Parsonage lost 1.0. Brother John was drunk & behaved himself most rudely as well as cruelly by words towards his good Wife—Poor Patty Clarke was quite unhappy about him. He kept us up till after 12 o'clock. Pray God give him a new mind & a better Heart. He made my Sister Jane almost faint this Evening. He always makes his Company miserable when he is so. Instead of spending a cheerful Evening it was quite other when occasioned entirely by him. I from my Heart pity his good Wife—Pray God comfort her. Brother Heighes did not sup at Parsonage.

28th. I breakfasted, supped & slept again at Parsonage. It being a fine morning I took a ride to Shepton-Mallett and dined & spent the Afternoon at Mr Figgus's with him, his Wife, old Mrs Paine & Mr Figgus's Sister. The Boy went with me on Mr Pounsetts Mare. I took Ditcheat & Doulting in my way to Shepton, & got a Testimonium* signed by Mr Leir of Ditcheat, and by Mr Pagett of Doulting, they being both at Home. I called on Mr Wickham of Shepton who was also at home and he signed it also. I called on Mr White at Shepton but Betsy White was not at home, she being in Devonshire at Mr Troits & is to remain there till Easter, was told. I called also on Mr and Miss Hole of Shepton. Gave to Mr Figgus's Servants 0.1.6. For my Horses at the George & to the Hostler 0.2.6. I returned in the Evening about 7 o'clock. It rained hard coming home some part of the way. To Will: for having my Mares Shoes new, pd 0.1.8. To Ditto for Turnpikes &c. gave 0.0.4.

* A letter of recommendation given to a candidate for holy orders witnessing to his piety and learning.

FEBRUARY *1st*. I breakfasted, & dined at Parsonage, and at one o'clock set of for Oxford in Ansford Inn Chaise. I put up at the Angel in West-Gate Street Bath, where I supped & slept. I met Mr Parfitt of Wells, the Bishops Secretary at my Inn at Bath and he supped & spent the Evening with me. He told me that I should have my Testimonium as soon as possible, it is now with the Bishop at London, pd him for it 3.6. N.B. The Bath Coach for to Morrow for Oxford quite full, so that I forfeit my half Guinea that I paid some time back, and must go to Oxford some other way, as I did not come last Week. However I met with a Young Gentleman from Devon at my Inn, who is going to Oxford, by name Coleridge of Ottery St Mary, and we agreed to take a Chaise to Morrow between us for Oxford—so far so good. He is of Christ-Church Coll. on the Students List, & Dr Kennicott there is his great Friend. He spent the Evening with us at the Angel Inn.

17th. I breakfasted, dined, supped & slept again at Coll. Mr Peddle Gent. Com., St Mary Hall, whose name is in the black Book put in by me in July last, waited on me this morning to desire me to take his name out of the same, which I promised to do upon his bringing me a Declamation on Nemo omnibus horis sapit,* & asking Pardon of Highway of Baliol.

20th. Mr Peddle brought me his Declamation this morning. I went to Highway of Baliol about him, and he is satisfied, therefore this Aft. I sent to the Senr Proctor for the black Book & erased his Name & put satisfecit. For Wine this Afternoon in M.C.R. pd 0.0.6. I went to the Music Room this Evening with Master & for going into the same being a Subscription pd 0.1.0. For Porter for myself & Cooke this Evening pd 0.0.6. I recd my Testimonium this Evening in a Cover from Parfitt of Wells signed by the Bishop there, but Parfitt sent me no Letter, only a blank Cover.

---

* 'No one is wise all the time'.

MARCH *13th.* At half past eleven this morning went with Cooke to see George Strap hanged, who was hung about a Qtr before one o'clock near the Castle. He confessed (just as he came out of the Castle) the Crime for which he suffered, but not before. He pulled up his Cap two or three Times to delay. A Methodist prayed by him in the Cart for some Time under the Gallows. He seemed full hardy. It is said that he declared Yesterday, if he had only his Liberty for one Qtr of an Hour, he would employ it in murdering of his Wife. I think I never saw such sullenness & Villainy on one Face, Jack Ketch kissed him twice before he went of. His Body was carried to Dr Parsons's, to be dissected, and anatomized pursuant to the Sentence. I do believe that there were more than six Thousand Spectators present when he was hanged.

APRIL *9th.* I breakfasted, dined, supped & slept again at College. Very busy all the morning in packing up things for my Norfolk Expedition, as I set of to Morrow Morning. I dined & spent the Afternoon by myself, in my Room. I went to Chapel this Evening at 5, being Sunday. Supped & spent the Evening in the Chequer, for Wine 1.6.

10th. I breakfasted in my Room this morning at 7 o'clock upon some Chocolate as did Cooke with me—after breakfast about 8 o'clock I set of in Jones's Post Coach for the City of London. Cooke went with me in the same, and I promised to frank him all the Way to Norfolk as he goes to oblige me. Mrs Prince and Osborne Wight of our Coll. went with us to London in the Machine or Post Coach. We all dined together at Maidenhead Bridge and then proceeded on to London. For Cooke and myself at Maidenhead pd 0.8.0. For the remaining fare for Cooke & myself, pd 0.15.0. We got to London about six o'clock. Cooke and myself then took a Hackney Coach and went to the Turk's Head Coffee House in the Strand opposite Catherine Street, kept by one Mrs Smith a Widow & a good motherly kind of a Woman, her Person and talking very like Mrs Carr of

Ivichester, and there we supped & slept. To the Oxford Coach-man gave 0.2.0. For an Hackney-Coach to the Turks Head pd 0.3.0. We went in the Evening to Mr Burnes in Duke Street Westminster, Secretary to the Bishop of Norwich to leave my Papers with him, and to desire the Bishop to give me Institution to Morrow, but he told me that he thought the Bishop wd not so soon. Trenchard and Lovel, late of the University, supped and spent the Evening with us at the Turks Head. Mrs Prince was a very agreeable & merry Traveller.

11th. We breakfasted, dined, supped & slept again at the Turk's Head Coffee House — at 11 this morning I went in my Gown in an Hackney Coach to upper Grovsenor Street to the Bishop of Norwich, but he was not within. I spoke to his Man. For the Hackney Coach back & forward pd 0.3.6. At 12 Cooke and myself took a Walk to Westminster Abbey, to the Horse Guards, to the Mall &c. We dined by ourselves at the Turks Head — in the Evening we went and called at Mr Strahan's the Kings Printer where Mrs Prince is, to talk with her about going to Norwich. We lounged about afterwards till supper Time. I saw Brewster and Courtney at the Coffee House to Day.

12th. We breakfasted, supped & slept again at the Coff. House. I went to the Bishop of Norwich this morning, found his Lordship at home & Dr Salter with him, recd my Letters of Institution & was instituted very soon, his Lordship behaved exceedingly handsome and free. Paid his Secretary Mr Burn for the same 4.17.6. Gave his Lordships Servant 0.5.0, returned to the Turks Head about 12 o'clock. For a Coach to the Bishops & back again pd 0.3.0. The Bishop told me that he heard that Mr Bookey of Whitchingham (one of our Livings) is dead. At about 12 Cooke & myself took a Walk round St James's Park, the green Park, to the Mews &c. We saw the Kings Horses at the Mews, gave 0.0.6. We dined & spent the Afternoon at Bridewell at Wight's Fathers with him, his Wife and Son Osborne & a Lady. The Bishop of Norwich is a short fat Man. We settled with Mrs Prince this Evening about going to Norwich to Morrow Morning, we are to go in a Post Coach. Mr Wight has noble Apartments at Bridewell. Mrs Prince & another Lady drank Tea &c. at Mr Wights. Mr Le Mesurier of our Coll. was at Mr Wights in the Afternoon.

13th. Cooke, myself, Mrs Prince and one Mr Millard who has a Brother at Norwich a Minor Canon, set of this morning early in an hired Post-Coach and four for Norwich over Epping Forest. At the Turks Head Coffee-House for myself and Cooke, paid and gave to Servants &c. 3.3.0. We changed Horses and Coach at the bald faced Stagg, on Epping Forest, and went on to Harlowe where we were obliged to take Chaises. From Harlowe we went on to Stansted where we had some Wine & Egg, & fresh Chaises. From Stansted we went on to Bourne Bridge took fresh Chaises & went on to New-markett where we dined & then went on in fresh Chaises to Barton Mills where we changed again, & then on again to Thetford where we drank Coffee, & then went on to Attleborough, & then on to Norwich where we got I thank God safe and well about 11 at night. We all supped & spent the Evening together at the Kings Head in the Market Place, Norwich. It being after 10 when we got to Norwich, we found the City Gates shut. We did not get to bed till after 2 in the morning.

14th. We breakfasted, dined, supped & slept at Norwich. We took a Walk over the City in the morning & we both agreed that it was the fairest City in England by far, in the Center of it is a high Hill and on that a prodigious large old Castle almost perfect & forms a compleat Square, round it is a fine Terrass Walk which commands the Whole City. There are in the City 36 noble Churches mostly built with Flint, besides many meeting Houses of divers Sects. A noble River runs almost thro' the Center of the City. The City Walls are also very perfect and all round the City but where the River is. On the Hills round the City, stand many Windmills about a dozen to be seen from Castle-Mount. We drank Tea & Coffee in the Afternoon with Mr Millard & his Wife Dr Salter's Daughter in the Lower Close

—Mrs Prince & Mr Millard there also. After Tea we got to Quadrille, lost o.1.o. Mrs Millard is a very impolite Lady, rather rude. We supped, spent the Evening & slept at our Inn. Our Journey from London to Norwich cost 11.14.4, which I paid, half of which I recd this afternoon from Mrs Prince & Mr Millards Brother 5.17.0. I waited on Mr Morphew the Archdeacons Secretary for Norwich to show my Letters of Institution and to get the Archdeacons Mandate for Institution—for which I pd him 1.12.0. Mr Morphew lives in the road from my Inn to the Cathedral at Norwich.

15th. We breakfasted at our Inn at Norwich and about 12 set forth for my Living at Weston in a Chaise. At Norwich at my Inn this morning pd 2.2.0 Chaise &c. to Weston included. We got to Weston which is about 9 Miles from Norwich by 2 o'clock in the Afternoon where we dined, supped & slept at the Parsonage House. To Turnpike & Driver from Norwich to Weston pd 2.0. My Curate Mr Howes came to us in the Afternoon. Beds &c. all in readiness for us when we came. We carried with us some Wine & Cyder from Norwich. Nothing but Bacon & Eggs to day for Dinner at Weston.

16th. We breakfasted, supped & slept at Weston Parsonage. A Man & his Wife, by name Dunnell live at the Parsonage House & are good kind of People. We went to Church this morning at Weston & Cooke read Prayers & Preached for Mr Howes. Mrs Howes & her Niece Mrs Davy were at Church, And they would make us get into their Chaise after Church & go with them to Hockering to Mr Howes's where we dined & spent the Afternoon, & came back to Weston in the Evening in Mr Howes's Chaise about 9 o'clock—gave the Driver 1.0. Mr Howes's is about 2 Miles West of Weston, Cooke likes my House & Living very much. For my Part I think it is a very good one indeed. I sleep in the Garrett at Weston as I would not let Cooke keep there, but immediately under, in the New Building which is very good. Cooke is mightily pleased with his Scheme. I also administred the H. Sacrament this morning at

Weston Church being Easter Day. I had near 40 Communicants. N.B. No mony collected at the Sacrament it not being usual at Weston. My Clerk is a shocking hand—the worst Singing I ever heard in a Church, only the Clerk and one more & both intolerably bad.

27th. We got up pretty early this morning and at 7 o'clock we got into the Yarmouth Coach to go to Yarmouth about 22 Miles from Norwich. We breakfasted on the road, and got to Yarmouth about 11 o'clock, where we dined & spent the Afternoon at the Sign of the Wrestlers kept by one Orton, near to the Market Place. We each took a Yarmouth Coach just big enough for one Person & drove down to the Fort, and so on upon the Sea Coast & close to the Sea the German Ocean, out of which I drank. We were close to the Sea & sometimes the Water came up to us. It is a sweet Beach—upon the Fort we saw the Porpoises playing in the German Ocean. The Tide was going out.

We had a very fine Day. After we returned from the Sea we went to the Church & saw that, and heard I think the finest Organ I ever did hear. The Organist, Mr Chicheley stone blind played on it. Between 3 and 4 this Afternoon we got into the same Coach and returned to Norwich about 7 o'clock. Yarmouth is a sweet Place indeed the Key very fine.

For our breakfast on the road this morning pd 0.1.6.

For our Dinner, Coaches &c. at Yarmouth pd 0.11.0.

The Yarmouth Coaches are very droll things indeed the wheels very low & directly under the seat—The Shafts very clumsy & very long, & up in the Air. A very small matter will overturn them, being so very narrow, and not more than a foot from the Ground.

For our Fare to Yarmouth & back again each pd 0.6.0.

Gave the Coachman—each of us—0.1.0.

We supped & spent part of the Evening at Mr Priests near the Market Place Norwich, with him, his Wife, and Mrs Davy who seems to be fond of Mr Cooke. She is a very young Widow but has two Children. We returned to our Inn about 10 o'clock where we drank a Bottle of Clarett this being Cookes Birth-Day, for which he paid, and then we went to bed. We were highly pleased with our Scheme to day.

MAY *16th*. At 7 this morning we got into the Ipswich Post Coach for London—two Strangers were with us. We breakfasted at Colchester, dined at Brentwood supped & spent the Evening and slept at the Turks Head Coffee House in the Strand, London.

18th. We breakfasted, dined, supped & slept again at the Turks Head Coffee House—after breakfast we took a Walk in St James's Park and whilst we were there the King & Queen with their Guards went by us in Sedan Chairs from the Queens Palace to St James's Palace, there being a Levee at St James's to day at 2 o'clock. The King did not look pleasant but the Queen did. In our return back I lost my Companion Cooke and therefore I took a Walk by myself to Westminster Hall, where I saw the Lord Chancellor presiding in the Court of Chancery & Lord Mansfield in the Kings Bench. I saw there also Peckham, Head, Caldecot &c. all in their great Wiggs & Gowns with a Hundred more. In the Afternoon went & saw the Exhibition of Pictures in the Strand—pd o.2.o. From thence we went to Covent Garden Theatre & saw a Play (the Merchant of Venice & for the Entertainment Love Alamode). The Theatre quite full being Miss Macklins Benefit. None of the Royal Family there. We sat in the Prince of Wales's Box, Cooke having two Ticketts for us from a Miss Saville who took the whole Box—we each pd o.5.o. Many returned there being no room for them. Mr Macklin acted Shylock in the Play & very well, Shuter, Quicke & Woodward capital Players also. Love Alamode (Author Mr Macklin) is a very merry & cheerful Entertainment indeed. We separated coming out of the Play House & Cooke went home by himself & I by myself. I met many fine Women (common Prostitutes) in my return home & very impudent indeed. The Turks Head very full after the Play—Thorpe &c. &c. there this Evening.

JUNE *13th*. I breakfasted, dined, supped & slept again at Coll. A Chinese Man about 28 Years of Age attended by a multitude of People came to see our College & Gardens this morning, I was in the Garden with him. He talks English very well. He had on his Head a Cap like a Bell covered with a red Feather & tyed under his Chin, a kind of a Close Coat on his Back of pink Silk quilted, over that a loose Gown of pink Silk quilted also which came down to his Heels, and over that a black Gauze or Crape in Imitation of a long Cloak, a Pr of Breeches or drawers of pink Silk also & quilted, and a kind of silk Boots of the same colour & quilted also, & a Pr of red Morrocco Slippers. His Hands were also covered with some thin silk of Pink. He had a Fan tyed to a Sash before him. He was of a moderate Stature, a tawny Complexion, black Hair tyed in a kind of Tail, small Eyes, short Nose, no Beard, in Short as to his whole Face, it was uncommonly ugly, not unlike some of the runabout Gipsies. The Warden dined & spent the Afternoon with us. For Wine this afternoon in M.C.R. pd o.o.6. I went to Chapel this Evening at 5 o'clock. After Prayers I went with Acton one of our Gen. Com. to have my Profile taken of by a Lady who is come to Town & who takes of great Likenesses. I was not above a Minute sitting for the same. At Bowls this Evening lost o.1.6. For Porter this Evening in Chequer pd o.o.6.

17th. This Day the following shocking Account was on the Oxford Journal—Extract of a Letter from Ansford, June 13: 'Thursday last, about six o'clock in the Evening the Inhabitants of this Parish were alarmed by a report that Mrs Tucker, Wife of Mr Reginald Tucker had dropt down dead in an apoplectic Fit. Several People immediately repaired to the house where a Scene the most shocking to human nature presented itself, one of the finest Women in these parts dead on the floor, weltering in her blood, with her Skull fractured, so that her Brains came out at the back part of her head; her face, breast, shoulders, arms, and one of her ears bruised in a barbarous manner, The Coroner was sent for and a Jury empanelled to sit on the body, before whom it was given in Evidence, that Mr Tucker left the House about half an Hour after twelve to go to Mr Petty's, at Hatspen, only about a Mile distant: that when he came there he was in such a Sweat as to be obliged to strip of his Shirt, & put on one of Mr Perry's, and on being asked how long he was coming, took out his Watch and said an Hour: that he staid in the neighbourhood till near 5 o'clock with some Sheep-shearers, and then went home, got into his house at a Window, and made the Outcry. It also appeared that a Person had been at the house about one o'clock, to call Mrs Tucker to an Afternoon Visit: that after calling at the Doors and Windows without receiving any Answer, she went away. Mr Tucker was examined, but persisted on his Innocence: Blood however appearing on his Cloaths, and strong grounds of Suspicion arising against him, the Jury brought in their Verdict Wilful Murder, and he was taken into Custody. A second Jury were summoned the next Day, who gave the same Verdict.' May God preserve poor Miss Tucker in her great distress.

For Wine this afternoon in M.C.R. pd 0.0.6.

JULY *11th*. Had a Letter this Evening from my Brother Heighes to let me know that Mr Pounsett so ill as to be given over, and he desired me to be at Ansford as soon as possible, as my Sister is much distressed. I am very sorry indeed for Mr Pounsett.

13th. I breakfasted, dined, supped & slept again at College. Bell one of our Fellows was at Masters Rooms this morning, who informed me of the same and I went & saw him, walked in the Garden with him, and had him to my Room afterwards, & he stayed with me till Dinner Time. I asked him to dine with us but he would not. He asked me to eat a bit of Dinner with him at his Inn—but he did not seem to be fond of my accepting his Invitation, therefore I declined going with him. I parted with him at 3. He appears to me to be quite cracked-brained— abuses the New Testament much but greatly praises the Bible and the Jews—a very strange Fellow. He is grown quite fat, wears a black Wigg with 3 Curls without any Powder in it. I have not seen him before as I know for the last ten Years. I drank no Wine in the Common Room after Dinner being rather out of Temper, Dawbeny Senr having made me angry. Was not in Spirits in the Evening.

18th. I got to Ansford to the old House about 3 o'clock where I dined, supped & slept at the Parsonage House. I was very glad to find that Mr Pounsett was alive but he is still very bad indeed, not able to move at all. I am afraid he will not get the better of it—but he is much better than he was, as they told me—my poor Sister is as well as can be expected. She has a very pretty little Maid about 2 Months old. A Mrs Coleman is at Parsonage & is very kind to Mrs Pounsett. Brother Heighes spent the Afternoon at Parsonage.

AUGUST *1st*. Whilst I was at breakfast this morning, Tuckers Attorney South's Clerk of Wells called upon me and served me with a Sub-poena to appear at the Assizes at Wells on Monday the 21 of the Month, in behalf of Tucker as to his Character. In the Sub-poena was a Shilling as is usual.

7th. Mr Pounsett brave to day, made a great Dinner, was below Stairs, & out in the Garden in my Aunts Chair of Bath who is at my Uncles. The Chair is very cleaver, any Person may move himself about in it by himself. It turns upon three Wheels — 1 behind & 2 by the side. The Hindwheel is very small & runs like a Castor. The Side Wheels are higher—and in the outside of the Side Wheels is placed a kind of another wheel within the Circle of the Others, by which it is moved about. It is a greater Chair with Arms—The Hinder Wheel in the Seat.

10th. I breakfasted, supped & slept again at Parsonage. Mr Pounsett brave again to day, but had a middling N. I dined & spent the afternoon at James Clarkes with him Mr White and Brother Heighes. I took a Walk in the Evening with James Clarke and returned to his House to supper, but Jack coming in soon after we returned, I marched of as he was merry. Jenny Clarke returned from Devonshire last Night. Betsy White of Shepton is to be married in a fortnight to a Gentleman of Devonshire by name Webster a Man reported to have 500 Pd per Annum, 18000 in the Stocks besides Expectations from his Father. He had settled 300 Pd Per Annum on Betsy.

25th. I breakfasted, supped & slept again at Parsonage. I got up this morning at about 5 o'clock and at six I set of again for Wells to the Assizes and go there about 8 o'clock. The Boy went with me again. Sam Pounsett with some others overtook me in the Road. I put up my Horses at the Goat again kept by Robin Coleman where I dined at half past 2 o'clock. At half past 8 this morning I went to the Assize Hall, The Judge came to the Crown Barr about 9 o'clock. Tuckers Trial was the first that came on. Tucker walked into the Hall very undauntably and behaved without any Concern for a long Time. The first thing

he did was to object to the major Part of the Jury and others put
& sworn in their Room. The People of the Jury he objected to
were all those that were near Ansford or Shepton Mallett. Mrs
John Perry of Hatspen was the first Witness examined. Wit-
nesses against Tucker were James Clarke, Charles Clarke, Mr
Hudson, Jenny Clarke, John Perry & Wife of Hatspen, Miss
Kelloway, Alice Gore, Lidia Troakes, Sylla Jeffries, John Cary,
Farmer Corpe, the Coroner Mr Goodson, Dr Galpin, Mrs Perry
of Ansford Inn &c. &c. For Tucker, Horner, his Daughter Miss
Tucker, Mrs Clarke & Mrs White, Mrs Pounsett of Cole &
Mary Swallow. Four Londoners also appeared for his Character. I stayed in the Hall till near 3 in the afternoon & then I
went to the Goat & eat a bit of Dinner, with Richd Clarke,
Andrew Russ and Sam Burge, and we stayed there till half past
4 and then went to the Hall again. Tuckers Trial was not then
finished. Just as we got there the Judge was summing up the
Evidence to the Jury which lasted a great while, and after that
the Jury was a long Time in debating how to bring him in. At
last however at about a quarter after six the Jury delivred in
their Verdict and brought him in Guilty. The Judge then immediately passed Sentence of Condemmation on him, and to be
executed Monday next. The whole Hall seemed to rejoice at the
Sentence, as it was the general Opinion that he was guilty. He
persisted still in his Innocence at the very last. When Miss
Tucker gave her Evidence most of the Ladies cried and greatly
pitied her in her Situation. The Judge greatly condemned the
Evidence given in by John Perry and his Wife of Hatspen, as
they varied greatly from their first Examination. Tucker spoke
for half an Hour in his Defence. He sometimes stood up & sometimes sat down, The Judge behaved very well to him & spoke
very impartially. Tucker cried when the Coat was produced in
Court. I could not get near the Judge as there was such a great
Croud. The Judge did not go out of the Hall any of the Time.
It lasted near ten Hours. Whilst Sentence was passing on Tucker
I returned to the Inn and got up on my Mare & went of for

133

Home. For myself, Horses & Man &c. to day pd 0.5.0. I got to
Parsonage about half past 8 o'clock. I most sincerely pity Miss
Tucker in her very great Affliction. Pray God comfort her—
And also make Tucker truly penitent by confessing his Crime
and that he might make what Satisfaction he possibly can by his
true repentance as his Time is so very short in this Life. Mrs
Pounsett of Cole & Sister White returned from Wells about 11
o'clock at night & they supped &c. at Parsonage. Mrs Pounsett
slept at Parsonage to night. Mrs Pounsett & Sister White informed me that my Name was called in Court this afternoon at
Wells three Times, to appear before the Court to Tuckers
Character but was not to be found. The Court soon passed over
my Name. N.B. It was at the Time that I was gone to Dinner.
I never heard of it before I came home—tho' I was in the Hall
for near two Hours after Dinner & saw many People that I
knew there & they never told me of it. I really never knew a
Breath of it till I came home.

28th. Poor Tucker was hung this Aft. about 5 o'clock near
Wells—& it is reported that he persisted in his Innocence to
the very last—however I cannot think him innocent: if he is I
doubt not but he will be amply rewarded, if he is not—Lord
be merciful unto his Soul.

SEPTEMBER *16th.* I breakfasted, dined, supped & slept again at
Parsonage. Mrs Coleman breakfasted, dined, supped & slept
at Pars. Mr Pounsett brave again, went to Cole this morning.
Sent an Answer to Smiths Letter of Bath. Dr Donne called upon
us this morning to desire me to come & dine with him on Venison to Morrow. Brother Heighes dined & spent the Afternoon
at Parsonage. Mr and Mrs Webster (late Betsy White) came to
Sister Whites on Horseback this morning, and they dined, spent
the Afternoon there, & returned to Shepton in the Even'. I did
not go to Mrs Whites to day tho' much pressed in the aft.
Brother Heighes & myself took a Walk in the Evening down to
Allhampton Field, and in our way back we met Mr and Mrs

Webster on the Turnpike Road. Mrs Webster spoke as usual to me, but I said little to her being shy as She has proved herself to me a mere Jilt. Lawyer White at Mr Whites—quite drunk this Evening. Paid Betty Chrich for Meat &c. this Evening o.7.6.

OCTOBER *6th*. I breakfasted, dined, supped & slept again at College. I had a very restless night last night, very frightful Dreams. I dreamed my Brother John was hanged. For Wine this Afternoon in M.C.R. pd o.o.6. Cooke came to College to day about Dinner Time. For Porter this Evening for Cooke & myself, pd o.o.6.

7th. I breakfasted, dined, supped & slept again at College. I thank God I had a tolerable good night last night. Cooke breakfasted with me this morning. For Wine this afternoon in M.C.R. pd o.o.6. The Senr Proctor (Head of Oriel) called on me this morning and stayed with me some Time, he caught me shaving. He asked me to dine with him to Morrow. I promised.

8th. I breakfasted, supped & slept again at College. Very much hurried in mind just after I got to bed last night, was in a violent Fever most of the former Part of the Night, but afterwards got some rest & waked brave. I went to Sermon this Afternoon at St Marys and heard a tolerable good Sermon by one Peach of St Johns College. After Sermon I went to Oriel Coll. and dined in their Common Room with Head the Senr Proctor, only him and Mr Fleming of Oriel Coll. spent part of the afternoon with us. I returned to Coll. at 5 o'clock and went to Chapel. For a Bottle of Cyder after Prayers pd o.1.o. For Porter for Cooke & myself pd o.o.6. I took a dose of Rhubarb going to bed to night.

NOVEMBER *7th*. Very busy to day in preparing things for Divinity Disputations for my Batchelor of Divinitys Degree. Harry Oglander and myself go up very soon.

8th. Harry Oglander & myself went this morning to Christchurch to the Professor of Divinity Dr Benthams for Leave to go up into the Divinity School Saturday next, and the Tuesday following, which he granted. We left our Questions and Names with him.

11th. I breakfasted, dined, supped & slept again at Coll. Cooke breakfasted with me again this morning. At one o'clock myself and Harry Oglander went into the Apodyterium adjoining the Convocation House and about a Quarter after one the Professor of Divinity came to the same Place, where we were with our Masters Hoods on, the Beadle of Divinity Mr Walker Walking before the Divinity Professor with his Staff from Christchurch, The Professor then put on his Robes, after which Harry Oglander the Respondent presented the Professor with a Copy of the Epigrams, reserving another copy for himself. The Professor then with the Beadle before him with his Staff, and we following him, nudatibus capitibus,* went altogether into the Divinity School thro' the Place commonly called the Pig-Market adjoining to the Divinity School, the Professor then went into his proper Pulpit, the Respondant into his (which is the left of the Professor), & the Opponent opposite to the Respondent; the Professor then reads the Lords Prayer in Latin, after that the Professor desires the responent to read the Epigrams and states upon both Questions, which being done the Professor reads the Epigrams and then proposes an Argument on the first Question, and goes thro' one entire medium to which the Respondent answers: then the Professor bids the Opponent read, his Opponent Speech, on the first Question then the Professor bids the Opponent propose an Argument on the first Question, & then begins the Disputations between the Respondent and Opponent, which lasted till near three o'clock in the whole. The States were about a Quarter of an Hour each before the Professor stopped us. The Professor then gives his Opinion of the whole Disputations and then concludes the whole in Latin with the Grace of our Lord &c. Our first Question was an Sacra Scriptura contineat omnia ad salutem necessaria—

* 'With uncovered heads'.

Affirmatur. Our Second was, An Sacra Scriptura sit satis per-
spicua in rebus ad Salutem pertinentibus—Affirmatur.* The
Beadle walks before the Professor with his Staff back again.
There was nothing paid by me or Harry Oglander. The Professor Dr Bentham behaved very polite, and exceedingly civil to
us indeed. We returned time enough to dine in Hall. For Wine
in M.C.R. pd o.o.6. I went to Chapel this Evening at 5 o'clock.
For Porter this Evening in Chequer pd o.o.6.

18th. After Prayers this evening I went to the Vice-Chancellor
(Dr Fothergill of Queens Coll.) to ask his Leave to preach a
Latin Sermon Monday Morn' next for my Degree which he
granted. Had a Letter this evening from my Norfolk Curate
who acquainted me that Mrs Ridley had a Survey taken on
her Side concerning Dilapidations, by a Clergyman the Revd
Mr Du Quesne and a Willm Timpson Carpenter at Hockering,
and they did not bring it to more than 26.9.0. N.B. a very wide
Difference between us indeed – My Curate Mr Howes is very
much for Mrs Ridley.

DECEMBER *9th.* I breakfasted, dined, supped & slept again at
Coll. I slept but very indifferent last Night, being much dis-
turbed by Company in Hawes's Room over my Head. For Wine
& Fruit this afternoon in M.C.R. pd o.1.6. For a Bottle of
Cyder this Evening in M.C.R. pd o.1.6. I went to Chapel this
Evening at 5 o'clock. Had a Letter this Evening from my Curate
Mr Howes, and in it a Norwich Bank Bill of the Sum of 150.0.0.
Being part of Mony for Tithes recd for me at Weston.

* 'Does the Holy Scripture contain all that we need for our salvation? Is the Holy Scripture sufficiently clear in matters pertaining to
our salvation?'

1776

JANUARY *5th*. I breakfasted, dined, supped & slept again at College. Took a Walk up the Hill this morning by myself. To Mr Wyatt Carpenter pd a Bill this morn of 4.6.0. For Wine this Afternoon in M.C.R. pd 0.1.0. Williams's Brother spent the Day with us again. Gave John Bignell a Xmas Box of 0.10.6. Went to Chapel this Evening at 5 o'clock. Had a Letter this Evening from a Revd Mr Pilgrim Hatton Street No. 98, London, on behalf of Mrs Ridley concerning Dilapidations at Weston, and which was very little to the Purpose indeed. His Preferment is in the Isle of Barbadoes. Gave the Porters Man this Evening a Xmas Box 1.0. Went to bed in tolerable good Time—no Cards.

14th. Recd a Letter this morning from my Sister Pounsett. The Post which should have come in last Night, did not come till 10 this morning on Account of the Snow. Scarce ever was known so deep a Snow as at present. Many Carriages obliged to be dug out near Oxon. No Curates could go to their Churches to Day. Not one from our College went to Day on Account of ye Snow.

18th. Williams Senr and Jeffries played at all fours this Evening in M.C.R.—They had Words at last & Williams threw the Cards in Jeffries's Face the whole Pack, being in a very violent Passion. They were both to blame, but Williams the much more so. Jeffries went to his Room soon after & there he stayed. For Oysters & Porter this Evening in Chqr Pd 0.1.0. Cutting the Cards with Jeffries this Evening won 1.1.0.

26th. Between 8 and 9 this morning went to Braze-Nose College to Napletons Rooms, went with him immediately to the Chapel to Prayers, sat next to the Principals Seat. After Prayers

138

I went into their Bursary and breakfasted with Napleton, Clever, Ratcliffe, & a Stranger. We had Chocolate, Coffee and tea for breakfast. Their Bursary is very handsome the Room immediately over the Gate-Way. Being the Senr Fellow in Coll. I went to Brase-Nose in a Visitational Capacity but did nothing at all only received for my trouble as usual 0.0.8. Some of us go every Quarter on the same Account. Was invited also to Dinner there and I went at 3 and dined & spent the Afternoon in the same Room with Napleton who is Bursar, Clever, Radcliffe, Bower the Stranger mentioned above, Dr Wall and Lucas of our College. We had a very elegant Dinner: First Course Cod & Oysters Sauce, Rost Beef, Tongue, and boiled Chicken, Peas Soup & Roots. The second Course a boiled Turkey by mistake of the Manciple which should have been rosted, a brace of Partridges rosted, 4 Snipes & some Larkes rosted, also, an Orange Pudding, Syllabubs & Jellies—Madeira & Port Wines to drink & a Dish of Fruit. Dr Wall, myself and Lucas came away about 7. Great Quantity of very fine Plate made use of there. Coming from Braze-Nose this morning lost one of my gold Buttons out of the Sleeve of my Shirt.

FEBRUARY *8th*. Sent a Letter to day to a Mr Francis Attorney at Law in Norwich to desire him to settle Dilapidations with Mrs Ridley or sue her for the same as I have not heard from her for a long Time. For Wine this Evening in Chqr pd 0.0.6.

16th. I thank God I got safe & well to Ansford about ½ aft. 6. I went to the old House & found all Friends there well. I supped & slept at Mrs Pounsetts at the old Parsonage House. Mr Pounsett was at Shepton Markett to day and returned very soon after me in about a Qtr of an Hour. Memorandums: My Journey from Oxford, every Expence included that was spent on the Road, cost me in the whole to the Sum of £5 9s 6d.

MARCH *5th*. I breakfasted, dined, supped & slept again at Parsonage. Brave this morning I thank God much more easy.

Brother Heighes told me this morning that my Disorder proceeded from eating great Quantities of Water-Cresses, Jenny Clarke was the same some Time back from the same Cause— I believe it to be true indeed: at one o'clock to day as a Leg of Mutton was rosting by the Kitchen Fire, a very dreadful Fire happened in the Chimney, It played above the Tunn near 2 Yards and very fiercely, I thought the whole House would have been in Flames every Moment, but the Wind being very high and to the South-West, blowed the Flame a quite contrary way to the Thatch, which blessed be God prevented the whole House from it &c. Our Cary & Ansford Friends were very good indeed & came to our Assistance in a very little Time, and brought Cary Engine with them, and by the Blessing and mercy of God in about 2 Hours it was happily extinguished, and for which Great Goodness O Lord, to whom I return my most unfeigned thanks and ever make me O Lord ever thankful & mindful for this so great a Deliverance to me and all in this House. My poor Sister was terribly frightened indeed. Thomas one of Ansford Inn Servants was the most active man in it, he was up to the Tun in a Minute and was the Man that threw down the first Pail of Water down it and many more were thrown down immediately, after that we got some wet Ruggs, & Whirn-Sheets & Blanketts and threw down the Chimney and covered over the Tunn upon top quite close, put out the Fire below, stopped up the Bottom also as close as we could, then continued pouring Water thro' the Cloth upon the Top of the Tunn. The Smoke came thro' the Wall in the Poining End. A Hole was made thro' the Ceiling also in the Kitchen Chamber to examine above, and all was safe—Robin Francis, James Lintern, our Boy, Jasorn Cock with many others very active indeed. Mr Willm Burge Junr came himself & sent all his Workmen immediately, James Clarke's Man & Richard, My Uncle's, Mr Whites & Perrys and many others came immediately, all Ansford & Cary almost came, and none but was greatly alarmed. My Uncle sent down some Cyder in Pails to the People & we

gave them more—I offered a Guinea to the People upon the
House, but they would not take it, Mr Burge would not suffer
it. I don't know what we should have done was it not for our
very kind & good Friends. It alarmed me very much indeed all
the Day after I could eat no Meat all the Day or scarce anything
else. Mr White sent us down some Victuals. It happened entirely for want of having the Chimney swept, it had not been
swept for above a twelvemonth not since Christmas twelvemonth. It is amazing that Mr Pounsett should neglect it so long,
very wrong of him indeed only to save one Sixpence. Sister
Clarke, Miss Patty Clarke, Sister White and Mr James Clarke
supped & spent the Evening with us. Brother Heighes &
Richard Clarke spent part of the Afternoon with us. Poor Patty
Clarke was greatly alarmed as was Sister Clarke & Nancy
Woodforde who were at it. I did not go to Bed till two in the
morning to Night and every thing I thank God was safe before

that. We had the Fire all the Day after in that Chimny. Mem:
A Wonderful Deliverance from Fire. N.B. when the Fire was
over I sent over a Note to Mrs Pounsett at Cole by our Boy. Our
Boy behaved exceeding well indeed at the Fire. N.B. Washing
Week—all the Cloaths out a drying when the Fire happened.

26th. Brother Heighes supped & spent the Evening at Parsonage. He acquainted me that Nancy Woodforde would not be
able to go with me into Norfolk, as one Dr Buckland had seen
her to day and had told her that her Disorder was the Kings
Evil* and that he could cure her in about a twelvemonth, therefore she is to be under him. Pray God she might be cured. The
Dr is a seventh Son & is a grazier and Farmer—But he has
cured many he says. Went in the Afternoon and saw Sister
Clarke as she goes for London to morrow. Jenny her Daughter
was there.

27th. Dr Donne called here this morning, Miss Patty Clarke
& Nancy Woodforde happening to be here at the same Time,
the Dr by my Desire looked at Nancy Elbow and Hand, and he
said he believed it to be the Kings Evil, he said he knew a Person
that was perfectly cured of such Disorder by a Man near Ax-
bridge a Gentleman Farmer but he had forgot his Name but
that he would recollect & send me his Name. The Person cured
by him had been under him & another very famous Surgeon
but that they could do nothing with her. She was cured by him
in 9 Months & has been well five Years. Mr Pounsett went to
Cole with Dr Donne & dined &c. there. Dr Donne said that
Alford Well Water had done great things in Complaints of the
Kings Evil, & very good for such Disorders.

APRIL *7th*. Went to Cary Church this morning being Easter
Day and recd the Sacrament from the Hands of Mr Thomas.
For an Offering at the Altar, gave 0.1.0. There was a poor

* Scrofula, a disease characterised by swelling and degeneration of
the lymph glands, formerly thought to be curable by a touch of the
King's hand.

crazy Woman at Church who made a Noise there, she stayed to receive the Sacrament And went up to the Altar but Mr Thomas passed over her, She afterwards walked up and down the Church. We had a Loin of Veal rosted as usual on Easter Day.

14th. Very much fatigued & hurried this morning by hearing that my Brother John had a Fall from his Horse in the Night coming from Evercreech & was found senseless about 1 in the morning a little below the turnpike. He has cut his Face much & much bruised inwardly, but no Bone broke—thank God he was not killed. He was bled & put to bed about 3 in the morning. In the Afternoon I went down to see him and he was up & below Stairs at Dinner but in Pain. I did not expect to see him so well as he was. I hope this will caution him from riding when merry—he has had many Falls before but none so bad as this.

MAY *8th.* Bill Woodforde & myself very busy all the Morning in packing the Portmanteau as we go to Morrow for Norfolk. I went this Afternoon to Mr Js Clarkes, Mr Richd Clarkes, Mr Willm Burge Senr and Junr and took my Leave of them as I go to Morrow. Bill Woodforde dined at Pars. Mr and Mrs White supped &c. at Parsonage. After Supper I went down to my Brother Johns & took Leave.

9th. This Morning at 9 o'clock took my final Leave of the old Parsonage at Ansford, and went up to Mr Whites and there I breakfasted with him, Sister White, Mr Pounsett and Jenny, Brother Heighes, his Sons Willm and Sam and James Clarke. Poor John Coleman the Baker being merry fell down Stairs in the Night about 11 o'clock & killed himself on the Spot by fracturing his Skull—am sorry for him. After breakfasting at Mr Whites about 10 o'clock I took my Leave of my Friends at Ansford & set forth on my Mare for Norfolk and Bill Woodforde on my Bay, Will Coleman went with me. I left my Friends very low on this Occasion. Bill Woodforde's great Newfoundland Dog Spring went with us to day & came to Wiley very well.

11th. We breakfasted at Hungerford & at 10 we went on. My bay Mare coughed exceedingly between Hungerford & Farnborough worse than I ever knew her. I believe it to be owing to eating Beans only for Corn. At 4 this afternoon we set forth for Oxford and got there I thank God safe and well at about 9 o'clock we came on slow on Account of my Mare—I gave her no Beans at Farnborough only Oats well watered and she came on brave afterwards. I rode my new little Mare quite to Oxford, but she strained my left Hand-wrist very much this Afternoon by my giving her a very violent Check on her making a false Step—it pained very much all the Evening & Night. I put up the Horses at the old Inn in Oxford the blue Boar kept by Mrs Ladds the Widow. The old Dog performed the Journey very well. I supped at the blue Boar but eat very little being taken ill on Account of the closeness of the Room & pain of my Wrist but I soon got tolerable again except my Wrist. I slept in my Rooms at College. Bill slept at the Boar.

12th. I went to Chapel this Evening. The Chapel and Anti-Chapel exceeding full on Account of our Organ being played. It played last Night for the first Time since its improved State —not quite finished yet. I wore no Surplice to Night being no longer Fellow of New College—my Fellowship expired April 12 last past.

14th. I breakfasted, dined and slept again at College. Bill Woodforde breakfasted with me this morning. Very busy this morning in packing up Books &c. for Norfolk.

16th. Bill Woodforde dined & spent the Afternoon in my Room by himself—I dined in Hall, spent the Afternoon in M.C.R. For Wine & Fruit this Afternoon in M.C.R. pd 0.1.0. Paid Gauntlett the Bursar my last Qtrs Kitchen Battels* 2.7.0. I went to Chapel this Evening at 5 o'clock. Took a long Walk this morning by myself up the Hill &c. Going over the temporary Bridge 3 Times & back Pd 0.1.6. Took a long Walk by myself in the Evening also. Bill Woodforde supped & spent the

* Food and drink bills run up by a member of an Oxford college.

144

Evening in my Room. For Cyder & Porter this Evening in my Room pd 0.1.6.

18th. Sent 4 Boxes by Jones's Waggon this morning for Norfolk.

Gave the Waggoner belonging to the same 0.1.0.

For a Collar of brass for my Great Dog &c. 0.5.6.

To my Laundress for washing & gave her 0.2.0.

Mr Calcot who succeeded me in my Fellowship bought most of my Goods & for the same paid me this morning 29.11.0.

Masters had Goods of me to the value of 3.4.0.

I dined in Hall to day and spent the Afternoon in M.C.R.— For Wine this afternoon in M.C.R. pd 0.0.6. I went to Chapel again at 5 o'clock. Went to Mr Wards this Evening and pd him on Balancing all Accounts with him in full of all Demands 14.0.0.

Paid Clarke & Castle the Mercers this Evening 1.1.0.

Paid Thorpe the Hosier this Evening also 2.19.0.

Paid Mr Wyatt the Carpenter this Evening also 0.19.6.

Gave Mr Wards Man this Evening 0.1.0.

Mr Lock sent my Clock by Jones's Waggon to day for Weston. Sent my Pictures also, by Jones's Waggon to day. Holmes supped & spent the Evening with us in my Rooms. For Wine this Evening in my Room & Porter pd 0.2.0. Gave Holmes my handsome Japan Inkstand and my gilt Leather Fire Screen both cost me 2.2.0. Mr Ward had what was left—£4 15s od. Mr Masters did not pay me for what he had to Day.

20th. We breakfasted at College and about 10 took my final Leave of my Rooms at College and set forth for Norfolk, myself, Bill Woodforde and my Serv. Will Coleman. Master Senr breakfasted with me in my Rooms.

Paid my Barber Pell for ½ Yrs shaving due at Lady Day 10.6.

Gave him for his trouble since I have been here now 5.0.

Gave Frank Payne's Boy this morning 1.0.

Gave a Person that led my Horses out of Town 1.0.

We got to Tame about 12 o'clock about 13 Miles from Oxon

and there we dined at the red Lion kept by one Powel. When we got to Tame was very uneasy on Account of my leaving at Oxford this Book and my Baldwins Journal, I sent a Man immediately from Tame with a Letter to Master Senr to send back the same, and in about 3 Hours he returned & brought me back both very safe. I was then quite happy—pd him for going 0.2.6 and for his Horse & Turkpikes paid him 0.4.9.

22nd. We breakfasted at Cambridge & then set forward. Bill & myself went after breakfast and saw Kings Chapel the finest I ever saw, all of fine carved Stone the Roof of the same—most capital Piece of Architecture indeed. Gave a Man that shewed it to us 0.1.0. the Gentlemen Commoners wear black gowns and gold Trimmings made slight upon the sleeves of the same, and very small gold Tossills to their square Caps of Cloth. The Members of Trinity Coll. undergraduates all wear Purple Gowns—Gentlemen Commoners wear purple Gowns trimmed with Silver instead of Gold & Silver Tossills. The Buildings are grand at Cambridge, but few of them.

24th. We breakfasted at Norwich and spent the morning there. I called on Mr Francis Junr and talked with him a good deal.* My first Box sent from Ansford is now at the Kings Head. Paid Mr Kerrison for the Carriage to Norwich 0.10.5. About noon I set forth for Weston about 10 Miles and got there about 2 o'clock—found there nothing to eat. As there was nothing to eat at Weston we rode down our Horses to Leonade Bridge about a Mile and there we dined & spent the Afternoon. We walked back to Weston in the Evening leaving our Horses behind to be taken care of. My Servant Will supped & slept there. Myself and Bill supped & slept at Weston at my House. We were very low in the Evening, as it appeared at present rather disagreeable to us.

25th. We breakfasted, dined, supped & slept at Weston. My

* The Norwich attorneys, Mr Francis Senr and his son, looked after all the legal and financial business between New College and the various incumbents of college livings in Norfolk.

Servant Will dined, supped & slept at my House to Night. My Horses are at Leonade and to remain there till I can get some Hay and Straw for them. Mr Wilson Junr called upon me in the Afternoon. We were very dull again in the Evening being in a strange Place and things very inconvenient at present.

26th. Mr Howes and his Wife called upon me this morning on their Road to Weston Church and I went with them to Church and heard my Curate Mr Howes read Prayers and Preach. No Service in the Afternoon therefore we took a walk round by Attlebridge to Leonade Bridge where we met Mr Wilson by appointment. He desired me to go to his House at Reepham and sleep there but could not upon any account. He stayed but a little Time at Leonade Bridge neither did we. At Leonade Bridge for Wine, Cyder, Ale, Pork, Cheese, Brandy, Rum & for my Servant pd 1.17.6.

27th. I dined & spent the Afternoon at Hockering at Mr Howes with him, his Wife, and Mr Du Quesne of Tuddenham. Gave Mr Howes's Servant Maid coming away 0.1.0. We played at Quadrille most part of the Afternoon. I spent a very agreeable Day there, and lost nothing. My Horses were brought to Weston about noon, and they are to stay with me now for the future. Had a Cart Load of Hay & the same of Straw from Mr Palmer one of my Farmers for which I owe him. Gave his Man that brought the same 0.1.0.

JUNE *3rd.* Two Servant Maids came to me this morning and offered their Services to me—I agreed with them both and they are to come to me new Midsummer Day next. One of them is to be an upper Servant, and she lived very lately with Mr Howes's —a very pretty Woman she is, and understands Cookery & working at her Needle well. I am to give per Annum & Tea twice a Day 5.5.0. She was well recommended to me by Mrs Howes, and the reason she was turned away from Mrs Howes's, was her not getting up early enough, as Mrs Howes told me. The other Maid was recommended to me by Mrs Howes—she is a Tenants Daughter of Mr Howes's, she is wooled.* I agreed to give her per Annum 3.10.0. She is to come at Midsummer also—she is to milk &c.—very bad all day in the Tooth Ach —The Tooth is faulty. Mr Hardy & his Boy Mason at work for me all day. Gave a Man this morning for bringing home our Dog 0.1.0. Dunnell the Carpenter at work for me all Day.

4th. My Tooth pained me all night, got up a little after 5 this morning and sent for one Reeves a Man who draws Teeth in this Parish and about 7 he came and drew my Tooth but shockingly bad indeed, he broke away a great Piece of my Gum & broke one of the Fangs of the Tooth it gave me exquisite Pain all the Day after and my Face was swelled prodigiously in the Evening & much Pain. Very bad in much Pain the whole Day long. Gave the old Man that drew it however 0.2.6. He is too old I think to draw Teeth, can't see very well.

5th. Very much disturbed in the Night by our Dog which was kept within doors to night, was obliged to get out of bed naked, twice or thrice to make him quiet, had him into my Room and there he emptied himself all over the Room, was obliged then to order him to be turned out which Bill did. My Face much swelled but rather easier than Yesterday tho' now very tender and painful—kept in to day mostly. Paid & gave Will my Servant this Evening 0.5.0. Paid Mr Dunnell this Evening part of a Bill due to him from me for 2 Cows, 3 Piggs, 3 Pr of Shoes, Flower, Tea, Sugar, News Papers, Pipes, Candles, Tobacco, Beer, Mustard, Salt, Washing, Halters, Comb & Brush, Crabs, Bread, & Porterage of 14.9.3 the Sum of, a Bank Note of 10.0.0.

JULY *19th.* Bill and myself took a ride in the afternoon to Mr Howes's at Hockering where we spent the remaining part of the afternoon with Mr Howes & his Wife. Mr Howes went to bury

* The tireless and splendid R. L. Winstanley has been unable to run this term to earth in any dictionary either standard or dialect.

a Corpse for Mr Du Quesne, & when he was gone Mrs Howes told us that she lived very unhappy with her Husband, as he wants her to make her Will & give every thing to his Family. I advised her to the Contrary, & to give to her own. We were wet coming back as it rained.

September *19th*. We breakfasted, dined, supped & slept again at Yarmouth. After breakfast we each took a Yarmouth Coach and drove down upon the Coast, and called again at the Fort. Will walked down there—at the Fort to Day pd 0.2.0. It was very pleasant and very delightful indeed nothing can beat what we saw to day—immense Sea Room, Shipps & Boats passing & repassing—the Wind being rather high, the Waves like Mountains coming into the Shore—we rode down to the Ocean, the Waves sometimes coming into our Carriages. We returned about 3 o'clock and we had some fine Smelts, Shoulder of Mutton roasted & Tarts. In the Evening took a Walk on the Quay, as fine a one as was ever seen—a great deal of Company walking backward and forward. We got a board an English Vessell, and were treated with Wine, Gin &c. the Sailors behaving civil indeed to us, had a difficult Matter to make them take any thing, but at last I did, and all the Silver I had, being only 0.1.0. She was a Collier and going soon back to Sunderland.

October *4th*. I breakfasted, dined, supped & slept again at Weston. Bill breakfasted, dined, supped & slept again at Weston. We had some more fishing this morning in some Pitts near the House—in that of Mr Dade we took out fifty brace but all very small, very good stock however—we put them & about 10 brace more all into the Barton Pond. Mr Bowles was with us & dined, & spent the afternoon with us. A Mr Roop a young Man & is a Brother of Mrs Davy's called on me this morning, he drank a Glass of Wine & decamped. I never saw him before in my Life —he is a Prig.

NOVEMBER *3rd*. This Morning about 11 o'clock Dr Thorne of Mattishall came to my House and inoculated* my Servants, Ben Legate and little Jack Warton, and in the following Manner —Ben is about 25 Years old, Jack about 9. The Dr took out of his Pocket a small — where the Matter was contained in Cotton Thread, they both present, and no Handkerchief or any thing over the Face's during the whole Time they then each stripped, and the Dr taking a small bit of the Cotton Thread saturated with Matter between his Left hand Finger & Thumb with the Launcet in his other hand, he then dipt the Point of the Lancet in the cotton Thread, and with the Point of Launcet made two Dotts like this: about two Inches apart in each of their Arms, dipping now & then his Launcet in Water & then with the Cotton Thread, scarce to be felt or to draw blood, they then stood with their Arms exposed to the cold Air for about 3 Minutes, till almost dried up: the Matter took effect almost instantaneously, and plain to be seen, the Place where the Dots were made a little above the other Flesh like a small sting of a Nettle. No Plaister or any thing else whatever put to their arms afterwards. They were allowed to make a good Meat Dinner, & then to take their Leave of Meat for some Time. They accordingly made a good Dinner on a Loin of Veal to day which we had for Dinner. For Supper they had Honey spread upon bread and their drink was Toast and Water. Just before they went to bed, they each took a Powder of Calamine in the Pulp of a rosted Apple—Ben's Powder weighed 17 Grains which I weighed in my Mony Scales, and Jacks was 14 Grains. I then took their Papers of Salts and poured some boiling Water on the same, and gave them to take early to Morrow Morning, charging them to drink plentifully of Water Gruel, about an Hour after to Morrow. Bens Paper of Salts weighed 19 Pennyweights, Jacks Paper of Salts weighed 9 Pennyweights and $\frac{1}{2}$. Pray God my People & all others in the Small Pox may do so well, several

* The purpose and principle are obvious, the method primitive but not so different from that of our own day.

Houses have got the Small-Pox at Present in Weston. O Lord send thy Blessing of Health on them all.

DECEMBER *3rd*. I breakfasted, dined, supped & slept again at home. Bill breakfasted, dined, supped & slept again at Weston. My Frolic for my People to pay Tithe to me was this Day & I gave them a good Dinner, Surloin of Beef rosted, a Leg of Mutton boiled & plumb Pudding in plenty. Recd to day only for Tithe & Glebe of them 236.2.0. Mr Browne called on me this morning and he and myself agreed & he paid me for Tithe only 55.0.0 included in the above, he could not stay to dinner. They all broke up about 10 at night—Dinner at 2. Every Person well pleased, and were very happy indeed. They had to drink Wine, Punch, and ale as much as they pleased, they drank of Wine 6 Bottles, Of Rum 1 Gallon and half & I know not what ale. Old Harry Andrews, my Clerk, Harry Dunnell, and Harry Andrews at the Heart all dined &c. in Kitchen. Some dined in the Parlour & some in the Kitchen. 17 dined &c. that paid me Tithe, that is to say—Stepn Andrews, Baker, Burton, Cary, Mann, Pegg Norton, Bowles, Dade, Case, Pratt, Legate Senrs Son of Ringland, Bidewell, Michl Andrews, Burrows and Legate Junr at the Horse. Mr Peachment came just at dinner time, but he had dined, he spent the Afternoon and Evening however. There was no Supper at all provided for them. We had many droll Songs from some of them—I made use of about 13 Lemons & abt 2 Pd of Sugar. Bill and myself both well tired when we went to bed.

10th. I breakfasted, dined, supped & slept again at home. Bill breakfasted, dined, supped & slept again at Weston. Mr Chambers the Schoolmaster who is lately come here called on me this morning to let me know that he would teach my Servants Ben & Will to write & read at 4/6 a Quarter each, which agreed for.

1777

JANUARY *13th*. I breakfasted, dined, supped & slept again at home. Bill breakfasted, dined, supped & slept again at Weston Went on my Mare & my Servant Will with me to Mr Du Quesnes where I dined, spent the afternoon and stayed till 8 at night, with him, Mr and Mrs Howes and Mr Donne. We had for Dinner a Leg of Mutton boiled, a batter Pudding & a couple of Ducks. It is a Clubb meeting & goes by the name of Rotation I became a Member of it to day and they all dine with me on Monday next — Every Monday is the Day. At Quadrille this Evening lost 0.1.3. I gave nothing at all to Servants. As there was no Moon to come home by, it was very disagreeable to come thro' the Wood that I did, but I thank God I got safe & well back, tho' very dark. When there is no Moon for the futur will get back before it is dark. This morning made a Contrac with Harry Dunnell before my Nephew to give him 6/6 Pe Week and a Dinner each Day to work for me from this Day fo one Year, and to which he agreed — A Dinner on Sundays. M Rat-Catcher came here this morning And he had some spor with a Rat which he soon killed. I gave him some Victuals an some Ale. Our People busy in washing to day. Mr Cary went to Norwich to day & brought me things.

FEBRUARY *14th*. To 36 Children being Valentines Day an what is customary for them to go about for in these Parts th Day gave 0.3.0 being one penny apiece to each of them. M Kerrs Waggon of Tuddenham and Mr Cantrells of Leonad brought me two Load of Brick apiece from Witchingham.
I gave the Waggoners Victuals & drink and each 0.1.0.
Paid my Servant Maid Betty Rix for things 0.1.2.

Paid Sukey Boxley for things another Maid 0.6.0.

MARCH 27th. I breakfasted, dined, supped & slept again at home. Bill breakfasted, dined, supped & slept again at Weston. We took half a large Basket full of Toads this Morning, out of the great Pond, put them into a Kettle and poured some boiling Water upon them which killed them instantaneously—I dare say we killed 200. Harry Dunnell and my Boy Jack Warton took them up in their Hands alive and put them into a Baskett. Great alteration of Weather to day the Morn' sultry hot, and Wind South. In the Evening very cold with a Fogg and Wind full North. Sowed some grass Seeds to day in my Garden.

   29th. I breakfasted, dined, supped & slept again at home. Bill breakfasted, dined, supped & slept again at Weston.
   To Js Smith Gardner this Evening, for Work pd 0.8.6.
   To Ditto for 18 Apple Trees pd 0.18.0.
   To Harry Dunnell for his Weeks Work pd 0.6.6.
   Andrews the Smuggler brought me this Night about 11 o'clock a Bagg of Hyson Tea 6 Pd Weight, He frightned us a little by whistling under the Parlour Window just as we were going to bed. I gave him some Geneva and paid him for the Tea at 10/6 Per Pd—3.3.0.

APRIL 17th. Sent my Servants Will and Ben with a Cart this Morn' to Norwich after some Wine from Mr Priest's & some Dishes and Plates &c. from Mr Beloes—China Merchant. Sent by them a Note to Mr Priest & one to Mr Beloe. They did not return till 7 in the Evening, they might have came much sooner I think. The things came home very safe however as well as Wine. I have now a compleat Table Service of the Cream coloured Ware, with some other useful things. Had a Note from Mr Beloe and Mr Priest. My Servants were both rather in Liquor and as for Will, he behaved very surly & went to bed before I supped—a pretty return for giving him half a Guinea last Week.

MAY *15th*. Mr Custance called on me this morning to go a fishing. We rode down to the River. Mr Custances Mistress a Miss Sherman & one Sandall an oldish Man a broken Gentleman & who keeps a Mistress also tho' he has a Wife living, went with us on horseback. I returned home to Dinner tho' very much pressed to dine with Mr Custance. We had but middling Sport — a Lease of Trout, & Pike & some flat Fish. Mr Custance behaved exceedingly civil to me. He sent me the finest Trout and the Pike this Evening by his Man Phillip — gave the Servant 0.1.0.

JUNE *4th*. Recd of Mr Legate Bens Father this morning for 2 small Piggs which Sukey sold him 0.15.0.

Gave Sukey out of them for selling them 0.1.0.

To Harry Andrews for making Laths 0.13.0.

The Toads in my great Pond made an extraordinary loud Noise for this last Week past. This being his Majesty's Birth Day had my blunderbuss fired of by Bill about 2 Hands high three Times in honours of the Day, and with Powder only. We had the fine Pike that Mr Custance sent me rosted for Dinner with a Pudding in his Belly and very good it was indeed — we dined on it chiefly, tho' we had a fine Piece of Beef boiled besides. The Pike was more than 2 Foot long after being rosted.

17th. Bill made me uneasy & very angry with him at breakfast by contradicting me in a very saucy manner — I therefore told him that I was determined that he should not return with me to Weston but that I would leave him in the West. This being my Rotation Day, the following Company dined and spent the Afternoon with me — Mr and Mrs Howes and with them Mrs Priest and Daughter from Norwich — Mr Bottom, Mr Donne and Sister with one Miss Church, a Lady rather deformed but dressed exceeding well with a prodigious high Head indeed but very sensible, and the Revd Mr Du Quesne Chancellor of St Davids. I have for Dinner a bad Leg of Mutton boiled scarce fit to be eat by being kept too long, and Capers, some Green Peas and a Piggs Face, a Neck of Pork rosted with

Gooseberries, a plumb Pudding, with Carrotts, Turnips &c. for Roots. Miss Church & Miss Donne came and went back in a common Market Cart. Most of the Company were wet by coming to day, as it rained much about 2 o'clock. They all returned about 9. At Quadrille this Afternoon after Tea with Miss Church, Miss Donne & Mr Du Quesne at 2d per Fish, lost 0.4.0. We were very merry with Mrs Howes to day. I gave them a plumb Cake with their Tea.

26th. At Dunstable this morning paid & gave 0.12.10. We set of from Dunstable before breakfast and went on to Tring where we breakfasted at the Rose & Crown, kept by one Brandon—very civil People. Paid and gave at Tring 0.2.10. From Tring we went on thro' Aylesbury to Tame and there we dined at the Red Lion kept by one Powel. From Tame we went on leaving Oxford to the right hand to Abingdon and there we supped and slept at the Hart kept by one Tramplett—at a private House at Abingdon this Evening paid and gave 7.0.

Ansford

JULY *5th.* I breakfasted, dined, supped & slept again at Mr Pounsetts. Brother Heighes and his Son Sam dined &c. with us. Sam brought his Violin with him and played several Tunes to us—he is amazingly improved both in Painting and in Musick—he is a very cleaver Youth. I gave Sam this Afternoon 0.2.6. Painter Clarke with Js and Richard Clarke supped and spent the Evening with us.

21st. I breakfasted, and slept again at Mr Pounsetts. Very low indeed all Day long, being afraid that I am not right in Health having something (tho' at present trifling) not right with my Privities, having a small Discharge from the same, owing to a private Connection when at Abingdon with one Miss Clarke, which I am much fearful of. I dined, spent the Aft. supped & spent the Evening at Mr Whites, with him, Sister White, Sister Clarke, Sister Pounsett, Richard Clarke, Bill Woodforde, Bob White, Sam Clarke, Jem White and Anne.

Js Lewis & Son spent part of the Afternoon with us, Richd Clarke did not sup with us. To Mr Whites Servant Maids gave 0.2.0. Tho' we had a very elegant Dinner was afraid to eat much. We had a whole Salmon, Ham & Fowls, Beans, a Neck of Pork rosted, with Puddings and Pies.

22nd. I breakfasted and slept again at Ansford. We were rather disturbed about an Hour after we got to bed, and Jenny came to my Door and waked me, and asked me if something did not fall down in my Room, and that she had heard something walk in the Passage to my Door, and also thought that I was ill — but it all ended in nothing. Mr Pounsett, myself and Sister dined, spent the Afternoon, supped, & spent the Evening at Richd Clarkes at Cary with him, Mr Thomas, Brother Heighes and Sam Clarke. Js Clarke, Sister White & Sam Woodforde supped &c. with us. In the Afternoon I walked down to Charles Clarkes and bought me 20 Yards of Huccaback Cloth for Kitchin Table Cloths in Norfolk $\frac{3}{4}$ wide at 1s 1d per Yd pd 1.1.0. To Richd Clarkes Servants coming away gave 0.2.0. Cousin Lewis and Son went of this morning for Nottingham. We had for Dinner at Richd Clarkes to day some Whiting, a Leg of Mutton boiled, a Couple of Ducks rosted & peas and a Plumb Pudding boiled. I was much better to day and more easy in my mind. Robert Biggen for stealing Potatoes was this Afternoon whipp'd thro' the Streets of Cary by the Hangman at the end of a Cart. He was whipped from the George Inn, to the Angel, from thence back thro' Street to the Royal Oak in South-Cary & so back to the George Inn. He being an old Offender there was a Collection of 0.17.6 given to the Hangman to do him Justice — But it was not much for all that — the Hangman was an old Man and a most villainous Fellow indeed. For my Part I would not contribute a Farthing to it.

30th. I breakfasted and slept again at Ansford. I dined, spent the Afternoon, supped & spent the Evening at my Brother Johns with him, his Wife, Miss Patty Clarke, Nancy Wood-forde, Brother Heighes & two Sons Willm & Sam. Bill Woodforde was very near being drowned last Night in Ansford River and in all probability would had not Bob White been with him as he pulled him out when sinking by the Hair of his Head. They went down to the River to go into the Water, the River was quite full. We had for Dinner at Jacks, three Fowls boiled & a Chop, a Leg of Mutton rosted & a Batter Pudding. Sister Clarke & Sam spent the Afternoon, supped & spent the Evening with us as did little Sophy Clarke. We spent the Day very agreeably till the last Hour and then Jack being merry began to be in his old Humours. I gave old Dinah Dyke & Jacks Maid 0.2.0.

AUGUST *29th*. We breakfasted at Thetford & then marched on. Paid and gave at Thetford this morning 0.15.9. We dined at the Cock at Attleborough—pd & gave there 0.5.3½. For some Corn for my Horse, & Beer for ourselves at a small public House between Attleborough & Weston not far from Sir John Wodehouses pd & gave 0.2.0. We called at Mr Du Quesnes as we came by his House but he was not at home. We got home to Weston & I thank God safe and well this Evening about 7—I found all my People well & things in decent Order. I sent a Letter by Cary this Evening before I pulled of my Boots to my Sister Pounsett to inform them that we were arrived at Weston safe and well. We supped and slept at the Rectorial House.

SEPTEMBER *16th*. We breakfasted, dined, supped & slept again at Weston. Very busy with the Engine this morning. Mr Du Quesne, Mr Donne & Sister, Mr Botham, Mr and Mrs Howes and Mrs Davy came to my House about 12 upon Account of seeing some fishing before Dinner as my great Pond* was near

* JW was very keen on his pond and always working on it in various ways—dredging it of mud, checking on its population of fish, bringing in machinery to drain it. At certain points, not necessarily recorded in this selection, he was more than interested in recording its daily level. It was, of course, a source of food. By April next year it was as full as he desired—at which point he ceases to refer to it.

empty. We were obliged to sink the Engine lower, and in doing the same in raising the Engine one of the triangular Poles broke and very near killed my Man Will Coleman, he was knocked down by the Pole falling on his Head, but it only stunned him for some Time, I then gave him a Dram and he was soon pretty well. It frightened us all very much. We caught a Number of small Tench with the casting Net, but could not get all the Water out to day for the Mud. The Ladies & Gentleman all dined & spent the Afternoon with us. I gave them for Dinner half a Dozen of very fine Tench (taken out of my Pond in the Yard) stewed, a Rump of Beef boiled and a Goose rosted & a Pudding — Mrs Howes found great fault with many things especially about stewing the Fish. She could not eat a bit of them with such Sauce &c. Mrs Davy fell down stairs but did not hurt herself. Miss Donne swallowed a Barley Corn with its stalk. Many accidents happened but none very bad.

At Quadrille this Evening won 0.1.0.

To Mr Burtons Harvest Men a Largess 0.1.0.

To Mr Palmers Harvest Men of Morton 0.1.0.

The Company went away about 9 o'clock. They all admired my plated Candlesticks & Snuffers. Bens Father & Barnard Dunnell who assisted at the Engine to day dined with our Folks. My Servant Will went to Mr Bowles Frolic to night & slept there as I gave him leave.

21st. I read Prayers and Preached this Morning at Weston. Harry Dunnell dined with our Folks to day. In the Afternoon my Dog Pompey came home shot terribly so bad that I had her hanged directly out of her Misery. My Greyhound Minx who was with her did not come and we suppose she has met with the same fate. It is supposed that Mr Townshends Gamekeeper who goes by the name of black Jack, shot Pompey. My Nephew and self took a Walk in the Afternoon.

22nd. Mr Burton brought me a brace of Partridges. My Greyhound Minx came home early this morning very much shot in one Side, but I hope not mortally. They were both shot by black

Jack and seen by John Bowles's Brother in Law as Mr Bowles told me. I intend to let Mr Townshend have knowledge of it.

30th. Finished carrying Mudd by Breakfast this Morning. Harry Dunnell found an old silver Spoon this Morn' in levelling Parts in the Pond to make it more even. It weighed one Ounce and marked with M.E. and I apprehend it belonged formerly to the Family of the Englands, one of which was Rector in 1575. I gave Harry Dunnell for finding it 0.2.6. To 2 Peck of Pears of Js Taylor 0.1.0.

OCTOBER *30th.* Bill took my little Mare unknown this morning out on my Clover Piece and put her into a Bath of Sweat by leaping her over a Rail which he had put up and trod my Clover to Pieces. I caught him at it and it made me very angry with him. I destroyed the Rail & about 12 Mr Du Quesne called on me and myself and Bill took a ride with him to Mr Priests at Reepham and there we dined & spent the Afternoon with Mr and Mrs Priest and two of their Children. We had for Dinner a Leg of Mutton & a Hare &c. We returned to Weston about 6 —Mr Du Quesne was left at Reepham where he stays till Saturday. My Nephew coming home from Reepham talked to me about his leaping my little Mare this morning and he grew rather saucy—after he came home he was very insolent and impertinent to me indeed. I had a large Piece of Thatch blown of my Barn after I was gone which made a great hole in it Harry Dunnell &c. who were in the Barn were obliged to keep out of it for an Hour, as they expected the Barn would otherwise fall upon them. But I thank God no great Damage happened to me through the high Winds—hope no other Person had more. Morn' wind very high indeed—WSW—& the wind made the Roof of the Barn all one Side move so plainly to be seen. Afternoon Stormy with high Winds still—SW.

Norwich

DECEMBER *12th*. I breakfasted at the Kings Head. I had but an indifferent Night as I thought my Sheets were not over and above aired. I heard the City Waits about 4 in the morning and their Musick was very entertaining indeed. After breakfast I took a Walk to Mr Locks my Coal Merchant and paid his Clerk a Bill of 8.1.6. From thence took a Walk to Mrs Davy's and chatted with her for about an Hour. From thence went to Mrs Le Neves and paid her a Yrs Rent for College Land—16.0.0. Mrs Le Neve would make me drink a Glass of Wine. From thence went to Mr Francis's and had a little Chat with Mrs Francis her Husband not at home. From thence went to Mr Adams Nursery Man & as I was going there met a poor Person a Man by trade a Mason carrying along upon a Hand Barrow, dead by falling from a Ladder between 12 & 1 and dashed his Brains out. Pray God the poor Man may be happy in another Life and his Family comforted in this. I paid Mr Aram a Bill of 3.19.0. Mr Aram is a very hearty Man & very large, and looks as if he was dropsical. He lives full half a Mile from St Stephens Gates. From thence went to my Inn—pd 0.9.9. Gave to Servants there 0.2.0. Then took my Mare abt half past two and set of for Weston where I got before 4 and I thank God safe and well & there dined, supped & slept. Went to the post Office this morning and recd a Letter from my Sister Pounsett

& another from Caldecot Bursar of New-Coll.—pd for them
1.3. To a Serv't at the Post Office gave 0.1.0. A very pleasant
& agreeable Day.

31st. Snow 6 Inches deep in the Ground this morning &
where the Wind drove it above a foot deep at lest. Bill went out
a Shooting again this Morning and he killed 3 Water Hens and
1 Blackbird. Gave my Nephew a pair of coarse worsted Stockings. Gave Will Coleman a pair of Ditto for him, put on a Pair
of the same myself to day. For half a Pound of Scotch Snuff of
Cary to day pd 0.1.4. We sat up to night till after 1 o'clock in
Honour of its being the Last Day in the old Year. After the clock
struck 12 we drank a Happy New Year to ourselves & Friends
in a Glass of Gin Punch.

1778

JANUARY *5th*. We breakfasted, dined, supped & slept again at home. Bill went out a shooting again this morning and he killed only one small Thrush. Mr Du Quesne sent me a Note this morning to desire me to put of my Rotation till Friday next, Mr Townshend being at Honingham, & if to Morrow he could not come. I therefore sent Will in the Afternoon with a Note to Mr Howes, another to Mr Donne & another to Mr Botham to let them know that I shall expect them on Friday. My Servt Man Ben spent the Day at his Fathers by my Leave. Sukey went out in the Afternoon and returned in the Evening with her Sister who laid at my House. N.B. I did not know of her going out, nor of her Sister staying here till after 10 any Night — I think it is taking too great Liberties with me to bring home a stranger to sleep here. I do not like it at all — as every Servant may do the same.

FEBRUARY *12th*. We breakfasted, supped & slept again at home. Mr Du Quesne called on me this morning about 11 o'clock and about 12 I took a ride with him to Ling and there we dined & spent the Afternoon at Mr Baldwins with him & his Wife & youngest Daughter and Mr Priest of Reepham. Mrs Baldwin seems to be rather of a gloomy Complexion, with a Beard. Before Dinner we went into Mr Baldwins Boat & went up the River a little way to take up some Hooks that were laid for Jacks, but never a Fish. Having done that Mr du Quesne, Mr Priest & self went and saw the Paper Mills close to Mr Baldwins. Mr du Quesne & myself bought a Ream of writing Paper 20 Quires belonging to the same I had one half and he the other 10 Quires apiece — I pd for mine 0.5.0. The Master

Mr Amerton went with us and shewed us the whole Machinery which is indeed very curious We had for dinner at Mr Baldwins some fricasseed Rabit, some Mutton Stakes, a Piece of rost Beef, a fine rich plumb Pudding, Tarts & Syllabubs. At Quadrille this Evening at Mr Baldwins lost 0.0.9. Gave Mr Baldwins Servant Man 0.1.0. I returned Home about 8 o'clock, Mr du Quesne & Mr Priest slept there.

27th. My Nephew & self walked up to Church this morning at 11 o'clock, and there I read Prayers only, being a Day appointed for a general Fast, on Account of the War with the Americans. I had a large Congregation. It was bitter cold with cutting Winds to day. My Servant Ben went after Dinner to his Fathers unknown to me and did not return home till near 11 at Night When he came home he went to bed without my seeing him, and I believe not very sober—it is very bad of him.

28th. I gave Ben a Lecture this morning for being out last Night. Paid Spaule my Blacksmith this morn' a Bill of 1.5.0. He paid me for some Bark had a great while ago 0.2.0. I had a vast deal of Snow rolled into my great Pond. Bill made a very high Place in the Pond with the same. Cary did not go to Norwich to Day therefore had my News Papers brought by Mrs Andrews, for which I paid 0.0.6.

MARCH *1st.* Read Prayers & Preached this morning at Weston. Neighbour Gooch's Father was taken very ill to day and thought to be dying. I sent him Port Wine and in the Afternoon went & saw him & read Prayers by him. He desired to have the Sacrament administred to him which I told him I would do it to Morrow Morning. Poor Gooch has been an Invalid for many Years. His Pulse I thought was pretty regular, he had been convulsed on one of his hands, but talked pretty cheerful & well. My Clerks Wife Jane Smith got immensely drunk I hear to day.

2nd. Poor Neighbour Gooch died this morning about 7 o'clock. I was quite surprised to hear of it indeed, as he did not appear to me Yesterday near his latter End. I hope that as his Intention was to receive the Sacrament this morning, that his Will will be to the Supreme Being, taken as if the Deed had been done.

17th. Very busy all the morning in taking down my Books, and removing the Book Shelves. My great Parlour was finished papering before Dinner. My Nephew, self & North dined to day in the Kitchen upon their Commons table there. Had 1 Upholsterer, 2 Gardners, 1 Carpenter & 2 Masons to day at work for me. I gave my Servants, Will, Nann & Jack leave to go to the Puppett Show (that is in Town) to Night & I gave them 1.0. They did not return till after 11 at Night.

19th. North was busy in putting up my Curtains for my Parlours and putting up a Tent Bed. North breakfasted & dined with us and in the Afternoon went for Norwich. Gave my Servant Maid Sukey this morning 0.6 to go to the Show or stay at home & she chose the latter.

APRIL *7th*. My Nephew Bill took a Walk about 11 this morning to Mr Howes's & there we dined & spent the Afternoon with him & his Wife, Mr Bodham, Mr and Miss Donne—We spent the forenoon a fishing in Mr Howes's Pond—I lent him my large drag Net, and my Cart carried it over for him—And Harry Dunnell, Will & Ben were with the Same. We caught vast Quantities of Fish, called Cruzers, they are a very beautiful Fish of a yellow hue but none very large, almost all the same size—some few small Carp & Tench. I gave Mr Howes 20 brace of stock Tench, and he gave me in return 50 brace of Cruzers. My Folks all dined at Mr Howes's & then came away. We had for Dinner some stewed Carp & some Cruzers Fryed which were very good indeed, A Fillett of Veal rosted and a Ham, and some Mince Pies & Tarts. At Quadrille this Evening lost 0.4.6. We got home about ½ past 9 o'clock.

11th. Had a Letter this Evening from my Sister Pounsett and a very agreeable one as it informed me that she was come to a Resolution of making me a Visit the beginning of May with her Husband.

15th. We breakfasted, dined, supped & slept again at home. Brewed a vessell of strong Beer to day. My two large Piggs, by drinking some Beer grounds—taking out of 3 Barrells to day, got so amazingly drunk by it, That they were not able to stand and appeared like dead things almost. I never saw Piggs so drunk in my Life—I slit their Ears for them without feeling.

16th. My 2 Piggs are still unable to walk yet, but they are better than they were Yesterday. They tumble about the Yard & can by no means stand at all steady yet. In the Afternoon my 2 Piggs were tolerably sober.

Norwich

MAY *15th*. We all breakfasted, dined, supped & slept at the Kings Head. After breakfast we all walked to Mousehold Heath and saw some Soldiers, regulars, perform their Exercise there which was a very pretty Sight. And it being a general Field Day they fired & did it exceeding well—a great Number of People were there to see them. It was too Miles from the City. Cousin Lewis knew one of the Serjeants, a fine Man, & his name is Langley. I gave Cousin Lewis to give to his Friend Langley 0.2.6. In the Evening we took a walk into St Georges Colgate to see a very remarkable & surprising little Boy, who is just 3

Years old and in Coats, and will play on the Organ some Tunes.*
He was rather sleepy this Evening and therefore could not be
prevailed on to play any Tune, but he would touch the Keys
indiscriminately, & not play any thing but what completely was
concord—Sharp & Flats the same. He would suck at his Mothers
Breast & play with one hand upon the Organ and every Note
in proper Tune. He is quite a miraculous Child & must be in-
spired. He is also a sweet pretty Boy & very engaging. His Name
is Crotch & his Parents very poor Mechanics. This Evening
after Supper I took a Walk by myself and called at a Friends
House and paid o.5.o. Had a Letter this morning from my
Sister Pounsett to inform me that my Sister and Mr Pounsett
will set of for Weston Wednesday last & come by way of Bath.

16th. We breakfasted & spent the morning at the Kings Head.
To Frank Clements at Norwich who is a Militia Man and lately
worked with me as a Gardner gave o.1.o. To Williams the
Welchman who lives at Lenewade Bridge and whom I saw at
Norwich gave o.1.o.

Gave Bill 2 Prs of Cotton Stockings for which I pd o.9.9.

To a Pr of Bath Garters for myself pd o.1.o.

To a Pr of Knee Buckles—for myself—pd o.o.9.

At 2 o'clock I took my Mare & set of for Weston and Mr Lewis
and Bill set of on Foot for the same Place.

To 2 New Basketts, o.2.6.

To a Cucumber in the Market pd o.o.6.

To 3 Pd of Salmon in the Fish-Market pd o.3.o.

* The remarkable little boy was William Crotch, born in Norwich
1775, died at Taunton 1847. At four years old he was giving daily
organ recitals in London; at eleven he was pupil-assistant to the
organist of King's and Trinity Colleges, Cambridge; at fourteen
composer of an oratorio performed in that city; at fifteen organist at
Christ Church Cathedral, Oxford; at nineteen B.Mus; at twenty-two
Professor of Music at the University of Oxford; and at twenty-four
D.Mus. He was later Principal of the Royal Academy of Music. He
was a talented artist too, but in no field fulfilled his excessively early
promise.

At the Kings Head I paid 1.17.6.

To Servants at the Kings Head gave 0.5.6.

We got here by 4 o'clock and dined, supped & slept at Weston. We were all pretty well tired & fatigued—about 7 o'clock this Evening who should arrive at my House in a Post-Chaise & Pair, but Mr Pounsett and my Sister Pounsett. They had come that Day 100 Miles. They set out from Ansford on Wednesday Morn' last & they came by way of London. They were much tired especially my Sister, but she was pretty tolerable. They supped & slept at my House. I was exceeding glad to see them, but did not expect them so soon. They slept in my Yellow Chamber, and Cousin Lewis and Bill slept up in the Garrett over my Chamber.

21st. We all breakfasted, dined, supped & slept again at Weston. I walked up to the White-Hart with Mr Lewis and Bill, to see a famous Woman in Mens Cloaths, by name Hannah Snell who was 21 Years a Common Soldier in the Army, and not discovered by any as a Woman. Cousin Lewis has mounted Guard with her abroad. She went in the Army by the name of John Gray. She has a Pension from the Crown now of 18.5.0 per Annum & the liberty of wearing Mens Cloaths and also a Cockade in her Hat; which she still wears. She has laid in a Room with 70 Soldiers and not discovered by any of them. The forefinger of her right Hand was cut of by a Sword at the taking of Pondicherry. She is now about 60 Years of Age and talks very sensible and well, and travels the Country with a Basket at her back, selling Buttons, Garters, Laces &c. I took 4 Pk of her 4d Buttons, & gave her 0.2.6. At 10 o'clock we all went down to the River with our Nets a fishing, and went by Lyng before we put in our Nets as we never fished there before and so up to Lenewade Bridge. We caught nothing at all till we came up to Lenewade Bridge. Mr Pounsett & Jenny went in Carys Market Cart. We had some cold Meat &c. with us and eat it by the River, which went down very well. Harry Dunnell, Bens Father, Will and Ben were the Principal Fishermen we had with us. We did not return home till 7 o'clock in the Even' and then dined, and which did for Supper too. We had Mr Custance's Boat to cross the River &c. At Lenewade Bridge we caught a prodigious fine Pike which weighed 8 Pound and half and it had in its Belly another Pike of above a Pound—We caught also there the finest Trout I ever saw which weighed 3 Pound and ten Ounces Good Pike & Trout also we caught besides. Sent Mr Custance my finest Trout for the Use of his Boat. In Liquor at Lenewade Bridge pd 0.2.0. The Pike was 33 Inches in length, The Trout 21 Inches in length.

JUNE 9th. In the Evening took a ride to Norwich & my Servt Will with me, & supped & slept at the Kings Head. In the Evening about 9 o'clock there was a great Riot upon the Castle-Hill between the Officers of the western Battalion of the Norfolk Militia, and the common Soldiers & Mob owing to the Officers refusing to pay their men a Guinea apiece as they to go Morrow towards the Place of their encampment—several of them refusing to go without it & would not resume their Arms after Roll calling for which they were put into the Guard Room & the mob insisting upon having them out, which occasioned a great riot. The Mob threw Stones & some of the Soldiers running their Bayonets at the Mob and wounded them. Some of each Side were hurt but not mortally wounded or any killed. it lasted till Midnight & the Officers behaved very well in it. I was at the Place for some Time till near 11 o'clock. To odd things this Evening pd 0.3.6. I did not go to bed till after 12 and then only pulled of my Coat & Waistcoat & Shoes, as there was such a Bustle & Noise all Night & a Riot expected again.*

* There is no mention of this incident in any Norwich newspaper beyond a report that the Eastern battalion, not mentioned in JW's account, had been moved out of the city. It is possible that editors were exercising voluntary censorship or that the diarist had got hold of a garbled and exaggerated story.

JULY *4th*. I sent Will to Norwich this morning early for things he returned about Dinner Time and brought a Letter from Sister White to Jenny & far from a pleasant one, Mr Guppy being very ill & all Cole Friends but indifferent. At Ansford however all were well. The Letter made Mr Pounsett very unhappy, as it did Jenny. They both intend setting forth for Ansford Monday next.

AUGUST *9th*. Bill behaved very saucy again this morning at breakfast and it made me very unhappy. It will not do at all. I read Prayers & Preached this morning at Weston. Mr Custance Senr & Lady with another Lady at Church this Afternoon. I read Prayers & Preached this Afternoon at Honingham. Had no Conversation with Bill all Day since breakfast.

17th. My Nephew got up this morning at 4 o'clock and took a long Walk by himself to Mounsely Clifts 7 or 8 Miles beyond North Walsham close to the Sea and return'd back to Weston a little after 9 in the Evening. It must be near 50 Miles that he walked this Day. He brought home a fine Piece of Sea Weed and some Star Fish &c. He was pretty well tired. Begun shearing my Wheat this morning and gave the Shearers according to the Norfolk Custom as under a good breakfast at 11 o'clock plumb Cakes with Caraway Seeds in them & some Liquor, a good Dinner with plumb Puddings and at 4 Beer again. N.B. the above are called elevens & fours's. Only Ben and Will my Shearers of Wheat. Before the Dew is of in the Morn' they mow Oats. My Wheat this Year not above 4 Acres. They Shear with Sickles instead of Reap-Hooks—The form of them like a Reap Hook but the Edge of it like a Saw—they do exceeding well. Will brewed this morning a Barrell of Ale before he went shearing Wheat at 12 o'clock.

26th. We breakfasted, dined, supped & slept again at home. Mr Baldwin called on us this morning and talked with us concerning a Midshipmans Place for Bill and desired us to drink a

Dish of Tea with him in the Afternoon which we promised him. Soon after Mr Baldwin went away my Maid Sukey came to me to inform me that she would be obliged to leave me at Michaelmas, and that the reason is that she was with Child and half gone, & that the Father was one Harry Humphrey, and that she was not concerned with any other Man, though she said that my Nephew had —— come into her Room when she was in bed and tried every way to get her to comply, but she said that she had got other ——. My other Maid Nann said she had heard the same. When this happened, Mr & Mrs Pounsett were here and it was talked of, and my name mentioned at —— as they thought I would give —— the business ——. I talked with Bill this morning very —— about his Behaviour with Sukey being in my House. In the Afternoon I took a Walk with Bill to Mr Baldwins at Ling & there drank a Dish of Tea with him, Miss Virtue Baldwin, Mr Hammerton & Dr Neale (Pringle of Reepham). Had a good deal of Chat with Mr Hammerton abt Bill. Bill is to go to London when Mr Hammerton goes which will be soon, to show himself to a Captain of a Ship & that Mr Hammerton will use all his Interest for him. I have been very uneasy & most unhappy all day about one thing or another. When Bill goes away I shall have no one to converse with—quite without a Friend.

27th. We breakfasted, dined, supped & slept again at home. Quite low and ill to day, no Appetite. Such dry Weather which we have had for so long, long Time together, was scarce ever known. All People (tho' in the midst of a Harvest) now wish for Rain. The Grass Ground about us instead of green looks quite rusty, being burnt up so long by the Sun, some are obliged to feed their Stock with Hay now.

28th. After Dinner I took a Walk to Ling to Mr Hammertons and there drank Tea with him, his Wife, Mr Wilson Junr and Wife of Reepham. They went soon after Tea. We sat & talked a good deal after about Bills proseeding with regard to the Navy—Mr Hammerton said that he would do what he could, and would advance him mony to rig himself out, if he succeeded, upon my promise of paying him again soon: it was so friendly in Mr Hammerton that I could not but comply in so critical an Affair. Bill is therefore to go in the London Coach on Sunday Evening & wait at the Swan & two Necks in Lads Lane London till Mr Hammerton calls on Tuesday morning early. Mr Hammerton rides. Very low and ill with all especially going to bed. Sukey went before Justice Buxton to day with her to Swear to the Father of the Child she is big with. I had a Note from Mr Buxton which Sukey brought to desire the Parish Officer the Overseer to come with her & then he would take her Information.

30th. I read Prayers & Preached this morning at Honingham. I read Prayers & Preached this Afternoon at Weston. Gave my Nephew to go to London this morning 5.5.0. About 6 in the Evening I took a ride with Bill to Norwich and there took a Place in the Coach for London We drank Coffee at the Kings Head this Evening. We supped at the Angel Inn, as the London Machine sets out from thence at 12 at Night. I stayed with Bill till 12 saw him safe into the Machine and then I went to the Kings Head where I slept but very little. I questioned Bill a good deal in the Evening at the Angel about his being great with my Maid Sukey, and he confessed something of it to me, that he had been great with her 3 or 4 Times. The first Time was Feb. 28 early in the morning in her Room. Sukey was in bed all Day last Monday and Mrs Hardy went to Norwich to get her a Gown which would fit her to give to Sukey there. A pretty picture. Sukey had admitted that Humphrey was great with her and that the first Time was in March, and if so Bill certainly had Sukey first ——. At the Angel I paid & gave 0.7.10. I was very restless & uneasy all night.

SEPTEMBER *3rd.* I breakfasted, dined, supped & slept again at home—I told Sukey this morning my Opinion of her respecting the late Affair that has happened to her.

171

7th. About 10 at Night my Nephew returned from London & he brought me a Letter from Mr Hammerton who informs me that Captain Allen of the Chatham a 50 Gun Ship will take my Nephew if he is properly & handsomely equipped which will cost about 60 Pounds. He must therefore go into the West and try his Friends. For my Part I cannot do it for him, I am sure. To a Poor Woman on Sparham Heath gave 0.0.6. Bill hired a Horse from Norwich to come to Weston. The Ship will sail from Sheerness in 10 or 14 Days.

9th. I breakfasted and slept again at home. I took a ride to Ringland about 2 o'clock and there dined & spent the Afternoon, supped & spent the Evening at Mr Custance's with him, his Wife and an old Maiden Lady by name Miss Rush. I spent a most agreeable Day there & was very merry. Mrs Custance & self played at Back-Gammon together. Mr & Mrs Custance are very agreeable People indeed, and both behaved exceedingly polite & civil to me. I there saw an Instrument which Mrs Custance played on that I never saw or heard of before. It is called Sticcardo pastorale. It is very soft Music indeed. It is several long Pieces of Glass lain in order in a Case resting on each End of every Piece of Glass—and is played on the Middle Parts of the Glass by 2 little Sticks with Nobbs at the Ends of them stricking the Glass. It is a very small Instrument & looks when covered like a working Box for Ladies. I also saw the prettiest working Box with all Sorts of things in it for the Ladies to carry about with them when they go abroad about as big again as a Tea Chest, that I ever I saw in my Life—it could not cost less than five Guineas. We had for Dinner some common Fish, a Leg of Mutton rosted & a baked Pudding the first Course, and a rost Duck, a Meat Pye, Eggs, & Tarts the second. For Supper we had a breace of Partridges rosted, some cold Tongue, Potatoes in Shells & Tarts. I returned to Weston about $\frac{1}{2}$ past Ten o'clock. To Servants at Ringland, 2, gave 0.2.0. Mr Custance also gave me to carry home a brace of Partridges which my Servant

Will brought home. They keep 6 Men Servants & 4 Maids.

20th. Die Solis. Another dreadful Misfortune happened to Mr Hammerton at Lyng this morning about 4 o'clock the Paper Mill on fire and burnt with such Rapidity that it burnt down the whole Mill and very near burnt down the dwelling House but that escaped. I sent Will down in the Evening after news And he brought me word that the Damage sustained was between 3 and 4000 Pound. The Mill was insured for 2000 Pound however—There was 1000 Pound worth of Paper burnt. No Body can tell how it came on fire at present. I am exceeding sorry indeed for the Event. I read Prayers & Preached this morning at Weston. Mr Custance Senr & Lady at Weston Church. I read Prayers & Preached this Afternoon at Honingham for Du Quesne who is not yet arrived. I buried poor Clement Allen this Evening at Weston aged 62 Years—He had been long ill. Gave poor John Grant this Evening 0.0.6.

30th. Rheumatic Pain very bad all night and still continues so—I took some Flower of Brimstone in some strong Beer about 11 this morning, before that took some Gin and after Gin some Brandy. My Pain continued all Day about me.

OCTOBER *1st*. I breakfasted, dined, supped & slept again at home. I got up this morning a little after 5 o'clock having griping Pains within me. I believe my Complaint proceeds from eating Walnutts on Monday last.

To Nann for getting Eggs gave 0.0.2.

To 2 Hndrd of Walnuts of Thos Rams Wife pd 0.1.0.

Something better this Evening.

5th. Mr Palmer called on me this morning and I had a long Chat with him about Sukey, also about the Highways & lastly about Methodists. To Mr Cary for things from Norwich &c. pd 0.8.4. About 11 o'clock at night just as I was going to bed my Nephew Wm Woodforde came to my House on foot. He came this Evening in the Norwich Coach from London. He was much disappointed at London on hearing that the Chatham was sailed and therefore prevented going on board her. He slept at my House but all the Folks were gone to bed & he obliged to sleep without any Sheets. The Ship was sailed about a Week & they kept him in the Country so long about raising 50 Pounds that occasioned his disappointment — 3 Weeks there.

14th. I breakfasted, dined, supped & slept again at home. Bill breakfasted, dined, supped & slept here again. Paid my Servant Sukey Boxly this morning a Yrs Wages due Oct. 10, the Sum of 4.0.0. Gave to her besides her Wages, as going away 0.4.0. I sent Cary's Cart with one of my Horses by Ben to little Melton about 4 Miles beyond Easton after my new Maid this Afternoon & she returned about 6 o'clock. Her Name is Eliz. Caxton about 40 Yrs of Age but how she will do I know not as yet, but her Wages are 5.15.6 Per Annum but out of that she is to find herself in Tea and Sugar. She is not the most engaging I must confess by her first Appearance that she makes. My other Maid came here also this Evening. Her Name is Anne Lillistone of Lenewade Bridge — about 18 Years of Age but very plain however. I like her better than the other at the first Sight. I am to give her 2.0.0 Per Annum and to make her an Allowance to keep herself in Tea & Sugar. Sukey this Evening left us but in Tears most sad.

NOVEMBER *4th.* Mrs Custance of Ringland taking an Airing by herself this morning in her Coach, called at my House and got out of her Carriage & went in and saw my Rooms & stayed about ½ an Hour & was well pleased with my House & Gardens and was very merry. This being my Rotation Day, the following Company dined & spent the Afternoon at my House, Mr Du Quesne, Mr and Mrs Howes, Mr & Miss Donne & Mr Bodham. The Dinner was put of one Hour on Account of Miss Donne being caught in the Rain and obliged to put in to Mr Howes's till Mr Howes's Chaise went after her. We had for Dinner a Dish of Fish, a Couple of Rabbits smothered with Onions & a Piece of rost Beef. I sent Mrs Custance of Ringland this morning a fine Pike & a brace of fine Trout by my Servt Will. At Cards this Evening lost 0.3.0. My Company left me about 9 this Evening. We spent a very merry, cheerful Day. I privately named a Child of the Parish of Attlebridge of one Crane's there by name Richard at my House. I was so so this morning, very hot & feverish.

6th. This morning I had some suspicion that Bill was concerned with my Maid Nanny and also that she appeared to me to be with Child. I was uneasy, But the Truth will appear e'er long if it be so. Sukey my late Maid was at my House all Day to day to show Nann to make butter & help in ironing. My Man Will Coleman went out after breakfast and did not return, till near 8 at night and then in Liquor, I said but little to him to night. He was at Js Bidewells to visit Bride &c.

17th. I breakfasted, dined, supped & slept at home. Bill told me this morning that he had the Foul Disease. —— at Norwich last. He is the Occasion of nothing but troublesomeness to me I will therefore get rid of him as soon as I can. Mr Bodham called on me this morning and stayed and dined with me. He went away about 4. To Tom Cushion this morning for killing and cutting up a Pigg for me gave 0.1.0. To a Boy for bringing some Porter for me gave 0.0.6.

21st. I breakfasted, dined, supped & slept again at home. Bill breakfasted, dined, supped & slept here again. Was very ill going to bed again last Night, I don't know the reason of it unless it be eating hash Mutton done in a Copper Sauce Pan on Wednesday last, or being made uneasy by my suspicions of Bill. Recd a Letter from Bathurst & one in it for Mr Wilson Junr. Recd of a Neighbour for 2 small Piggs 0.10.0. Bill was very saucy this Evening & said that he never did any harm in his Life, & after all that has passed ——. I told my Maid Betty this morning that the other Maid Nanny looked so big about the Waist that I was afraid she was with Child, but Betty told me she thought not, but would soon inform me if it is so.

23rd. I told Bill this morning that I should have nothing more to say to him or do for him—And I gave him his Mony that he desired me to keep for him. He was very low on the Occasion and cried much. I lent him as he desired me my little Mare to take a ride to Dr Thornes to take his Advice. I had very little Conversation with Bill again to day. To a poor Norwich Weaver in distress gave o . o . 6. Sold Mrs Dunnell 10 young Geese to day for o . 15 . o for which she owes me as I would not be paid. Privately named a base born Child of my late Maids Sukey Boxly by Name Thomas. Harry Dunnell dined with our Folks in the Kitchen—his Wife being from home.

DECEMBER *7th*. About 3 this Afternoon I went to Norwich with my Nephew who goes in the London Machine this Night on his Sea Expedition, which if he does not succeed in on board the Chatham, is not to return here but go into the West & get into a Bristol Privateer. Mrs Hammerton sent up a Bottle of Catchup to be carried to her Son, but we could not carry it. I put up my Horses at the Kings Head this Evening and we supped together at the Angel Inn in the Coffee Room there, from whence the Coach went of, which was exactly at 12 at Night, I saw Bill safe into the Coach & then returned to my Inn to sleep. Bill set of in tolerable good Spirits. I gave him to spend between Young Hammerton and self as we could not carry his Catchup o . 10 . 6. Gave to Bill besides for himself 1 . 1 . o. My Servant Will went with us to Norwich and carried behind him two very fine Turkey Cocks which went in the Coach, and they were Presents from me to Mr Toulmin & Mr Charles Hammerton. Mr Toulmin is Agent to the Chatham, and Mr Hammerton is Brother to Mr Hammerton of Lyng and who behaved particularly civil to Bill when last in London where he slept &c. For our Supper &c. at the Angel, I paid o . 4 . 6.

19th. I breakfasted, dined, supped & slept again at home. I shot a Rook and a Jack Daw at one Shot this morning and I believe 50 Yards from me. I had a long Letter from my Sister Pounsett this Even'. Admiral Keppell and Sir Hugh Palliser two of our Chief Admirals have had a grand Quarrel and are both to have a Court Martial set upon them soon.

20th. I breakfasted, dined, supped & slept again at home. I read Prayers, Preached & publickly presented Sukeys Bastard this Afternoon at Weston Church. I was very strange this Evening after Supper—fainty.

23rd. Mr Du Quesne, Mr and Mrs Howes, Mr Bodham, Mrs Davy's 2 Children Betsy & Nunn, Mr and Miss Donne and their Cousin a little Boy by name Charles Donne of London dined & spent the Afternoon with me being my Rotation—and all but Mr Du Quesne supped & spent the whole Night with me being very dark & some falling Rain. Mr Bodham, myself & Mr Donne sat up the whole Night and played at Cards till 6 in the Morning. Mr and Mrs Howes went to bed in my Bed Room about 2 in the Morning. Miss Donne, Betsy & Nunn Davy slept together in the Yellow Room. Mr Donnes Nephew slept in Wills Room with Mr Donnes Man Charles. All my Folks sat up. About 6 in the Morning we serenaded the Folks that were a bed with our best on the Hautboy. Mr Du Quesne went home about 10 o'clock. I did all I could to prevail on him to stay, but cd not. I gave them for Dinner 3 Fowls boiled, part of a Ham the major Part of which Ham was entirely eat out by the Flies getting into it, a Tongue boiled, a Leg of Mutton rosted & an excellent Currant Pudding I gave them for Supper a Couple of Rabbitts smothered in Onions, some hash Mutton, & some rosted Potatoes. We were exceeding merry indeed all the Night. I believe at cards that I lost about 0.2.6.

1779

JANUARY *1st*. I breakfasted, dined, supped & slept again at home. This morning very early about 1 o'clock a most dreadful Storm of Wind with Hail & Snow happened here and the Wind did not quite abait till the Evening. A little before 2 o'clock I got up, my bedsted rocking under me, and never in my Life that I know of, did I remember the Wind so high or of so long continuance. I expected every Moment that some Part or other of my House must have been blown down, but blessed be God the whole stood, only a few Tiles displaced. My Servants also perceived their Bedsteds to shake. Thanks be to God that none of my People or self were hurt. My Chancel recd great Damage as

did my Barn. The Leads from my Chancel were almost all blown up with some Parts of the Roof, The North West Window blown in & smashed all to Pieces, the East Window also damaged but not greatly the North W. Leads on the Top of the Church also, some of them blown up and ruffled, besides 2 Windows injured — The Clay on the North End of my Barn blown in and the West Side of the Roof, the Thatch, most all blown away, leaving many holes in it. The Damage sustained by me will amount I suppose to 50 Pounds, if not more. However I thank God no Lives were lost that I hear of & I hope not. Mr Shaddelows Barn, Michael Andrews's, with many others, all blown down. Numbers of Trees torn up by the Roots in many Places. In the Evening the Wind abated and was quite calm when I went to bed about 11 o'clock. Since what happened this morning, I prolonged the Letter that I designed to send to my Sister Pounsett to relate what had happened here by the Storm — And this Evening sent it by Mr Cary. A smart Frost this Evening. As the Year begins rather unfortunately to me, hope the other Parts of it will be as propitious to me. Morn', dreadful high Winds with Hail & Snow terrible Morn' indeed, Wind — NW. Afternoon, Wind still very high but not so rough as in the Morning with Snow — NW. Mem: A Dreadful Morning.

3rd. There was no Service to day at Weston Church, as the Church & Chancel is so much injured. I sent Will to Mr Hamertons at Lyng this Afternoon to enquire after Bill & by a Letter recd there, Bill has altered his Mind. N.B. Bill is gone into Somersett & does not intend going into the Chatham.

22nd. Sent a Letter this Evening to my Sister Pounsett. Mr Hammerton & I had some talk about my Nephew, he said that he believed him to be a very unsteady Man. That he was very desirous & eager after the Chatham before he returned & that when he did, he altered his Mind, forsook her & fled into the West. Mr H. told me also that the Captain had kept a Place open entirely for him, and that he wd have been very soon promoted. The Captain was much displeased as well as Mr Hammerton, who had both been very kind to him & did all they could for him. He will never I believe turn out very well any where, and his Parents whatever they may promise, will do nothing. His Father had wrote a Letter to him to let him know that he would get a Lieutenancy of Marine for him that his Uncle Thos Woodforde had promised to speak to my Ld Guildford for him about the same. I wish my Head might never ake before that Time.

30th. I breakfasted, dined, supped & slept again at home. I took a Walk to Church to see how my Chancel goes on this morning a little before Dinner. I advanced to Spaule to Day or lent him 2.2.0. Had a pure quiet Day of it & went to bed in good Time. Had a Letter this Evening from Bill Woodforde at Cary, Had another from Lewis in Nottinghamshire.

FEBRUARY *16th*. I breakfasted, dined, supped & slept again at home. Paid Mr Wetherell my Plumber this morning a Bill for mending the Lead &c. of my Chancel 28.17.6 as follows, re-casting of old Lead 42 cwt 3 qtrs 14 lb at 4/0 per Hndrd 8.11.6. For new Lead added 14 cwt 2 qtrs 6 lb at £1 0s 0d Per Hndrd 14.12.6.

Workmens Wages at 2/0 per Day 4.16.0.

For 23 Pound of Solder at 9d 0.17.3.

Coals ½ a Bushel, 0.1.3.

To Mr Cary for things from Norwich &c. 0.2.9.

I allowed for Waste &c. in re-melting the old Lead 4 Pound in the Hundred — Wetherell charged me 7 Pound but I would not allow it, as one Mr Fox of Norwich a capital Plumber & who did St Andrews Church lately, and of whom I asked a few Questions when last at Norwich relating to the same informed me that 4 Pounds was what he allowed for Waste &c. There was Plowing to day for a Hat at the Hart. The Man that plowed the best & straightest Furrow was to have the Prize, Valued at 18 Shillings.

MARCH *5th*. Sent a Letter this Evening to Dr Oglander Warden of New-College to petition for him for Assistance in repairing my Chancel with the Society. Sent another Letter to my Sister Pounsett. The fine Weather still continues & not likely to change as yet. Never known I believe so mild a Time.

30th. I spent most of the morning at Church to day. Whilst I was at Church this morning I recd a Note from Mr Custance of Ringland to desire me to dine with him to Morrow, and I sent a Verbal Answer back that I would. Never known perhaps such a long Continuance of dry and fine Weather, we have had no settled Rain for any time for almost two Years last Past.

31st. I breakfasted and slept again at home. I took a ride about 2 o'clock to Mr Custance's at Ringland, and there dined, supped & spent the Even' with him and his Wife and Lady Bacon. We had for Dinner for the 1 Course a Dish of Fish, a Leg of Mutton rosted & some Ham & Chicken Tarts; The 2nd Course an Orange Apple Pudding, some Asparagus, Veal Collops, Syllabubs and Jelly; For Supper some fricassied Rabbit, hashed Fowl, cold Ham and Jelly. Soon after Dinner was obliged to return to Weston to bury old Mrs Pegg at 5 o'clock, which I did aged 73 Yrs. I had a Hatband and a pair of white Kidd Gloves. I returned to Mr Custances by Tea Time and after Tea, we got to Cards to Whist at which I lost 0.1.6. Mrs Custance & self attacked Lady Bacon & Mr Custance. I spent a very agreeable Day there to day. We had some Parmesan Cheese after Dinner & Supper, of which I eat very hearty & like it exceedingly. I gave to one only of Mr Custance's Servants 0.1.0. I got home about 11 at night.

APRIL *4th.* I breakfasted, dined, supped & slept again at home. Quite a Summers Day again very fair & very hot. I read Prayers & administred the H. Sacrament this morning at Weston Church. Mr and Mrs Custance of Ringland & Lady Bacon at Church this morning and were at the Sacrament. When they recd the Sacrament they went into my new Seat and there sat till I had finished at the Altar. My Clerk Js Smith dined here being Easter Day. My Chancel is now much approved by all People. There is nothing more to be done to it, but painting it.

11th. I breakfasted, dined, supped & slept again at home. Between 11 and 12 o'clock this morning I went to Church & publickly christned Mr Custance's Child of Ringland, it had been privately named before, and the name of it was Hambleton Thomas. The Gossips* were Sir Edmund Bacon Proxy for Sir Thomas Beauchamp, Mr Press Custance & Lady Bacon. Mr and Mrs Custance also present at the Ceremony. There were

* Godparents or sponsors.

two Coaches at Church. Mr Custance immediately after the Ceremony came to me and desired me to accept a small Present, it was wrapped up in a Piece of white Paper very neat, and in opening of it, I found it contained nothing less than the Sum of 4.4.0. It was exceeding handsome of him I am sure. He gave the Clerk also 0.10.6. He asked me to dinner but could not as I have duty to do at 3 o'clock—but am to dine there Thursday. I read Prayers, & churched a Woman this Aft. at Weston.

28th. Mr Priest of Reepham made me a short morning Visit. I went and shewed him my Chancel, which he likes much. In the Afternoon took a ride to Lenewade Bridge to meet Mr and Mrs Baldwin &c. there, but no body came. I then took a ride on to Sparham and made a Visit to the Revd Mr Attle who behaved very complaisant and civil, tho' a Visit so long due to him from me. I drank a Dish of Coffee & one Dish of Tea there and returned home—He has a noble House and his Fields about him look exceeding neat & well. He built his House himself & it cost him 1000 Pound.

MAY *2nd.* I read Prayers, Preached and churched a Woman this morning at Weston—for churching recd 0.0.6. Mr and Mrs Custance not at Church this morning, they being not as yet returned from Sir Edmund Bacons. My Mare was very ill this Evening owing to eating so much of the Garden Grass to day. I had her rode out for an Hour and afterwards gave her some Gin and small Beer—And she soon was better.

4th. We breakfasted at Weston, and at 12 o'clock after eating some cold Meat we mounted our Horses to put into Execution a Scheme upon the Northern Coast of Norfolk, which had been some time talked of. My Servant Will carried some Shirts &c. for us. We got to Aylsham at ½ past 2 refreshed ourselves & Horses for about an Hour and then proceeded on to Cromer where we supped & slept at the Kings Arms, (an ordinary House) kept by one Alsop, a civil and intelligent Man—I paid & gave at Aylsham 1.6. At the Inn at Cromer we were not much more than 20 Yards from the German Ocean—which highly delighted us, Cromer is famous for catching of Crabbs & Lobsters—and could see Men catching them at Sea by a Glass. We had some hot Crabbs & Lobsters for Supper that were just brought from Sea and exceeding fine Eating they were. An agreeable young Man in the travelling way supped & spent the Evening with us.

6th. We breakfasted at Wells and after breakfast we got a small Boat and went to Sea in it, we carried some cold Meat & some Beer with us in the Boat. My Man Will went with us also. We had two Men to manage the Sails &c. for us. When we got to Sea we fastened our Boat to a Sea Mark & regaled ourselves —but I could eat but very little being very near sick as was Will, it being the first Time of my being upon the Sea—and the Waves so large that frightened me, as I thought it dangerous. We saw several Cormorants flying about the Sea. Mr Hall having been often at Sea did not mind it. We returned from Sea about 12 o'clock and I was glad to set my Foot on Land again. We hired the Boat for half a Crown only. At Wells I paid and gave for my Share 0.13.0. About 1 o'clock we left Wells and went for Houghton Hall, the Seat of Lord Orfords—in our way thither we called at great Walsingham and saw some fine old Ruins of an Abbey and also some good Gardens of a Mr Warners there, and in which are some curious Ruins of an old Monastery. We gave to see the Gardens &c. 0.1.0. From thence we went on to Houghton, we neither eat nor drank at Walsingham. About 3 o'clock this Afternoon we reached Houghton, where we dined, supped & slept at the Kings Head, close to Ld Orfords Park & about half a Mile from the Hall. Musgrave the Landlord. After we had regaled ourselves with a cold Collation about half an Hour we walked down to the Hall. Saw the whole House and the fine Pictures there The House & Furniture the grandest I ever saw and the Pictures are supposed to be the best Collection in Europe. We stayed there till after 8 o'clock. We each gave for seeing the House 0.2.6.

31st. I breakfasted at home, and at 6 this morning set Forth on my Mare for the West Country, and took my Man Will Coleman with me, he riding my great Horse.

JULY *9th.* I breakfasted, supped & slept again at Ansford. I went a fishing by myself this morning down to Week Bridge and angled from there to Cole, and there I dined & spent the Afternoon at Mr Guppeys with him his Sister and Mr Pounsett. We had for Dinner some bacon & beans, a Shoulder of Mutton & Currant Pye. I caught 3 Trout, the largest being 14 Inches & half long Which I caught with 2 Grasshoppers & a small hook. Whilst I was a fishing this morning, Bill Woodforde came to me on Horseback to take his Leave of me as he was then going of for Portsmouth to go aboard the fortune Sloop of War, of 12 Gunns, and in the same Capacity as he was to have went in the Chatham of 50 Gunns. The latter would have been much better and he repents much of not going, but is now too late. I wished him well, but gave him nothing at all. To Mr Guppeys Maid Sybbyl for a poor Woman in distress at Shepton Montague gave 0.1.0. To Mr Guppeys Man Ellis Coleman gave 0.1.0. Sister Clarke supped & spent this Evening with us again we got back.

21st. I breakfasted and spent the morning at Ansford. About 12 o'clock I got into the Weymouth Machine from Bath and set of by myself for Weymouth. There was only one Man in it who was dressed as a Gentleman and behaved as such. His name was Watson. We dined at Sherborn at the George a shabby Inn and had a most miserable Dinner, about 2 Pound of boiled beef and a old Tame Rabbitt. I paid for my Dinner &c. at Sherborne 0.1.6. We then went on to Dorchester & there we had a Bottle of the famous Dorchester Beer & very good it was. For the Bottle of Beer I paid myself 0.0.6. We got to Weymouth about 8 o'clock and there I supped & slept at the Kings Head kept by one Loder a very good Inn and very civill People.

22nd. I breakfasted, supped & slept at the Kings Head. After breakfast I took a Walk on the Beach, and in my Walk met with

Mr Sam Burge & another Gentleman on Horseback going to Portland. I wanted a Horse much to go with them. I then walked back to my Inn and hired a Tim Whiskey*, got into it immediately and drove down to the Ferry opposite Portland Isle, and there had my Whiskey put into a Boat and carried over to Portland where I stayed till 5 in the Evening, but saw nothing of Sam Burge. I drove and walked about the Island most part of the Time. I dined at the Hotel there kept by one Child—I paid and gave at the Hotel o.1.8. After Dinner I drove down to the Castle to see it—It was formerly a good Place, but now much impaired. There are 8 Cannon there, but they looked bad. I gave to the Man that showed it o.1.o. Then went to the Ferry & returned—paid at the Ferry for having my Whiskey back & forward o.1.6. For some Beer &c. at the Ferry pd o.o.6. Portland Isle is about 9 Miles in Circumference and about 8 in Diameter. It seems to be one entire Rock of Stone and prodigious fine Stone. To some Stone Masons at Work in the Island gave o.o.6. I picked up a great Number of Sea Weeds there, but lost a Pair of Gloves in so doing. I returned to Weymouth about 8 in the Evening. I saw nothing of Mr Watson since the Morning as he has taken Lodgings in the Town. Weymouth is a very pretty agreeable Place and the Sea close to it. I was quite tired this Evening.

AUGUST *19th*. I breakfasted, supped & slept again at Ansford. I took a ride & Will with me this morning to Milton. We fished at Milton till 7 in the Evening but caught only a brace of small Trout and a brace of small Eels. We dined on some bread & Cheese under a Tree by the River. For some Beer & for the Horses standing at an Inn pd o.o.8. Going thro' the Turnpike at Creech Hill pd o.o.2. When I returned home I found the People at Ansford in a great Consternation, a report being spread by John Burge of Castle-Cary, that the French & Spanish Fleets were engaging at Portsmouth, that 3 of our Line were

* A kind of light, two-wheeled, one-horse carriage.

sunk & that the Spanish & French Fleets consisted of more than 60 Ships of the Line, and ours only of 40 Ships, That the stones in Portsmouth Street were taken up &c. As it came from such Authority I don't credit it at all. John Burge said he had it from a Man who saw the Engagement, and saw also our 3 Ships sunk and that the Sea looked on fire where the Engagement was. It frightened my Sisters White & Pounsett very much.

20th. In the Evening I walked to South Cary to old Mrs Pennys & there Mr Pounsett & self smoked a Pipe with Dr Penny. Nothing true about the French as mentioned Yesterday. Richard Clarke a small matter better to day. Brother John sent for me this Evening from Mr Whites to desire me to come to him, which I did, found him quite in Liquor & a Pain in his Side which made him low. I did not stay long with him.

28th. Isaac Francis pd me this morning half a Years Rent for an House & Orchard, due Lady Day last 3.3.0. I gave him out of it, as he is poor 0.2.6. I took a Walk this morning with Mr Pounsett and my Tenant Farmer Corpe into some Fields belonging to me to see some Trees that the Farmer want to have cut down. We marked down 22 Trees mostly Pollards. I called at my Brother John & Sister Clarkes—Jack is very angry about Nancy's coming into Norfolk.* Mr Pounsett & self dined, spent the Aft. supped & spent the Evening at Js Clarkes, with him, his Brother Richard & Wife, Mr and Mrs White, and Sam Clarke. Sister Pounsett dined & spent the Aft. with us but did not sup with us, her Child's Nose bleeding. Brother Heighes spent the Afternoon with us. Sister Clarke supped & spent the Evening with us. We had for Dinner some Beef Stakes, 3 Fowls

* This is the first we hear of Nancy's coming to live in Norfolk since 1776 when she was reported as too ill with scrofula to accompany the Diarist. Brother John was angry at her departure; he had probably taken her in out of charity and was annoyed when she withdrew her household services in favour of a more attractive offer. As Winstanley points out, poor relations often held a very ambiguous position, half kin, half servant, in the homes of their better-off relatives.

rather stale boiled & a Pigs Face, a Chine of Mutton stale also
rosted and an Apple Pudding. Js Clarke talked rather strange
after Supper about my Poor Houses near his House now let to
the Parish.

SEPTEMBER *8th*. I breakfasted at Ansford and after breakfast
set forth for Norfolk and my Servant Will Coleman with me.
We dined at Chicklade, pd and gave there 0.4.4. From Chicklade we went on to Salisbury, the Bourne-Road, got there about
8 and supped and slept at the 3 Lions, kept by one Newman
very civil People & a very good Inn. To a poor Woman this
Evening gave 0.1.0. I lost one of my best Silk Handkerchiefs
out of my Pocket this Evening, very likely to be picked out. To
Turnpikes to Day paid 0.0.6. I went and saw 150 French
Prisoners this Even' that are on their March to Winchester.
Things left at Mr Pounsetts at Ansford—6 Shirts, 4 Stocks,
1 Pr of Shoes, 1 Pr of Bath Metal Buckles, 2 Prs of my coarse
worsted Stockings, 1 Pr of coarse dark ribbed Do.

OCTOBER *1st*. I breakfasted, dined, supped & slept again at
home. Very busy this morning and afternoon in my Garden
trimming up my Shrubbs and transplanting some.
    2nd. I breakfasted, dined, supped & slept again at home. As
I was out in my Garden this morning in my Ermine, old Hatt
& Wigg, Beard long & a dirty Shirt on who should walk by at
the End of my Garden, but my Squire and a Mr Beauchamp
with him, Mrs Custances Brother. They walked into my Garden
and went over it, they like it exceedingly. They would not walk
into my House. Got a bad cold in my Head. All our Folks but
Betty and Will have got bad Colds, particularly Nanny and my
Boy Jack has the hooping Cough very bad.
    To Stephen Andrews Man for bringing some Coal gave 1.0.
    To Ditto, for loading the same at Norwich pd 0.4.
    12th. About 8 this Evening, my Sister Clarke, Nancy Wood-
forde and my Nephew Saml Clarke arrived at Norwich in the

London Machine from the West greatly fatigued by being up all last Night—they drank some Tea immediately and soon decamped to bed. They slept at the Kings Head.

21st. I breakfasted and slept again at home. Sister Clarke, Nancy & Sam breakfasted & slept here again. Mr and Mrs Kerr sent over to us this morning to desire that we would dine with them we sent word back that we could not having no Carriage to go there he then sent word that he would send his one Horse Chair after the Ladies—which we could not refuse complying with—therefore at about 1 o'clock Sister Clarke & Nancy went in the Chair and myself walked to Mr Kerrs and there dined, spent the Aft. supped & spent the Evening with Mr and Mrs Kerr and Mr Bodham of Mattishall. We had for Dinner a Leg of Pork boiled a Turkey rosted and a Couple of Ducks. We had for Supper a Couple of Fowls boiled, a fine Pheasant rosted & some cold things. Dinner & Supper served up in Chelsea Dishes & Plates, Melons, apples & Pears, Walnutts & small Nutts for a Desert. We played at Quadrille after Tea, at which I won 0.0.6. My Servants Will & Ben went out a Coursing this Morn by my Order and did not return till after we were gone. They coursed a Brace of Hares but killed never a one. We returned as we went & got home about 11 o'clock. Mr Kerr would make me accept of a Hare also.

To Mr Kerrs Servants gave 0.1.0.
Sister Clarke gave the Servants 0.3.0.
We spent a very agreeable Day indeed at Mr Kerrs.

NOVEMBER *13th.* I breakfasted, dined, supped & slept again at home. Sister Clarke breakfasted &c. &c. as did Nancy & Sam. Du Quesne made us a morning Visit. Mr Hall breakfasted with us & set of soon afterwards for Winborough. Had a Letter this Evening from Mr Kingston Bursar of New College with a Draught in it on Hoare the Banker for the Sum of $73.10.11\frac{1}{2}$ being a Present from that worthy Society for the loss I sustained the first of January, owing to the high Wind concerning my

Chancel—very handsome indeed was it of them. At Quadrille this Evening at pence lost 0.2.0.

18th. At 3 o'clock myself & Nephew took a ride to the Hon. Charles Townshends at Honingham where we dined and spent the Afternoon, by Invitation. Just as we got to Mr Townshends Mr Du Quesne overtook us and went with us there & dined &c. &c. A Mr Hill and Son from Wells a rich Merchant & Owner of the Standard Inn at Wells where Mr Hall and self slept when at Wells—kept by one Smith—He with another Wells Merchant by name Springle a very droll sensible Man & who has travelled much abroad, also dined & spent the afternoon with us. Mrs Townshend was dressed in a scarlet riding Dress her Head dressed very high & no Cap at all on. We had for Dinner a Loin of Mutton rosted, rost Beef, a boiled Chicken, Soup, Pudding &c. First Course—A Turkey rosted, a rosted Hare, Mushrooms, Tarts Maccaroni, and a Custard Pudding &c. Neither Turkey or Hare above half done—I never made a much worse Dinner I think. We dined at 4 drank Tea at 7 or after. At 9 we returned home—left the other Company there. I gave nothing to the Servants at Mr Townshends. Mr Townshend is going next Week for London.

DECEMBER *4th.* Mrs Dunnell paid me for Tithe &c. 20.1.0. I paid her out of it for divers things 5.8.7½. Had a Letter this Evening from my Sister Pounsett. This Evening by Mr Cary came Bills Present to me, viz a large Moorish Sword and a curious Moors Purse, made of Morocco Leather with some Coins in it. He also sent me two Curious Shells and a Quill that came from Falklands Island. It is some gratitude in him I must confess—but he expects something in return as he complains in his Letter to me of being very low in Pocket. At Quadrille this Evening won 0.2.0.

1780

JANUARY *12th*. I breakfasted, dined, supped & slept again at home. Sister Clarke, Nancy & Sam breakfasted &c. here again. Mrs Davy & Son from Hockering walked to my House this morning about 11 o'clock and they dined and spent the Afternoon with us till near 5 o'clock and then they walked back again to Hockering and Mr Sam and myself walked with them back and drank Tea at Mr Howes's with him & his Wife and Mrs Davy. Sad work there on Account of the Chaise not being retired but laid down. Borrowed a Pair of Skates of Mr Press Custance this morning and skated round my great Pond. but not having put on any for near 10 Years had many Tumbles but did not hurt myself at all. My Man Will Coleman had a most terrible fall on my great Pond as he was sliding, he fell directly on his Face, cut his Lip, Eyelid, & Nose bleeding. It affected his Head very much all Day after it. We had for Dinner a rosting Pigg & a Neck of Mutton boiled & Capers, and some mince Pies. To little Nunn Davy, coming away gave 0.1.0. Excessive cold and Wind very high & a bitter Frost.

22nd. Sister Clarke had a Letter this Evening from my Brother Heighes, rather an unpleasant one, as it mentions that he is in great distress & likely to go into Limbo,* as Jeanes has brought an Action for Damages on losing his late Trial of 20.10.0. My Brothers Letter to my Sister made me uneasy as it did all with me. My Brother wants me to be bound for him, which in my present Circumstances cannot as I am distressed in many ways at present, and if I do more than I have done already for him, I must want myself. I have taken his Daughter Nancy to live

* Prison, it being evident from the context that more than a state of mind is meant.

190

with me & have been kind to his Son Will during his living with me for near 3 Years.

FEBRUARY *4th*. This being a Day for a general Fast to be observed thro' the Kingdom to beg of Almighty God his Assistance in our present troubles, being at open rupture with America, France & Spain, and a Blessing on our Fleets & armies;* I therefore went to Weston Church about 11 o'clock and read the proper Prayers on the Occasion—but there was no Sermon preached. My Squire & Lady at Church and there was a very respectable Congregation that attended at it. Most of my Family went—Sister Clarke & Sam & 3 Servants. We did not dine till 4 o'clock this Afternoon. Sent a long Letter to my Sister Pounsett this Evening. Sister Clarke, Nancy, Sam & myself all took it in our heads to take a good dose of Rhubarb going to bed.

11th. Sister Clarke & Nancy had a few words at breakfast. My Sister cant bear to hear any one praised more than herself in any thing, but that she does the best of all.

20th. I read Prayers, Preached & churched a Woman this morning at Weston Church—very thin congregation owing to the Snow—it snowed all Day almost. Sister Clarke could not go to Church—Sam & self did. For churching a Woman recd 0.0.6. Neither my Squire or Lady at Church. Very high Wind with much Snow & very cold. Sister Clarke & self had high words at breakfast to Day. In the Afternoon we made it up again.

29th. After Breakfast I took a Walk to Church, and there married one James Knights and Patience Spinks by Banns— recd for marrying them 0.5.0. Sam went with me & was a

* Britain was now dangerously isolated, war breaking out with France in 1778, with Spain in 1779, with Holland in 1780. The northern nations formed the League of Armed Neutrality to put a stop to British searches of neutral shipping believed to be trading with the American rebels.

Witness to the Marriage. I privately baptized a Child this morning at my House of one Bushells by name, Sarah. My Sister & self taught the Young Folks Piquet this Evening, but did not play for any thing. Morn' mild but windy — WNW. Afternoon, ditto — WNW. In the Evening about 9 o'clock very remarkable Northern Lights very bright & very red — the Center seemed to be very near over my House, & not unlike a fiery Furnace.

MARCH *8th.* We were very quere after Dinner to day, having but a plain Dinner, viz. some hash Mutton, a plain Sewet Pudding and a couple of Rabbitts rosted. Sam made me rather angry at Dinner when I asked Sister Clarke if she would have the Outside of the Pudding or the first Cut of it, upon which Sam said, I hope you will not Madam, for you know that I always give the outside to the Dogs. Busy in seeing the Seat in the Garden getting on.

APRIL *4th.* A Guinea and one of the Rings of Sam's Purse were found by my little Maid Betty this morning among the Ashes in the Kitchen Grate — Sam in taking out his Handkerchief out of his Coat Pocket (where he always kept his Purse) must take the Purse out with it, and standing by the Fire, might fall into the Fire — both Guinea & Ring quite black. The Servants were very glad the above was found as they were very uneasy on being suspected.

17th. I breakfasted, dined, supped & slept again at home. Nancy breakfasted, dined, supped &c. here again. Sister Clarke and her Son Sam breakfasted, dined, and spent part of the Afternoon with us. About 5 o'clock my Sister and Sam went of in Lenewade Chaise for Norwich, to take Coach for London this Night. I sent my Man Will with them to Norwich. Will returned about 10 at Night and informed us that they got safe to Norwich, but could not go from thence till to Morrow Night, the Coach being full. I lent my Sister towards bearing her Expences 5.5.0. I gave Sam my little Book of Mapps, Atlas Minimus.

Recd of Mr Herring this Aft. for Tithe last Year 5.5.0. We were all very low at parting with each other, poor Nancy very low indeed.

I gave to Nancy this Evening 0.5.0.

Paid Mr Cary for things from Norwich &c. 0.10.1½.

Paid to Ditto—for Snuff at ½ a Pound—0.1.6.

My Head Maid slept with Nancy and is so to do.

18th. Mr Du Quesne sent his Chaise here to day about 1 o'clock to carry us to the Rotation, and about half past one we both got into it & sent to his House and there we dined, spent the Afternoon and part of the Evening with him, Mr and Mrs Howes, Mr and Mrs Dawson, little Miss Roupe, a Captain Lodington and Mr Bodham. We were very merry till just at last, when Mr Howes behaved strangely, that is Mrs Howes had invited all the Company to dinner on Thursday next and all settled—but just as Mr Howes was going away, he desired to be excused from having Company at his House to Dinner on the above Day, but should be glad to see them at Tea. It made all the Company stare again. We had for Dinner, some Skaite & Oyster Sauce, a Breast of Veal boiled, a Leg of Mutton rosted, a Pidgeon Pye, a Pudding and the Charter.* At Quadrille this Evening won 0.1.6. Nancy & myself got home about 10 in Mr Du Quesnes Chaise, but was rather afraid as the Driver was merry, but he drove us very well and very safe. Will was very much in Liquor. The Servants went to a public House at Honingham and there they all got merry.

I gave the Driver, Stephen, 0.2.6.

I gave also to a Lad behind the Chaise 0.1.0.

Captain Lodington is a cheerful little Man and not above 20 Years of Age if so much. He was aboard the Monmouth when last engaged by the French. He has seen a good deal of Service abroad in the E Indies has been in the Service about 4 Years— is first Lieutenant in the 6 Company of Marines.

* A dish of cream, eggs and apricots.

193

MAY *3rd*. I breakfasted, dined, supped & slept again at home. About ½ past nine o'clock this morning my Squire called on me, and I took my Mare and went with him to the Hart just by the Church Where most of the Parish were assembled to go the Bounds of the Parish, and at 10 we all set of for the same about 30 in Number went towards Ringland first, then to the breaks near Mr Townshends Clumps, from thence to Attertons on France Green, where the People had some Liquor, and which I paid, being usual for the Rector 0.4.6 and Press Custance was with us also. From France Green we went away to Mr Dades, from thence towards Risings from thence down to Mr Gallands, then to the old Hall of my Squire's, thence to the old Bridge at Lenewade then close to the River till we came near Morton, then by Mr Le Grisse's Clumps, then by Bakers and so back till we came to the Place where we first set of. Mr Custance Senr then called the six following old Men (that is) Richd Bates, Thos Cary, Thos Dicker, Richd Buck, Thos Cushion and Thos Carr, and gave each of them half a Guinea. To George Warton who carried a Hook and marked the Trees, my Squire gave also 5 Shillings. To Robin Hubbard also who carried a Spade he gave 5 Shillings, and sent all the rest of the People to the Hart to eat and drink as much as they would at his Expence. The Squire behaved most generously on the Occasion. He asked me to go home and dine with him, but I begged to be excused being tired, as I walked most of the Day. Our Bounds are supposed to be about 12 Miles round. We were going of them full 5 Hours. We went of at 10 in the morning and got back a little after 3 in the Afternoon. Nancy was got to Dinner when I returned. Ben, Will, & Jack all went the Bounds. Ben's Father Wm Legate in crossing the River on horseback was thrown of and was over head & Ears in the River. My Squires Man John was likely to have had a very bad Accident in leading the Squires Horse over a boggy Place both Horses were stuck fast up to their Bellies, and by plunging threw him of in the Mire and was very near being hurt by the Horses plunging to get out, but

194

by great & providential means escaped free from any Mischief. The Horses also were not injured at all—the Man had his new Suit of Livery on & new hat which were made very dirty. Where there was no Tree to mark, Holes were made & Stones cast in.

9th. To a Man (whose Name was Pedralio an Italian & who is the Manager of the Fire Works at Bunns Gardens at Norwich) and who makes Thermometers and Barometers and carries them about the Country, called at my House this morning with some of them and I bought one of each for wch I paid him 1.16.0.

18th. Busy in planning out the Foundation for a small Temple in my Garden opposite the Front of my House, and the other Side of my great Pond.

JUNE *3rd.* Had a very long Letter from my Sister Clarke and a very civil one—I wished she had sent it before especially as I had sent a Letter to my Sister Pounsett wherein I upbraided Mrs Clarke for not writing.

9th. About 2 o'clock who should make his appearance at my House but Nancy's Brother Willm who is a Midshipman aboard the Ariadne of 20 Guns. He came from Yarmouth on Horseback this morning. He wore his Uniform, and he dined, supped & slept at my House. Nancy was very happy to see him indeed.

16th. I breakfasted, dined, supped & slept again at home. Nancy breakfasted, dined, &c. &c. here again. Bill breakfasted, dined, &c. &c. here again.

To H. Dunnell's Wife for Veal 18 Pd at 4, Pd o.6.o.

To a travelling Man for 4 brass Cocks pd o.6.o.

To Ditto for a Pound of Stone blue pd o.1.6.

Bill painted a Coat of Arms to Day on the Front of the Temple in my Garden—Venetian Blinds of plain Deal to keep out the Afternoon Sun made to day. About 11 o'clock at Night and just as we were going to bed, an express Messenger from Norwich on horseback came to my House with a Letter to let us know that Bills Ship the Ariadne was in the Yarmouth Roads. I gave the Messenger some Victuals, Drink & o.2.6. Probart of the Kings Head sent the Letter to me and in it an Account of our taking Charles Town in Carolina and had killed & taken 5000 Men.* Bill sets of to Morrow for Yarmouth.

19th. This being my Rotation Day, Mr and Mrs Howes, Mr & Mrs Howes from Hampshire, Son of Mr Howes Senr and who is a Clergyman and has the Living of Fordingbridge, their 2 Children a Daughter & Son, little Nunn Davy, and Mr Du Quesne and Mr Hall, all dined & spent the Aft. with us and stayed till after 8 in the Evening. I gave them for Dinner a Dish

* Charleston was taken by General Clinton on 12 May and, with lesser victories at Camden and Guildford early in 1781, represented perhaps the most important success of the British forces in America. But the strategy of which it formed a part, and the war effort itself, collapsed with the surrender of Cornwallis at Yorktown on 19 October 1781.

of Pike & Eels, a Neck of Mutton boiled & Capers & Carrotts, a Breast of Veal Rosted, a plain Pudding, a very fine green Goose & some green Peas, and some Gooseberry Tarts. After Dinner for a Desert gave them 3 large Dishes of Strawberries, the scarlet and Wood Strawberry and some Cream & Sugar. After Dinner the Gentlemen walked about and smoked a Pipe in the Temple. And while we were at Tea the 2 Boys got into the Temple where was left some Wine & some strong Beer, and little Nun got himself very drunk & vomited a great Deal — the other was very well. Nunn is a sad unruly Lad indeed. At Cards neither won or lost. Nancy lost 0.0.9. My Squire called on me this Morn' and talked to me a good deal about his Brothers Mistress sitting in my Seat Yesterday and whether she had Leave and also that she strutted by them in a very impudent Manner coming out of Church — & stared at Mrs Custance.

23rd. After breakfast this morning I sent my Maid Betty to Mr Press Custance's Mistress (Miss Sherman) to desire her not to make use of my Seat in the Chancel any more, as some Reflections had been thrown on me for giving her Leave. I likewise sent Will to Mr Kerrs on the same Account as I was willing to make in General. Miss Sherman sent word back by Betty that she was much obliged to me for the Use she had already made of it, and did not take it at all amiss with me, she knew from whence it came — and that she would get a new Seat made. Mr Kerr sent me word that he was not the least angry with me, and he expected it. About 2 took a ride to Ringland and dined and spent the Afternoon with my Squire, his Wife, Lady Bacon, and a Mr Prideaux, Grandson of the famous & learned Dr Prideaux who wrote the Connections. We had for Dinner some Maccarel, green Peas-soup, a Fillet of Veal rosted — fricassied Rabbit, a Couple of Ducks rosted, Patties &c. Oranges, Strawberries &c. after. I returned to Weston about 9 o'clock. We did not drink Tea till after 7 o'clock in the Evening. Mrs Custance asked for Nancy, but Mr Custance said nothing at all about her — which I think not right.

197

AUGUST *5th*. Mr Bodham and his Father dined & spent the Afternoon with us—Mr Bodhams Father is a very sensible Man and an Antiquarian, and highly pleased with my Medals, which I shewed him & likewise my Microscope. I had for Dinner 3 Fowls boiled, part of a Ham, Beans, a Breast of Veal rosted & some Apple Tarts. Mr Bodham Senr highly pleased with my Garden &c. They left us about 7 in the Evening.

11th. My great Horse much worse this morning, was walked up to Reeves again and Ben with him, the Dr gave Ben a Draught for him to take—but the poor Horse was so ill on his return, that he could not give it to him, and about 10 o'clock this morning died. I endeavoured to bleed him a little before and sent Will to Gould of Attlebridge to come and see him, but he was dead long before he came. Gould said that he died of a Fever in the Bowels—and that he should have been bled, had a Clyster & some cooling Physic also. Am very sorry for him as he was so goodnatured a Beast. Dont intend to employ Reeves any more as a Farrier. I could not have thought that he would have died so soon. The Death of my poor goodnatured Horse (by name Jack) made me very uneasy all the day long. Ben and Will skinned him, we kept one half of him and we gave the other half to Mr Press Custance. Whatever the Skin fetches, is to be divided between Will, Ben & Jack.

SEPTEMBER *20th.* Mr and Mrs Donne, Mr Bodham & Miss Donne dined and spent the Afternoon with us. I gave them for Dinner 3 boiled Chicken & a Tongue, 2 Couple of Rabbitts smothered with Onions, a Neck of Mutton rosted, a Melon, Grapes, Figgs and Filberts. The Melon was of my own rising in my Garden. At Quadrille this Afternoon won 0.3.0. The Company left us about 7 o'clock. Sent a Note to Mr Howes, to desire him, his Wife and the Company with them to dine with me on Friday next as I could not have them here to day. Sir Edward Astley & Mr Coke returned Members for the County again this Day at Norwich.

21st. Recd a Note from Mr Howes's that they cannot dine with us on Friday next. They are affronted I apprehend, at not being asked here Yesterday to meet Mr & Mrs Donne &c. Mr Du Quesnes Man Robert brought me a large Baskett of Plumbs and Pears this morning. My Squires Lady brought to bed of another Son this Morn'.

22nd. My Squire called on me this morning to desire me to come over in the Afternoon and privately name his new born Son. I married one John Vout and Rose Branton this morning by Licence at Weston Church—a compelled Marriage. N.B. am owed by Mr Mann the Church Warden for Marrying them, as I could not change a Guinea 0.10.6. Took a ride in the Afternoon to Mr Custances of Ringland and privately named his Child by name, Edward. I stayed & drank a Dish of Coffee with the Squire and one Mr Martineau of Norwich a Doctor & Man Midwife. Recd a printed Letter from the Bishop to send him an Account of the Roman Catholicks in my Parish—but I do not know of one in it.

NOVEMBER *12th.* I read Prayers & Preached this Morning at Weston. Neither my Squire nor Lady at Church this morning. As I was returning from Church this morning Mr Press Custance overtook me and acquainted me that Mr Custance had lost his last Child this morning—it had been ill some Time. I walked with Mr Press Custance back to Church and fixed on a Place in the Church where the Child is to be buried. We heard this morning by Mr Press Custance that many People were robbed Yesterday between Norwich & Mattishall by two Highwaymen. They are both known and were very near being taken. One of them is a Nephew of one Parferoy (a Gardner at Ringland) and his Name is Huson—My Man Ben knows him very well. These two Fellows slept at Bens Fathers on Friday Night & were in the Parish of Weston most of the Day, Yesterday. Nancy was much alarmed on hearing the above. It was lucky that I did not go to Norwich last Week.

13th. I breakfasted, supped & slept again at home. About 11 o'clock this morning took a ride to Norwich and my Servant Willm Coleman went with me. I carried with me upwards of 150 Pound in Bills and Cash, and got to Norwich very safe with the same. Went to Mr Kerrison's Bank and there recd a Bank Note of 150 Pd which I immediately inclosed in a Letter and sent it of by the Post to Dr Bathurst of Christ Church, and which I hope will get safe to him there. Kerrison the Banker asked me to dine with him, but cd not. I called at Mr Francis Junr in Surry Street but did not stay. I dined at an Ordinary at the Kings Head for which I paid only for my Dinner 0.1.0. Extra-ordinaries after Dinner pd 0.2.0. We had a very good Dinner, that is, a Piece of boiled Beef some Peas Soup, a neck of Pork rosted & a rost Turkey. At 4 o'clock this Afternoon set of for Weston, and got home safe & well thank God about 6 in the Evening. For my Horses & Servant at Norwich pd 0.2.0. Called at Mr Priests also, but did not make any stay.

15th. Went to Church this morning at 11 o'clock and there buried Mr Custances Son Edward—aged 7 Weeks & 3 Days. The Corpse was brought in a Coach & four attended by two Servant Maids in very deep mourning & long black Hoods. Mr Press Custance was the chief Mourner, none of their Relations attended besides—Neither Mr nor Mrs Custance there. The Coffin was lead with a Copper Breast Plate on it & on that was engraved the Age & Name of the Child. The breast-Plate was plain, & made thus. The Child was buried in the Chancel in the North Aile. The Coach came up close to the Church Door. The Driver & other Servants had hatbands & Gloves, I had also a fine black Silk Hatband and tied with white Love-Riband and a Pair of white Gloves. After the Funeral Mr Press Custance gave me a Bit of White Paper sealed up with Mr Custances Arms on it and in which there were 5.5.0. Only a clean white Napkin covered the Lead Coffin. Very rough with much Snow this Morning & very cold.

DECEMBER *15th*. Nancy & myself being rather out of Spirits & ill last Night, took a Dose of Rhubarb each, last Night & this morning we were both brave. Mr Hall dined & spent the Afternoon with us. He also dined here the Day I went to Norwich with Nancy. Nancy was not well pleased with him, and about leaving a Dog here behind him which however he did not, as Nancy was against it. I gave him for Dinner some Fish, a Shoulder of Mutton rosted—he left us about 4 o'clock. Mrs Davie called here this Aft. in Mr Howes's chaise with her Daughter Betsy, who is just returned from School and is to spend a few Days with Nancy, therefore Mrs Davie left her with us, and returned in the Chaise to Mr Kerrs where Mr and Mrs Howes of Hockering spent the Afternoon & herself. Paid for some fish this morning 0.1.2. Mrs Davie's Daughter Betsy supped & slept here. Betsy slept with my Niece Nancy Woodforde.

30th. I breakfasted, dined, supped & slept again at home. Nancy breakfasted, dined &c. &c. here again. Betsy Davie breakfasted, dined &c. &c. here again. At Cribbage with Nancy this Evening neither won or lost. Nancy had her new Cotton Gown brought here this Evening from Norwich by Mr Cary and I think very handsome, trimmed with green Ribband—a Cotton of my Choice.

31st. I read Prayers & Preached this Afternoon at Weston. Nancy & Betsy Davie walked to Church to day being fine Weather and not dirty under foot. Neither my Squire or Lady at Church, they being from home. This Being the last Day of the Year we sat up till after 12 o'clock, then drank a Happy new Year to all our Friends and went to bed. We were very merry indeed after Supper till 12. Nancy & Betsy Davie locked me into the great Parlour and both fell on me and pulled my Wigg almost to Pieces—I paid them for it however.

1781

JANUARY *11th*. I breakfasted, supped & slept again at home. Nancy breakfasted, dined &c. here again. Betsy Davie breakfasted, dined &c. here again. About 1 o'clock took a Walk and Will with me to Hockering and there dined spent the Afternoon & Part of the Evening till near 9 o'clock at Mr Howes's with him, his Wife, Mrs Davie, Colin & George Roupe, Mr Du Quesne and Mr Hall. Rotation Day. I walked back again to Weston in the Evening.

At Quadrille this Evening won 0.3.0.

Gave little George Roupe this Evening 0.1.0.

This Day heard the News that Jersey was taken by the French and retaken by the Islanders afterwards—between 4 and 6000 French landed there, but were all destroyed or taken Prisoners by us. It is too good news to be true I am afraid the whole of it. Country News very bad, hearing of nothing but Highwaymen and breaking houses open at Norwich. Trade at Norwich never worse. Poor no Employment.

FEBRUARY *3rd*. Mrs Davie, Betsy & Nancy breakfasted, &c. here again. Had but indifferent Night of Sleep, Mrs Davie and Nancy made me up an Apple Pye Bed last Night. Mr Du Quesne promised to dine with us to day, but he sent me a Note in the morning that he could not, having a very bad cold & gone home to nurse the same. He slept but very poorly last Night at Priests of Reepham, He was to have taken my House in his return home & dined.

12th. I breakfasted, dined, supped & slept again at home— Mrs Davie, Nancy & Betsy breakfasted, dined &c. here again.

To Mr Cary for things from Norwich &c. pd 0.8.7.

To Betty for things pd 0.2.7.

We did not get to bed till after 12 this night the Wind being still very high. We were as merry as we could be. I took of Mrs Davie's Garter to night & kept it, I gave her my Pair of Garters & I am to have her other to Morr'. Mr Charles Roupe called here this morning & stayed dined & spent the Afternoon with us.

APRIL *14th*. I got up very ill this morning about 8 o'clock, having had very little Sleep all the Night, owing to the Pain in my Ear which was much worse in the night and broke and a good deal of blood only came away. The Pain continued still very bad all the morning, tho' not quite so bad as before—It made me very uneasy abt it. A throbbing Pain in my Ear continued till I went to bed. I put a rosted Onion in my Ear going to bed to night.

MAY *16th*. Between 7 and 8 o'clock this morning went down to the River a fishing with my Nets—Ben, Will, Jack, Harry Dunnell, and Willm Legate (Bens Brother) were my Fishermen. We begun at Lenewade Mill and fished down to Morton, And we had the best Day of fishing we ever had—We caught at one Draught only ten full Pails of Fish, Pike, Trout and flat fish— The largest Fish we caught was a Pike, which was a Yard long & weighed upwards of thirteen Pound after he was brought home. We caught about 20 brace of Pike, but threw back All the small ones, also we caught abt 15 brace of Trout, the largest not more than a Pound & half—all the smallest we threw back. 3 brace also of Perch, one tolerable Tench and I dare say near or not quite five hundred Brace of Roach & Dace. Prodigious Sport indeed we had to Day tho' cold & wet. As we were fishing by Coplins, he came out and ordered my Men of from his Land, & behaved quite contrary to the Opinion I had of him. After talking with him some little Time, he then said I might fish, but then I would not, at which he seemed rather uneasy. We eat some cold Meat which we carried about one o'clock and returned home to Dinner at 4. For Beer at Barnard Dunnells of Morton pd 0.1.0. Gave Beeston, Cantrell, Palmer of Morton & Barnard Dunnell some Pike, & most of the flat Fish to the Poor at Lenewade & Morton and of my own Parish. Harry Dunnell & Will Legate dined &c. with our Folks. Paid them also for their labour to Day. I was rather fatigued this Evening by fishing.

17th. Mr Priest of Norwich came to my house about 1 o'clock and he stayed & dined with us & spent the Afternoon and in the Evening returned to Norwich. I was very glad to see him, as he & Wife behaved very civil to Nancy. Mr and Mrs Howes, Mrs Davie, and Mr Du Quesne dined and spent the Afternoon with us also. I gave my Company for Dinner my great Pike which was rosted & a Pudding in his Belly, some boiled Trout, Perch & Tench, Eel and Gudgeon fryed, a Neck of Mutton boiled and a Plain Pudding for Mrs Howes. All my Company were quite astonished at the Sight of the great Pike on the Table. Was obliged to lay him on two of the largest Dishes, and was laid on part of the Kitchen Window Shutters covered with a Cloth. I never saw a nobler Fish at any Table, it was very nice cooked, and tho' so large, was declared by all the Company to be prodigious fine eating, being so moist. At Quadrille after Tea, neither won or lost. At about 9 they all left us. I put a large Pike into the Boot of Mr Howes's Chaise before they went back.

31st. The Land begins to burn and scorch the Corn. The new Lays of Grass greatly hurt by the dry Weather.

JUNE *3rd.* I read Prayers and administred the Holy Sacrament this morning at Weston Church being Whitsunday. It rained very heavy in the Night, a Thunderstorm with little Thunder or Lightning, but much Rain. All Nature seemed this morning greatly refreshed by the Rain, as it was so much wanted. Thanks be to the Lord for so blessed & gracious a Rain. My Squire & Lady at Church & at the Sacrament. Nancy also was at Church & at the H. Sacrament by my Desire, and was the first Time of her ever receiving it. My Clerk Js Smith dined with our Folks to day.

30th. Nancy by being with Mrs Davy has learnt some of her extravagant Notions and talked very high all Day. I talked with her against such foolish Notions, which made her almost angry with me, but when we went to bed we were very good Friends and she was convinced.

JULY *13th*. Mackay, Gardner at Norwich called here this Even', and he walked over my Garden with me and then went away. He told me how to preserve my Fruit Trees &c. from being injured for the future by the Ants which was, to wash them well with Soap Sudds after a general washing—especially in the Winter.

17th. Mr Galland & Mr Howlett called on me this Evening, to advise them what to do with one Norton who threatens to burn half the Parish, he has burnt this Afternoon all the Break upon the Common that Mr Howlett had cut to put under his Stacks. He is a sad Rogue I believe. I advised them to have a Warrant to secure him. He was therefore this Evening secured by the Constables.

30th. To Mr Cary for things from Norwich pd 0.10.0.

To my Maid Eliz. Caxton for things pd 0.7.0.

I rode to Mr Dades this morning and privately named a Child of his by name William. Nancy and myself get up every morning before 7 o'clock under the penalty of forfeiting sixpence each Day, Sundays only excepted.

AUGUST *1st*. Very hot and sultry this Afternoon. The Earth very dry. The Ponds, River &c. never known so low scarce—my large Bason was amazingly shrunk. Cary's Pitt which was scarce ever known dry is so much so now that People can come at no Water.

8th. Mrs Davie breakfasted with us, and soon after was sent after by a Man & Horse or rather her own ordering. She set of from Weston about 10 o'clock this morning. About 2 o'clock a strange young Man called at my House (shabby dressed with one Shoulder higher than the other) to ask me Leave to set up a School in this Parish, said he came from Yarmouth & was recommended he said by a Mr Gosling of Yarmouth to this Parish, brought no Character with him, said also he was a Scotchman. I told him that I thought it strange that he should apply without any kind of Certificate, Character &c. A Suspicious Man I take him and might belong to a base Crew, but hope not.

17th. Gave Nancy 5 Yards of Muslin this morn' to make a Gown. Mr Priest of Reepham dined & spent the Afternoon with us. We had hash Mutton & a Pudding & some baked Kidneys for Dinner. My Squires little Boys with their Nurses made me a Visit in the Evening & supped here on bread & Milk. The Nurses had Tea. Mr Custance sent me a Note in the morning to take a Family Dinner with them on Tuesday. He will send after Nancy. He also sent us the London Papers to read. My Harvest finished this Evening.

21st. I breakfasted, supped & slept again at home. Nancy breakfasted, supped &c. here again. Nancy and myself dined & spent the Afternoon at Mr Jon Custance's at the New Hall with him & Mrs Custance—they sent their Coach after us & carried us back home in it. We had for Dinner a Ham & 2 Fowls boiled, some young Beans, Veal Collops & hash Mutton for the first Course, a rost Duck, baked Puddings, Apple Tart &c. second. They behaved very civil & very friendly to us—Mrs Custance gave Nancy a Pearl Necklace & Pearl Chain to hang from the Necklace, a Pr of Pearl ear-rings & another Pr of Ear-rings. Mrs

Custance is exceedingly kind to my Niece indeed. We returned home about 8 o'clock in the Evening—After spending a very agreeable Day there.

22nd. I took a ride to Du Quesnes this morning stayed with him about an Hour, found him rather low still, and fretting himself about being so tyed by the Leg, in dancing backward & forward to Townshends with his great Company. The Archbishop of Canterbury & Lady are there &c. The Arch bishop & Lady go from Townshend Saturday next. Du Quesne is then determined to visit his Neighbours, tho' Townshend be ever so much affronted at it. Townshend & Lady are to remain at Honingham. From Du Quesnes went on to Mr Howes's but did not stay long, saw him, his Wife, Mrs Davy, Alexander Payne & Wife. I acquainted them that my Rotation Day was Tuesday next. I returned home to Dinner by 3 o'clock.

SEPTEMBER *24th.* At 8 this morning took a ride to Aylsham, about 10 Miles from Weston, with my Man Will Coleman—we got there about 10 put up my Horses at the 3 black Boys and then sent for a Barber, dressed myself in my Gown & Cassock & Scarf, being the Arch-Deacon's Visitation to Day, and went about 11 o'clock to Church, where Mr Farwell read Prayers, and after Prayers I ascended the Pulpit & gave them a Sermon. From Church we returned to the 3 Boys to Dinner. The Church of Aylsham is large and handsome and an Organ at the West End of it & which was played. We had for Dinner part of a Rump of Beef boiled, a Loin of Veal rosted, 3 Fowls rosted and an Ham with some plain Puddings. It was a shabby Dinner & overdone—Plates, Knives and Forks very shabby indeed. To Mr Morphew pd for Procurations & Pascals 0.9.7¼. I drank some spruce Beer of Mr Taswells at Dinner and liked it very well—It was in Bottles.

OCTOBER *4th.* Mr Burroughs of Morton called on me this morning to let me know that Captain Le Grisse had heard that I had carried from his Gravel Pit a large Quantity of Gravel lately, and more than was permitted me, and that I would make some acknowledgement for the same. But I believe it is Burrough's Scheme to get some Mony for himself. I intend waiting on Mr Le Grisse concerning it, when I go to Norwich. Mrs Custance (tho' only brought to bed about a fortnight) called here this morning in her Coach, and took Nancy with her to spend the Day with her, at the New-Hall. She is very finely and brave indeed, am heartily glad for it. At 2 o'clock took a Walk to Mr Custances and there dined, spent the Afternoon & Evening till 8 o'clock. Mrs Custance dined by herself above Stairs. Mr Press Custance, a Mr Walton who is a Portrait Painter from London & is drawing Mr Custances Picture, and Mr Rawlins the Architect dined with us there. We had for Dinner a jugged Hare, a Leg of Mutton rosted, stewed Beef, and hashed Duck for the first Course, besides a fine piece of boiled Beef on the Side Table. For the second Course we had a brace of Pheasants rosted, some frilled Oysters, Pudding and Tarts & Custards. After Tea Mrs Custance, Nancy, Mr Custance, Mr Press Custance, Mr Walton & self played a Pool of Commerce of one Shilling Apiece, drawing Two Pences, at which I lost 6d, Nancy lost 1/6 having bought in a second Time, Mrs Custance won the Pool—in all neat 0.4.6. Myself & Nancy returned home in Mr Custances Coach. We spent a very agreeable Day at the new Hall. The Weather also very fair, Evening cold rather.

5th. Mr Charles Townshend of Honingham called on me this morning about 11 o'clock and walked round My Gardens with me and afterwards came in and sat with us about half an Hour & then returned. He caught me on the hop, being in my Garden and dressed in my Cotton morning Gown, old Wigg and Hat. Soon after Mr Townshend left us, Dr Thorne of Mattishall made us a Visit, walked about the Garden, eat some Grapes, and after spending half an Hour with us in my Study, he went away. About 2 o'clock Mr Du Quesne and Mr Priest of Reepham in Mr Priests Chaise came to us and dined and spent the Afternoon with us and part of the Evening till 8 o'clock and then they went on to Du Quesnes. I gave them for Dinner a Bit of boiled Beef, a boiled Fowl with Pork and Greens and a Hare rosted. After Tea we played one Pool of Quadrille. Neither won or lost. This has been quite a Levee Day with us.

NOVEMBER *21st.* Just as I was returned from Church Mrs Howes and Mrs Davy came to us and stayed with us about an Hour. Mrs Howes better but still very weak. One Mr Aldridge who goes about with a Cart with Linens, Cottons, Lace &c. called at our House this morning to know if we wanted any thing in his way. He called here whilst Mrs Howes and Mrs Davy were here. I bought of him some Cotton Yards 6 for a morning Gown for myself at 2/6 per Yard pd 0.15.0.

Some Chintz for a Gown for Nancy 5 Yrd & $\frac{1}{2}$, I pd 1.14.0.

For an East-India Silk Handkerchief for self pd 0.5.6.

Nancy also bought of him a Linen Handkerchief &c. of him, Mrs Howes bought a Silk Handkerchief of him also.

DECEMBER *28th.* I breakfasted, dined, supped & slept again at home. Had my Study Chimney-Piece altered to Day by Mr Hardy and to prevent its smoking, but am still afraid of it. This is, I believe the 4th Time of altering it. I was hurried all Day about it and also vexed. Mr Hardy and his Man Tom Carr dined in Kitchen.

1782

JANUARY *7th*. I breakfasted, dined, supped, and slept again at home. Nancy breakfasted, dined &c. here again.

To Mr Cary for things from Norwich &c. pd 0.11.6.

To my Servant Man Ben Legatt paid this morning a Years Wages due to him the 6 Instant 10.0.0.

To my Senior Maid Elizabeth Claxton paid also this morning a Years Wages due the 6 Instant 5.15.6.

To My Servant Man Will Coleman paid this morning a Years Wages due to him the 6 Instant 4.4.0.

To Ditto also for 20 Coomb* of Grains pd 1.0.0.

To Ditto also for dressing my Wiggs a year 0.10.0.

To my under Servant Maid Lizzy Greaves paid this morning also a Years Wages due 6th Instant 2.0.6.

To my Boy, Jack Warton, gave this morning 0.10.6.

Mr Cary dined with our Folks to-day. My Taste very indifferent and so it was yesterday at Dinner. Everything tastes very disagreeable to me—I don't know what occasions it unless it is my having taken some Brimstone and Treakle—or having made use of some strong sage Tea every Day about 11 in the Morn' lately, I have also a small Cold, which might be the cause.

25th. My lower Maid Lizzy went to her Mothers this evening to sleep there, as she has my leave to go with her Mother to-morrow to Norwich to get a pair of Stays for herself.

FEBRUARY *8th*. This Day being appointed to be observed as a Fast on the present Troubles and Wars abroad, I went to Weston Church this morning at 11 o'clock and there read Prayers

* A dry measure, equal to four bushels or thirty-two gallons.

proper on the occasion—but there was no Sermon after.*
I had a large Congregation—Mr Custance was at Church—
Mrs Custance not, being so cold. After divine Service I walked
with Mr Custance to his New Hall, and there spent an Hour or
better with them. We sent over after Church to Hockering to
enquire after Mrs Howes, and about 3 my Servant Boy returned
and greatly surprized us by acquainting us that poor Mrs Howes
was no more—she died at one o'clock this morning—Pray God,
she may be happy, and the Family comforted under so sore an
affliction—She will be greatly missed by all the Rotation &c.
Nancy and myself were greatly concern'd to hear of it and more
so, as it was so unexpectedly. One Christopher Breeze from
Lyng, a young man and lately a Driver of Mr Custances, and
who came after a copy of the Register, dined with our Folks
in Kitchen. I gave him a Copy and would take nothing for
it. Nancy sent a long Letter to her Aunt Jn Woodforde this
Even'.

12th. At 10 o'clock this morning took a walk to Hockering to
attend poor Mrs Howes's Funeral there to-day. The Snow was
very deep in some Places as I went. My Man Will went with me
—We got to Mrs Howes's before 11 and there met Mr Shelford
senr, Mr Du Quesne, Mr Priest senr of Reepham, Mr Potter of
Scarning, Mr Bodham, Mr Smith, Dr Thorne and Mr Priest of
Norwich. I found all the the Clergy in gowns and some in
Cassocks also—I did not carry my gown, as I did not know
whether or not the Clergy appeared in them—I borrowed one
however, of Mr Howes and likewise a Band. Before we went to
Church there was Chocolate and Toast and Cake with red Wine
and white. At half past 11 o'clock we went to Church with the
Corpse in the following Procession. The Corpse first in an
Hearse and Pair of Horses, then followed six Chaises, in the first
which was Du Quesnes went Du Quesne and Dr Thorne, in the

* The British were fighting the American War of Independence, in
conflict with both the Spanish and the French in the West Indies,
and in no little trouble again with the French in India.

second which was Mr Shelfords went Mr Shelford and Mr Smith, in the third which was Mr Priests, went Mr Priest and myself, in the fourth which was one from Dereham, went Mr Potter and Mr Bodham, in the fifth which was from Norwich went Mr Priest of Norwich and a Mr Forster the Undertaker, in the sixth which was Mr Howes's, went Mrs Howes's two Servant Maids in deep mourning. The Underbearers and Servants all in Hatbands black closed the Procession and an handsome appearance the whole Procession made — we returned to Mr Howes's in the same manner as we went from it to Church — Mr Du Quesne buried her — The Pall-Bearers were Mr Shelford, Mr Priest, Mr Potter, Mr Bodham, Mr Smith and myself — we had all black Hatbands and Gloves, but they were white. Poor Mrs Howes if she had lived till to Morrow wch was her birth Day — she would have been 69 Years. It was as decent, neat, handsome Funeral as I ever saw and everything conducted in the best manner — and by its being so I conclude that it was Mrs Davy's good management. Mr Howes, Mrs Davy &c. kept above stairs all the Time — They desired me to walk up to them which I did after the Funeral, but did not stay long with them — found them low and left them so. After our return from Church we had Cake and Wine and Chocolate and dried Toast carried round. My Servant and all Servants that attended and all the drivers all had Hatbands and gloves given to them. We walked back again and got home about half past 2 o'clock — and a bitter cold walk we had back, the Wind in our Faces and it snowed most of the way, which was beat in our Faces. We walked over France Green and by Hockering Park House.

MARCH *17th*. A great deal of Snow fell in the Night, and many heavy Storms of Snow, Hail &c. most of this Day. I read Prayers and Preached this afternoon at Weston. Had a small congregation, owing to the Weather. None of Mr Custances Family at Church. Having heard that Thos Thurston's Wife (who is and has been ill a long while) longed for some rost Veal from my

House, having therefore a Loin rosted for Dinner, I sent her a good Plate of it.

20th. I got up rather early this morning being disturbed by a noise in my Study, in cleaning of it, at which I was rather angry and scolded a little.

21st. The poor Woman whom I sent some Veal to Sunday died yesterday morning—She eat nothing afterwards till she died, But she eat hearty of the Veal I sent her.

22nd. I buried Eliz. Thurston Wife of Thos Thurston this afternoon at Weston, aged 45 Yrs. It snowed all the whole Day with very cold high Wind.

APRIL *1st.* Mr Custance sent after Nancy this morning to spend the Day with Mrs Custance and to have her Hair dressed by one Brown, the best Ladies-Frisseur in Norwich. About Noon the Weather turned out very wet and the Wind very high and so continued till 9 at Night. The Barometer sunk from this morning at 10 o'clock to 10 at Night 13 Degrees from No. 28–17 to 28–4. Nancy returned home about ½ past 9 o'clock this Even', with her head finely dressed of but very becoming her. Mrs Custance would not let Nancy pay the Barber, but she paid for her and it cost no less than half a guinea. Mrs Custance gave the Barber for dressing her Hair and Nancys the enormous sum of one guinea—He came on purpose from Norwich to dress them. Mrs Custance (God bless her) is the best Lady I ever knew.

MAY *29th.* Very busy all the Morning, packing up our things for to go into the Country, as we set out in the Evening. Mr Du Quesne, who goes to London with us dined and spent the Afternoon with us—and about 5 o'clock this Evening Nancy and myself went in Lenewade Bridge Chaise, and Mr Du Quesne in his own Chaise, for Norwich and there we drank Tea at the Angel where the London Coach puts up and in which we are to go in to Night.

To the Driver of the Lenewade Chaise gave 0.1.6.

Paid and gave at the Angel for eating &c. 0.2.6.

My Servant Will Coleman went with us and is to go into the Country with us. We met Mr Priest of Reepham and his Son St John at Norwich—The latter is going to Bury in the outside of the London Coach. No inside Place vacant.

For 2 inside Places in the London Coach pd at Norwich 1.16.0.

For 1 outside Place in Do. pd at Do. 0.10.6.

To extraordinary weight of Luggage at $1\frac{1}{2}$ per Pound pd 0.8.6.

At 9 o'clock this Evening we all set of for London.

30th. We travelled all night long and I thank God safe and well. We breakfasted at Sudbury—and I paid there 0.2.6. Our Coach was quite full having six in it—4 gentlemen and 2 young Ladies. We got to London about 2 o'clock in the Afternoon all safe and well, thank God for it. To Coachmen from Norwich gave 0.4.0. We did not like the Inn where the Coach put up (which was the Swan and 2 Necks in Lad-Lane.) therefore we got into a Hackney Coach and drove to the Bell Savage on Ludgate Hill and there dined, supped, and slept. Mr Du Quesne went with us there and dined and spent the Afternoon with us —In the Evening he went to the Arch-Bishops at Lambeth where he supped and slept. Nancy bore her Journey very well as did Will and myself. We were all very glad to get to bed to night, being tired.

31st. We breakfasted, dined and spent the Afternoon at our Inn. Before we breakfasted, I hired a Coach and we went in it to St James Park. Will also went with us. From the Horse Guards we all walked up the Park to St James's Palace and saw the Guards relieved at 9 o'clock—a very pretty sight. We also saw most of the State Rooms in the Palace. Gave to People at St James's Palace 0.3.6. From thence we walked up the Park to the Queens Palace but did not go into that—the Royal Family being there. After that we walked down the Park back to the Horse-Guards and there took a Hackney Coach and returned to our Inn to breakfast. Mr Du Quesne came to us at breakfast—and after breakfast, Nancy, myself and Will took a Coach and went to the Tower and saw the Horse Armory, the small Armory, the Artillery, the Regalia, and the wild Beasts.* Mr Du Quesne went with us in the Coach as far as the Royal Exchange and there he took his Leave of us. At the Tower gave in the whole 0.9.0. From Breakfast to Dinner we were taken up in seeing the Tower, and did not dine till 5 o'clock at our Inn. For Coach hire to Day pd 0.5.6. After Dinner we walked to a Milleners Shop and I bought 3 dressed Caps for Nancy, for my Sister Pounsett and her little girl, with about 10 Yards of Ribband besides—pd there 1.10.6. To a small Paper Caravan for the above pd 0.1.6. I went by myself and gave a Peep into St Pauls Church this aft. To a Barber this Afternoon for shaving &c. gave 0.1.0.

For 2 inside Places in the Salisbury Coach pd 2.2.0.

For 1 outside Place Do. pd 0.10.6.

Paid and gave at the Bell Savage for all of us abt 1.15.0. They were very civil People at the Bell Savage Inn by name Barton and a very good House it is. About 10 o'clock at Night we set of in the Salisbury Coach from the same Inn for Salisbury, and the Coach guarded. I was bit terribly by the Buggs last Night, but did not wake me.

JUNE 20th. I took a Walk by Myself about Noon to Ansford and there dined and spent part of the Afternoon at my Brother John's, with him, his Wife, Nancy and Mr Thomas. Mr Pounsett came to us in the Afternoon and then my Brother John, Mr Pounsett, Mr Thomas and self took a walk to Cary and drank Tea and smoked a Pipe at Mr Thomas's. We had for Dinner to day at my Brothers' a Leg of Lamb boiled and Spinnage, a couple of Fowls rosted and Asparagus and a nice Batter Pudding with Currant Jelly. Sister Pounsett and her little Maid went to

* In the days before the establishment of the London Zoo, wild and unusual animals, especially lions, were to be seen at the Tower.

Ansford in one of the Bruton Chaises (which I hired to bring back Nancy to Cole) this Afternoon and drank Tea at Mrs Whites. Mrs Jn Woodforde and Nancy met them at Mr Whites. We all returned to Cole about 9 o'clock at Night. Mr Pounsett and myself walked back again to Cole. Had a very long Letter whilst I was at my Brother Johns, from Mr Du Quesne dated the 18 Instant from Lambeth Palace—wherein he acquaints me that in Norfolk the 31 of May there happened at Weston and adjacent Villages a most terrible Tempest of Thunder, Lightning

and Hail there which did great Damage to Mr Custances new House and likewise broke many of my Windows—The Corn in Weston Field almost all destroyed by the Hail which were as big as Bulletts and were 12 Inches deep in Weston Field—Thank God! no lives are said to be lost. Nancy supped and slept at Cole. My Letter from Du Quesne was franked by Mr Townshend. Very sickly in London in the Influenza. Very few escape—Mr Du Quesne has been confined to his Room in it—Mrs Townshend was very dangerously ill in it.

JULY *20th*. Mr Thomas spent the Morning with us Yesterday, he came to ask me to preach for him on Sunday but I could not, as I brought no Sermon with me—The last Time I was in the Country I had some Sermons with me and was never asked to preach therefore I thought it of no Use to bring any now.

Weston

OCTOBER *24th*. Nancy came home about 12 o'clock and Mrs Davy and another Lady (a Mrs Church) with her. Mrs Davy and the other Lady did not stay long—Nancy stayed and dined, supped and slept here. Mr Hall, just returned from Andover in Hants, came here about Noon and he dined, supped and sat up all Night at my House, having no bed but mine which I offered to him, but he would not accept of it, therefore obliged me to sit up with him all Night. We had for Dinner a Piece of boiled Beef, some Herrings which Mrs Davy brought here and a Couple of Ducks. Mr Pyle dined with our Folks—his men at work here.

25th. I breakfasted, dined, supped and slept again at home. Hall went away about 10 o'clock. I was quite ill all day by setting up last night and will not do it again for any Hall in the Kingdom—He might have as well went to Lenewade and slept as he used to do—but he minds nothing but self and his Money. I slept about noon for 2 Hours and tolerably well. Nancy breakfasted, dined, &c. &c. again at home. Nancy sent a Letter this Evening to her Aunt Woodforde.

NOVEMBER *20th.* Mr Custance made me a Morning Visit, and desired that we would dine with him Monday next. Mrs Custance soon after Mr Custance was gone made me a Visit and stayed with me till near 2 o'clock. Very soon after Mrs Custance was gone Mr Howes with Mrs Davy and Nancy came here and they stayed and dined and spent the afternoon with me—and Mr Howes with Mrs Davy prevailed on me after many Entreaties and at last with great reluctance on my Part, to let Nancy return with them to Hockering as they are going to Norwich to-Morrow, which I did, tho' much against me. Poor Mr Howes and Mrs Davy had set their hearts so much on it, that they were made very uneasy at my refusing them at first, and they almost cried and said that they would never be friendly with me if I did not admit of it. Mr Howes said he would never enter my Doors more. The chief and principal Reason I gave, was, I did not approve or ever could that my Niece should make so free at Mr Priest's — Mrs Davy having sent a note this morning before they came here, that she with Nancy intended dining with them to Morrow at Norwich. It made me rather uneasy after they were gone back as I cannot by any means approve of it on any Account neither should I at last, unless to make old Mr Howes easy. Mr Custance told me this morning that he had a few Days ago about 80 Turkies, geese, Ducks, and Fowls stolen from him in one night — many of them that were fatting. This is the time of the year that many idle Fellows from Norwich go about the Country stealing Poultry to send them to London to make a Penny of them. I never had any stolen yet, but daily expect it. Burrows of Morton had but a few Days ago also taken from him Poultry to the Amount of 3 or 4 Pds value. We had for Dinner to day one Fowl boiled and Piggs face, a Couple of Rabbitts smothered with Onions, a Piece of rost Beef and some Grape Tarts.

DECEMBER *25th.* This being Christmas Day I went to Church this Morn' and then read Prayers and administred the Holy Sacrament. Mr and Mrs Custance both at Church and both received the Sacrament from my Hands. The following poor old Men dined at my House to day, as usual, Js Smith, Clerk, Richd Bates, Richd Buck; Thos Cary; Thos Dicker; Thos Cushing; Thos Carr — to each besides gave 1/0 — in all 0.7.0. I gave them for Dinner a Surloin of Beef rosted and plenty of plumb-Pudding. We had mince Pies for the first Time to-day.

1783

JANUARY *7th*. I breakfasted, and spent most of the Morn' at home. Nancy breakfasted, and spent part of the Morn' at home. Betsy Davy breakfasted, and spent part of the Morn' here. Mrs Davy breakfasted with us this morning. As soon as the Ladies had breakfasted, they set of for Norwich and Nancy with them. I stayed till near 12 before I set forth for Norwich and my Servant Will went with me—We all went by appointment to Mr Priests and there dined, supped and spent the Evening. Mrs Davy and Nancy slept at Mr Priests. I slept at my old Inn the Kings Head. Mr Du Quesne dined, supped and slept at Mr Priests. We had for Dinner some fresh Salmon and Oyster Sauce, a boiled Turkey and Oyster Sauce, a fore Qtr of London Lamb, mince Pyes, &c. After Tea we had a vocal and instrumental Concert—Nancy sung. Mr Du Quesne, Mr Reeves, Mr Starkey and Mr John Priest played on their violins. Mr Fearman on the Base-Viol and Mr Mulley on the Organ—a very good Concert. We did not sup till near 10 at night—and then we had a very handsome supper—A Couple of boiled Fowls and Oyster Sauce, a rosted Hare wch I sent them—one Duck rosted, a hot Tongue, Tarts, Italian Flummery—Blamanche black Caps and sweet-Meats. I did not get to bed till after 12 to-night. Gave Mr Priests Maid coming away 0.1.0.

25th. This Evening the Ipswich News brought us the joyful News of Peace being signed at Versailles the 20 of this month and recd at London the 25. No mention of the same in either of the Norwich Papers. The above Peace is with America, France and Spain, but not with the Dutch—Tho' daily expected by them.

MARCH *5th*. Much colder than yesterday—Wind much higher and Frost more severe—The coldest Day for some years. I was very low and indifferent all day long. The Barometer very low, and the Wind being very rough when I went up to my Chamber to go to bed, being not the lest sleepy, I lighted my Fire, and sat down and read the Life of Lewis 14 of France till after 2 o'clock in the morning and then went to bed, the Wind still high. I heard some Noise between one and two but it did not last.

6th. The first thing I was informed of when I came down stairs, was, that my Stable had been broken up, in the Night and that there was stolen out of it, a Hatchet, a Hook, a Bridle, and a pair of hedging Gloves of Bens. There was seen Yesterday a Couple of idle Fellows passing and repassing my House, I saw them once go by, one of them was in a long blue Coat, the other in a brown one. They came in at the back Window of the Stable, which they cut away, to wrench it open with a large stick wch was found just by, they left behind them a Pr of Sheep Sheers broke directly in the middle—They also took Bens Cart Whip, which they left on the Muck-heap. I think myself well of, in having so few things stolen as there were so many in the Stable and in the Corn Room. I sent for Harry Dunnell to mend the Window and to John Spaule to make some new iron work for the same, all which were done by the Evening and all right again. Harry Dunnell dined with our Folks and for his work to day I gave him 0.1.0. There were several Stables in the Parish broke into besides mine last night, Peachmans, Bucks, Widow Pratts, Manns and Forsters—and several things stolen. Nancy was very much alarmed on hearing the above. I did not go to bed to Night till after 12 o'clock.

8th. To a poor Boy by Name Allison of Lyng, turned out of doors by his Parents as he says—gave this Even' 0.0.6. A change of the Ministry will soon take place as mentioned on the Papers—Ld North and Charles Fox have shook hands—O North, how low art thou fallen.

23rd. I read Prayers and Preached this Afternoon at Weston.

I buried this Evening at Weston poor old Thos Reeves commonly called Dr Reeves—aged 71 years. Mrs Davy came here about 7 in the Evening in Mr Howes's Chaise and she supped and slept here as did the Driver and the Horses—She came here by appointment this Evening to carry Nancy with her to Norwich early in the Morning to see the Grand Procession of Bishop Blaize* &c. It was very kind of her indeed. No Person besides ever gave her the most distant offer. And if Mrs Davy had not been so kind, she could not have gone, as I could not by myself have made it agreeable to Nancy without some Lady being with her.

24th. About 6 o'clock this Morning we all got up to go to Norwich and after breakfast we set forth at 8 o'clock, Mrs Davy and Nancy in the Chaise, myself on Horseback, Will, Ben and Lizzy on horseback, Jack went behind the Chaise as I was willing that all shd go that could. Betty, my Upper Maid stayed at home being Washing Week. We all got to Norwich about 10 o'clock—The Road we went was filled with People on Horseback and foot, going to see the fine Sight—Ben carried Lizzy behind him on Phyllis and the first Time she ever carried any one, double, and she carried her very well and safe, to Norwich and back again. I put up my Horses at the Kings Head—Mrs Davy and Nancy were at Mr Priests. The grand Procession began about 11 o'clock this morning—I saw them first beyond Black Friars Bridge near St Saviours Church and a very pretty and grand Sight it was. Mr and Mrs Custance, Sir Edmund Bacon and Lady at the Kings Head, I called on them about 11 o'clock, and gave them an Account of the grand Sight and left with them a Paper of the Procession. I never saw so great a Multitude of People in my Life collected together, the Market-

* Patron saint of the Norwich wool trade, Blaise was a third-century bishop of Sebaste in Armenia. He died after suffering terrible tortures; his flesh, for example, was torn with iron combs 'such as are used to card wool'. The other characters in the procession represented those who joined the Argonauts in search of the Golden Fleece.

Place was as full as it could be, both in the area, at the Windows and on the Tops of the Houses—and every Street besides full of People from all Parts of the County. The Procession proceeded thro' every principal Street of the City and it lasted till 4 in the Afternoon. We eat some cold Ham and Veal at Mr Priests about 2. A Mrs Goddard an old Maid, Du Quesne's Maid Betty and a Miss High with her in Du Quesne's Chaise were at Mr Priests, as was Miss Priest of Reepham. About ½ past 4 we all set forth for Weston and got home about 7 o'clock, rather fatigued. Mem: Just without the Gates Mr Howes's Chaise broke down, one of the Axle-Trees being broke, which my Servant Boy Jack, behind the Chaise, found out—but luckily for it we were near Mr Howes's Coach Maker, a Mr Baldwin, who lent them a carriage leaving the old Shatterdan behind to be mended. Paid and gave to day at Norwich abt 2.6. We were all highly delighted indeed with this Days Sight—it far exceeded every Idea I cd have of it. Hercules, Jason, and Bishop Blaize, were exceedingly well kept up and very superbly dressed. All the Combers were in white ruffled Shirts with Cross-Belts of Wool of divers Colours—with Mitred Caps on their heads—The Shepherds and Shepherdesses were little Boys and Girls on horseback, very handsomely and with great Propriety dressed. Orations spoke in most of the principal Streets. I never saw a Procession so grand and well conducted.

MAY *1st*. The 2 Fellows who were suspected breaking open my Stable and many others, were tried this Day at the Sessions at Norwich and convicted of the Robbery of stealing a Sack from Mr Howlett and are to remain in Prison for three years—which I hope will do good.

6th. To a Man who comes from Windham and carries about stuffs for Gowns &c. for 27 yards and half at 9d per yard pd 1.0.6. Gave both my Maids a Gown apiece of it and of the same Colour, something of the Pea Green. Gave Nancy also, to make a Skirt for her of a light blue 6 yds. Nancy much better to day tho' not quite well yet. Cobb the Rat-Catcher dined with our Folks to day. We caught and killed about 3 Dozen of Rats in the Barn before Dinner to day—3 old female Rats with their young ones—2 old dog Rats and some half grown.

26th. I buried poor Joe Adcocks Wife this Evening aged 43. Pray God comfort the poor Man in his distress, he having buried, his Father and Mother and Wife within 6 Weeks.

JUNE *5th.* I breakfasted at the Kings Head—and after being shaved I walked to Mr Francis's—then to Priests to taste some Port Wine and there bespoke a Qtr of a Pipe. Called at Beales in the Fish Markett and bought 3 Pairs of fine Soals—2 Crabbs —and a Lobster—Pd him for the above and for some Fish I had before of him 0.8.4. About 11 o'clock sent Will home with the Fish to have for Dinner as I have Company to dine with me to-day.

At Mr Bakers for a Pr of large Scissars to trim Horses pd 1.6.

At Dittos—for 2 Pounds of Pinns for Nancy and Mrs Davy pd 4.8.

Called at Buckles and bespoke a large Lock for my Back-Door. At Quantrells Gardens for a Glass of Gin and Water pd 0.3. Paid and gave at the Kings Head 0.8.9. Called on my Sadler Allum and bespoke a Pillion for Nancy. Called on my Upholsterer Horth and bespoke a Bolster Tick and some Paper to paper one of my Garretts. Gave my Barber—Milsham—this morning 0.1.0. About 1 o'clock I mounted my Mare and set of for Weston and did not get home till near 4 o'clock on Account of my poor Mare, she having filled herself so much on dry Meat last Night—I was afraid that she would have dropped on the road as she puffed and blowed so terribly—I walked her most part of the way—and I got of and walked many Times—It vexed and fretted me much on Account of having Company to Dinner—It was also very hot and was obliged to wear my great Coat, the Pockets of which also were loaded with 2 Pounds of Pins &c., however I did get home at last as did my Mare—And

I found Mr Smith and Mr Baldwin with my Ladies at home. I was pretty much fatigued with the Heat and fretting. Mr Smith and Mr Baldwin dined and spent the Afternoon and part of the Evening with us till 9 at Night. Nancy and Mrs Davy dined, breakfasted, supped &c. again here. We had for Dinner 3 Pr of fine Soals — a Leg of Mutton rosted, and some Gooseberry Tarts. After Tea we got to Cards, at Loo, at which I won 4.0. I dined, supped and slept at home.

25th. Very uncommon Lazy and hot Weather. The Sun very red at setting. To a poor old crazy Woman this morn' gave 0.0.6. Nancy and myself dined and spent part of the afternoon at Weston House with Mr and Mrs Custance — Mr Rawlins dined also with us — whilst we were at Dinner Mrs Custance was obliged to go from Table about 4 o'clock labour Pains coming on fast upon her. We went home soon after dinner on the Occasion — as we came in the Coach. We had for Dinner some Beans and Bacon, a Chine of Mutton rosted, Giblett Pye, Hashed Goose, a Rabbit rosted and some young Peas — Tarts, Pudding and Jellies. We got home between 5 and 6 o'clock. After Supper we sent up to Mr Custances to enquire after Mrs Custance who was brought to bed of a fine girl about 7 o'clock and as well as could be expected.

JULY *29th.* About 1 o'clock I took a ride to Mattishall to Mr Bodhams and there dined and spent the Afternoon with him, Mrs Bodham, Mr and Mrs Ball of Catfield, Sister to Mrs Bodham, Mrs Davy, Mr Smith, Mr and Mrs Howes, Mr Ashull and Nancy. We had for Dinner a Piece of boiled Beef, some Beans and Bacon, a couple of Ducks rosted, a Veal Pye and some Apricot Dumplins. At Quadrille this Evening won 0.2.0. As we were coming away Mrs Howes came to me and asked me to their House it being their Rotation next, but I entirely refused to go, as they had not only kept away from mine very lately, but would not let Miss Howes come who was very desirous of coming to Weston. I gave it to her, and most of the Company seemed pleased with my behaviour. We did not get home till after 9 in the Evening. Nancy was obliged to change Horses, the flies teazing Phyllis very much which made her kick a little.

AUGUST *14th.* I sent Will early this morning to Hockering, after Mrs Davy who returned here to breakfast, and she dined, supped and slept here with Nancy. My Maid Lizzy very ill today, worse than ever, and kept her Bed most part of the Day. Dr Thorne came here whilst we were at Dinner, and he dined with us but obliged to leave us immediately after Dinner, having a great many Patients to visit. He ordered that Lizzy should begin to take the Bark* immediately as the fever was abated, and which I sent for to his House this Evening. She begun taking the Bark at 10 this Night and is to take it every two Hours till she has taken a Dozen Papers. If it purges her she is to have 4 Drops of Laudanum in her Bark when she takes it then 3 Drops — then 2 then 1 Drop which will take of the purging. Betty is to set up till 4 in the morning to give her the Bark and then Will: as he brews to Morrow, will give it her. We had for Dinner to day a boiled Leg of Mutton and Capers, a Duck rosted and one of Nancy's Pudding with Jelly.

28th. I breakfasted, supped and slept again at home. Nancy breakfasted, supped and slept again at home. Lizzy's Mother breakfasted, dined and spent the Afternoon here and in the Evening returned to her home. My sick Servants but indifferent again to day. About 2 o'clock Mr and Mrs Custance called here by appointment and took Nancy and self with them in their Coach to Mr Townshends at Honingham where we dined and spent the Afternoon with Mr and Mrs Townshend, Mrs Cornwallis, Widow of the late Arch-Bishop of Canterbury's and who is also Sister to Mr Townshend, Mr and Mrs Custance, and Mr Du Quesne—The latter of whom we were glad to see, as it was so long since we saw him. Mr and Mrs Townshend behaved

* Peruvian bark (in other words, quinine), the use of which in medicine was extended by Sir Hans Sloane (1660–1753).

very genteel to us. The drawing Room in which we drank Tea &c. was hung with Silk. The Chairs of the same kind of Silk and all the woodwork of them gilded, as were the Settee's. The looking glass which was the finest and largest I ever saw, cost at secondhand 150.0.0. The Height of the Plate was seven feet and half, and the breadth of it was five feet and half, one single Plate of glass only. The frame and Ornaments to it, was carved and gilded and very handsome. There was two Courses at Dinner besides the Desert. Each course nine Dishes, but most of the things spoiled by being so frenchified in dressing. I dined on some Hare rosted, but very insipid. After Coffee and Tea we got to Cards to Loo at which I had the good Luck to win abt 0.1.0. Mrs Cornwallis and Nancy did not play Cards with us but with the Children, Miss Caroline and Miss Amelia Townshend, about 3 or 4 years old. Nancy sung one Song, then Mr and Mrs Custance, Nancy and self came away about half past seven o'clock, we got home about 8 o'clock. To Page's Harvest Men gave a Largess of 0.1.0.

SEPTEMBER *4th.* About 1 o'clock Mr and Mrs Custance called here in their Coach and took me with them to Norwich to dine with the Bishop. I was dressed in a Gown and Cassock and Scarf. We got there to the Palace abt 3 o'clock, and there dined and spent the Afternoon with his Lordship Dr Bagot,* and his Lady Mrs Bagot, whose Name before Marriage was Miss Hay, the two Miss Hay's her Sisters, two Mr Hay's her Brothers, a Mr Gooch the Bishop's Chaplain, Dr Brook of Yarmouth, Mr Buxton of Easton, and his Nephew the Revd Mr Buxton, Mr Du Quesne, Mr Priest of Reepham, and 5 strange Clergymen. There were 20 of us at the Table and a very elegant Dinner the Bishop gave us. We had 2 Courses of 20 Dishes each Course, and a Desert after of 20 Dishes. Madeira, red and white Wines. The first Course amongst many other things were 2 Dishes of pro-

* Dr Lewis Bagot (1741–1802), an almost exact contemporary of JW, served as Bishop of Norwich between 1783 and 1790.

digious fine stewed Carp and Tench, and a fine Haunch of Venison. Amongst the second Course a fine Turkey Poult, Partridges, Pidgeons and Sweatmeats. Desert — amongst other things, Mulberries, Melon, Currants, Peaches, Nectarines and Grapes. A most beautiful Artificial Garden in the Center of the Table remained at Dinner and afterwards, it was one of the prettiest things I ever saw, about a Yard long, and about 18 Inches wide, in the middle of which was a high round Temple supported on round Pillars, the Pillars were wreathed round with artificial Flowers — on one side was a Shepherdess on the other a Shepherd, several handsome Urns decorated with artificial Flowers also &c. &c. The Bishop behaved with great affability towards me as I remembered him at Christ Church in Oxford. He was also very affable and polite to all the Clergy present. Mr and Mrs Custance were exceedingly pleased, with both Bishop and Mrs Bagot, as seemed everybody else. About half past 6 o'clock we all withdrew from the dining Room to the Library or Drawing Room, where we had Tea and Coffee brought round to each of us. There was a strange Lady that came to Tea with us. Abt half past 7 Mr and Mrs Custance and self took our Leave as did the rest of the Company, we got home between 9 and 10. It lightned a good deal as we came home. Mr Custance would carry me quite to the Parsonage as we returned home, tho' I desired him to put me down at the Church. I was exceedingly pleased with this Days excursion. Nancy recd a long Letter from her Brother William dated the 29 June from Staten Island in North America brought by Mr Custance's Servant from Norwich this Evening. The Letter came to 0.2.4. He is very well and has escaped many Dangers in America. He sent inclosed in his Letter some Continental Money Paper valued there at 10 Shillings and which he desired to be given to me.

OCTOBER *12th*. Had another disagreeable Letter this morning from the Bishop's Register to preach at the Cathedral of Norwich on the Sunday Morn' Feb. 8 next. I read Prayers and Preached this Aft. at Weston Church. Neither Mr or Mrs Custance at Church.

24th. I breakfasted, supped and slept again at the Kings Head. After breakfast I dressed myself in my best Coat and Waistcoat and then walked down in my Boots to the Bishops Palace and had a long Conversation with the Bishop abt many things — but what I went to his Lordship chiefly on, was my being appointed on the Combination List to preach at the Cathedral the 8 of February next, when my Name had been inserted but a few Years back. To which his Lordship replied, that as I did not then preach in propria Persona was one Reason, and the Second was that he was willing that the Pulpit at the Cathedral should be filled properly by able and beneficed Clergy, and that it was rather a Compliment conferred by him on those that he so appointed.

NOVEMBER *7th.* Mr Custance made me a long morning Visit and offered to send his Coach after me to dine with him to day by appointment, but I told him that Mr Du Quesne who dines also at Weston House to day would take me with him in his Chaise thither as he promised and therefore abt 2 o'clock Du Quesne did call on me, stayed with me abt half an Hour and then we both went to Weston House in our Gowns and Cassocks (as we are to meet the Bishop of Norwich there to day) and there we dined and spent the Afternoon with Mr and Mrs Custance, The Bishop and his Lady Mrs Bagot, his Lordships Chaplain Mr Gooch, and Sir William and Lady Jernegan. Mr and Mrs Branthwaite were also invited but did not come, the former having sent word in the Morning that he had the Gout. The Bishop was not dressed in his Gown and Cassock, but in a purple Coat and a short silk Cassock under it. The Company all broke up about half past seven o'clock. I got home by 8. Could not prevail with Du Quesne to Stay and sup with me on his return. We had for Dinner some stewed Carp, Ham and Fowls, a fine Cygnet rosted &c. &c. — the first Course — a brace of Pheasants rosted, a fine Hare rosted, Blamange, Green Peas, Jelly &c. &c. the second Course. Many Dishes of Desert afterwards but nothing extra. The Bishop took Du Quesne very genteelly in to preach a Charity Sermon the ensuing Year at Norwich towards the Support of the Charity Schools there. Sir Willm Jernegan is a very fine Man, very easy, affable and good natured. Lady Jernegan is a fine Woman but high and mighty. They are both of the Romish Persuasion. It being Friday and a Fast Day of Course to them, they however eat Fowl, Pheasant and Swan and Sir William eat some Ham. Upon the whole we spent an agreeable Day, but must confess that being with our equals is much more agreeable.

DECEMBER *2nd.* This being my Tithe Audit Day, we had this Year a very agreeable meeting here, and were very agreeable — no grumbling whatever.

Total recd this Day for Tithe 286.15.0.
Paid out of the above to Steph. Andrews 0.15.0.
Ditto to Mr Dade 6.17.0.
Ditto to Mr Mann 4.14.0.
Ditto to Mr Bidewell 0.13.0.

After the Company was all gone and we thought everything were agreeable and happy in my House, we were of a sudden alarmed by a great Noise in the kitchen, and on my immediately going out there found my Servant Man Will Coleman beating about the Maids in a terrible manner and appeared quite frantic and mad. I seized him by the Collar and as soon as he was loose, he ran out into the Yard and jumped into the Pond there in a moment but he was soon taken up by Ben, which frightened us so much that we were obliged to sit up all night. We got him to bed however about 1 o'clock and after some time he was somewhat quiet — but it frightned us so much that Nancy and self did not go to bed till 6 in the morning. Ben and Jack did not go to bed at all. The reason of his being so, was on Lizzy's Account, as he wants to marry her and she will not, and he is very jealous. Am afraid however that it proceeds from a family complaint, his Father having been crazy some time. It is therefore now high time for him to leave me which I shall endeavour to do the first opportunity. It made me very ill almost instantly and made my niece very unhappy as well as ill also.

30th. Mr Custance's Servants, George, Harry, Haylett the Gardner with the Cook Maid, Betty and Sukey Chamber-Maids all supped and spent the Evening with our Folks in Kitchen. They stayed till 10 o'clock and then walked home. I gave them a Couple of rost Fowls and some good Punch. Won of Nancy at Cribbage this Evening 0.2.0.

1784

JANUARY *21st*. Bitter cold, very hard Frost, and much Snow in the Night. I went out with my Man this morning tracing Hares, we found one fine one which the Dogs killed. At Cribbage this Evening with Nancy won 0.2.0. She was very sulky and sullen on loosing it, tho' not paid. She did not scarce open her Mouth all the Even' after. Mr and Mrs Hardy supped and spent the Even' with our Folks.

26th. I rejoiced much this morning on shooting an old Woodpecker, which has teized me a long Time in pulling out the Reed from my House. He had been often shot at by me and others, but never could be a match for him till this Morn'. For this last 3 Years in very cold Weather did he use to come here and destroy my Thatch. Many holes he has made this Year in the Roof, and as many before.

FEBRUARY *7th*. I breakfasted and spent part of the Morn' at home. Nancy, Mrs Davy and Betsy did the same. Snow very deep indeed and bitter cold Weather. About 11 o'clock this morning myself, Mrs Davy, Betsy and Nancy got into Lenewade Bridge Chaise to go to Norwich as I am to preach to Morrow at the Cathedral. We were obliged to have four Horses the Snow being so very deep. We got to Norwich I thank God safe about 2 o'clock. We were obliged to go round by Mr Du Quesnes to get to the Turnpike road as soon as we could on Account of the Snow wch was very deep indeed especially over France Green and no Tract of Wheels to be seen. We were very fearful going over that Green as it was very dangerous. It was very hard work even for the four Horses to get over that Green. It was much better on the Turnpike. The Snow in some Place was almost up to the Horses Shoulders. Towards Lynn the Snow is much deeper and the Road to it almost impassable. Will went on horseback with us to Norwich. We all dined, spent the Aft. supped &c., at the Kings Head.

8th. We breakfasted and slept again at the Kings Head. At 10 o'clock this morning we all went in a Coach to the Cathedral. I went full dressed and being Preacher sat next to the Sub-Dean Dr Hammond. Whilst the Anthem was singing I was conducted by the Virger to the Pulpit and there Preached a Sermon from these Words 'Let your light so shine before Men that they may see your good Works and glorify your Father wch is in Heaven'. After Sermon was over I walked back to the Vestry, had my Hood taken of, and then a Person came to me and gave me for Preaching 1.1.0. I gave the Virger for the Use of the Hood 0.1.0. Neither Bishop, Dean or Mayor at the Cathedral. The Cathedral was not crowded owing to the cold. Lady Bacon was at the Cathedral and immediately after I had conveyed the Ladies back to the Inn and I had undressed myself, I waited on Lady Bacon and sat with her some Time at her Lodgings at one Hirsts. We all then went to Mr Priests where we dined, spent part of the Afternoon, supped and spent the Evening with him, his Wife, and their Son John. In the Afternoon we took Coach and went to Alderman Starling Days where we drank Tea with him, his Wife, his Mother, and Sister in Law, his Son and a Capt. Poole, a very good kind of a young Man. Mr Day behaved with great Politeness and everything very genteel. As we returned in the Coach from Mr Days we were very near being overturned before we got to Priests. To Coaches this Day for us pd 0.8.0.

9th. We breakfasted at the Kings Head and stayed in Town till near 2 this Afternoon and then we had a Chaise and four from the Kings Head and set of for Weston to get there by Dinner. I walked down to Mr Frosts this morning and pd him a Bill for things had of him in 1780, 2.16.0.

To my Barber this morning gave 0.2.0.

At Chases for Books pd 0.3.1.
At Scotts for a Pr of Gloves pd 0.2.2.
At Bakers for things pd 0.4.0.
Paid and gave at the Kings Head abt 3.0.0.
Called at Mr Francis's, Priests, Buckles, Smiths my Mercer
and Garland my Taylors. We got I thank God safe home to
Weston about 4 this Afternoon—the Snow as deep as we went
and harder work for 4 Horses than going to Norwich. Gave the
Drivers as they brought us home safe 0.3.0, some strong Beer
and some Victuals. We did not dine till near 5 this Afternoon.
Lent to Mrs Davy this morning at the Kings Head 2.2.0. Mrs
Davy, Betsy, and Nancy dined, supped and slept at Weston.

MAY *18th*. This being Mr Smiths Rotation I rode to Mattishall
about 1 o'clock and there dined and spent the Aft. with Mr
Smith, Mr Du Quesne and a Mr Codman with him, Mr and
Mrs Bodham, Miss Bodham and a Miss Betsy Donne of London,
a fine showy Girl. After Coffee and Tea we got to Quadrille at
wch I won 0.0.6. We had for Dinner some Cods Sounds* and
Tongues with Egg Sauce, a Couple of Fowls rosted, a Piece of
rost Beef, Tarts, Trifle, Plovers Eggs &c. It was also Mattishall
Gaunt to day, and a great many People were there being a fine
Day.

JUNE *5th*. Nancy recd a Letter from her Brother Sam this Evening which gave her great Spirits, he having lately been intro-
duced to the Queen and presented her a Picture of his Painting
being her Son Prince Frederick. Sam talks of great things, of
being soon knighted. Am very glad that his Lot fell in so for-
tunate a Soil—And his Merit is deserving the same. Sam's News
too great to be true, am afraid.

10th. About 3 o'clock this Afternoon Mr and Mrs Custance

* The swimming bladder of certain fish, in particular sturgeon and
cod, also mentioned by Pepys: 'This day dined ... upon a fin of ling
and some sounds.'

called on us, took us into their Coach and carried us to Mr Micklethwaites where we dined and spent the remaining part of the Afternoon and part of the Evening with Mr and Mrs Micklethwaite, Mrs Branthwaite Senr of Norwich, Miles Branthwaite and Wife, a Miss Howes, and Mr and Mrs Custance—we returned as we went in Mr Custance's Coach between 8 and 9 o'clock. We had a very genteel Dinner, Soals and Lobster Sauce, Spring Chicken boiled and a Tongue, a Piece of rost Beef, Soup, a Fillet of Veal rosted with Morells and Trufles, and Pigeon Pye for the first Course—Sweetbreads, a green Goose and Peas, Apricot Pye, Cheesecakes, Stewed Mushrooms and Trifle. The Ladies and Gentlemen very genteely dressed. Mr Micklethwaite had in his Shoes a Pair of Silver Buckles which cost between 7 and 8 Pounds. Miles Branthwaite had a pair that cost 5 guineas.

17th. Prodigious fine growing Weather indeed. Very busy all the Morning in writing.

30th. Mr Cantrell sent me word this morning early that his Chaise was pre-engaged to Miss Lombe unknown to him— therefore was obliged to send Will to Mattishall to acquaint them of being disappointed and could not send for them—Ben also being gone to Norwich for Fish. The Rotation therefore is to be put of, and only the Priests Families and Du Quesne to dine here to day. To Mr Cary for things from Norwich &c. pd 0.5.6. Sent by Will to Mrs Davy a Couple of nice Spring Chicken, half of a plumb Cake, and Tongue and some Potatoes. Thus far at 2 o'clock—when lo! a Market Cart arrived at my House from Mattishall with Three Ladies in it, Mrs Davy, Miss Betsy Donne and Nancy who all stayed and dined, supped and slept here. Mr and Mrs Priest and Son Richd of Norwich, Mr Du Quesne and Mr Smith dined and spent the Afternoon here. We had for Dinner some fryed Soals—4 boiled Chicken with some Bacon—a Goose rosted—Neck of Mutton boiled and Capers—Peas—and Pudding and Tarts. Mrs Davy brought back the Chicken I sent to her which we had for Supper—with other things. About 8 in the Evening most of the Company left us. Mrs Davy and Miss Betsy Donne slept in Nancy's Room and Nancy in the Garrett over me. Miss Donne is a most agreeable young Lady, full of vivacity, very pretty with an excellent Voice.

JULY 2nd. About 1 o'clock I took a ride to Mattishall and there dined, supped and spent the whole Night at Mr Smith's, with him, Mr and Mrs Thorne, Mr and Miss Pinching, Mrs Davy, Miss Betsy Donne and our Nancy. We had for Dinner at Mr Smith's, boiled Beef, rost and boiled Chicken, part of a fine ham, a Couple of Ducks rosted and Peas — Pudding, Tarts and Cheese-cakes. For Supper a cold Collation, with Lamb-Stakes and Gooseberry Cream and green Peas &c. We were very merry the whole Day and all Night, singing all Night long by Miss Donne. She is an excellent lively girl indeed and about 17 Years Old. We broke up at 4 in the Morning. I immediately sat of for Weston — got home about 5 o'clock — and went to bed directly — Saw the Sun rise coming home. To Mr Smith's Boy — Robin gave 0.1.0. I went to Mr Hewitts in the Afternoon to desire that Miss Donne might sleep at Mr Thornes to Night.

3rd. I got up about 9 o'clock and soon after breakfast I took a ride to Mattishall to see Mr and Mrs Bodham and there dined and spent the Afternoon with them, Betsy Donne and Nancy Woodeforde. I called at Mrs Davy's and Mrs Thornes. Mrs Davy gone this morning for Pulham. My Man Ben came after Nancy about noon in a Market Cart — After Tea I returned to Weston as did Nancy, but she was at home before me: I was very flat and dull on leaving my dear Miss Betsy Donne. Nancy supped and slept again at home. We are both glad that this Week is over. Nancy recd this Week from her Brother Sam from London a neat genteel and pretty Baloon hat. Mr and Mrs Custance are gone to Sir Thomas Beauchamps to spend a few Days with them at Langley Park.

5th. After Dinner I paid Lizzy half a Years Wages due this Day, and then dismissed her from my Service, as she is going on my recommendation to Weston House. I gave her extraordinary o.2.6. I paid her for Wages 1.6.6. In the Evening sent Ben with a Market Cart for my New Maid who lives at Mattishall and she came here about 8 at Night and she supped and slept here. Her Name is Molly Dade about 17 years of age—a very smart Girl and pretty I think. Her Friends bear great Characters of Industry &c.

15th. We were to have had Betsy Davy and Mary Roupe over from Mattishall to have spent this Day with us but Mrs Davy's going to Pulham yesterday on a Love Affair with a Mr Rand who went with her and came back with her, but Matters however could not be settled then. Mr Rand is a Man of very good Fortune, keeps a Carriage and is an Apothecary and has great business—A very sensible Man, a Batchelor about 50 years of Age. And lives at Snettisham near Burnham. To a Man this morning that brought a very pretty kind of a Monkey to shew gave 1.0. He called it the Mongooz from Madagascar.

16th. About 10 o'clock this morning Mr Matthews with a Cart full of young Folks came to my House—viz, Betsy Davy, Hannah Thorne, Mary Roupe and Nunn Davy—they all spent the Day with us, and a pretty Day it was. Nothing but Noise the whole Day long.

17th. Mr Love finished painting my Parlours this Day at Noon. Hylett, Mr Custance's Gardener was this morning turned out of his Place and payed of—being found out by Mr Custance in sending Fruit &c. to Norwich by the Elsing Carrier—Mr Custance went after the Carrier himself this morning and took from him 4 Quarts of very fine Strawberries and some Cucumbers packed up by Hylett for to be sold. Mr Custance in a very great Passion.

19th. Nancy went this morning before 7 o'clock behind my Man Will to Mrs Davy's at Mattishall where she is to spend a few Days with her.

20th. At 4 this Afternoon I mounted my Mare and rode to Mattishall where I drank Tea and stayed till 9 in the Evening at Mrs Davy's with her, Mr and Mrs Bodham, Miss Donne,

Mr Du Quesne and Nancy Woodforde—Mr Smith was to have been there also—but went for London this morning very suddenly and much discomposed. The Cause of it is this, Mrs Davy had a Letter this morning from Mr Rand who is distracted after her, the Contents of which were communicated to Mr Smith, which made him almost frantic, he immediately made Mrs Davy an Offer to marry her after his Mothers Decease, what answer was returned I know not, but he marched from Mattishall directly. Mrs Davy was extremely low and uneasy about it. After one Pool of Quadrille we had a Syllabub and some Rasberries with Cream and Sugar—and Wine. We all broke up about 9 o'clock rather after. At Quadrille this Evening won 0.1.0. To Mrs Davy's Maid gave coming away 0.1.0.

AUGUST *4th.* About 10 o'clock this Night a Clergyman by name Cambell (Vicar of Weasingham in this County and formerly of Oriel Coll. Oxford and afterwards Fellow of Worcester Coll. in the same University) came to my House and he supped and slept here—himself and horse. I remember him at Oriel Coll. but not so intimate as to expect that he would have taken such freedom especially as he never made me a Visit before. He slept however in the Attic Story and I treated him as one that would be too free if treated too kindly. It kept me up till after 12 o'clock.

SEPTEMBER *22nd.* At 2 o'clock took a Walk to Mr Micklethwaite's and there dined, spent the Afternoon, supped and spent the Evening with him, his Wife, his Father and Mother, old Mrs Branthwaite, Captain Micklethwaite and Wife, Mr Jonathan Micklethwaite and my Niece. About 5 o'clock we dined. Before Dinner I publickly baptized their little Boy at home, which I did not much like, but could not tell how to refuse—He was privately named before at Norwich I believe—His Name is Nathaniel. Old Mrs Branthwaite and old Mrs Micklethwaite were the Godmothers—and old Mr Micklethwaite and his Son Captain John Micklethwaite were Godfathers. We had a very genteel Dinner and Supper. Old Mr and Mrs Micklethwaite and his Son the Captain, the strangest kind of People I almost ever saw. Old Mrs Branthwaite almost as strange and vulgar. Nancy was sent for in their Carriage and we returned home in it about 12 at night—very windy, very wet, and very dark; I thank God we got home however safe. I gave the Driver and the Man behind it each 1.0—0.2.0. After Tea and Coffee We got to Whist at which I won 0.1.0. Coming away this Evening Mr Micklethwaite made me a present, for christening his Child, of 1.1.0. Upon the whole spent an odd disagreeable kind of a Day —as did also Nancy—we laughed much after we got home.

OCTOBER *7th*. Jack told me this morning that he is advised to get another Place being too old for a Skip-Jack any longer. He wants to be a Plow Boy to some Farmer to learn the farming Business as he likes that best—I told him that he was very right to try to better himself, and at Lady Day next he is to leave my House for that purpose. He has been a very good Lad ever since he has been here. Widow Greaves here again all Day and Night.

10th. My New Maid (in Betty's Place) Sally Dunnell came here this Evening, which was sooner than we expected her by a Day—but we contrived for her to sleep here &c. tho' my other Maid nor Mrs Greaves were as yet gone. They all slept here to night. I published Bettys Banns for the last time this Aft. at Church—I suppose she will marry very soon. My new Maid seems to be a mighty strapping Wench.

14th. Finding my new Maid (who came as Cook to us) to know nothing of her business, I therefore this Evening gave her notice that she must leave my Service and as soon as possible— I believe her to be a goodnatured Girl but very ignorant.

15th. My new Maid Sally Dunnell left my Service this Morn'. Gave the Maid as she was going away for the Time she had been here at 6d per Day 0.3.0. My poor Maid Molly Dade, not so well to day as I could wish her, having somewhat of a Fever on her. She is one of the best Maids that ever we had and very much liked by us both and would wish to keep her but am very much afraid it will not be in our Power tho' we are both most willing to keep her. She is one of the neatest, most modest, pretty Girls I ever had. She is very young, but tall, only in her 17th year. Ben went early this Morning beyond Dereham to buy me a Cow, now in her full profit, but could not. It was at a Sale of Colonel Dickens's near Dereham. Widow Greaves came to us again this Evening to be with us till we can get another Maid—I sent for her.

19th. I sent my Maid Molly Dade this morning behind Ben to Mattishall, to stay a few Days at home, to see if change of Air would do her Cough good. Her Sister Betty, continues in her Place.

NOVEMBER *2nd.* Soon after breakfast I took my Men with me a coursing. Set out about 11 and stayed till after 4 in the Aft., we brought home a brace of Hares and a Rabbit, both Courses with the Hares very fine indeed. Whilst we were out, a Servant Maid came to offer her Service here, who lately lived at Mr Eatons at Elsing and but a very little time indeed only a Quarter of a Year—Nancy could not recollect her Name or give any direct answer as I was out. By the Account that Nancy gave me, don't think she will do—she being rather high and her late Wages 8 Pounds per Annum—Her Friends live at Foxley a place I by no means approve of—as it has proved that many from that Place have been guilty of many felonious Acts and but very few Years ago. She formerly lived at old Mr Gurdons at Letton and for 9 years—She afterwards lived with his Son— N.B. Old Mr Gurdon's House of Letton about 3 years ago was broke open and robbed of all his old family Plate, but was never discovered. The above Robbery was supposed to have hastened the death of poor old Mr Gurdon a most worthy Man.

3rd. Sent Will this morning to Mr Smiths at Mattishall with a Hare—told him to call on Molly Dade, during the Time that he was gone Molly's Father called here—he gave us a very poor

Account of our worthy Maid poor Molly Dade—that he believed she cannot recover. We were extremely sorry for her. He came after her Stays that were here, the others being too large for her—so much of late has she fallen away. Mr Dade could not stay to dine with us to day. Will on his return also told us that Mr Thorne had given poor Molly over and that he could do no more. Pray God Almighty comfort her—and with patience wait the Almighty's Will—As good a Girl as ever lived.

7th. My Maid Betty Dade (in the room of her poor Sister Molly) went to see Molly this morning—My Man Ben carried her behind him. We sent her a Knuckle of Veal for Broth and a Jar of Black Currant Jamm. Betty and Ben returned about 5 this Evening—she left her sister but very poorly and very weak. I read Prayers and Preached this Aft. at Weston. Mr and Mrs Micklethwaite at Church. Nobody from Weston House at Church to day.

9th. After breakfast I rode down to Lenewade Bridge to attend Dr Bathursts Tythe Audit and there dined and stayed till after 4 o'clock in the Aftr and then returned home—All safe and snugg. I was far from being well however to day. This Evening I had a new Servant Maid come as Cook, Molly Peachman, she is to have 5 Guineas Per Annum, Tea included —Nancy prevailed on me to take her.

DECEMBER *25th.* I read Prayers and administered the H. Sacrament this Morning at Weston Church, being Christmas Day. Mrs Custance at Church and at the Sacrament. Mr Custance not there being ill at home. Js Smith, my Clerk, Richd Buck, Thos Cushing, Thos Carr, Richd Bates, Thos Dicker, and Thos Cary, all dined at my House as usual on Christmas Day, I gave to each of them a Shilling to carry home to their Wives before they went away—in all—o.7.o. I gave them for Dinner a Piece of rost Beef and plumb Puddings—and after dinner half a Pint of strong Beer apiece. N.B. All old Men.

1785

JANUARY *16th*. I was very dull and low this Evening, having no company at all, now Nancy is from home. And not used of late to be much by myself—better soon.

22nd. About 1 o'clock Mrs Davy with Nancy in Mr Thorne's Chaise came here and Mr Thornes Man with them. Mrs Davy stayed here about half an Hour, would not dine here, and then set of back for Mattishall, leaving Nancy with me—Very glad she is come home. Nancy dined, supped and slept at home. Paid Nancy this Evening for some Patty Pans &c. 0.2.6 and which she had paid for me to Mrs Davy. Mrs Davy did not by any means behave as she used to do towards me—was scarce civil to me.

23rd. Very fair and fine to day, quite a Summers Day. I read Prayers and Preached this Aft. at Weston. Mr Dade of Mattishall came over here this morning to let his Daughter know, that her poor Sister Molly died last Night—poor Soul! I doubt not of her happiness in a future Life—She was long expected to die. Pray God bless her Spirit and comfort her Relations. Mr Dade did not stay long here this morning. Mr and Mrs Custance both at Church this Aft. And they desired that we would dine with them on Friday next—and that they would send their Coach.

FEBRUARY *28th*. The Frost severer than ever in the night as it even froze the Chamber Pots under the Beds. Wind very rough and tho' the Sun shone all the morning very bright yet it continued freezing every minute. Most bitter cold to day indeed, and likely to continue.

MARCH *14th*. Poor Neighbour Clarke's Wife and 4 Children are taken down in the small Pox—Their Neighbour Gooch, his Wife, nor any of a large Family of children belonging to them, have none of them had the Small Pox.

15th. Sent poor Clarkes Family a large Bushel Basket of Apples, to make Apple Dumplins for poor Souls. Sent another basket of same to Goochs Family. To Nortons and Downings Family sent each a Basket of Apples.

16th. Dr Thorne called here this morning—He has been inoculating John Gooch and whole Family. Nancy complained very much this morning of the Wind in her Stomach—I desired her to drink some strong Beer after Dinner instead of Wine, which she did and was better after it—She was much oppressed by Hysteric wind before—She also by my desire had some Milk for breakfast and is to continue it. Neighbour Clarkes Wife and Family as well as can be expected. It is a good kind of small Pox they have.

APRIL *12th.* I buried poor old Widow Pully this Aft. aged— 80 yrs. My Servant Willm Coleman was out all the Evening till just 11 o'clock—came home in Liquor behaved very rudely and most impudently to me indeed, I told him that I was determined never more to bear with such Behaviour, and that he shd certainly go to Morr'. Mr Peachman called here about 7 o'clock and paid me for 4 acres of Turnips at 30s per Acre—6.0.0. He did not stay long with us—drank some fresh ——.

15th. Will came to me to day to desire I would give him a Character if wanted, which I promised him. He seems to be rather cast down to day and at no work.

16th. Will Coleman I hear went of early this morning for Norwich and in high Spirits. I had 2 yong Men offer themselves but neither wd do as they never waited at Table in their lives.

18th. Saw the first Swallow this Season this Morning. Will Coleman called here this morning very early to take his Leave of his late Partners—He was gone before I was below Stairs—He has got a Place at Catton—at 10s 6d per Week and no Board or 1s od Per Day and board. Mr Du Quesne came here about 2 o'clock in his Chaise and he dined and spent the Afternoon here and abt 4 o'clock we went with him in his Chaise to Norwich got to Kings Head about 6 o'clock—there met Mr and Mrs Custance, just going to the Play, we stayed after that and drank a Dish of Tea—and then we took a Coach and drove to the Theatre. Got there just as the first Act was over—We sat in the Mayors Box—The Mayor (Partridge) was there also. Lady Bacon and Mrs Custance in the next Box to us. Sir William Jernegan came and spoke to us. The Play was the Duenna—and Farce the Divorce. Both bespoke by Sir Will and Lady Jernegan. After we came from the Theatre which was abt 10 we all supped at the Kings Head and there slept. Mr and Mrs Custance returned to Weston after the Play. The Kings Head was quite full of Company, Mr Du Quesne and myself were obliged to sleep in one Room and down the Yard—Nancy just by us in a single Room and a very good one. We did not go to bed till after 12 o'clock.

25th. Will Coleman came to us this morning as we were walking in the Garden, and said that he could not be easy after his late bad behaviour, till he had spoke to me and asked pardon for it—I then told him that I would employ him as a Gardener and give him a shilling a Day and his Board for 2 Days in a Week—but that he must get a Lodging from my House, and if he can somewhere in the Parish. He appeared then quite happy and went directly about his work in the Garden.

To Mr Cary for things from Norwich &c. pd 0.7.6½.

To Nancy for Butter at 10d pd 0.2.6.

26th. Bretingham Scurl a new Servant came here whilst we were at Dinner, I ordered him into Parlour directly and made him wait at Table and he did pretty well. He appears to be a good-natured willing young Fellow. Will Coleman who is gardening for me looked rather shy upon Scurl at first—We call him Briton.

JUNE *1st.* Mr and Mrs Custance called here about 11 o'clock and took Nancy with them in their Coach to go to Norwich. They would have taken me up also but I preferred going on horseback, about 12 therefore, I went to Norwich and took Briton with me, and we got there about 2 o'clock—but was wet getting thither. About 3 o'clock this Afternoon a violent Tempest arose at Norwich in the North East, very loud Thunder with strong white Lightening with heavy Rain—which lasted about an Hour—immediately after which Mr Deckers Balloon with Decker himself in a boat annexed to it, ascended from Quantrells Gardens and very majestically. It was out of Sight in about 10 Minutes, but appeared again on his Descent. It went in a South East Direction—I saw it from Brecondale Hill, and it went almost over my Head. Mr and Mrs Custance and Nancy were at Mackay's Gardens. They saw it also very plain from thence. A vast Concourse of People were assembled to see it. It was rather unfortunate that the Weather proved so unfavourable—but added greatly to the Courage of Decker that he ascended so very soon after the Tempest. It also bursted twice before he ascended in it, upon the filling it, if it had not, a Girl about 14 was to have went with him in it—but after so much Gas had been let out—it would not carry both. Mr Du

Quesne was there and in the Gardens. Mrs Thorne, Mrs Davy and Captain Thorne overtook me going to Norwich just by the Turnpike — I parted with them just by St Giles's Gate and saw nothing more of them afterwards — They were wet as well as we on the Road — I put up my Horses at the Woolpack. The Tempest happened as I was on Brecondale Hill. I went directly to a red House adjoining, and was very kindly asked to walk in to a Parlour, which I accepted — Whilst I was there I found that I was got into Mrs Thornes Brothers, Mr Thos Agges. I saw a very pretty Quaker there, a young Woman. After I returned from seeing the Balloon — I went to a Perfumers Shop in the Haymarket by name Amyot and bought some Essence of Jessamine, Lavender, Bergamot for all which I paid o.2.3. I then called at Bakers and bought a Habit Brush for Nancy with a looking Glass at the back of it pd o.2.o. I then called at Priests, there saw Du Quesne, but neither eat or drank there — For some

Amber Grease, Oil of Time, Lavender, and Spermaceti pd 0.2.3. After that I mounted my Mare and sat of for Weston—got home about 8 o'clock this Evening and then dined, supped and slept in the old House—Nancy was at home about an Hour before me—very much tired. We were very wet coming home this Evening. At Norwich for 1 half Pint of Porter and gave the Maid 0.3. Mr and Mrs Custance, Nancy, myself, and in short all that went to see the Baloon were highly pleased. We were all sorry that the Weather was so bad for it. Decker however has gained great Credit by it.

8th. I dreamt very much last Night of Mr Smith and Mrs Davy and the connection entirely broke of—I told Nancy of it at breakfast—Just as we were going to sit down to dinner, Mr Matthews brought a Note to my Niece from Mrs Davy—to let her know that she was in great distress, having recd a Letter this morn' from Mr Smith to break of any farther connection with her—his Friends being so very averse to the Match And that he was going to leave England directly. Mrs Davy desires my Niece to come over to her directly—but she could not go.

10th. Nancy made part of a breakfast at home and at 8 o'clock this morning she sat of in Mr Bucks Market Cart and Ben with her for Mattishal Burgh to Mrs Davys where she is to spend a few Days with her, as she is very low from what has lately happened by Mr Smith. Sent a very long Letter to my Sister Pounsett by Cary. Sent also one for Nancy to her Brother Sam.

JULY *13th*. Mr Thomas of Dereham called on us this Morn' but did not stay. Sent Ben very early to Norwich this morning after Fish, he returned about 11 o'clock and brought with him eight pair of small Soals with two Couple of Chicken. Mr and Mrs Thorne and their Daughter Hannah and a Miss Pinching, and Mr Thorne's Nephew Mr Walker an Attorney about 18 Years of Age, Captain Thorne, Mrs Davy, Betsy and Nunn, came to our House about 3 o'clock and they all dined, supped and spent the Evening, and stayed till 3 o'clock in the Morn with us. We had for Dinner some Pyke and fryed Soals a nice Piece of boiled Beef, Ham and a Couple of Fowls, Peas and Beans, a green Goose rosted, Gooseberry Pies, Currant Tarts, the Charter, hung Beef scraped &c. For Supper fryed Soals, a Couple of Chicken rosted, cold Ham &c. &c. Artichokes, Tarts &c. Fruit after Dinner and Supper—Strawberries, Cherries, Almonds—Raisins &c. &c. Miss Pinchings Brother came to us from Norwich about 10 o'clock this Evening just as we were going to sit down to Supper and he supped &c. with us. Just as the Ladies and Gentlemen were going to drink Coffee and Tea in the Garden, I was sent for to go to Weston House to name a Child of Mrs Custances who was brought to bed this Afternoon about 2 o'clock—I therefore walked up directly to Weston House and named the Child by name Mary Anne, the smallest Infant I think I ever had in my Arms—The Child came 10 Weeks before its Time, therefore afraid that it would not live. I soon returned to my Company but lost my Coffee and Tea. After Tea the Ladies and Gentlemen got to dancing and danced and sang till Supper Time—About 12 o'clock this night we all got to dancing again—We had many droll Songs from Mr Walker who sings with great good humour and very well—He is a mighty lively and agreeable young man indeed—They all stayed with us till 3 o'clock in the Morning and then they all returned to Mattishall but Betsy Davy who was left here to spend a few Days with us. Upon the whole we spent a very agreeable, merry and cheerful Day, and every thing conducted and done extremely well by our Servants.

SEPTEMBER *15th*. Mrs Davy, Betsy, and my Niece, after Tea this Afternoon about 6 o'clock went from my House in Clark Hewitts Cart (which was left here Yesterday) to Mattishall Parsonage where Mrs Davy boards with a Mr and Mrs Matthews (which Mr Matthews is an Exciseman and came from Lambourne in Berkshire) whose House Mrs Davy and Betsy leaves at Michaelmas next, on Account of the Affair being broke of between her and Mr Smith, therefore Nancy went with them to spend a few Days there before they left Mattishall. They carried with them in the Cart some cold boiled Beef, stuffed with Parsley, some Turnips, Radishes, Colliflowers and 4 Cucumbers. My Boy Jack Secker drove them with my Horse in it.

OCTOBER *1st.* Mrs Davy and Betsy with Mr Ashill, in a Dereham Post-Chaise called here this morning about 8 o'clock, breakfasted here and then took Nancy with them to a Place called Thurning about 10 Miles from Weston NEN to look at a boarding Place for Mrs Davy and Betsy — I did not like that Nancy should crowd into the Chaise with them and for no Purpose whatever — It made me rather cross. They all returned to dinner about 3 o'clock to my House. I gave them for Dinner, a fine Rump of Beef boiled and Dumplins, a rost Fowl and a rost Duck and a large Damson Pye — Mrs Davy, Betsy and Mr Ashull sat of for Mattishall about an hour after Dinner. Mrs Davy and Betsy have agreed to board at Thurning at a Mr Elwin's, very good, creditable People and genteel. They go there at the half Quarter after Michaelmas. Mrs Davy seemed displeased and uneasy all the Day. Nancy had a Letter from her Brother Sam in London — who tells her that he is going to Italy to finish his Studies in Painting — Mr Richd Hoare* made him the Offer and with it £100 per Annum during the Time that he is abroad.

10th. In the Afternoon my Maid Molly Peachman left my Service, being to be married to Morrow Morning. I paid her for 11 Months Wages at 5.5.0 per Ann. 4.16.6. She paid me out of it, what I lent her being 1.1.0.

11th. I went to Church this morning and Married my late Maid, Molly Peachman to one Js Shipley by Banns. Received for marrying them only 0.2.6 having had half a Crown before

* Richard Hoare (1758–1838), antiquary and historian of Wiltshire, succeeded his banker father to the baronetcy in 1787.

on publishing the Banns. Hambleton Custance, with his two Brothers George and William, with their Nurse Maid were present at the Marriage being a very fine morning.

NOVEMBER *8th.* Went down to Lenewade Bridge this morning to attend at Dr Bathursts Tithe Audit, dined there and stayed till near 6 o'clock this Evening — then returned home safe (thank God) with the Cash. All but one Person attended which was one Neale. Had not been home much more than an Hour before Nancy's Brother Willm came on horseback to our House from the West — he supped and slept here. He came thro' London, called on his Brother Saml who will also come to Weston in a few Days.

10th. About 11 o'clock this morning Mr Press Custance called on me in a Post Chaise, and I went with him in it to Weston Church, clerically dressed, and there buried in the Church Mr Custances youngest Daughter Mary Anne.

19th. As I was dressing for Dinner, Nancy's Brother Saml from London came here in a Chaise, and he dined supped and slept here with his Brother — He sat out of London, last Night at 8 o'clock, travelled all night in the Mail Coach — came here about 3 this Afternoon.

20th. Nancy and her two Brothers, Willm and Saml, breakfasted, dined, supped and slept again at Weston Parsonage. I read Prayers and Preached this morning at Weston. Mr Micklethwaite at Church — none from Weston House. It gave me much pleasure to see Nancy and her two Brothers appear so happy here — and so in each other.

DECEMBER *3rd.* My Nephew Samuel drew my Picture to day in Crayon. He likewise drew his own Picture, his Brother's and Sister's, Mrs Davy's and Betsy's.

4th. I made my Nephew Saml a present this Evening of 5.5.0.
18th. The Captain* breakfasted, dined, &c. here again. I
* JW is making ironical reference to his nephew Bill.

read Prayers and Preached this Morning at Weston. Mr Custance was at Church this morning. Whilst I was at Dinner to Day, a Letter was brought me by my Butchers Lad, from the Bishop of Norwich to request me to preach the 19 of March next at St Clements at Norwich, for the Benefit of the Charity Schools there. I did not relish it.

20th. I breakfasted at the Kings Head and afterwards walked about the City and paying Bills. About 11 o'clock this morning I walked down to the Bishops Palace and stayed there about an Hour with the Bishop—and I acquainted him that I had preached a Sermon at St Stephens in the Year 1780 for the benefit of the Charity Schools. His Lordship said he did not know that I had and therefore told me that he would appoint another Clergyman to preach instead of me. My Servant, Briton, came to Town about 11 o'clock and about half past 1 I sat of for Weston and got home to Dinner at half past 3 o'clock, and there supped and slept at the Parsonage House.

21st. This being St Thomas's Day, had a great many poor People of the Parish to visit me, I gave to each of them that came, sixpence. Gave in all to day to the poor 1.5.6. About 12 o'clock Mr Ashill of Norwich called here in his return home from Thurning, after visiting Mrs Davy and Daughter there— The former sending for him on being taken exceeding ill about the late disagreeable Affair with Mr Smith. Mr Ashill says that it has almost made her distracted, she is very unhappy. Mr Ashill eat some cold Mutton &c. and then at 2 o'clock sat of for Norwich again.

29th. Had a very long Letter from Mr Smith this morning concerning Mrs Davy and himself, wherein he lays the whole blame on her in a late affair accusing her for her too great familiarity to one Clarkson.

To my Butchers Man, Billy Stonton, Xmas Gift 0.1.0.
To Neighbour Howes's Wife for 5 Chicken pd 0.2.6.

1786

JANUARY *7th.* I walked with my Nephew before Dinner up to our Church, but had great difficulty to get thither for the Snow, in the Lane by Billy Bidwells the Snow was full 4 foot deep in many Places—we were pretty near half an Hour getting there. In the Lane leading from Church Street to Car-Cross was quite full of Snow and up almost to the top of the Hedge. We returned home rather a better way by Js Smiths and down Blacker-Field. I sent Ben to Norwich this Morning as Cary did not go, but gave him orders not to run risk or danger if he met with difficulties from the Snow. He returned home safe about 4 o'clock this Aft.

FEBRUARY *12th.* I sent Nancy and Betsy Davy Yesterday Morn' to Coventry and have not as yet spoke to either of them.

13th. Nancy and Betsy not sent for from Coventry as yet.

14th. To 53 Valentines to Day gave 0.4.5. Nancy and Betsy Davy called home this Aft. from Coventry. The Captain after breakfast took a ride to Thurning to see Mrs Davy and there stayed and dined and spent the Afternoon, but returned home to Supper.

18th. Mr Smith of Mattishall sent me a note this Morn' to desire me to meet him in Weston Churchyard privately, which I accordingly did, and there I stayed with him near an Hour, talking over the Affair between him and Mrs Davy—by which he made out that Mrs Davy was as artful and bad as any Woman could be. It surprised me astonishingly indeed. After breakfast the Captain took a ride to Mattishall and did not return till 12 at Night, just as I was going to bed after sitting up for him till that Time—I cannot say but I was rather displeased at it especially being Saturday Night.

MARCH *4th*. My Maid Betty Dades Father came here, just as we were going to dinner, and his too frequent Visits here of late being far from agreeable to me, I went out into the Kitchen and told him that he had better have his Daughter home, as I did not like for him to make too free here, and I also gave Betty notice to leave my House at Lady Day next, on his Account. Rec'd an oil Picture from my Nephew Saml from London, this Evening from Norwich. The Picture was drawn from Nature from some Forest near London — a small Picture.

11th. Betsy Davy breakfasted, dined, &c. &c. here again. The Captain breakfasted, dined &c. &c. here again. Mr Custance called on us this Morning, stayed with us about half an Hour, and desired our Company at dinner on Wednesday next with our Company. This Evening about 6 o'clock Mrs Davy came here in a Post Chaise from Norwich in her way from Pulham having been there and in Suffolk on Account of the Death of a Brother of hers at Woodbridge. Mrs Davy drank Tea this Aft. supped and slept here.

12th. I read Prayers and Preached this Morn' at Weston Church. Mr and Mrs Custance at Church. Neither any from my House at Church but self and 2 Servants. Mrs Davy took on a good deal to day, and soon after Tea this Evening she took it in her head to go to bed. I had been persuading her not to go to Mattishall.

17th. Mrs Davy breakfasted, dined, supped and slept here again. Betsy Davy breakfasted here and about 12 she took leave of Weston Parsonage and went on horseback to Mr Thorne's at Mattishall, and there she dined, supped and slept — poor dear soul — She was much hurried by her Mother on going away. Am much afraid it will be a very long time before she will be at Weston Parsonage again. The Captain took a ride to Mattishall with Betsy Davy and he dined with her there, and returned home to Supper. Dr Thorne being from home at the assises at Thetford which begins this day.

18th. Mrs Davy breakfasted and spent part of the Morn' with us. About 1 o'clock Mrs Thorne of Mattishall came after Mrs Davy to spend a few Days with her and they returned to Mattishall about 2 o'clock. Our Parting was rather cool than otherwise.

28th. Nancy breakfasted and spent the Morning with us till after 1 o'clock, then Mrs Bodham of Mattishall came after her in her Chaise, and she returned with her to Mattishall before Dinner and is to stay some Days with Mr and Mrs Bodham at South-Green. Nancy's Brother breakfasted, dined &c, here again. I married this morning Harry Andrews, Widower and Mary Horner, Widow—recd for it 0.5.0.

APRIL *15th.* The Captain busy in making a small Sloop out of a Piece of Deal Balk or large Beam, which we got at Mr Frosts when at Norwich and had it brought home in my Cart this Day Sennight from Norwich.

19th. Mr Walker from Mattishall came here about 12 o'clock and he dined and spent the Afternoon with us—a very droll Young Man he is and an excellent Singer. About 1 o'clock who should come to my House but Mr Jeanes the New Rector of the Witchinghams, I mounted my Mare immediately and went with him to great Witchingham and inducted him into the Church &c. He then returned with me and dined and spent the Afternoon with us—In the Evening he returned to Norwich to his Wife and another Lady who are at Lodgings in the City—Jeanes was only married last Thursday in London, she is very young it is said. We had some Fish and a Surloin of Beef rosted &c. Betsy Davy returned with Mr Walker in the Evening to Mattishall to Mr Thornes. Nancy had a Letter from her Sister this Evening.

JUNE *10th.* My Ear pained me very much all the Morning. Mr Custance sent us a nice Melon this Morning. The Captain very busy this Morning with his Ship. Sent Briton early this Morning to Norwich after Fish &c. he returned before 12 o'clock with Maccarel &c. He went in the little Cart and had the Horse

Punch. Mr and Mrs Bodham with Miss Anne Donne from Norwich, Mr Du Quesne, Mr Smith, and Mr Lane of Hingham who is to officiate for me at Weston during my Absence dined and spent the Afternoon with us. Just before Dinner the Captain launched his new Ship, before the Ladies and Gentlemen present but to his great Chagrin and the Company's disappointment it upset and went down to the starboard side almost immediately and took in Water and could not be righted. She was far too much overmasted. We were all exceedingly sorry on the Captains Account. We had for Dinner some Maccarel, a fore Quarter of Lamb, 3 boiled Chicken and a Pigs Face, Pigeons and Asparagus, Lobster, Apricot and Gooseberry Tarts and Custards. After Dinner by way of Desert—A Melon, Oranges, Almonds and Raisins. The Company left us about 8 o'clock this Evening.

12th. My Ear pained me much again this morning.

To Mr Cary for things from Norwich &c. pd 0.8.6.

To my Man Briton for things from Norwich &c. pd 0.14.8.

Took a good large Dose of Rhubarb last Night, as did also Nancy, made her get up at 4 o'clock this Morn'. The Captain got up early this morning and sat of for Mattishall to my Glaziers, Hubbard, after some Lead to put on at the bottom of the Ship by way of a false Keel and returned home with it 10 o'clock, with a long piece which weighed 25 Pound—After he had breakfasted he put on the Lead to the bottom of the Vessel and then she sailed as well as our most sanguine wishes could desire.

18th. I read Prayers and Preached this Morning at Weston Ch. Mrs Custance with her eldest Son at Church and my Niece. Mr Custance at home on the late Death of Mr Morris, a Relation. Nancys Brother not at Church also, not being dressed in time. Mrs Custance with her three Sons drank Tea with us this Afternoon—Mr Custance not at home—Mrs Custance &c. came to see the Ship on the Water. She admired it very much indeed.

23rd. Nancy and Brother breakfasted, and dined here again.

After dinner we all went to Norwich in a Post Chaise which we had from thence, and carried our Baggage with us, Briton went also in my Cart with a Trunk for the Captain—We all got to Norwich about 6 o'clock and drank Tea at the Kings Head, and stayed there till half past 6 o'clock and then went to the Angel Inn and at 7 o'clock this Evening, myself, Nancy and Brother went in the heavy Coach for London with three strange Women in it also. Paid at the Kings Head at Norwich for Chaise from Weston, Tea &c. about 0.15.0.

For 3 Peoples Fare to London I pd 4.10.0.

For extra Luggage—12 St. I pd 0.15.0.

It was very hot this Evening, especially with a Coach full.

24th. We all got to London (thank God) safe and well by 3 o'clock this Afternoon—to the Swan and 2 Necks in Lad Lane where we had some Rum and Water. To the last Coachman gave 0.3.0. After staying some little Time in Lad Lane we had a Coach and went with our Luggage to our old Inn the Bell Savage at Ludgate Hill where we supped and slept—and kept by the same People, Burton and his Wife. Nancy and her Brother walked out in the Evening by themselves, giving me the Slip, and did not return till Supper time, at which I was much displeased and gave it to them smartly, and to make it still worse soon as Supper was removed and having ordered a Bottle of Wine, they left me without drinking a drop and went to bed leaving me by myself—I sat up by myself very uneasy till about 12 and then I went.

25th. We breakfasted, supped and slept again at the Bell Savage. Very much pestered and bit by the Buggs in the Night. After dressing ourselves, after breakfast we walked down to Charing Cross, and there took a Coach and went to Kensington Gardens and there we walked about till near 3 in the Afternoon —and then we walked back to the 13 Cantons near Charing Cross where we dined on Beef a la mode and which was very good.

26th. We breakfasted, supped and slept again at the Bell

Savage. I was bit so terribly with Buggs again this Night that I got up at 4 o'clock this Morning and took a long Walk by myself about the City till breakfast time. After breakfast we walked to Osborn Place, Spital Fields to deliver a Letter for Mrs Bodham to Miss Eliz. Donne at that Place, but she was from home, after leaving the Letter we immediately returned back—We went thro' a most black-guard Place going to the above House. We took Coach part of the way coming back and went to the 13 Cantons again at Charing Cross where we dined again on beef a la mode pd there 0.2.0. For the Coach hire thither and back pd 0.3.0. In the Evening we took Coach and went to the Circus in St Georges Fields and there saw wonderful Feats of Horsemanship &c. performed by Hughes and his Children.

For Coach hire thither pd 0.1.0.

For 3 Pit Tickets at the Circus I pd 0.9.0.

For Oranges &c. to day pd 0.1.0.

For a little red Book of Prints pd this Evening 0.12.0.

I saw a vast number of strange Prints at the Shop. We were obliged to walk back this Evening from the Circus as we could get no Coach.

28th. We breakfasted again at the Bell Savage. I did not pull of my Cloaths last Night again but did as the Night before, and slept tolerably well. After breakfast George Pace called on us and then went out with the Captain—Nancy walked with me to one Smiths in Surry Street, Strand, a Barber and there had her Hair full dressed—Smith was Sam Woodfordes Hair Dresser—I was shaved and had my Wig dressed there. I gave him for shaving and dressing 0.1.6. After that, the Captain and George Pace joined us and we walked about Town, shopping &c. till 3 this Aft. and then went to the 13 Cantons again and there dined again on Beef a la mode, I pd for all 0.2.6. The Captain and George Pace then left us and Nancy and myself walked back to our Inn, packed up all our things and were ready for our Journey by 6 o'clock. I paid at the Bell Savage, our Bill 3.14.0. To Servants at the Inn gave 0.10.6. At a Qtr before 7 this Evening

Nancy and self got into the Bath Coach, and were just setting out, after some time waiting for Bill, when he luckily arrived, but it was enough to make one very mad, he was at last obliged to leave some things behind him. We had four of us in the Coach and Guard on top. It carries but 4 inside, and is called the Baloon Coach on Account of its travelling so fast, making it a point to be before the Mail Coach. We trimmed it of indeed, tho' only a Pr of Horses.

30th. We breakfasted and spent all the Morning at Bath, and about Noon we got into a Post Chaise and set forth with our Luggage for Shepton Mallet about 19 Miles from Bath, got there about 5 o'clock, had some Rum and Water at the George Inn, took a fresh Chaise and sat of for Cole to Pounsetts—thro' Ansford. At the Castle Inn at Bath for Chaise to Shepton, our own eating, Lodging &c.—paid and gave there 2.7.4½. For some Fish, Soals and a Crab to carry to Cole pd 0.3.2. To the Bath Driver and for Rum and Water at Shepton pd 0.3.0. We saw my Nephew Js White at Shepton Mallett. When we got to Ansford Turnpike Gate we dropt the Captain and his Trunk &c. there—who went to his Fathers. Nancy and self went on to Cole, driving pretty fast thro' Ansford, calling no where—and thank God got to Cole to my Sister Pounsetts about 8 o'clock this Evening and found both my Sister and Mr Pounsett and Daughter brave. For the Shepton Chaise and Driver—pd and gave 0.10.6. To Turnpikes to day pd about 0.2.0. We supped and slept at Mr Pounsetts, very little fatigued.

JULY *1st.* My Brother John called on us this Afternoon, he looks but poorly—I wish to God he would take more care of health.

15th. After breakfast I walked out a fishing, had not put my Line in Water more than five Minutes before I caught a fine Trout of one Pound and a Quarter with a Grasshopper. It measured in length 14 Inches and in the highest Season. Mrs Pounsett Senr dined and spent the Aft. with us. After Tea this Aft. walked out again with my Rod and Line up the Bruton

River and there caught another fine Trout which weighed 1 Pound and $\frac{1}{4}$ and measured $14\frac{1}{2}$ inches. Mr Sam Pounsett supped and spent the Evening with us.

AUGUST *10th*. Nancy and self very busy this morning in making the Charter having some Company to dine with us—But unfortunately the Cellar Door being left open whilst it was put in there to cool, one of the Greyhounds (by name Jigg) got in and eat the whole, with a Cold Tongue &c. Sister Pounsett and Nancy mortally vexed at it.

SEPTEMBER *21st*. Nancy, Sister Pounsett and self went to Ansford this Morn' on foot with Nancy's Brother Willm who came over to breakfast and we all dined at Castle Cary at R. Clarkes with her, my Brother John and Wife and Juliana Woodforde and her Father—We had for Dinner, a Neck of Mutton boiled and Capers and a rost Shoulder of Pork alias mock Goose and a nice plumb Pudding. Js Clarke spent part of the Afternoon with us. My Brother John indifferent to day being merry last Night and very near being killed last Night going home from Ansford Inn to his own House on horseback and falling of—His face is cut but little however.

OCTOBER *4th*. After taking Leave of our Cole Friends, Nancy and self set forth in a Chaise from Bruton for Weston. We called at Wincaunton to see Miss Tucker, but she was gone. From Wincaunton we went on to Meer and there changed Chaises and went on to Hindon—there we were obliged to bait the Horses as we could get no Chaise and then went on in the same Chaise for Sarum. N.B. At the same Inn at Hindon was Mr Pitt the prime Minister, in the same Dilemma as we were all the Horses being engaged—He was going to Burton Pynsent.* We got to Salisbury to the White Hart about 6 in the Evening and there we supped and slept, a good Inn, kept by one Weeks —The Inn almost full being the Salisbury Musick Meeting this Week.

5th. We breakfasted, dined, supped and slept again in Sarum. We walked about Salisbury a great deal to day, saw the Bishops Garden—and the Cathedral—and also the Company returning from another Church after the grand Musick. All the Ladies highly dressed.

To the Girl that shewed us the Cathedral gave 0.1.0.

For a pair of Scissars and a Penknife to day pd 0.5.0.

For 2 Places in the London Coach for to Morrow Morn early —paid half price on taking the same 0.18.0.

---

* At the age of twenty-seven, in the third of his seventeen years of unbroken premiership, William Pitt the younger was on his way to Burton Pynsent, a Somerset estate left to his father Lord Chatham (together with a munificent £3,000 a year) by Sir William Pynsent Bt. This spectacular benefactor had never met Chatham, but admired him greatly.

Paid our Bill this Evening—which with Servts came 1.15.0. Nancy also bought a neat pr of Scissars for 0.4.6.

London

8th. We breakfasted, dined supped and slept again at the Angel. A Miss Stevenson, No. 33 Greek-Street-Soho, Nancy's London Millener breakfasted with us this Morning. I went by myself and saw the Guard relieved again this Morning at St James's Palace. Miss Pope drank Tea with us in the Afternoon at the Angel—and after Tea we took Coach and went to Magdalen Chapel in St Georges Fields being Sunday and heard Prayers read and a Sermon. Very excellent singing at Magdalen Chapel. The Women had a thin green Curtain before them all the Time, one of them played the Organ. Dr Milne preached from these Words 'And Nathan said unto David thou art the Man.' Another Clergyman read Prayers—We had a first Seat. Gave towards the Charity at going in 0.3.0. We kept the Hackney Coach all the time in waiting for us, and after Divine Service we returned in it to the Angel, and Miss Pope supped and spent the Evening with us.

11th. After travelling all Night (thank God safe and well) We got to Newmarket to breakfast, and there stayed half an Hour —paid for our breakfasts 0.2.0. To the Coachman and Guard gave 0.3.0. Whilst we were at Newmarket and changing Coaches and Luggage, found that a small red Trunk of my Nieces was left behind in London, in which were all her principal Matters—It vexed her at first very much—but on my assuring her that I saw it safely lodged in the Warehouse, she was more composed. I would not pay the remaining part of our fare or for our Luggage till the Trunk was forthcoming.

12th. We breakfasted, dined and slept again at the Kings Head. Mr Priest called on us this Morning at the Kings Head. We drank Tea, supped and spent the Evening at Mr Priests, with him, his Wife and their Son John. Mr Barker and his Wife (a very pretty and agreeable Woman) drank Tea with us this

Afternoon at Mr Priests. After Tea we played a Pool at Quadrille won 0.2.6. We got back to our Inn soon after 10 this Evening. Made all the enquiry I could and sent the same to London. Nancy but indifferent and thinking too much on her Trunk, as no Trunk was brought by either of the Mail Coaches.

13th. We breakfasted at the Kings Head at Norwich and about 12 set off for Weston Parsonage in a Post-Chaise of Ravens at the Kings Head and (I thank God) about 2 o'clock we got safe and tolerably well to the old Parsonage House at Weston, found all my Servants tolerably well and things tidily. To the Norwich Driver besides a Dinner gave 0.1.6. We dined, supped and slept at our old House again. My Niece seemed something better on being at home.

NOVEMBER *3rd.* To John Pegg ½ Years Land Tax, ditto Servants Tax—ditto House Tax—ditto Window Tax—ditto Horse Tax in all paid him 11.0.0.* Sent Mr and Mrs Jeanes this Morning a large Sack of Apples (Beefans) a Couple of Pigeons and a very fine fat Duck ready for the Spit—to them at their Parsonage at Witchingham, they being very lately got in there with almost every inconvenience, they were highly pleased with the above. Had my brewing Copper new set by Mr Hardy.

22nd. Nancy very well when she came down Stairs this Morning, but very soon after taken very ill in an Ague, vomited very much, was laid on the bed most of the Morn', could not get up to dinner—but rather better about 5 o'clock this Afternoon and came down Stairs and was much better after Tea. I buried this Afternoon about 4 o'clock, John Plummer an Infant aged only 5 Weeks. I knew nothing of burying the above Infant till 3 o'clock this Afternoon, then on hearing the Church Bell, I sent to Church to enquire the reason, and word was brought me, that there was a Child then at the Church Gate for Interment—It being my

* To his shock JW's taxes had risen to twenty per cent since the drastic increases imposed by Pitt (for the American War) in 1784 and 1785.

Dinner Time, I went as soon as ever I had finished my Dinner—
Some Mistake of my old Clerk or the Father of the Child—in not
acquainting me.

DECEMBER *10th*. I read Prayers and Preached this Afternoon
at Weston C, Mr and Mrs Custance at Church and a large
Congregation besides at Church being fine, cheerful Weather.
Nancy had two Letters from Mrs Davy this Afternoon done up
in a parcel, and with the same a little Lump of something, but
what, I know not—as Nancy never mentioned a word of what
it was, nor of a single word in either of the Letters—I care not
for it, but shall take care to be as private myself in matters.

19th. Henry Baker, my Butcher, called here this Morning by
my desire, and I paid him a Bill for Meat for the last Year, the
sum of 33.2.6 for which I took a stamp Receipt in full. Mr
Custance made us a morning Visit on foot and stayed with us a
full Hour—during his being with us, Mr and Mrs Jeanes came
to our House and they dined, supped and slept here by appointment. Mrs Jeanes does not look by far so well as she did. Has
been much hurried by change of Servants &c. We gave them
for Dinner some Soup, a boiled Neck of Pork, a fine rost Turkey,
Apple Pye and Puffs. After Coffee and Tea we got to Cribbage
lost 0.1.0. We did not get to bed to Night till 12 o'clock. Mr and
Mrs Jeanes slept in Nancys Room and Nancy slept over my Bed
Chamber. Mr Jeanes's Servant Lad George England about 15
Years of Age dined supped and slept here. Mr Jeanes's one
Horse Chaise was put into my Barn. Two of Mr Jeanes's Horses
also were with my Horses all Night. Mr Jeanes's Servant Lad
G. England seems fonder of Kitchen Fire than any Work.

29th. Had another Tub of Gin and another of the best Coniac
Brandy brought me this Evening abt 9. We heard a thump at
the front Door about that time, but did not know what it was,
till I went out and found the 2 Tubs—but nobody there.

31st. We breakfasted, dined &c. &c. again at home. I read
Prayers and Preached this Morn' at Weston C. Neither Mr or

Mrs Custance at Church this Morn'. They sent us a wild Duck this Morning. This being the last Day of the Year, we sat up this Night till after 12 o'clock—then drank Health and happy New Year to all our Somersett Friends &c. and then went for Bedfordshire alias to bed.

1787

JANUARY *18th*. Nancy very indifferent indeed all day—worse. Sent Briton to Reepham on foot this Morning with my Watch to be mended, the main Spring being broke, owing to my putting it forward by the Key. Briton did not return till 4 this Afternoon and then very wet and dirty, owing to the very sudden Thaw. It was quite a hard Frost when he set out, and I thought it more safe for him on foot than horseback but poor Fellow he had a terrible bad walk back being both very dirty and very wet. I gave him a glass of Gin on his return. Betty being gone to her Friends at Mattishall and Briton also out at dinner Time, I was with pleasure under the necessity of assisting at Dinner. Nancy complained a good deal in the Evening. We diverted ourselves at Cribbage this Evening at which neither won or lost.

25th. Nancy had a very indifferent Night and rather worse today, being still weaker. She did not come down Stairs till 2 o'clock this afternoon. However she made a good Dinner on a boiled Leg of Mutton and Caper Sauce and was better after. Rode to Ringland this Morning and married one Robert Astick and Elizabeth Howlett by Licence, Mr Carter being from home, and the Man being in Custody, the Woman being with Child by him. The Man was a long time before he could be prevailed on to marry her when in the Church Yard; and at the Altar behaved very unbecoming. It is a cruel thing that any Person should be compelled by Law to marry. I recd of the Officers for marrying them 0.10.6. It is very disagreeable to me to marry such Persons.*

* These so-called compulsory marriages were not legally enforceable. They were, however, the inevitable result of the law as it stood, especially of the Bastardy Act of 1773. Under that Act a woman (on

28th. I read Prayers and Preached this morning at Weston Church neither Mr or Mrs Custance at Church, nor above 20 People in all at Church—The Weather being extremely cold and severe with much Snow on the ground and still more falling with cutting Winds. After Service I buried a Daughter of Harrisons an Infant aged only 5 Weeks—I think that I never felt the cold more severe than when I was burying the above Infant. The Wind blowed very Strong and Snow falling all the time and the Wind almost directly in my Face, that it almost stopped my breath in reading the funeral Service at the Grave, tho' I had an Umbrella* held over my Head during the Time. Nancy brave all day but still very lame, she did not go to bed till after 10 o'clock this Evening. Mr Thorne called again on his Patient this After. about 3 o'clock—soon after we had dined.

FEBRUARY *3rd.* Mr Thorne called here this Morning accidentally having been to bleed Mrs Custance at Weston House. He was not pleased on hearing that Nancy was so bad as not to be seen by him being above Stairs. I am afraid she caught cold, as her pain within her was so bad that she could not get from the close-Stool for near 2 Hours together. I went up to see her in the Evening, and she was very low and cried a good deal—but seemed rather easier—after she had her Tea and Toast she seemed something better and soon after came down Stairs and stayed the rest of the Evening. When she went to bed she was

oath before a justice) had only to name any man the father of her child to cause his instant arrest and imprisonment, unless he offered security to indemnify the parish. Another clause permitted the man's release if the woman married. Not unnaturally, in numerous cases, a man unable to indemnify the parish preferred wedlock to prison.
* JW's first mention of an umbrella—not surprisingly, for umbrellas came into general use in England only during the 1780s. A poor fellow who put one up in 1778 was jeered by the London mob. They were considered effeminate. It is even less surprising (as Beresford points out) that JW succumbed to someone else holding one over his head only during an appalling blizzard at a funeral.

tolerably easy. I was very uneasy indeed the whole Day on my dear Nieces Account. 'Pray God give her more ease.' I sent Briton to Norwich this Morning after News, &c., in my little Cart—he returned by dinner time. No letters from the West, or elsewhere, as there were none from the West, I wonder much at it; as Nancy has long expected one from her Aunt and one from her Sister Juliana.

10th. Nancy tolerable this morning but did not come down to breakfast, nor was below Stairs till Noon', just as she was coming down stairs Mrs Custance came to us and stayed till near 3 o'clock. She seemed far from well, having a low nervous Fever hanging about her, and very far gone with Child. I tried to divert her as much as I could, showed her some Medals of mine &c. I was quite sorry to see her so very low and weak. Nancy dined, supped &c. below Stairs and was tolerably well and cheerful all Day.

MARCH *13th.* Whilst we were at breakfast, Mrs Davy from Thurning with a Servant with her, called here and drank a Dish of Tea with us, stayed about half an Hour afterwards and then went on to Mr Thornes at Mattishall. I did not ask her to stay and dine with us. She talked of returning back to Thurning Thursday or Friday next—I did not ask her to call on her return. Nancy was highly pleased to see her. Mrs Davy behaved as free as if nothing had been said respecting her Character by Mr Smith. She is grown much fatter than she was. I never knew a Woman of much greater Effrontery. The Election for the City of Norwich comes on Thursday next, a strong Contest is expected.

17th. Sent Briton on horseback to Norwich after News &c. He returned about 4 o'clock with the same. No Letter or any Tidings whatever of Mr and Mrs Jeanes. Mr Hobart had only 80 Majority of Sir Thos Beevor. The Election at Norwich conducted with great credit to the City. No appearance of a Riot or any disturbance whatever, but all things were carried on in the greatest Order and Peace. No Stavesman whatever on the Occasion. Sir Thos Beevor is said to have demanded a Scrutiny at first, but has since dropped it, is said. For Churching a Woman at Witchingham recd 0.0.6. Briton returned home from Norwich with a Hobart Favour in his Hat, and highly pleased.

18th. I read Prayers, Preached and churched a Woman at Witchingham this Morn', for Mr Jeanes. Mr Jeanes Man is gone to London to his Master with Mr Jeanes Stallion, being sent for by him. Mr Jeanes is expected in the ensuing Week. I read Prayers and Preached this Afternoon at Weston C. Also churched 2 poor Women at Weston Church. Mr and Mrs Custance at Church this Afternoon and a very full Congregation at Church this Aft. I gave the two poor Women the Churching Fee. I met Mr Custance on my return from Witchingham this Morning on the little Common, and he very genteelly desired me for the future to go thro' his inclosures by his House whenever I wanted to go to Witchingham or Lenewade Bridge, &c. as that way is somewhat nearer than the other. Nancy told me this Evening that Mrs Davy had had an offer of marriage made her, but not said whom—also that her Daughter Betsy has had an offer also from young Walker who was lately at Mr Thornes. The above are very great Secrets.

27th. Mrs Custance made us a morning Visit and stayed with us an Hour—She is quite hurried and uneasy on Account of her little Boy, William, having got the Measles, and herself never having them, and also that she is very near her Time of being brought to bed, having scarce a Month to go with Child. Am exceeding sorry for poor Mrs Custance indeed and likewise for Mr Custance who must be very much concerned. Busy brewing some strong Beer to day.

30th. Mr Custances Coach damaged my great Gates last Night. About Noon, Mr and Mrs Jeanes from London came here in their road home to Witchingham, and stayed an Hour with us, and refreshed themselves with some cold rost Beef and Porter &c. and then went for home. Mrs Jeanes looks much better. Mr Jeanes whilst in Town bought a close Carriage and a pair of black Horses to go in the same. Mrs Jeanes came down in it. It looks smart. Mr Jeanes came down on his fine Stallion as he could not dispose of him for so much as he asked. For a fine Eel 2 pound weight pd 0.0.6.

MAY *6th*. Soon after my return from Church, one of Mr Custances Servants called here to let us know that Mrs Custance was brought to bed of a Boy about 11 o'clock this Morn'. She with the little stranger as well as can be expected. I buried this Evening one Willm Hill aged 65 yrs. He was ill but a very little Time—was well respected and a great many People at his burial.

21st. Mr Jeanes made us a short morning Visit. Of John Gooch for Turnips for his Cow almost all the Winter recd of him 1.1.0 but I returned it to him again immediately. Very busy all the morning in cutting the Weeds in my Bason and cleaning the same, and likewise in launching the Ship Anna in the same.

28th. Mr and Mrs Jeanes with Miss Short dined and spent the Afternoon with us. We had for Dinner a nice boiled Leg of Lamb, a very nice small rosting Pigg, Apricot and Gooseberry Tarts Oranges and Nutts by way of desert. Soon after Coffee and Tea, They returned for Witchingham and took my Niece with them in their Carriage to spend a few Days with them.

JUNE *24th*. I read Prayers, Preached and Christned a Child by name John, this Morning at Weston Church. Mr and Mrs Custance, Mrs Michlethwaite and her Sister Miss Branthwaite at Church. Nancy was at Church this morning and walked there and back. My Niece has not been able to go to Church since she returned from Somersett in October last.

JULY *9th*. Mr Jeanes made us a short morning Visit, and he acquainted us that his Wife was brought to bed of a Daughter this morning about 7 o'clock, and as well as he could wish her to be in her state. She was not more than 10 hours in labour. Mrs Jeanes's Mother, Mrs Springer, was to have been with them at the time, but is expected to Morrow. Mrs Custance 2 Daughters Fanny and Emily came to our House this Evening on a Walk, and they drank some Milk and Water and eat some Cakes. I walked with them and the Maid Sally good part of the way back, as far as John Bakers, and there the Rain overtook us but not much, and there another Maid Sukey, met us, and there I left them. I was wet thro' on my return back to my House. The little Folks, I hope, got home without being wet. I gave to each of the little Ladies a Medal apiece in imitation of an half Guinea in kind of brass. My Folks busy in bringing our Hay home and stacking it all Day long. The Major Part of it stacked to day.

11th. I was very busy all the Morning long in helping them in the Field, as we were busy carrying our Hay. We finished about 8 this Evening and then came Rain.

21st. Nancy very busy this morning in making some Rasberry Jam and red Currant Jelly. She made to day about 8 Pound of Currant Jelly and about 9 Pound of Rasberry Jamm. This Evening as we were going to Supper, a covered Cart drove into my Yard with 3 Men with it, and one of them, the principal, was a black* with a french Horn, blowing it all the way up the Yard to the Kitchen Door, to know if we would like to see a little Woman only 33 Inches high and 31 Years of Age. As we did not give our Dissent, she was taken out of the Cart and brought into our Kitchen, where we saw her and heard her sing two Songs. I dont think she was any taller than represented, but rather deformed, seemed in good Spirits, sang exceedingly high with very little Judgment and was very talkative. She was called

* Plenty of black people were brought to England during this century as a natural consequence of the slave trade—indeed they were treated as slaves until the Somerset case of 1772 in which Lord Mansfield judged that a slave was free by the mere fact of landing on English soil.

by the black Polly Coleshill of Glocester. The Black told me that he formerly lived with the Earl of Albermarle I gave him 0.1.0. Ben returned from Norwich about 4 this afternoon.

31st. About 9 o'clock this Morning Mrs Davy with her Daughter came to my House in a one Horse-Chaise and they dined and spent the Afternoon with us—In the Evening Mrs Davy returned home to Thurning but left her Daughter to spend a few Days with Nancy, Betsy being far from well, having a violent palpitation of the heart—she is now however much better than she has been of late. We had for Dinner some Veal, Beans and Ham, a piece of boiled Beef, a Green Goose and some tarts. Betsy Davy supped and slept here.

AUGUST *10th.* About 1 o'clock this Morning there was a most violent Tempest—very much Lightning and the most vivid, strong and quick I think I ever saw before—Not so much Thunder but very loud what there was—The Rain was some time before it came but then it was very heavy, the Rain did not last long. We were much alarmed, the Maids came downstairs crying and shrieking at 1 o'clock. I got up immediately and thinking when I went up Stairs to bed last Night that there was likelihood of a Tempest being so hot, I had lighted my little Lamp, and only laid down on my Bed with most of my Cloathes on and was just dozing when I heard the Maids all of a sudden shrieking at my Door. We lighted some Candles. Nancy had one in her Room, they were much frightned. It continued incessantly lightning from before 1 till 4 this Morning—then it abated and then I went to bed and slept comfortably till 9 o'clock. Thank God Almighty, for preserving us all safe from so violent a Tempest. May all others escape as well. It was most dreadful to behold the Lightning. Mr Massingham, Dr Thornes Apprentice, just called here in the Evening to enquire after Betsy Davy &c.

28th. My Greyhounds being both very full of fleas and almost raw on their backs, I put some Oil of Turpentine on them, which soon made many of them retire and also killed many more.

SEPTEMBER *4th*. About 11 o'clock this Morning walked to Weston Church to christen Mr Custance's last little Boy, but the Company not being arrived Mr Custance sent his Coach after me to go to Weston House which I did and there stayed about half an Hour with Mr and Mrs Custance, Sir Thomas and Lady Durrant, the latter is Mr Custances own Sister and a very fine Woman, there was a Daughter with them about 11 Years old, her Name as her Mothers Susannah. Mr and Mrs Collyer of Wroxham then sent word that they were waiting at Church, we all then went in two Coaches and four to Weston Church where I publickly presented (being privately named by me before by name John) the young Gentleman. Sir Thomas Durant and Mr Collyer, God Fathers, and Lady Durant the only Godmother. Two Coaches and four and a Post Chariot at Church. After the Christning we walked about Weston Church about 20 Minutes, then the Company went for Weston House — and I walked home to the Parsonage. About 2 o'clock I dressed and walked up to Weston House and there dined and spent the Aft. with Mr and Mrs Custance, Sir Thomas and Lady Durrant and Daughter, Mr and Mrs Collyer, and Mr Press Custance — After Coffee and Tea Sir Thos and Lady and Daughter set of home to a place called Scottow — Sir Thos invited me to his House. After they were gone, Mrs Custance, Mrs Collyer, Mr Press Custance and self sat down to Cribbage at Shillings, at which I won 0.3.0. Mrs Collyer and Self against Mrs Custance and Mr Press. About 8 this Evening I walked home. N.B. Mr Custance very genteelly made me a present for christning the Child, wrapped in White Paper of the Sum of 5.5.0. In the Morn' I sent a Dozen of very fine Anson Apricots to Weston House which were on the table after Dinner and all eat, but not a word mentioned from whence they came, therefore suppose that neither Mr or Mrs Custance knew anything of the Matter.

28th. I spent a good part of the Morning at the Church and in the Church Yard, my People being busy in laying some Gravel upon the Walks there and making the Church Yard more decent.

OCTOBER *2nd*. Nancy went in her little Cart with Briton, and I on my Mare to Witchingham about 1 o'clock and there we dined and spent the Afternoon at Mr Jeanes's with him, his Wife, Mr Du Quesne, Mr and Mrs Priest of Reepham with their two Daughters, Rebeccah and Mary. We had for Dinner a Couple of small Chicken boiled, and a Tongue, one stewed Duck, a fine Haunch of Venison and a baked Pudding. Mr Du Quesne fell backward from his Chair in the Afternoon and bruised himself much. The Ladies were not in the Room at the time. We returned as we went directly after Coffee. Mr Du Quesne went with me, he complained a good deal of his Fall when on horseback in giving him much Pain. Mr Du Quesne should have went in his Carriage especially as Mr Jeanes desired him, and to take up my Niece with him in the same, and which he might have done. We spent a very agreeable Day and did due justice to the Venison which came out of the New Forest from Mr Jeanes's Father.

NOVEMBER *12th*. Soon after breakfast I walked out a Coursing and took Ben and the Boy with me, did not return till near three, afternoon, we had tolerable Sport, coursed one Hare and a Couple of Rabbitts, all of whom we killed, it was a very large Hare. I think I never knew so pleasant a day so far in November, it was more like Summer than Autumn. I was very indifferent the whole Day, could eat but very little for Dinner being over fatigued and likewise my Spirits but very bad.

DECEMBER *11th*. I took a ride this Morning to Weston House and spent half an Hour with Mrs Custance — Mr Custance being walked out — I went to ask them to dine with us to

Morrow to meet Mr and Mrs Bodham. Mrs Custance seemed much pleased with it, but could not promise till she had seen Mr Custance. Mrs Custance having ordered her Coach to go to my House, I desired her not to counter-order it, therefore she with 3 Children went and spent half an Hour with my Niece and then returned back again. About ½ past 2 o'clock Mr and Mrs Bodham with Miss Mary Donne of Norwich came to my House to spend a day or two with us. Mr and Mrs Bodham with Miss Mary Donne, dined, supped and slept at my House — Miss Donne slept with my Niece in the Attic Story over me. Miss Mary Donne is a very genteel, pretty young Lady and very agreeable with a most pleasing Voice abt 21 Yrs very tasty and very fashionable in dress. Mr Bodhams Coachman Js returned home to Mattishall with his pair of Horses before Dinner and is to come again on Thursday Morning after them. Mr Bodhams Footman Thos dined and slept here. We had for Dinner to day a boiled Leg of Mutton with Capers, a Couple of Chicken rosted and a Tongue, a Norfolk plain batter Pudding, Tripe, Tarts and some blamange with 4 Sorts of Cheese. For Supper some Oysters, a wild Duck rosted, Potatoes rosted, and some cold Chicken &c. After Coffee and Tea we got to Quadrille, viz: Mr and Mrs Bodham, Miss Donne and self. I won 0.3.0. I did not get to bed to Night till after 12 o'clock.

1788

JANUARY *13th*. I read Prayers and Preached this Afternoon at Weston C. Mrs Custance and her 2 eldest sons at Church, but not Mr Custance, he being detained on Justice business, having had a Felon by name Wakefield of Booton brought to him this Aft. on very great suspicion of his being guilty of the Murder of one Thos Twaites of Honingham, when a great many Poachers were at Mr Townshends about 3 years ago, and at which time the above poor old man was murdered by having his skull fractured by a Bludgeon. The above Wakefield was impeached by an Accomplice one Beales who was of their Party, and is now in the Castle at Norwich as one of the Gang. It is also reported that he has impeached about ten more of the said gang.

25th. Sent the Hare I killed yesterday to Mr Bodham by Briton. Of Nancy for not being below Stairs for 2 Mornings before 10 o'clock, forfeit each time 6d recd 0.1.0. Briton returned before Dinner and informed us that Mr Bodham continued still very indifferent.

FEBRUARY *1st*. Mr Carter of Ringland sent me a Note this Morn' before breakfast, to desire my Sentiments on a particular Question relating to the tolling of a Bell for a Child that died without being baptised at its decease, at any time from thence to its being interred and at the putting of it into the ground. I sent an Answer back to Mr Carter, that as the Funeral Service could not be read over it, the tolling of the Bell at any time to be inadmissable.

11th. Nancy not being below Stairs this morning before the clock had done striking 10 forfeited — 0.0.6.

29th. Mr Taswell sent early to me this morning that he would take a Family Dinner with us to day and desired us to send to Mr Custance that they might not wait dinner for him. He went from Weston House early this morning to go to Aylsham to read Prayers there to day being Friday. At 11 o'clock this Morning I sent Briton to Weston House to let them know that Mr Taswell was to take a Family Dinner with us to day, Briton returned pretty soon and informed us that Mr and Mrs Custance, Lady Bacon and Son and Master Taswell would also come and partake of the Family Dinner, and they sent us some Fish, a wild Duck and a Sallad. It occasioned rather a Bustle in our House but we did as well as we could—We had not a bit of White bread in House, no Tarts whatever, and this Week gave no Order whatever to my Butcher for Meat, as I killed a Pigg this Week. We soon baked some white bread and some Tartlets and made the best shift we could on the whole. About 3 o'clock Mr and Mrs Custance, Lady Bacon and Son, Mr Taswell and Nephew arrived and they dined, drank Coffee, and Tea and returned home about 7 o'clock this Evening to Weston House. Mr Taswell with his Servant came here a little time before the other Company on horseback from Aylsham, he dressed himself at my House. We gave the Company for Dinner some Fish and Oyster Sauce, a nice Piece of Boiled Beef, a fine Neck of Pork rosted and Apple Sauce, some hashed Turkey, Mutton Stakes, Sallad &c. a wild Duck rosted, fryed Rabbits, a plumb Pudding and some Tartlets. Desert, some Olives, Nutts, Almonds, and Raisins and Apples. The whole Company were pleased with their Dinner &c. Considering we had not above 3 Hours notice of their coming we did very well in that short time. All of us were rather hurried on the Occasion.

MARCH *11th.* Mr Custance's Servant brought me a Letter this Evening from my Brother Heighes, he having been at Norwich to day, in which he presses us much to come into the Country this Summer, his Daughter Juliana being very ill, and apprehended to be in a decline, and is very desirous of seeing her

Sister, but she is far from being able at present to take such a journey and being so lame as unable to walk without holding. Very bitter cold all the day long and severe frost tho' fair. I dont know when the cold Weather affected me more than it has this very day. My Brothers Letter affected Nancy very much, made her quite low.

APRIL *19th*. Recd a Letter this Evening from Mr Du Quesne at London, intends being home to night, it was dated April 14— He talks very highly of Cole, and the many Civilities recd from our Somersett Friends. Recd also a very short Letter from my Brother Heighes informing me that his Daughter Juliana is entirely given over by the Faculty—poor Girl—Nancy recd also a very melancholy Letter from her Brother Willm concerning poor Juliana, that she was at the last stage of Life, and to desire Nancy to come down immediately into Somersett. Am afraid by this time that poor Juliana is no more. Nancy was half distracted almost on the Account. She cried incessantly the whole Evening, I sincerely pity her—no two Sisters could love one another more. Mr Du Quesne's Head Maid, Betty, called on us this afternoon to let us know that Mr Du Quesne would be at home this Evening.

21st. I breakfasted, dined, &c. again at home. Nancy breakfasted, dined, &c. again at home. After breakfast we took a ride to Mr Du Quesnes, Nancy in her little Cart and myself on Horseback. We found Mr Du Quesne at home and very well after his long Journey, stayed with him near 2 Hours. Mr Du Quesne told us that he never met with More Civility than he received from our Somersett Friends when he was with them, particularly from my Sister Pounsett, Mr Pounsett, and from my Brother John Woodforde and Wife and Mrs R. Clarke. He spoke very much of my Brother Johns Genteel Behaviour towards him —and of the kind Attention of Nancy's Brother the Capt. to him. He saw Nancys poor Sister Juliana, she would go to my Brother Johns to dinner to meet Mr Du Quesne—and she liked him very much. Mr Du Quesne said that she was extremely weak and no hopes of her getting the better of it. He brought for Nancy a little Parcel from her poor Sister and gave it to her —which she opened on her return home. It was a small roundish red Morrocco Purse with a small silver lock to it and in it was a new half guinea of 1787 and 2 Queen Anne's Sixpences. It made her very uneasy and unhappy for a long time after, was rather more composed before she went to bed. It made my heart ache to see her so miserable.

MAY *8th.* Sent Briton to Norwich early this morning for things wanted from thence, he returned by dinner, and brought a Letter for Nancy from her Brother Willm upbraiding her for not coming to see her Sister, who is still alive and that is all—poor Girl I am sorry for her but am not pleased with Willm for such a Letter to her Sister, as it made her very unhappy and very ill, vomited a good deal and could eat nothing at all for Dinner. Instead of condoling with her about her poor Sister and sorry for her not being able to go into the Country he rebukes her with want of humanity &c. It is quite cruel and unfeeling of him I think. His Letter was composed of a great many fine Epithets and sentimental thoughts.

17th. I breakfasted, dined &c. again at home, Nancy breakfasted dined, &c. again at home. Sent Ben very early this Morning to Norwich with ten Coomb 2 Bshls of Wheat. He sold it to Mr Bloome at 24s od per Coomb—I recd for the same 12.0.0. He also brought me 2 Letters—One from My Sister Pounsett and the other from my Brother Heighes both which brought the disagreeable news of Nancy's Sister's Death, poor Juliana Woodforde, she died on Monday Morn' last about 11 o'clock. Poor Nancy greatly affected on hearing of the same. Nancy had a Letter by Ben from Mrs Davy. Sent a Dozen, hollow little Cakes to Weston House. In my Sister Pounsetts Letter was a Bank Bill of the value of 10.0.0. To John Greaves and Brother pd this Even' 0.8.0 for Carpenters work and sawing.

JUNE *6th*. To my Man Ben for things pd 4.4.8 that is, £1 18s od for a Tub of Coniac Brandy of four gallons by Moonshine Buck and £2 6s od for two Tubbs of Geneva of 4 Gallons each by ditto and the odd 8d for Horses Shoes removed.

11th. I breakfasted, supped and slept again at home. Nancy breakfasted supped, &c again at home. Betsy Davy breakfasted, supped, &c. here again. About 1 o'clock Mr Du Quesne called here on horseback and I went with him on my Mare to Mr Jeanes's, and Nancy and Betsy Davy went thither also in my little Cart, where we all dined, with Mr and Mrs Jeanes Junr, Mr and Mrs Jeanes Senr, Mr and Mrs Locke (who came to Mr Jeanes's last Night) Miss Short, Mr Charles Springger, (Brother to Mrs Jeanes Junr) Mr and Mrs Priest and Miss Mary Priest from Reepham. We had a very excellent Dinner, that is to say, a fine Piece of fresh Salmon with Tench and Eel, boiled Ham and Fowls, the best part of a Rump of Beef stewed, Carrots and Peas, a fore Qtr of Lamb rosted, Cucumbers and Mint Sauce, a Couple of Ducks rosted, plain and Currant Puddings. After Dinner 2 large Dishes of Strawberries, some Blanched Almonds with Raisins and Aples. We were much crowded at Table, rather unpleasant. Major Lloyd with his 2 eldest Daughters joined us at the Tea Table in the Evening which made the whole Company then consist of 18 in Number. After Coffee and Tea we had two or three Songs from Miss Kate Lloyd who sings delightfully indeed. It was sometime after 9 o'clock before we got back to Weston—we returned as we went. Upon the whole we spent a very agreeable Day. Mr Jeanes Senr is a mighty cheerful good natured plain downright Man. Mr Locke a very neat well looking old gentleman, and Country Esq. fond of Hunting, keeps 16 fox Hounds, talks plain Hampshire and Delights also in farming. Mr Charles Springer a very modest young Man about 17 or 18 yrs, in some branch of Trade belonging to the India House.

JULY *7th*. Mr Custance sent me a Melon and with it a Note to

278

inform us that Mrs Custance was this morning about 2 o'clock safely delivered of another Son and that both Mother and Child were as well as could possibly be expected in the time. Mr C. also desired me (if perfectly convenient) to wait on him in the afternoon and name the little Stranger. After Dinner therefore about 5 o'clock I took a Walk to Weston House and named the little Infant, in Lady Bacons dressing Room by name, Neville. The Revd Mr Daniel Collyer of Wroxham was with Mr Custance when I first went in but he soon went. I stayed and drank Tea with Mr Custance and Sons and did not return home till after 8 this Evening.

28th. I was very low-spirited this Evening after Tea. I believe that Tea made me worse rather I think. I shot a Wood Pecker this Morn' in my Garden.

29th. I breakfasted, dined and spent the Aft. at home. In the Evening took a ride to Norwich and Briton with me, and there I supped and slept at the Kings Head. In the Evening before Supper I walked into St Stephens and saw the Polish Dwarf, Joseph Boruwlaski and his Wife who is a middle sized Person, he is only three feet three Inches in height, quite well proportioned everyway, very polite, sensible and very sprightly, and gave us a tune upon the Guitar, and one Tune of his own composing. The common price of admittance was one Shilling, but I gave him rather more 0.2.6.

AUGUST *11th.* Mr Walker and Betsy Davy came over on single Horses this Morning from Foulsham and they breakfasted, dined, and spent the Afternoon with us. We had a good deal of singing to Day from my Niece and Mr Walker—the latter sung many new Songs. We spent a very agreeable Day together. We had for Dinner a boiled Leg of Mutton and Capers, a Couple of rost Chicken, Apple Pye and black Currant Tarts—Apricots, Apples and black Currants for a Desert. Mr Walker and Betsy Davy came to us about 9 o'clock this morning and stayed till half past six in the Evening. We had a

Note that Mr and Mrs Bodham would dine here on Wedn.

16th. Mrs Davy with one Harris in a Cart called here, this Evening about 5 o'clock and drank Tea here in her road from Norwich to Foulsham. Soon after Mrs Davy came also Mr Walker and with him another young Man by name Viol, both almost wet thro' and they drank Tea also here in their road from Norwich homewards, so that my House was more like an Inn this Evening than anything else.

Norwich

SEPTEMBER *25th.* Very soon after Dinner, Mrs Davy and Betsy, Miss Walker and my Niece went in an Hackney Coach to St Andrews Hall to hear the Concert this Evening. Mr Walker and myself walked thither. The Tickets to the Miscellaneous Concert to Night were 7 Shillings and 6 pence each. Mrs Custance being a Subscriber and having a transferable Ticket, was so kind as to lend my Niece hers for this Evening. Mr Walker procured Tickets for the rest of us. He is to pay for Tickets, Coaches, Lodgings &c. and when finished Mr Walker and self are to divide the expenses between us. A great deal of Company indeed at the Hall and full dressed — 911 supposed to be present. The Concert was very fine indeed, and Madame Mara, the famous Singer, sung delightfully. I never heard so fine a Voice — Her Notes so high. The Kettle Drums from Westminster Abbey sounded charmingly, beat by a Mr Ashbridge. Near 100 performers in the Orchestra. The Concert was over between 10 and 11 at Night but we were obliged to wait a full Hour before we could get to our Hackney Coach, so many Coaches before it and some an Hour after us. I went back with the Ladies in the Coach to our Lodgings and there we supped and slept. I dont know what our Company would have done without my Servant Briton, being with me.

26th. As I only laid down on the Bed last Night with some of my Cloaths, I got up pretty early (considering we did not go to bed till near 2 this morning) and I took a Walk in the City, went to Bacons and got Tickets for the Oratorio this morning at St Peters Church—went also to Browns my Barber and was shaved—paid him also for a new Wigg I had sometime back the sum of 1.1.0. Gave him also for dressing my Wigg &c. 0.2.6. Called at Beales and paid for Soals 0.3.0. Then returned to my Lodgings to breakfast about 9, and there breakfasted with Mrs Davy and Betsy, Miss Walker, my Niece, and Mr Walker. Soon after breakfast. I walked to the House of Mr Priests and there waited for Mr Custances Coach to return Mrs Custance's Ticket to her, the Coach called about 11, with Mr and Mrs Custance in it, and I went with them to St Peter's Church and there heard the fine Oratorio of Judas Maccabeus which was performed very capitally—Madame Mara also performed her part very well indeed. There was supposed to be present 1200 People. The Church was quite full, I got as near to my Party as I could. Mrs Davy during the performance made some little disturbance, fainting away, but she soon came to herself again, quite a fine Air. Betsy Davy did not mind it at all, as she knows her well. The Oratorio was not over till 3 this Afternoon. We all walked back from St Peters to our Lodgings and there I left them and went to the Wool-Packet in St Giles's, where my Servant Ben was waiting for me with my Horses. I then mounted my Mare, and went home with Ben to Weston did not get home till 6 o'clock this Evening and there dined, supped and slept at the Parsonage House. I was highly entertained by the Musick both Days. Scarce ever seen so much Company at Norwich. Lodgings scarce to be got and some exceeding dear indeed—two Rooms it was said, was let at 10 guineas. Almost all the principal Families in the County there.

OCTOBER *11th*. Mr Walker called here this morning but did not stay he had been out with the hounds. Sent Briton early this Morning to Norwich after News &c. He returned by dinner time. Received by him a long Letter from my Brother Heighes, who informs me that his Son Willm is going to marry a Miss Jukes a fortune of £5000.

17th. Mr Jeanes sent me this morning a large Hamper of common Apples, I sent the same Hamper back full of my Apples called Beefans with a great many Shrubs, Laurels &c. &c.

NOVEMBER *5th.* Soon after breakfast (young Rose called here and desired me to lend him my Greyhounds, having found a Hare sitting) Mr Walker and self took a Walk with the Greyhounds and saw the Hare coursed which gave great Sport indeed, but was killed at last. I never saw a better Course. I let Mr Rose have the Hare for a Friend of his. After we had killed that Hare we went after another and found one in about an Hour, but we had very little Diversion with her, the Greyhounds scarcely seeing her, She soon got of. Saw never another tho' we stayed out till 3 o'clock. Mr Walker almost knocked up by walking so long, we were out from 11 till 3 in the Afternoon. Whilst we were out again this Morning Mrs Custance with 3 Children called at the Parsonage, and spent an Hour with my Niece and Betsy Davy. Mrs Custance brought a brace of Partridges for us. After Tea again this Evening we got to Whist, Partners the same, Betsy mine, Nancy Mr Walkers and we beat them again won 0.1.6. So that Nancy owes me now 0.17.0. Very fine Evening tho' cold for the Holkham Jubilee.

11th. Two Men from Hockering by names, Bugdale and Ames, called here this Morning to see 8 Piggs, Shots of mine which I have to sell, I asked 10 Pound for them, they offered me 8 Pound. I then told them that they should have them at 9 P. but they would not give that, so we parted. Brewed a Barrel of small Beer to day. Reported this Day at Norwich that our good King was dead, pray God it might not be true.*

* On 5 November it looked as though George III's insanity was finally incurable. His own physicians were pessimistic as he lived out the winter at Kew Palace, but a doctor famed for his knowledge of insanity, Dr Willis, predicted a rapid recovery—correctly, for early in February 1789 the King was markedly better and later in the month bulletins were discontinued.

14th. After breakfast Nancy, and Betsy Davy would go to Norwich with Mr Walker, and there they dined at the Kings Head and returned home to Tea about 6 o'clock and Mr Walker instead of going to London as proposed returned with them. A pretty expensive and foolish Scheme indeed—I was not pleased. To Neighbour Case for Pork at 4½d pd 0.2.3. After Tea this Evening we got to Whist lost 0.3.0. The News relating to the Kings Health this Day at Norwich, was, that he remains near the same, by no means better—still in the greatest danger. Mr Walker paid me what I lent him at Cards 0.2.6.

15th. Mr Walker breakfasted here and then sat of for Norwich in my little Cart and Briton with him, who is to bring back News &c. Mr Walker goes by the Mail Coach this Aft. for London. Briton returned about 5 o'clock this Afternoon. Brought me a Letter from my Sister Pounsett to let us known that Nancys Brother William was gone of with Miss Jukes to be married, and that they were at Portland Island. Briton also said that Mr Walker did not go to London this Day neither, and that he would return to my house again this Evening, which he did to Supper and also slept here again. It was after 12 before I got to bed this Night. Mr Walker brought us a brace of Pheasants.

16th. I read Prayers and Preached this Afternoon at Weston Church—none from Weston House at Church. Nancy, Betsy Davy, and Mr Walker also from Church. I prayed at Church for our most gracious and truly beloved Sovereign King George the third. I did it out of my own head, no prayer yet arrived.

18th. Soon after breakfast Mr Walker took a ride to Norwich to take a place in the Mail Coach for this Afternoon for London—but he returned to us this Evening between 7 and 8 o'clock and it being very dark, he hired a Man to come with him on another horse—Joe at the Kings Head. After Joe had refreshed himself and Horse also he returned back to Norwich. Mr Walker said that there was no Place in the Coach but all that is nothing, his inclination was to stay. Betsy Davy's Birth Day now 18 Years of Age.

19th. Mr Walker breakfasted here, and then sat of once more for Norwich to go in the Mail Coach this Afternoon for London —I still think it rather dubious where he goes or not this Day. On his taking leave he went up to Nancy and wished her well shaking her by her hand, and then went to Betsy and did the same, but to me (altho' in the Room at the same time) he never said one word or took the lest notice of me (tho' I also helped him on with his great Coat) after he was mounted and just going out of the great Gates then he said good Morning and that was all—very slight return for my Civilities towards him of late and which I did not expect. It hurt me very much indeed. Mr Walker did not return however this Day to us.

20th. To one Platten of Hockering sold 8 fine Piggs, littered in April last for 8.8.0. I gave him for good luck out of it— 0.1.0. Mr Jeanes made us a morning Visit and brought us some fine Prawns just arrived from Hants. Miss Woodforde rather pert this morning.

21st. Mr Walker's Birth Day now 21 Years of Age.

22nd. Sent Ben early this Morning to Norwich after News and other things from thence, he returned about Dinner time. No Letters for us. Betsy Davy had a Letter from Mr Walker from Thetford and with it a Parcel in which was nothing but a Fox's Brush or Tail.

DECEMBER *6th*. Sent Ben to Norwich on horseback after News &c. He returned home to dinner with the same. Betsy Davy had a Parcel and a Letter from Mr Walker in Town. The Parcel contained a very handsome red Morocco Almanack and Pocket Book, gilt with a silver Clasp to the same—quite new fashioned. Nancy also had a Letter from Mr Walker and a Barrel of Oysters sent her by him also.

20th. Mrs Custance with her two Sons Hambleton and George who are just returned home from School, made us a long morning Visit. They both looked well, but George has Child-blains on one foot. Sent Briton early this morning to Norwich with my little Cart, after News &c. he returned abt 4. Received a Letter by him from Mr Walker in which he mentions having sent me 2 Gallons of English Gin, but he mentioned nothing of when it was sent, by what Conveyance, or where left.

23rd. To Mr Ames my Cooper, paid a Bill of 0.18.0. Just as we were going to Dinner a Man came express from the Kings Head at Norwich, with a Letter for Betsy Davy from Mr Walker at London to desire her to meet him at Norwich at the Kings Head on Christmas Day next Thursday and that Nancy would accompany her. He mentioned in his Letter that he had ordered a Post-Chaise from the Kings head to be at my House for them in the Morning. Very wild, unsteady, and thoughtless Work indeed.

25th. I read Prayers and administered the H. Sacrament this Morning at Weston Church being Xmas Day. For an Offering at the H. Sacrament gave 0.2.6. Mr and Mrs Custance at Church and at the H. Sacrament. Before I went to Church this Morning Nancy and Betsy Davy went of in a Norwich Chaise which came to my House by 7 o'clock this morning for Norwich to meet Mr Walker at the Kings Head, and there they dined, but returned home to Tea in the Afternoon and Mr Walker with them. Mr Walker supped and slept here. Js Smith, my Clerk, Thos Cary, Thos Carr, Richd Buck, John Peachman, and Nath. Heavers had their Christmas Dinner and each 1s 0d —0.6.0. Poor old Richd Buck and old John Peachman being both Lame, could not come to my House to dinner, so I sent their Dinner to them, &c. Sent also a Dinner to the poor Girl Betty Deeker.

1789

JANUARY *2nd*. Mr Custance came to us this Morning on foot and spent above an Hour with us—tho' so bitter cold. I slept but indifferent last night, so bitter cold. After Tea we got to Cards—nothing lost or won. As cold today as it has been yet. Mr Walker's Cough somewhat better. Nancy, Betsy Davy, and Mr Walker are all confederate against me and am never let into any of their Schemes or Intentions &c. Nancy I think ought not to be so to me.

3rd. Did not get to bed till near 1 o'clock—being very uneasy. The treatment I meet with for my Civility this Christmas is to me abominable.

6th. Bitter cold day again with high wind, it froze in all parts of the House. Sent Ben round my Parish with some money to the Poor People this severe Weather, chiefly those that cannot work at this time, some 1 Shilling apiece—some at 1s/6d apiece. In all, Ben gave for me this Day 1.14.6.

20th, Tuesday.* I breakfasted, dined, &c. again at home. Nancy breakfasted, dined, &c. again at home. Betsy Davy breakfasted, dined, &c. here again. I could not get to sleep last Night till quite late thinking on such Variety of things and People. Mr Howlett and Mr Forster called here this Afternoon as they were going to a Parish Meeting at the Heart to speak to me respecting the Rent due for the Poor Cottage where Dick Buck &c live, which belongs to the Widows Charity—I told them that I expected the Parish would pay the Arrears. Mr Howlett brought with him in a Baskett a Couple of Guinea Fowls, a Cock and a Hen, as a present from him and his Wife.

* From this date JW always, or nearly always, inserts in his heading not just the date but the day of the week.

24th, Saturday. Sent Briton early this morning on horseback to Norwich after News &c. returned home by Dinner. Brought a Letter for Nancy from Mr Walker. An old Man came express from Foulsham with a Letter for Betsy Davy from Mr Walker in Town. Betsy gave the old Gentleman for coming over with it 1s. 6d. I gave him some Victuals and Drink. The Wind was so high in the Night that I got up about 2 o'clock but did not come below. Went to bed before 5 o'clock. N.B. Not a Word mentioned to me by either Betsy or Nancy concerning anything in the Letters sent by Walker. Betsy very busy all the Evening writing since she recd Walkers Letter—but to who not one Word to me. They are both artful.

MARCH *4th, Wednesday.* Mr Du Quesne dined and spent the Aft. with us. He was not in good Spirits, owing to disagreeable things happening in his Family with regard to Servants, his Man Servant James Atterton having been too familiar with his two young Servant Maids, Lizzy Greaves, an old Servant Maid of Mine about 23 Years of Age, and another Girl by name Mary, both of which are with Child by James. The former Maid Lizzy, was married Yesterday to James, and the other discovered her Situation only last Night. James also had kept Company with Lizzy's Sister, Sukey, now Servant at Weston House for the last four Years. James never appeared to have been such a sly Fellow as he has proved to be, but much the contrary. We had for Dinner to day a boiled Chicken and a piece of bacon, some rost Beef and Tarts. Mr Du Quesne left us before Tea.

17th, Tuesday. This morning settled Money Matters with my Niece for the last year—paid her the balance in ready Cash—which was—4.4.0. The whole that I had paid for her and gave her the last Year—amounted to 31.2.9. Brewed some strong Beer to day. Nancy very discontented of late, and runs out against living in such a dull Place.

24th, Tuesday. Nancy recd a very disagreeable Letter from her Brother William this Evening by Mr Custances Servant, respecting the dangerous State of my Brother Heighes's Health, his case is a violent Stranguary* and if some remedy or other does not soon, very soon do good, it will terminate fatally to him. Pray God! grant a Blessing to those made use of for his Recovery and that we might have better News in our next Letter from the West. Nancy as well as myself very uneasy on the above melancholy Account. I hope he is not so bad as said.

26th, Thursday. Very sharp Frosts of Nights still prevail and very cold Weather, no appearance of Spring yet to signify. The Wall fruit Trees seem to promise very well, the Apricots as full in Blossom as can be, but they are not full out, otherwise the Frost would cut them.

28th, Saturday. I took a Walk to Weston House this Morning to see Mr Custance who is ill in a swelled Face. I stayed with him an hour and half and returned home to dinner. Mr Custance pressed me much to dine with him as he was alone, and Mrs Custance at Raveningham, at Sir Edmund Bacons, but I could not as I expected a Letter from the West by my Servant, Briton, who went to Norwich this morning after News &c. and which in all probability would be most unwelcome to me and likewise to my poor Niece — accordingly when I returned which was about 3 o'clock to my House, Briton was returned, and with him brought a Letter sealed with black Wax to me, which on opening I found to be from my Brother John, informing us, that my dear Brother Heighes died on Sunday last the 22 Instant about 11 o'clock in the Morning from a violent inflammation in the urinary passage which finally terminated in a Mortification in a very short time, pray Almighty God that he might be more happy in a future State than he has experienced in this, and all his frailties in this Life forgiven. We heard nothing of his being ill till Tuesday night last, and now gone, O Lord make us wise to think on futurity. We were both most unhappy, on hearing the fatal News, my Brothers Letter was dated on the 22 Instant

* A disease of the urinary organs resulting in painful emission of urine.

the Day my poor Brother died. My Brother John rather bad in a cold but all our remaining Friends well. Pray God comfort my Nephew Willm in his great distress. My Brother mentions that he believes that my late Brother Heighes had left his Sons Willm and Samuel executors, and that they are to pay Nancy a share of his Estate in Sussex in money.

APRIL *11th, Saturday.* Sent Briton this morning early with my little Cart to Norwich after News &c. &c. He returned abt 4 o'clock this Afternoon and with him brought me a Letter from my Sister Pounsett, in which she says that our late poor Brother Heighes had made a Will and left his Estate in Sussex equally between his Sons Willm and Saml and their Sister A. M. Wood-forde which I think very good and just of him. It is rather apprehended that the Widow will have the Estate during her natural Life. Briton also brought all our Mourning home, viz. a black Coat and Waistcoat for me. A Black Bombasine Gown and Coat for Nancy with long Sleeves, and also a black stuff German Great Coat for her to wear in common. Mr Du Quesne sent a Servant over to our house about 2 o'clock with a fine Trout, and that if we were not engaged he would dine with us to day and at 3 he came and dined and spent the Afternoon with us. We had for Dinner the Trout, some minced Veal, and a Neck of Mutton rosted.

19th, Sunday. Between 7 and 8 this Evening Mr Walker and Betsy Davy came to my House they were on horseback. They stayed and drank Tea and at 8 sat of for Foulsham, as I was determined not to offer them beds. They came from Lynn this morning, in Post Chaises from Lynn to Dereham, and afterwards on horseback.

20th, Monday. Soon after breakfast Mrs Davy of Foulsham with a Servant Boy with her on single Horses came to our House and she stayed and dined and spent the Afternoon with us, but went away before Tea back to Foulsham. We had for dinner a Fillet of Veal rosted and a nice boiled Ham, Tartletts &c. Mrs

Davy was not well pleased with me nor I with her. She is without exception the most bold Woman I know.

23rd, Thursday. This being a Day of public thanksgiving to Almighty God for his late great mercies to our good and gracious King George the third, in restoring him to Health after so dangerous an illness, I walked to Church at 11 o'clock and there read Prayers proper for the Occasion with the other morning Prayers, a good many People at Church but neither Mr or Mrs Custance or any of the family. Mr Custance went for London yesterday I heard. He is to stay a Week in Town it is reported. Mr Custance being one of the Gentlemen of the privy Chamber to his Majesty, I apprehend is the Occasion of his going, as this Day the King goes publickly to St Pauls to return thanks, both Houses of Parliament attend him etc. It is to be a grand Procession thither. It is to be a great day of rejoicing every where almost. We heard firing of Guns from many Quarters abt Noon There was nothing at all done at Weston in that way.

29th, Wednesday. I breakfasted, and spent most of the Morn at home. About 1 o'clock took a ride to Mattishall and Briton with me to Mr Bodham's, got there about 2 where I dined supped and slept. Only Mr and Mrs Bodham and my Niece there. Briton slept there. As I was putting on my Boots in the Kitchen this morning to go to Mr Bodhams, Mr Walker and Betsy Davy called at the Kitchen Door on horseback, to whom I went out to speak to with only one boot on. I asked them to unlight and have some refreshment but they neither would They both looked very cool on me, particularly Betsy Davy who scarce deigned to cast a look on me when I spoke to her, they behaved with great reserve. We had for dinner today at Mr Bodhams some boiled Beef, a Fillet of Veal rosted and a Tongue a boiled Pudding and some Tarts. Mr and Mrs Hewitt drank Tea and spent part of the Evening with us. At Cards after Tea lost 0.2.6. We did not get to bed till near 12 o'clock tonight.

MAY *3rd, Sunday.* I read Prayers and Preached and christned a

Child by name Joseph this afternoon at Weston Church. None from Weston House to day at Church. Mr Custance not returned home as yet. Recd a letter this Evening from my Niece at Mattishall to let me know that she goes to Morrow to Mr Thorne's to spend a few days with Mrs Thorne &c. Betsy Davy and Mr Walker are I believe there. I was very much displeased at it and shall send for her home to Morrow early. I am almost continually vexed and tormented by her connection with the Davy's &c. They have almost alienated my regard for my Niece.

4th, Monday. I got up at 6 o'clock this morning and sent of Briton after Nancy as soon as I could. Nancy returned with Briton which was very good of her about 2 o'clock and she dined and slept at home.

20th, Wednesday. Mr Walker with Betsy Davy behind him, called here about 2 o'clock and after staying with us about half an Hour Mr Walker mounted his horse and went of for Foulsham leaving Betsy Davy behind to spend the Day and the Night with us, and she therefore dined, supped and slept here. She looks very poorly and is very bad again in her old Complaint the palpitation of the heart and Cramp in her head. Too much raking about has been I think the cause of her being so ill again, much beyond her Strength.

21st, Thursday. Betsy Davy breakfasted, dined, and spent part of the Afternoon with us. About Noon Mr Walker came here and he dined and spent part of the Afternoon with us till 4 o'clock, and then Mr Walker and Betsy Davy behind him went of for Foulsham. We had for Dinner some Skaite, and a nice Neck of Pork rosted and Apple Sauce, and Tarts and Tartlets. My Maid Nanny Kaye lost her poor old Father this week and is to be buried to Morrow, therefore she desires to go to the Funeral to Morrow at Foulsham. And as it is supposed that she and her Sisters must be at the expense of burying their Father, I gave her towards defraying the same the sum of 1.1.0 with leave to go to Foulsham to Morrow.

28th, Thursday. I breakfasted, dined, &c. again at home.

Nancy breakfasted, dined, &c. again at home. I had a very odd Dream last Night, I dreamt that I should die the Friday before the fifth of Novbr next; not my Will o Lord but thine be done, if it be thy good pleasure thus to fulfil the same. And may thou O Good God forgive me all my Sins.

Somerset

JULY *11th, Saturday.* I breakfasted, supped and slept again at Cole. Nancy breakfasted, supped and slept again at Cole. Mr Du Quesne breakfasted, supped and slept again at Cole. Sister Pounsett and Daughter, my Niece Nancy and self with Mr Du Quesne dined and spent the Afternoon at Ansford, at Mr Frank Woodfordes with him and his Wife, at Ansford Parsonage the Place and House in which I was born and lived many Years but had not been in it before this day, for almost fifteen years, owing to a disagreement between us, which now I hope will be ever done away. The House and Garden greatly altered for the best. We had a very good Dinner, a fine Piece of fresh Salmon, a Leg of Mutton rosted, fricasseed Rabit, a Couple of Ducks rosted and Peas, a currant Pye and Syllabubs &c. A good Desert of Fruit after Dinner, Strawberries, Cherries and Currants. Mr Frank behaved very hearty and generous to us as did his Wife, who seemed to be very attentive. Between Dinner and Tea I took a Walk by myself to my Uncle Toms and saw him and his Wife who were both glad to see me, both very old. We returned to Cole before 9 o'clock this Even' as we went, that is, Mr Du Quesne, Sister Pounsett and Daughter and Nancy in Ansford Inn Chaise. I walked thither and back again with Briton. Some small Rain fell during my return back. Sister Clarke drank Tea with us at Ansford Parsonage this Afternoon.

24th, Friday. I breakfasted, dined &c. again at Cole. To a Fisherman for a fine Crab, 4 Pound, pd 0.1.0. Very great Rebellion in France by the Papers*—The Bath Paper (the only Paper taken in here) comes every Friday Morning.

    * The Bastille had fallen ten days earlier.

AUGUST *4th, Tuesday*. Dies Memorabilis. I breakfasted, supped and slept again at Cole. I rose this morning at 6 o'clock, shaved and dressed, and at 7 I went in a Bruton Chaise and my Niece Jenny Pounsett with me, to my Brothers at C. Cary and there we made a second breakfast, after that all sat of about 9 o'clock for Sherborne to see the Royal Family. We got to Sherborne about 11 o'clock, had some White Wine Negus at the Antelope, and then we all went down to Lord Digby's Park, and there walked about till about 12 o'clock, at which time, the King, Queen, Princess Royal, Princess Elizabeth, and Princess Augusta arrived in the Park in three Royal Coaches with 4 Horses to each. We were very near them as they passed by. After they had taken some refreshment, they all walked upon the Terrace before the Crowd. We were all very near indeed to them, the King looked very red and is very tall and erect, The Queen and Princesses rather short but very pleasing Countenances and fair. After the Royal Family had walked round the Garden, they returned into Lord Digby's for a time. The King walked first with Lord Digby who held his hat in his hand, The Kings Hat was on, then the Queen with her Lady in waiting, then the Princess Royal and her Attendant Lady, then Princess Elizabeth and her Attendant Lady, then Princess Augusta and her attendant Lady. The King was in his Windsor Uniform, blue coat with red Cape and Cuffs to the Sleeves, with a plain round Hat with a black Ribband round it, The Queen was in a purple Silk, and white Bonnett, The Princesses all in Pink Silk and white Bonnetts. After they had been within Doors about an Hour They all came into the Park, the King on horseback, The Queen and Princesses and their Ladies, in two open Carriages, and they all passed thro' the Multitude, I was close to them as they passed. They took a ride quite round the Park, and were I suppose in performing it near 3 Hours. The King returned to the House by Water—The Queen and Princesses returned in their Carriages. They then went to Dinner at Lord Digbys. It was 5 o'clock this Afternoon before they got into Lord Digbys.

Our Company then made the best of our way to our Inn to dine also. Nancy and the other Ladies bore the fatigue pretty well, we were obliged often to sit on the grass in the Park, being there almost 6 Hours. It was a most delightful Day, thank God for it.

SEPTEMBER *7th, Monday.* Sister Pounsett very low on the thoughts of our leaving Cole to Morrow. Pray God comfort her.

OCTOBER *16th, Friday.* I breakfasted, dined, &c. again at home. To a poor old man of Hockering by name Thomas Ram, having lost a Cow gave 0.2.6. Brewed another Barrell of Table Beer to day. Sad News from France all anarchy and Confusion. The King, Queen and Royal Family confined at Paris. The Soldiers joined the People, many murdered.

24th, Saturday. Sent Briton early this Morning to Norwich with my little Cart after many things. Recd for 2 small Piggs of Tom Carr's Wife 12.0. Briton returned from Norwich about 4 o'clock brought me a long and pleasing Letter from my Sister Pounsett, whom I thank God to find by her writing that she is better in health. She also informed us that my Brother John and Wife and Mrs Richd Clarke, intend setting out for Norfolk in about a fortnights time to spend the Winter with us. We shall be very happy to see them. Pray God! they may have a safe and pleasant journey.

31st, Saturday. Very high Wind with much Rain in the Night but about 5 o'clock this Morn' it was highest, it shook the House, but thank God we received no damage. It was a very strong NN Easterly Wind. It blew down a great many apples and split a large weeping Willow in the Rasberry Garden.

NOVEMBER *7th, Saturday.* Very melancholy News on the Papers respecting the Ships wrecked and lives lost at Yarmouth and near it by the very high Wind early in the Morn' Saturday the 31 of October. May those poor Souls lost be O Lord better of. And send thy divine Comfort to all their Relatives. Mr Custance sent us a brace of Partridges. Billy Bidewell brought our News-papers from Norwich to day. We had no Letters whatever. We were in great expectation of hearing from Somersett, as we now daily expect my Brother and Wife, and Mrs Richd Clarke, to be with us.

11th, Wednesday. To James Pegg this morning paid 11.2.3 that is, half a Years Land Tax 6.0.0, Half a Years House and Window Tax 2.15.0. Male-Servant Tax, for half a Year 1.5.0. Female ditto, for ditto 0.10.0. Horse Tax, for ditto 0.10.0. Additional Horse Tax, for 1 Quarter, 0.1.3. Cart Tax, for Half a Year 0.1.0. Bottled of Mr Palmers Rum this morning, it is strong, but nothing near so fine flavoured, as what we had last from Mr Priest of Norwich. Sent Briton early this morning to Norwich with my little Cart, for many things from thence but more particularly for Letters as we are in daily expectation of seeing my Brother &c. Killed another fat Pigg this Morning, and the weight was 9 Stone and half. Briton returned home from Norwich about 4 o'clock this Afternoon, brought me a Letter from my Brother John, informing us of the Death of Mrs James Clarke on Friday Sennight last, 'pray God she may have a happy change'. I sincerely pity the 2 infant Children that she has left, and likewise her disconsolate Husband poor Doctor Clarke I heartily pity him. My Brother also informed us that himself, Wife and Mrs Richd Clarke intend being at Norwich Friday.

13th, Friday. I breakfasted, dined, supped and slept at Nor-wich. Nancy breakfasted dined &c. at Norwich. About 11 o'clock this Morn' our Somersett Friends my Brother and Wife and Mrs Richd Clarke arrived at Norwich from London in the Expedi-tion Coach after travelling all night. We were very happy to see them arrived safe thanks be to God for the same, considering their great fatigue they all looked very well, they breakfasted, dined, supped and slept at the Kings Head. Bought this day of Willm Hart, Cabinet Maker on Hog Hill Norwich 2 large second hand double-flapped Mohogany Tables, also one second hand

Mohogany dressing Table with Drawers, also one new Mohogany Washing-Stand, for all which paid 4.14.6 that is, for the
2 Tables 2.12.6. Dressing Table 1.11.6. Mohogany Wash-
stand 0.10.6. I think the whole of it to be very cheap.

To my Barber, Browne for a wig pd 1.1.0.

To a Quart Bottle of nice Mushrooms of Mrs Nutter paid
0.6.0.

To a Quart Bottle of Mushroom Catchup 0.3.6.

To a Baskett for packing up the same 0.0.6.

To 4 handsome Glass Salt-Cellars cut Glass at Cooks Glass
Shop paid 0.16.0.

To 12 Patty Panns &c. at Studwells pd 0.2.6.

To 12 Yards of Diaper for Towells pd 0.15.0.

To 6 Yards of Huckaback for Do. pd 0.6.0.

27th, Friday. Mr Custance very kindly called on me this Morn
to enquire how I did, he did not stay long as he was going on to
Mr Townshends on a Visit. I thank God had a better night of
rest than I have had the 3 last Nights. Had no Cramp at all. My
Brother recommending me last Night to carry a small Piece of
the roll Brimstone sewed up in a piece of very thin Linnen, to
bed with me and if I felt any Symptom of the Cramp to hold it
in my hand or put it near the affected part, which I did, as I
apprehended at one time it was coming into one of my legs, and
I felt no more advances of it. This I thought deserving of notice,
even in so trifling a book as this is.

DECEMBER *1st, Tuesday.* I breakfasted, dined, &c. again at
home. My Brother and Wife, Mrs Richd Clarke and Nancy
breakfasted, dined, &c. here again. Mrs Custance called at our
Gate this morning but did not come in—It being my Tithe
Audit. Mr Du Quesne also called on us this morning and stayed
about ½ an Hour with us. He is going to dine at Mr Jeanes's and
from thence to Mr Priests. The following Farmers paid me for
Tithe this Morning, and dined and stayed till after 12 at Night
at my House. Stephen Andrews, Js Pegg, John Rose, John

Norton, Henry Case, Charles Hardy, Robt Rising, Jonas Silvey, John Buck, Thos Reynolds, John Girling, John Peachman, Willm Howlett, Charles Cary, Robt Emeris, Willm Bidewell, John Greaves, John Baker, Js Pratt and John Heavers. We had for Dinner, some Salt Fish, a Couple of boiled Rabbitts and Onions, a boiled Leg of Mutton, boiled Beef and rost Beef and plumb Pudding. My Brother dined with us in the Parlour and the Ladies by themselves in the Study. There was drank, about half a Dozen Bottles of Port Wine, 8 Bottles of Rum, besides as much strong Beer, as they wished to have. I was far from well the whole Day, having a very bad Cold and a very troublesome Cough. Recd to day for Tithe about 245.11.0. Paid John Buck a poors Rate at 10d in the Pound from Michlms 1788 to Lady Day 1789. I am rated at £30 5s 0d, therefore I paid him 1.5.2½. We were all very merry, and very harmonious. My Brother sung 2 or 3 Songs.

28th, Monday. Recd of Edwd Gooch this morning for Tithe 0.6.0.

To one Willm Mason of Sparham who goes about at Christmas playing on 10 Bells gave him 0.1.6.

To my Malsters Man James Barrett Xmas Gift 0.1.0.

I walked to Church about 2 o'clock this afternoon and buried poor John Gooch who has left a Wife and several Children but most of them out. He was lately a near Neighbour of ours for some Yrs. I thought that he had been older only 48 Yrs. At Quadrille this Evening lost 0.0.6.

1790

JANUARY *28th, Thursday*. I breakfasted, supped and slept again at home. My Brother and Wife, Mrs Clarke and Nancy breakfasted, supped and slept again here. About 2 o'clock Mr and Mrs Custance called here in their Coach and took up Mrs Woodforde and Mrs Clarke and went to Mr Du Quesnes where they dined and spent the Afternoon. Mr D Quesne sent his Carriage after my Brother, self and Nancy and we also dined and spent the Afternoon at Mr Du Quesnes with him and the above Company. We returned as we went about 9 o'clock this Even'. Mr Custance shewed me a Letter when at Du Quesnes from Mr Walkers Uncle of Woodstock to a Mr Barker, Wine Merchant, at Norwich informing him that Mr Walker was a profligate abandoned young Man, and to guard Barker from trusting him with any more Money or any one else, that he should allow him 30 Pound per Annum to keep him from starving provided he made a better Use of it than he has hitherto done, and if he did not, he should even withdraw that. Mr Custance also told me that he had made use of his Name, Sir Thos Beauchamps and mine to get money raised for him at Norwich particularly the above Mr Barker of whom he has had 300 Pound, besides many others. Among the others Hylett, Hostler at the Kings Head to whom he owes 50 Pound. Also Mr Custance told me that Walker should say that he was coming over to my House for a few Days, was to be married to Betsy Davy very soon, that I was her Guardian and he was to have her fortune of me directly on the Marriage &c. I was astonished to hear such things, but not so much as I should otherwise, had I not been an eye-witness in some degree of his profligacy and extravagance. I have a long time given him up, his behaviour to me last Winter made me despise him utterly. Nancys encouraging him to come to my House after such behaviour has greatly lessened my esteem for her, as she shewed no regard for me. After Tea and Coffee we got to Cards won 0.1.0. The Wind being very high about 12 o'clock I did not get to bed till after 2 o'clock in the Morn'.

30th, Saturday. Sent Ben to Norwich this morning after News &c., he returned by Dinner time. No Letters. Walker is talked of very much at Norwich, there are two Writs out against him, he is gone of but is supposed to be at Thetford at an Inn. Neither won or lost at Quadrille this Evening.

FEBRUARY *4th, Thursday*. My poor Cow very weak indeed not able to get up. My poor Greyhound Patch died in the Night in her Kennel, she had fresh strained herself a Day or two ago, and hurt herself so much that she could not stand at all and groaned very much. Mr Du Quesne made us a long Morning Visit and brought over his Violin and played a good deal. Mr Priest and Son, Robert of Reepham called also on us whilst Mr Du Quesne was with us. Mr Priest and Son returned with Mr Du Quesne to spend the Day and night with him at Tuddenham. Dr Thorne of Mattishall called on us whilst we were at dinner, had about half dined, and he sat down and eat very hearty of a rosted Pigg, drank Tea with us and left us a little before 8. Not a word mentioned concerning Walkers Situation.

5th, Friday. My poor Cow rather better this morning, but not able to get up as yet, she having a Disorder which I never heard of before or any of our Somersett Friends. It is called Tailshot, that is, a separation of some of the Joints of the Tail about a foot from the tip of the Tail, or rather a slipping of one Joint from another. It also makes all her Teeth quite loose in her head. The Cure, is to open that part of the Tail so slipt lengthways and put in an Onion boiled and some Salt, and bind it up with some coarse Tape. I took a Walk to Weston House this Morning and after chatting with Mrs Custance, christened a

Child of Mrs Alldis the Housekeeper by name Betty. My Brother complained a good deal to day of a pain in his Stomach, which he is afraid that it proceeds from something gouty there.

28th, Sunday. I read Prayers and Preached this Morning at Weston Church, and also churched a Woman. None from Weston House at Church, Mrs Custance being in the Pains of Child-birth, 'Pray God Almighty befriend her and grant her a happy moment' is the sincere Wish and Prayers of not only myself but of all my Friends now at Weston Parsonage. Sent up this Evening to Weston House again and to our great Joy received the good News that Mrs Custance was safely brought to bed of a Boy and both as well as possibly could be wished.

MARCH *3rd, Wednesday.* I breakfasted, dined &c. again at home. My Brother and Wife, Mrs Clarke and Nancy breakfasted, dined &c. here again. Nancy had a Letter by Mr Cary from Mrs Davy of Foulsham relating almost the same bad Actions that Walker had been guilty of &c. I wish now to break of every Connection with Mrs Davy and all her long train of Acquaintance. I desired Nancy to drop her Acquaintance by all means, which if she does not (after their Characters are so well known) she will disoblige me as much as she possibly can do, and so &c. Mrs Davy in her Letter desires her to look for a House to board at in her Neighbourhood as she intends leaving Foulsham very soon. N.B. I dont think Nancy has had a Letter from her before for the last twelvemonth. Nancy's Character (being too intimate with Miss Davy) is not talked of so well: as she used to go with Betsy Davy and Walker to Norwich &c. by themselves. They all spent the Day and slept at Mrs Davy's at Foulsham when Mrs Davy was gone from home. Betsys Character is entirely ruined by her indiscreet ways, many times out by themselves, suffered herself to go for his Wife at public Places &c. Walker even boasts (as people say) of his behaviour to Betsy and says the worst of things of her. He now proves to be one of the most profligate, wicked, artful, ungrateful and deceiving Wretches I ever heard of, I never liked him. I believe both Mother Davy and Daughter also to be very cunning, close and not without much Art. I never wish to meet them again at my House none of the 3.

APRIL *6th, Tuesday*. When I got up this morning, perceived a violent pain in my right great Toe on my Foot about the middle Joint and swelled a great deal indeed could scarce get on my Slipper, and then could not keep him on long, but get into a pair of Shoes. I should think it must be the Gout. This is the first Attack I ever met with before now. One Woods belonging to this Parish with a Wife and Family now living at Dunham, called on me this Morning to ask some Charity, his House wch he rented at Dunham being burnt down last Thursday whilst he was out at work and all his goods burnt. I ordered Betty to give him for me 0.5.0. The Parish also has promised him 2 Guineas. At Quadrille this Evening won 0.0.5. I was rather better this night going to bed altho' late but still much pain in my great Toe.

27th, Tuesday. Recd a Note this Morning from Dr Thorne informing me of the death of his Nephew Walker, and that he should be glad to have him buried at Weston on Thursday next. I returned an answer to it.

29th, Thursday. Between 1 and 2 o'clock this Afternoon walked to Weston Church and buried Mr Thorne's Nephew Robert George Walker, aged 23 Years. He was brought in a Hearse with 4 Horses, but from whence I know not. Dr Thorne was present, and a young Man Son of Mr Thorne of Kimberly, and a short Man at whose house Walker was at, were all that attended. My Brother walked with me to Weston Church. I had a black silk Hatband and a pair of Beaver Gloves. And the Dr also gave me 1.1.0. There was not the least Description on the Coffin or any kind of Ornament, quite plain and uncoloured. At Quadrille this Evening won 0.1.0.

MAY *4th, Tuesday*. Mr and Mrs Forster of Lenewade Bridge

called on us this morning. They came to talk with me about the behaviour they have lately received from Mr Jeanes since Mr Forster has purchased the College Estate at Witchingham of the Le Neve's. That Mr Jeanes behaved very strangely to him and his Wife on Sunday last at Church and after Mr Jeanes in such a violent Passion with Mr Forster. About 1 o'clock took a walk by myself to Weston House and chatted an Hour with Mrs Custance and Miss Custance.

10th, Monday. Between 12 and 1 o'clock we all sat of for Norwich in two of the Kings Head Chaises. Got to Norwich about 2 o'clock, partook of a cold Collation at the Kings Head and at 3 got into one of the Yarmouth Coaches and of for Yarmouth and about 7 in the Evening (thank God) got safe thither to the Angel Inn in the Market Place, kept by a Mr and Mrs Dark.

At Norwich I paid and gave abt 0.5.0.

To the Yarmouth Coachman gave 0.3.0.

At Accle for Rum and Water pd 0.0.6.

My Brother and Wife and Mrs R. Clarke, very highly pleased with Yarmouth and the Sea View. We supped and slept at the Angel at Yarmouth. My Servant Briton I took with us.

12th, Wednesday. I breakfasted, dined, supped and slept again at the Angel Inn at Yarmouth, as did likewise My Brother and Wife, Mrs R. Clarke and Nancy. As soon as we had breakfasted we got into the Yarmouth Coaches again and took a ride on the Beach, called at a public House on the Coast and had some refreshment, and returned home about 2 o'clock to our Inn to dinner. Paid and gave the public House on the Beach 0.2.0. In the Evening I called on Lady Bacon who is in Lodgings near the New-Chapel Yarmouth. I stayed with her about half an Hour.

To a small Box Compass pd 0.1.0.

To a small Book with some Poems of Goldsmith 0.0.9.

At a Pot-House on the Quay with my Brother amongst some jolly Tars, for Porter 0.0.4.

For some Cakes at a Confectioners pd 0.1.0.

302

At a Hospital for old Sailors gave 0.1.0.

13th, Thursday. I breakfasted and dined at the Angel Inn at Yarmouth, as did also my Brother and Wife, Mrs R. Clarke and Nancy. After breakfast I walked out with the Ladies to see the New-Chapel and to attend divine Service there this Morning being Holy-Thursday, but when we got thither, there was no Duty at the Chapel, however the Clerk shewed us over the Chapel. I gave to the Clerk for shewing it 0.1.0. We then walked down to the Quay and called at a Mr Ramey's to see some very curious drawings of Mrs Rameys, done by a red hot Poker on Box. They were very curious indeed and highly finished. To the Servant Man that shewed it us gave 0.1.0. We then returned to our Inn and dined on some cold Meat and Sallad and some Tarts. My Brother did not go with us, but went out by himself and did not return till we had almost dined; he had been out with some Tars and had been drinking with them and was a little merry.

JUNE *3rd, Thursday.* Two of the Kings-Head Chaises came to my House this Afternoon according to order, and at 5 o'clock we all sat of for Norwich—My Brothers Wife, Mrs Clarke and Nancy in one Chaise, and my Brother and self in the other, we got to Norwich by Tea-time to the Kings Head where we all drank Tea, supped and slept. Gave to my Brother this Evening my Silver Cork-Screw with a five Guinea Norwich Bank Note wrapped round it—'Pignus Amicitiae'*—St Peter's very musical Bells rung this Evening which highly pleased our Somersett Friends as they never heard them before. We were all rather low at our leaving Weston Parsonage this Afternoon. Our Somersett Friends go of for the West to Morrow Aft. 3 o'clock.

4th, Friday. I breakfasted, dined, supped and slept at Norwich. Nancy breakfasted, dined &c. &c. at Norwich. My Brother and Wife, and Mrs Clarke, breakfasted and dined with us at the Kings Head, and at 3 o'clock, this Afternoon, after taking leave

* 'Pledge of friendship'.

of us, they went of for London in the Expedition Coach, from the Kings Head—a double-Coach. Mrs Clarke but very indifferent with a swelled Face. It being the Kings Birthday St Peters Bells rang most part of the Day and at 1 o'clock Lord Heathfields Light Horse were drawn up in the Market Place and fired 3 Vollies in honour of the Day. We also saw St Andrews Hall and likewise the Mayor and Aldermen go from thence full dressed to the great Church to Prayers and a Sermon this Morning about 11. I gave to a Man at St Andrews Hall 0.1.0. Shewed the Ladies also Bunns Rural Gardens and the Iron-Foundery this Morning. At parting we were all very low on the Occasion. Pray God send them a safe Journey into the West. Nancy and self took a Walk in the Evening to Mr Priests Senr and there drank Tea with Mr and Mrs Priest and their Son John. Soon after Tea a Dr Hooke and one Mr Taylor joined us, and I played one Rubber at Whist with Mr Priest Senr, Dr Hooke and Mr Taylor, I lost 0.1.6. At 7 o'clock I took Nancy with me in one of the Hackney Coaches down to Bunns Gardens to hear a Concert and see some Fireworks. We stayed there till near 11 o'clock—the Concert was midling, the Fireworks very good. Paid at the Gardens for 2 Tickets 0.2.0. We returned as we went and in the same Coach. Paid the Coachman there and back, 0.3.0. There was very little genteel Company there, but as Nancy never saw any publick Gardens before, she was well pleased with the sight. Lord Orfords droll-dressed Militia Men at Norwich, red Cloth Slops and long white Trowsers. Paid Nancy for her Pigg that was lately killed 9 Stone 1.11.6.

JULY *15th, Thursday*. Paid a Qtrs Land-Tax to Js Pegg this morning 3.0.0. To a poor Woman from Dereham by name Hall with a small Child with her was taken very ill with a violent Pain within her by my great Gates and was laid down in the road, I went out to her and gave her a good Glass of Gin and gave her sixpence to go to the Inn, but she did not go there but returned back towards Dereham. She is a Widow and belongs to the House of Industry near Dereham. I hope she is no Impostor. Mr and Mrs Custance with Mr George Beauchamp and his new Bride drank Tea with us this Afternoon. After Coffee and Tea we got to Cards to limited Loo at one penny a Fish, at which won, about 0.4.0. Nancy lost at it 6s 1d. Nancy owes me at Cards this Even' 7s 1d. Mr B lost upwards of a Guinea. They left us a little before 9 o'clock. Mrs Beauchamp much like her sister Lady Beauchamp not so handsome, but taller and larger. Thank God! something better after taking Rhubarb last night.

AUGUST 3rd, Tuesday. I thank God, had a tolerable good Night last Night. I drank but very little Wine Yesterday or to day only 2 or 3 Glasses. I used myself before and all last Winter to near a Pint of Port Wine every Day and I now believe did me much harm.

28th, Saturday. Briton went early this Morning to Norwich on horseback, after News-papers &c. I sent a long Letter to my Sister Pounsett by him. He returned home to dinner—No Letters. In shearing Wheat this Afternoon Briton cut off part of his left hand Thumb with the Sickle, owing in a great Measure to his making too free with Liquor at Norwich to day, having met his Uncle Scurl there who treated him with Wine. It bled very much I put some Friars Balsam to it and had it bound up, he almost fainted.

SEPTEMBER 10th, Friday. We breakfasted before 7 o'clock this Morning: at half past eight Mrs Custance took us up into her Coach and carried us to Norwich and put us down at St Peter of Mancroft Church before eleven o'clock and there we stayed till three in the Afternoon highly delighted indeed with the Musical performance. Select Pieces from the Messiah, Joshua &c., a great Band with the Abbey Double Drums; between 8 and 900 People present. Tickets 5s 0d each. Segniora Storace the principal Singer, Miss Pool the second. Saw Sir Edmd and

Lady Bacon, Sir Thos and Lady Beauchamp, Sir John Wood-house, Mr Hobart, Mr Windham and our New Bishop Dr Horne and Family &c. We returned with Mrs Custance to Weston House about 5 in the Afternoon and there took a Family Dinner with her and Mr Custance. The latter was but just returned from Scottow having been there ever since Monday last in adjusting the late Sir Thos Durrants Affairs, he being left joint Executor with Lady Durrant. We returned home to Weston Parsonage by 8, rather fatigued with the hurry of the Day. On our return home found a Note on my Table from Mr Jeanes, to put off our dining with him, on Monday next instead of to Morrow. As the Haunch of Venison will be better by being kept till then as supposed by some—Hope it will be sweet.

17th, Friday. The young Woman Spincks (who lately had a Bastard Child by one Garthon of Norwich) called on me this morning to acquaint me that her Child is dead, died last night, owing it is supposed to her given him a Sleeping Pill which she had of her Neighbour Nobbs whose Husband is very ill and had some composing Pills from Mr Thornes, one of which Nobbs wife advised her to give her Child to put him to sleep whilst she was out. The Child slept for about 5 hours, then he waked and fell into convulsion fits wch continued for 4 Hours and half and then died in great Agonies. If the Child died owing to the effects of the Pill, I believe it not intentionally given to destroy the Child as she always had taken particular care of him and looked remarkably healthy. I advised her to make herself easy on that respect. Mr Peachman and Mr Buck also called on me this morning soon after and talked with me a good deal on the death of the Child. They both think that the Childs Death was owing to the Mothers giving the Pill to it. I had no objection I told them of burying the Child without the Coroner Inquest, as It was possible the Child might have died without taking the Pill, however it ought to be well considered on for the public good. I took a walk with my Niece to Weston House this morning, in our way there we met with Mr Custance in Weston

Field, and soon after Mr Press Custance with another gentleman by name Mitchel out of Devonshire, on a shooting party, Mr Du Quesne also we saw in Weston Field whilst with Mr Custance in his return home from Reepham. If I mistake not the above gentleman by name Mitchel who was with Mr Press Custance I saw at Bruton Church when last in Somersett, and I believe Son of Mr Mitchel the School-master at Bruton and a Clergyman and who came from Devonshire. He looked exactly like him I must confess. We stayed about an Hour with Mr and Mrs Custance and returned home to dinner. In the Afternoon I walked to Mr Bucks and advised him and the Woman Spincks to inform the Father of the Child of its death and to send for Mr Thorne to have his Opinion whether the Childs Death was owing to the Pill being given it, as Mr Thorne made them. Mr Buck sent immediately to Mr Thorne. I returned home to Tea before the Dr came. To Largesses to day gave o.2.o.

18th, Saturday. Sent Briton early to Norwich this morning with my little Cart, returned not till 3 this Afternoon the Cart being obliged to have something done to it. No Letters at all. He brought 2 pair of Soals and half a Dozen new Maccarel the first this Season. Mr Thorne called here about Noon having been to see the dead Child and said that its Death was owing to the Mothers giving it part of the Pill. Soon after the Doctor went, the Mother of the Child Eliz. Spincks came here to know what to do, I told her to go to the Overseer (Emery) to send for the Coroner and inspect the Body before I could bury it. To Largesses to day, gave o.4.o.

19th, Sunday. I read Prayers and Preached this Afternoon at Weston Church. Mrs Custance with her 2 Daughters at Church. It being a fine Day Nancy was at Church. But few Farmers at Church this Afternoon on Account of an Inquest being taken by a Coroner from Norwich on the Body of Eliz. Spincks Boy. They were from 1 till near 5 on the above business. The Jury brought in their Verdict—not intentionally given by the Mother to her Child. This Evening between 6 and 7 I buried the Child (by name Garthon Spincks) in the Churchyard. As we were walking back from Church we met with Mr Forster in his Market-Cart and with him Mr Priest of Norwich whose intention was to have been at Weston Church this Aft. but they were too late. We saw them just by our House. I asked them to walk in but they did not. Mr Priests Wife is at Lenewade Bridge at Forsters. Mr Forster asked us to drink Tea to Morrow in the Afternoon to meet the Priests of Reepham there.

24th, Friday. Nancy was taken very ill this Afternoon with a pain within her, blown up so as if poisoned, attended with a vomiting. I supposed it proceeded in great measure from what she eat at Dinner and after. She eat for Dinner some boiled Beef rather fat and salt, a good deal of a nice rost duck, and a plenty of boiled Damson Pudding. After Dinner by way of Desert, she eat some green-gage Plumbs, some Figgs, and Rasberries and Cream. I desired her to drink a good half pint Glass of warm Rum and Water which she did and soon was a little better — for Supper she had Water-gruel with a Couple of small Table Spoonfuls of Rum in it, and going to bed I gave her a good dose of Rhubarb and Ginger. She was much better before she went to bed — And I hope will be brave to Morrow.

OCTOBER *18th, Monday.* I walked to Weston Church this morning about 11 o'clock and there married Thomas Arthurton and Mary Newel both single Persons by banns for which I received only 0.2.6 having recd half a Crown before on their banns. After my return from Church I mounted my Mare and rode to Mr Du Quesnes, to enquire how he was, having heard yesterday that he was but very indifferent. On my arrival there found him tolerably well and cheerful, stayed with him an hour and returned home to dinner. He told me that he had lately a palpitation of the heart which alarmed him. I advised him when attacked by it again to take a small Tea-spoonful of Ether in a Wine Glass of Water. I am inclined to think that his Complaint proceeds from flatulencies, as People advanced in Years are much subject to. He seemed much inclined to my Opinion. He was sorry that I could not dine with him on friday next to meet Mr and Mrs Custance, Mr and Mrs Townshend and with them, Lord and Lady Stawel of Holte-Forest near Farnham, Surrey. The present Lord Stawel is Son of the late Hon. Henry Bilson Legge. Lady Stawel, late Miss Curzon, is Daughter of Asheton Curzon Esq. Brother of Lord Scarsdale. Mr Custance and self cannot wait on them—Mr Custance being obliged to go to Lady Durrants and myself obliged to attend the Arch Deacons Visitation at Reepham on that Day. Mrs Custance goes and takes my Niece with her. St Faiths Fair to day. Weather against it. My Servant Maid, Nanny Kaye, was desirous of going there, had my Leave and went on foot, returned home about 9 in the Evening.

NOVEMBER *20th, Saturday.* To Mr Cantrell's Servant Lad for bringing me one Dozen of Port Wine and 2 Gallons of Rum in a small Cask, gave him 0.0.6. Returned by him 13 Bottles and the empty Cask. I buried about 2 o'clock this Afternoon poor Lydia Betts, Widow of the late old Richd Betts. I did not know that she was ill, till she was dead. She was above 70 Years of Age, I was told. The Corpse was carried by my House, and what was remarkable a recruiting Party with a Drum and fife and Flag flying, passed just before all by chance—Drum beating and fife playing. They came from Lyng, Lyng fair being Yesterday in pursuit of a young Fellow who had listed Yesterday and had run away, and who shd that young Fellow be but Barber, Mr Hardy's the Mason's Lad, to whom I gave a Shilling to last Saturday, hearing he was a good sober Lad and particularly kind to his aged Mother. Mr Cary brought our News from Norwich. No Letter.

25th, Thursday. Nancy repeated to me this Evening seventy two Verses taken out of a Magazine of some of the Kings of England from 1066 the time that William the Conqueror began to reign till 1737 when George the 2nd succeeded his Father

George the 1st. She repeated them without missing one Word. I sent Ben after breakfast round the Parish to let them know that my Tithe Audit will be Tuesday. He returned about 4 in the Aft. pretty full of Liquor. Every Farmer almost asked him to drink.

DECEMBER *8th, Wednesday*. Paid Charles Cary, Shoemaker, this Morn', 2.8.0.

Paid Mr Palmer my Malster this morning a Bill for Malt &c. for the last Year, 22.18.6.

Paid Mr Baker my Butcher this Morning a Bill for Meat for the last Year, 46.5.0.

Paid Mr Cantrell for Porter &c. last Year, 4.13.0.

Poor old John Clarke departed this Life, and I hope for a better, this Morning. I walked over this Evening to my Neighbour John Clarke's, whom, as I heard was rather worse but I found him better than I expected to find him, but still very indifferent and very low. I gave him to buy Oatmeal for Water Gruel 0.1.0 and when I got home I sent him over a Bottle of white Wine to put into his Gruel and likewise part of a cold rost Loin of Veal.

12th, Sunday. I read Prayers and Preached this Afternoon at Weston Church. Mr and Mrs Custance at Church. Being a dry fair Day there was a large Congregation. Lent my Servant Man, Ben Leggatt, this Morning my Mare Phyllis to go to a Place called Crownthorpe on some particular Business of his own and he stayed out the whole day and was not returned home when I went to bed which was not till after one o'clock in the Morning. It made me and the whole Family very uneasy, thinking some Accident must have befallen him. It made me quite unhappy.

13th, Monday. When I came down Stairs this Morning could hear no tidings of Ben at all, which still made me more uneasy. I then sent for Willm Large and sent him on horseback after him. And about 2 o'clock Ben with Willm Large returned and

I thank God safe and well. Ben went Yesterday in the Afternoon with a Mr Watson Steward to Sir John Woodhouse to Kimberly Hall, where having made too free with the Baronets strong Beer, fell of his Horse coming home and lost her, so that he walked about all the Night after her and did not find her till about Noon, she was found at Kimberly in a Stable of Mr Hares, a boy happening to see and put her in there. I ordered Willm Large to dine here and to have 2s od. Thank God! that Matters turned out no worse. Windy and wet and my Study Chimney smoaked. Nancy also had a Note from Mrs Bodham to let us know that they with Miss Anne Donne from Norwich would dine with us on Wednesday next and sleep that Night. I was very indifferent all day long could eat but very little and not relish that, tho' we had a fine fat rost Goose for Dinner.

15th, Wednesday. The Wind was exceeding high indeed in the Night, or rather very early this Morning, it was almost as high as the first of January 1779. I got up at about 3 o'clock this Morning but did not go out of my Bed-Chamber, and did not return to bed till 7 o'clock after or thereabout, The NW Wind very high and alarming during that whole time, had a little rest when I returned to bed (tho the Wind still rather high) till near 10 o'clock. I then got up and the Wind rose again and at 12 was as high as ever it was in the Night and greatly alarmed me again and continued so till after 2 in the Afternoon and then (blessed be God for it) it gradually abated. Both my Rooms below stairs smoaked a good deal this Morning, and expecting Company to dinner also it vexed me. And my Maid Betty Dade breaking likewise the only Tea China-Slop-Basin at breakfast or after in the Kitchen made me more fretful. May God Almighty protect those on the Sea who were exposed more immediately to such high Wind and may we not hear of any very great damage either by Sea or Land—And may all escape thro' the blessing of God as well as we have done. It shook our Rooms above Stairs and below. We received no Injury (thank God) whatever. About half past two o'clock this Afternoon Mr and Mrs Bodham with Miss Anne Donne of Norwich came to my House and they dined, supped and slept here. Soon after they came Mr Jeanes of Witchingham came to us and he dined and spent the Afternoon with us, and after Tea and Coffee he returned home to his Wife. We had for Dinner a Couple of Chicken boiled and a Ham, the best part of a large Rump of Beef boiled, a plumb Pudding, a very fine fat Turkey rosted Tarts &c. We dined and supped in the best Parlour, neither smoaked but little. After Tea we got to Quadrille, at which I won, o.2.6. Mr and Mrs Bodham slept in our best Room — Miss Anne Donne with Nancy in the Attic's. Mr Bodhams Coach Horses with Coachman returned home after staying a very little time. Mr Bodham's Servant Lad, Thomas, stayed here and slept with my Servant Man, Briton. We gave our Company for Supper a rost Duck some rosted Potatoes, Artichokes, Red Herrings, hashed Turkey, Tarts &c. It was after 12 o'clock before I got to bed. The Wind (thank God) quite down by bed-time. Miss Anne Donne, second Daughter of Doctor Donne of Norwich, is a very merry, agreeable, fashionable, young Lady but not handsome.

28th, Tuesday. To my Chimney-Sweepers Son, Frank Holland for his Christmas Box as usual, gave, o.1.0. To Willm Mason of Sparham who used to go about at Christmas with 10 Bells, and has this Year got a Bell-Harp, gave, o.1.6. Nancy had a Letter this Evening from her Brother William at Gallhampton near C. Cary Somersett. Mr Custances Servant brought it from Norwich. All Friends tolerably well in the Country, his Mother he says is crazy and calls herself Lady Woodforde. William talks in a very high Stile of his House and furniture and improvements he is still making.

1791

JANUARY *1st, Saturday*. I breakfasted, dined, &c. again at home. Nancy breakfasted, dined, &c. again at home. We did not set up last Night to usher in the New Year, as it might be as well omitted and by the blessing of God hope that this Year may bring more pleasant Days than the last Year to me. Since our Somersett Friends left us in June last my Niece hath been almost daily making me uneasy by continually complaining of the dismal Life she leads at Weston Parsonage for want of being more out in Company and having more at home, tho' I enjoy no more than herself. It was not so in 1780.

8th, Saturday. Ben went early with my great Cart to Norwich, and carried in it 10 Coomb 2 Bshls of Barley to Mr Bloomes at the Duke's Palace. The high Wind waked me about 2 o'clock this Morning and tho' I did not get up yet the Wind continued near the same, without my sleeping any more, at half past 8 got up, very much deranged for want of more sleep, the Wind still continuing the same, and is still very high at my writing this tho' past seven o'clock in the Evening. At 11 calm. Holland with his two Sons Franck and George, Chimney Sweepers, were here this Morning about four o'clock and swept my Study, Parlour, Kitchen and Back Kitchen, Study Chamber and Parlour Chamber Chimneys, and thank God recd no hurt tho' the Wind was very high all the Time. I gave his youngest Son George a Xmas Box, 0.1.0. They all made a comfortable Dinner on cold Meat. Ben did not return till 5 o'clock this Evening. Mr Bloome had my Barley upon honour, no price sent back, as he always gives me as much as any. He brought back ½ Chldrn* of

* A chaldron is a dry measure equal to 36 bushels when applied to coal and 23 for other substances.

Coal from Mr Bloome. Nancy sent a long Letter by him to her Aunt John Woodforde. No Letters for us. No News I hope recd is better for us.

FEBRUARY *20th, Sunday.* I read Prayers and Preached this Afternoon at Weston Church—Mr and Mrs Custance at Church. I was rather out of temper this Aft. on Account of my Maid's (Nanny Kaye) Banns being not published this Afternoon by me, as she never mentioned it to me before I went to Church. Pray God! forgive me.

21st, Monday. To a little Boy (Edward) of one of Downings Girls by Mr Barton late of this Parish—gave 0.1.0—As he was assisting my Boy pulling Turnips. Had a Couple of Tubbs of Gin brought me this Evening about 8 o'clock—soon safely lodged.

27th, Sunday. I read Prayers and Preached this Morning at Weston Church. None from Weston House at Church—It being a very cold, windy, and wet Day, as bad a Day almost and as cold, as any during all Winter. I published the Banns for the first time between my Maid Nanny Kaye and Willm Spraggs of Attlebridge. recd for publishing the same 0.2.6 which I gave to my Maid (Nanny) on my return from Church, and at the same time told her that I hoped she might repent not of what she was about to do. She is about 34 and he about 20 with an indifferent Character.

MARCH *8th, Tuesday.* Gave poor Roberts one of my old Shirts to put on in the small-Pox—His, poor Fellow, being so extremely coarse and rough, that his having the small-Pox so very full, his coarse Shirt makes it very painful to him. I sent his Family a Basket of Apples and some black Currant Robb.* There are many, many People in the Parish yet have never had the Small-pox. Pray God all may do well that have it or shall have it. Went this Afternoon and saw poor old John Peachman Who

* A conserve of fruit, rather like jelly, made by boiling the juice of a fruit with sugar.

is very lame, found him unable to walk and having no relief from the Parish gave him money. Called also at Tom Carys Shop and left some money for Roberts's Familys Use for such useful things as they might want and they have. Recd for 4 Pints, ½ Butter, at 9d, 0.3.4. Lady Durrant at Weston House.

11th, Friday. Mem. The Stiony on my right Eye-lid still swelled and inflamed very much. As it is commonly said that the Eye-lid being rubbed by the tail of a black Cat would do it much good if not entirely cure it, and having a black Cat, a little before dinner I made a trial of it, and very soon after dinner I found my Eye-lid much abated of the swelling and almost free from Pain. I cannot therefore but conclude it to be of the greatest service to a Stiony on the Eye-lid. Any other Cats Tail may have the above effect in all probability — but I did my Eye-lid with my own black Tom Cat's Tail.

15th, Tuesday. My right Eye again, that is, its Eye-lid much inflamed again and rather painful. I put on a plaistor to it this morning, but in the Aft. took it of again, as I perceived no good from it. I buried poor John Roberts this Afternoon about 5 o'clock, aged about 35 Yrs.

APRIL *6th, Wednesday.* I walked to Church this Morning and married my late Maid, Anne Kaye, and Willm Spraggs Junr of Attlebridge, by Banns, I gave my fee which I received of the Man, to the Woman. The Man's Brother Andrew Spraggs was Father. Brewed a Barrel of Strong Beer.

15th, Friday. Quite a Summer's Day to day. All Nature gay. Turnips quite a dead Load upon the Land. Many are obliged to throw them into Ditches &c. I am obliged to carry many off from Carys Close.

MAY *1st, Sunday.** I read Prayers and Preached this Afternoon

* From this date JW almost invariably notes the daily dinner at the Parsonage. Hitherto he has merely set down the more elaborate meals provided for guests.

315

at Weston Church and also christened a Child. None from Weston House at Church, had but a small Congregation being very wet. Dinner—Breast of Veal rosted.

JUNE *27th, Monday*. Mr and Mrs Jeanes and Mr Springger called at the bottom of our Garden this morning abt 10 o'clock in their Journey into Hampshire but did not stay with us above 10 Minutes and were off. Mrs Jeanes and Mr Springger with two Children were in Mr Jeanes's close Chaise, and Mr Jeanes was in his little low Cart. He had his grey Horse led by a Man. Hired Horses from Norwich to go in the Close Chaise. They were to call at Mr Du Quesnes and have a Snap.* They go to Attleborough, Thetford &c. to London. Mrs Custance with her two eldest Sons, Hambleton and George spent an Hour with us this Afternoon. Counter-Revolution in France, the King, Queen and Dauphin have made their escape. Dinner to day Hash-Mutton and a Suet Pudding &c.

29th, Wednesday. The News of to day, is, that the French King and Queen &c. are retaken and carried back to Paris.† I hope that it is not true, tho' on Lloyds Paper.

JULY *14th, Thursday*. I hope this Day will be attended with no bad Consequences, this being the Day that the French Revolution first took Place there last Year, and many Meetings advertised to be held this Day in London, Norwich &c. throughout this Kingdom to commemorate the above Revolution. Pray God! continue thy Goodness to this Land and defeat all the designs of the Enemies to it. Dinner to day, Giblet Soup and Shoulder Mutton rosted. Very busy all day about painting the Doors of my Coach House &c., quite tired at Night.

21st, Thursday. Shocking Accounts on the Papers of dreadful

* A snack.

† These references are to the French royal family's abortive flight to Varennes.

Riots at Birmingham, Nottingham &c. on Account of commemorating the French Revolution the fourteenth of this Month. The Presbyterian and Independent Meeting Houses pulled down to the Ground and the inside furniture burnt, many of the Dissenters Houses destroyed, amongst the rest Dr Priestlys, both Town and Country Houses burnt.

AUGUST 2nd, Tuesday. My Servant Maid Nanny Golding had another Fit this morning, screamed out most hideously and so loud that Ben heard her in a Field beyond the Cover, where he was hoeing Turnips. I never heard so frightful a Shriek or crying out. She continued in the fit near an Hour and then went to bed with a violent headache, and there lay all Day and night. It frightned us all. I must part with her at Michaelmas. Brewed a Barrell of Beer to day. Nancy recd a Letter this Afternoon by Mr Custance's Servant from her Brother Saml who is just arrived in England from Italy, it was dated from Dover July 30, last Saturday, he was very well and going for London and from thence into Somersett, says nothing of coming here. Dinner to day rost Beef and Gooseberry Pye.

7th, Sunday. I read Prayers and Preached this Morning at Weston Church. Mr Custance at Church, as was Nancy. Poor Love the Painter who lived with his Father at Norwich was buried Yesterday, he had been in a low way some time owing to his being very deaf, and one day last Week cut his Throat— pray God forgive him. He was a great Support to a very infirm and aged Father, and afraid that he might be reduced to want. He was a young Man of good Character and much respected, he used to be much at Weston House, and has painted some Rooms for me, and gilded my Weather Cock the last thing he did for me. I am sorry for him.

14th, Sunday. I read Prayers and Preached this Afternoon at Weston Church. St Edmd Bacon was at Church and the only Person in Mr Custances Seat. There was a large Congregation at Church. Poor old Js Smith my Clerk made a shocking hand of it in singing this Afternoon at Church, much laughed at. Dinner to day, Fillett of Veal rosted.

SEPTEMBER *12th, Monday.* Gave my Servant-Maid, Nanny Golding, warning this Morning to leave my Service at Michaelmas next, on Account of her being subject to bad fits. I was sorry to do it, as she was or at least appeared to be, a very good Servant. I should have been glad to have kept her—if I could, but fits are dreadful, they are so very alarming and come on so suddenly.

To Andrews's Men, a largess, gave, 0.1.0.

To Howletts Ditto, gave, 0.1.0.

To Pratts Ditto, gave, 0.1.0.

Dinner to day Veal Soup, Veal Collops, and Bacon and a brace of Partridges rosted and Apple Dumplins.

16th, Friday. A Hare being seen near my House by Ben I went out with my Dogs, found her, had a very fine Course and killed her. Dinner to day Jugged Hare, very good.

OCTOBER *12th, Wednesday.* I paid my Maid Nanny Golding this Morning her half Years Wages due Oct. 10, 2.12.6. And about 2 o'clock this Afternoon her Mother came after her and she returned with her to her own home. I was sorry to part with her as she was a very good Servant I believe and had it not been that she was subject to fits, should not have parted with her so soon. Pray God! she might get better of the fits. Since she has taken Assafoetida Drops by my desire she has not had a fit since. I gave her the remaining part of a bottle to carry home. My new Maid Winfred Budery came home this Evening about 5 o'clock. I hope she will do. Dinner to day a Couple of rost Chicken and Piggs Face and a broiled blade bone of Veal.

28th, Friday. Nancy had a Letter from her Aunt Jon Woodforde this Evening by Mr Custance's Servant George—In which is mentioned the Death of Mr James Clarke on the 27 of September last. Mr Franck Woodforde and Mr Messiter Executors for his Children—Nothing mentioned of Mrs R. Clarke having anything. My Sister Pounsett was said to be very indifferent. Pray God! she may soon get better. Mrs Thornton of Hatspen also dead, and Mr Perry late of Ansford Inn died lately at Glastonbury. Mr Willm Ashford said to be in a decline. Sister Clarke but poorly and her Son as strange as ever.

NOVEMBER *15th, Tuesday*. About Noon (being fine) I walked out a coursing taking only Briton and the Boy with me, Ben being in Weston Great Field plowing. We stayed out till near 4 o'clock, saw no Hare but coursed one Rabbit and killed it. We walked over most of the large Brakes by Ringland. Nancy very busy with the Maids all the Morning in making some black Puddings &c.

DECEMBER *12th, Monday*. Most piercing cold indeed this morning and a sharper Frost if anything than Yesterday, it froze within Doors in a very few Minutes this Morn. The Thermometer was this Morning at nine o'clock down to No. 42, tho' in my Study. Norton and Bush had some Words I heard to day at my Tithe Audit in the Kitchen, which was never mentioned to me before or known by me till Norton himself came and told me this Morn' he having applied to Mr Custance for a Warrant against Bush for assaulting him. Mr Custance told him to come to me. I advised him to make it up with Bush. Norton is in one of his crazy fits. It vexed me to hear of it. I thought all was harmony and Mirth that Night in the Kitchen.

25th, Sunday and Xmas Day. This being Christmas I walked to Church this Morning and read Prayers and administered the Holy Sacrament to 22 Communicants. Gave for an Offering at the Altar 0.2.6. None from Weston House at Church this Morn' the Weather being very cold, wet and windy and extreme bad Walking, being all Ice under. My Foot extremely painful, hard Matter to get to and from Church, but thank God I went thro' it all better than I expected. The following old Men dined at my House being Christmas Day and each had a Shilling apiece to carry home to their Wives, 0.6.0. James Smith, Thomas Carey, Thomas Carr, Christopher Dunnell, Nathaniel Heavers, and John Peachman. Dinner to Day Surloin of Beef rosted, plumb Puddings and mince Pies. My large Wax Candle lighted up as usual for one Hour (being Christmas Day) in the Evening. It froze again sharp this Evening. Thank God my foot was much better at Night. I laid my Foot up in a Chair almost all the Aft.

26th, Monday. To Js Fisher, blacksmiths Man, Xmas Gift, 1.0.

To Jon Austin, Butchers Man, Xmas Gift, 1.0.

It froze again all last Night and this Morning which makes it worse walking than ever.

Paid Mr Cantrell of Lenewade Bridge for Porter, Wine and Rum for the Year, 3.6.0.

To Weston Ringers, gave 0.2.6.

To Jon Short Junr, Wheelwrights Son Xmas Gift, 1.0.

To Js Barratt, Malster's Man, Ditto, 1.0.

Dinner to day, boiled Beef and Pork and Greens. Blessed be God for it, my foot is much better. Mrs Custance was brought to bed of a Daughter last Night, in about half an Hour after the Dr came. We did not hear anything of it till this Evening and then by chance. I sent up almost immediately.

1792

JANUARY *3rd, Tuesday*. Gave Betty Leave to go home for a
couple of days to see her Friends at Mattishall. Ben carried her
in my old Cart to E. Tuddenham. Master Custance with his
two Brothers, George and William made us a morning Visit,
stayed about half an Hour with us, and then I took a Walk back
with them to Weston House and there privately baptized Mrs
Custance's last Child (Born on Christmas Day last) by name
Charlotte. I was ready dressed and just going to take a Walk to
Weston-House as the young Gentlemen came. Poor Mrs Custance still extremely ill, not able to move. Mr Custance most
unhappy abt it tho' Mr Martineau* says, he sees no danger.
Pray God Almighty restore her to her former Health soon, is the
earnest Prayers and Wishes of her many many Friends, particularly to her dearest Friend and deservedly so, my much ever
respected Squire Mr Custance. It is my daily, Morning and
Evening Prayer, that she might get over it and that soon. Poor
Lady Bacon I sincerely pity on her Sister being so ill. I never
knew two Sisters in all my life testify more regard one to another
more than Lady Bacon and Mrs Custance, and I believe them
to be as good Women in every respect as England ever produced.
A Hare was found setting near the Church by John Baker Junr,
sent Ben out with my Dogs and they soon killed her. I told Ben
to give John 1s od. It was a very large Hare its weight was 8lb ½.
Dinner to day boiled Beef.

6th, Friday. Sent Briton to Weston House again this Morn'
brought me bad News of poor Mrs Custance, that she had had
a very bad Night, and all very uneasy about her at Weston-

* Doctor and man-midwife.

House. Pray God Almighty bless the means that are made use of for her Recovery and preserve her, and likewise comfort her distressed Husband, Children, and her dear Friends allied to her. Her present distressed Situation makes me very unhappy, as she has been so kind to us. Mr Thorne called on me about dinner time stayed about half an hour, left Compts to my Niece and should be glad to see her at his House to meet Miss Davy in February. I made little or no Answer to him on that Account as our Connection with the Davys are at an End. I asked him to dinner but he declined it. Nancy still at Mr Du Quesne's with Miss Priest.

14th, Saturday. Mrs Custance still continues getting better. Betty also a good deal better this Morning. The most severe Frost last Night and this Morning as I ever felt. The Milk in the Dairy in the Pans was one Piece of Ice and the Water above Stairs in the Basons froze in a few Minutes after being put there this Morn'. I don't know that I ever perceived the cold so piercing as this Morning, have kept a Charcoal-Fire in my Celler since we brewed. Dinner to day a boiled Chicken with Pork and Greens and a fat Goose rosted, and Damson Tarts &c. Billy Bidewell brought our News for us.

FEBRUARY *3rd, Friday.* Nancy now thinks that she hears better to day. Took a Walk this Morning to Weston-House stayed better than half an Hour there and then returned home to Dinner. Mrs Custance still confined to her bed and as helpless as ever, quite lame of one Side, in every other respect tolerably well. Mr Custance gone out. Dinner to day boiled Rabbit and Leg Mutton rosted. At Cribbage this Evening with Nancy, won, o.o.6. I am neither well or ill, have at times strange feeling about me, cold streams running over my Shoulders &c. at times, and restless Nights.

8th, Wednesday. Nancys hearing almost entirely recovered. Had a Note this Evening by Js Atterton from Mr Du Quesne, sent an Answer back by him, and also sent by him a Quart

Bottle of Tent Wine* and a Couple of Lemons to his Sister in Law Susan Greaves who is in the last Stage of a Consumption. Pray God comfort her in distress and soon release her. Dinner to day, boiled Leg of Pork and Peas Pudding, a rost Rabbit and Damson Tarts. At Cribbage this Evening, lost os 6d.

15th, Wednesday. Mrs Custance sent her Coach and four after Nancy this morning to spend an Hour with her in her Room which she did and returned about 1 o'clock. She found Mrs Custance better than she expected but nevertheless so bad as to be unable to move herself in bed or likely to do so perhaps for the next two Months, owing it is supposed to some violent strain in the back-bone on Child-bearing. In every other respect very well, can eat and drink heartily and now in tolerable good Spirits. After Nancy was gone I took a Walk with my People a coursing and stayed out till 3 o'clock. Coursed one Hare and one Rabbit and killed both. On my return home I privately baptized a Child of Johnny Reeves that was at my House by name Sarah. As I was a coursing this morning a Gentleman smartly dressed rode up to me and enquired whether I had seen Mr Peachman. His name was Jarrett Dashwood as Briton informed me. We had just killed a fine Hare.

APRIL *13th, Friday*. Quite Summer-like Weather. Dinner a fine Pike boiled and Veal-Cutlets. Gave my Boy Billy Downing, he having been a very good lad and of most good natured turn and having asked Leave to go to Norwich with his Mother to Morrow-Morning to buy a Pair of Breeches &c. gave him this Even' 5.0.

26th, Thursday. We dined and spent the Afternoon at Weston-House with only Mr Custance at dinner with us. We drank Coffee and Tea in the Octagon Room alias Mrs Custances dressing Room, and Mrs Custance being finely drank Tea with us, she looks very well considering her long Confinement. Tho' she

* A Spanish wine of a deep red colour (*tinto*), of low alcohol, and often used as sacramental wine.

is now able to sit up in a Chair, yet she cannot walk a step without great Assistance. This is the first time that I have seen her for the last four Months, No Gentlemen besides those of the Families have as yet been admitted to her presence, I was the first. Mr Custance sent his Coach after us, but it being fine Weather I walked thither and back. Nancy had a long Letter from her Brother Willm. Paid Mrs Custance this Afternoon my Subscription-Money for Penn's Sermons, 2 Vol. Octavo, 0.12.0.*

27th, Friday. Sent Mrs Jeanes a Couple of fat Spring Chicken by Winfred, as she cannot get any. Sent Mr Jeanes by the same Hand a black-Pudding. Mr Du Quesne dined and spent the Aft. with us He made a Visit to Weston-House before Dinner. Paid Mr Emeris this Evening, half Years Poor-Rate at 10d, in the Pound, 1.5.2½. Mr Du Quesne looked but poorly, thin and very weak. He eat however very hearty and drank much small-Beer.

MAY *21st, Monday.* Sent Briton this Evening after Nancy in my new little Curricle, she returned safe and well abt 8 o'clock, she met with a Storm on her Journey. She supped and slept at home. She gave me a worse description than ever of the bad management in Mr Jeanes House and dirtier than ever. Had not Miss Lloyd been there Nancy would not have liked it at all. Mrs Jeanes more affected. Miss Lloyd told Nancy that she could not endure being there, as she is treated by them like almost unto a Servant, being ordered about so — And as for Mrs Jeanes Brother Springer she never saw or heard so poor a *Honey*.†Dinner to day rost Shoulder of Mutton &c.

30th, Wednesday. Great Rejoicings at Weston House &c. Bells

* James Penn (1727–1800) wrote tracts and sermons, some of which, according to the *DNB*, 'show considerable humour and power'. Let one title suffice: 'By way of Prevention; a Sleepy Sermon, calculated for the Dogdays, with an Address to the Clergy and another to the Laity of the City of London'.
† A term of endearment as old as Chaucer, though obviously employed by JW to ironical effect.

ringing, Guns-firing &c. on Account of Mrs Custance coming down Stairs for the first time for the last 5 Months. I gave my People on the Occasion a bottle of Gin to drink this Evening in Kitchen. I am most heartily glad that Mrs Custance is so much recovered, hope she wont make too free. Dinner to Day boiled Chicken and Oyster Sauce, a Pigs Face, cold Loin of Veal rosted &c.

JUNE *17th, Sunday.* I read Prayers, Preached, and churched Mrs Custance this Afternoon at Weston-Church. The first time of Mrs Custance being at Church since December last, having been so long ill, she is still very weak, not able to go without a Stick. Mr Custance at Church and 3 eldest Sons and both Daughters.

AUGUST *2nd, Thursday.* I breakfasted, supped and slept again at home. After breakfast about 9 o'clock I drove Nancy to Norwich to be at the Musical Meeting at the Cathedral, for the Benefit of the publick Hospital. We got to Norwich by 11 o'clock we went immediately to the Cathedral, I gave at the entrance of the Church, 1.1.0 for the Charity, which is reckoned handsome but we were some time before we could get Seats, the Church being so exceedingly crowded. Nancy got a seat under the Orchestra and very little after I got a most excellent Seat along with the Stewards of the Charity. After Prayers, Our new Bishop gave us a very good Discourse on Charity, more particularly that for which we were assembled. His Text was from the 25 Matthew 35, 36 Verses 'I was a Stranger and ye took me in: Naked, and ye clothed me; I was sick, and ye visited me.' We had very select and grand Pieces of sacred Musick from Handels Compositions before and after the Sermon. All together it was not only delightful but seemed heavenly and gave us Ideas of divine Musick. It finished about half past two o'clock. For Musick Books at Bacons, pd 1.0. We walked, immediately as it was over, to Nosworthys where we were showed a very good room above Stairs where we had some refreshment, some Mutton

325

Stakes and a Cucumber, Porter and Port-Wine—all very cleaver. Nosworthy, when we were going away, on my asking him what we stood indebted to him said only for the Port-Wine to be paid for, but I told him that would not do, therefore I desired or insisted on his taking, 7.6 which after much intreaty he took. From thence we went to St Giles's Gate, got into our Curricle about six o'clock and thank God! arrived safe and well at home about eight o'clock, not so much fatigued as Yesterday but Nancy was pretty much tired and very hot. We called at the Falcon at Cossey on our return home and had a Tankard of Porter, pd 0.4. We had delightful Weather and we spent a very pleasant day indeed upon the whole. We never went near the Priests, they never invite us on any public Doings whatever at Norwich. Briton went with us, our Horses at the Woolpocket.

SEPTEMBER *1st, Saturday*. Mr Custance made us a long morning visit, he was on foot. He made us very uneasy by what he told us, which was, that they were going to leave Weston-House and reside at Bath in about a Month from this time, that their Children might be educated there, the Misses.

15th, Saturday. Had a Tub of Rum brought me this Evening.

16th, Sunday. We were much agitated this Evening about what I had brought me Yesterday. Bad reports about the Parish.

17th, Monday. I got up very early this Morning and was very busy all the Morn' in very necessary business.* Recd for Butter this Morn' at 10d, 3.4. Dinner to day boiled Beef very salt indeed, very much out of sorts—much jaded, and had no Appetite. Mem. John Norton is supposed to have informed against his Neighbour Buck.

* JW was presumably busy hiding or even burying the smuggled rum. By statute he was liable to a fine of £10 for each offence of buying smuggled goods, while the supplier could expect a fine of no less than £50. The Act encouraged informing, moreover: if the seller gave away the buyer within twenty days he would be let off his own offence. However, in this case Buck the blacksmith supplier got off with a small fine and JW was soon back to his secret purchases.

OCTOBER *4th, Thursday.* Took a Walk with Nancy this Morning to Weston-House to take leave of Mr and Mrs Custance and see the little folks before they set out for Bath. They go on Sunday next. We stayed an Hour with Mrs Custance saw the 5 youngest Children. Mr Custance was gone to Mr Du Quesne's, but we met him on our return home, at the bottom of the Croft (alias Field adjoining to our Garden) he having been at our House enquiring after us. He was on horseback, and stopped and talked with us some time, and then parted, we wishing him Good Health and a safe Journey to Bath &c. Mrs Custance looked very well indeed, altho' she has been fatigued in ordering matters relating to their removal. We wished her &c. Health &c. Knights and his Wife are the only People to be at Weston-House during their absence. Mr Custance intends being at Weston in January or February next, but will make a short stay here. We shall most severely feel the Loss of such good and very friendly Neighbours and pray God bless them and theirs wherever they go and send them a safe Journey. Dinner to Day Skaite and Veal Collops &c. Recd this Evening for Butter at 10d 0.3.4.

6th, Saturday. Sent Ben early this morning to Norwich with three Hampers and 159 empty Bottles in them to be carried to Mr Priest Senr in lieu of those sent by him to me with the last Cargo of Wine. Nancy sent by him two Letters, one to her Br William at Gallhampton and the other to her Br Saml at Sir Richd Hoares, Stourhead, Wilts. Mr Custance sent us this morning a fine Cock-Pheasant. Mrs Custance also sent a large square Bottle of pickled Mushrooms, and a common Quart Bottle of preserved Gooseberries. Ben returned about 5 o'clock this Afternoon.

7th, Sunday. Our very good and worthy Friends Mr and Mrs Custance with five of their Children with two Nurses and Rising the Butler, left Weston this morning about 10 o'clock and gone for Bath. They had their own Coach and four, and a Post-Chaise. As we were walking in the Garden at the time Nancy saw them at the opening in Church Street, I heard them very plain. Their own Horses carry them to Attleborough, and there the Horses return with their Servants the drivers back to Weston House. Pray God bless them and theirs, and may every thing turn out to their most sanguine wishes. It made us quite low all the whole Day. It is a great, very great loss to us indeed. I read Prayers and Preached this Afternoon at Weston Church, churched a Woman and published Banns of Matrimony and read four Briefs. Weston Singers sung this Afternoon. Nancy walked to Church with me being fine Weather. Am very glad it was so good a Day for Mr and Mrs Custance &c. travelling. Dinner to day, boiled Neck of Mutton and a very fine and tender Cock-Pheasant rosted.

12th, Friday. Mr Jeans made us a Morning Visit, eat a Fig or two, carried some to his Wife, but could not stay to dine with us, tho' asked so to do. Mr Jeans informed us that he had heard it rumoured about, that there would be a great Mob collected at St Faiths Fair on Wednesday next, on Account of the dearness of Wheat and other Provisions, but I believe rather from the late long propensity of the discontented to a general Disturbance, so prevalent at present in France. The Norwich Mob to meet the Country Mob on the above day at St Faiths. John Buck, the blacksmith, who was lately informed against for having a Tub of Gin found in his House that was smuggled, by two Excise Officers, was pretty easy fined. Dinner to day boiled Tongue and Turnips and a fine Couple of Ducks rosted.

23rd, Tuesday. Had a Tub of Brandy and a Tub of Rum brought this Evening. Gave one of the Men that brought it 1/0.

24th, Wednesday. Very busy between 8 and 10 o'clock this Morn in bottling off Brandy and Rum.

25th, Thursday. Mr Du Quesne called here about 2 o'clock in his way to Mr Priests at Reepham, being so late he did not get out of his Carriage, he brought a Letter for Nancy from Mrs Custance at Bath inclosed in one to Mrs Townshend from Mrs C. They all got to Bath very safe and well on the Thursday after they left Weston-House. Mrs Custance writes in high Spirits. Bath seems to do her much good respecting health. Dinner to day

328

boiled Skaite, boiled Chicken and Oyster Sauce and Shoulder Mutton rosted.

NOVEMEBR *1st, Thursday.* My right foot worse this morning than yesterday. Mr Jeanes was here this morning before I was stirring, tho' was down Stairs before 8 o'clock. Soon after Mr Priest from Mr Du Quesnes came here on foot, and soon after him Mr Priest's Chariot from Reepham with Miss Mary Priest in it, and with her Mrs Jeans and her two Daughters Mary and Caroline with their Nurse Susan Harrison arrived at my House and they all breakfasted with us on Tea and Toast. Immediately after breakfast Mr Jeans got on his Horse and went for Windham, where he gets into the London Expedition about 4 this Afternoon for London for a few days. Mr Priest and Daughter went for Reepham soon after. Mrs Jeans, two Daughters and Nurse were left at Weston Parsonage and there dined, supped and slept. Mrs Jeans slept with Nancy in the best Chamber, with Miss Jeans on a Mattress on the floor of the same Room, and the youngest about 7 Months old with her Nurse, Susan Harrison in the Attic Story. We had for Dinner to day, some boiled Skaite, a Leg of Mutton rosted and Damson Tarts. For Supper one rosted Partridge &c. It is rather disagreeable to be so lame just at this time — but thank God! it is no worse.

9th, Friday. I breakfasted, dined, &c. again at home. Nancy breakfasted, dined, &c. again at home. Mrs Jeans, her two Daughters and Nurse breakfasted, dined, supped and slept again at Weston Parsonage. At Noon put on my common Shoe on my right foot, it being almost quite well and swelling gone. Mr Du Quesne called here about one o'clock stayed about an Hour with us and then went home, as he came, on horseback, on old Fox. I asked him to dine with us, but there being no Moon, he could not. Dinner to day hash-Mutton and Suet Pudding — Mutton Stakes and a rost Goose &c. No tidings of Mr Jeans as yet, how long they stay with us cannot tell, they only begged to be taken in for 3 or 4 Days and now it is more than a Week —

The Children particularly the smallest very great trouble, continually a fire above Stairs, washing, &c. &c.

10th, Saturday. I breakfasted, dined &c. again at home. Nancy breakfasted, dined, &c. again at home. Mrs Jeans, her two Daughters and Nurse breakfasted, dined and spent part of the Afternoon here. As my Servant Lad, Billy Downing, was going to Lenewade Bridge after some flour for the House, he saw Mr Jeans with a young Lady in a Post-Chaise, going to Witchingham, and the Chaise went thro' our Parish. Mr Jeans asked him if his Wife was gone home, to which the Boy answered, no — however they went on for Witchingham Parsonage, and about 3 o'clock or rather after a Note came to Mrs Jeans from Mr Jeans with a Servant Boy and a little Cart to convey Mrs Jeans and Children home. Accordingly as soon as they had dined, Mrs Jeans with her two Children got into the Cart and went for Witchingham. The Nurse, Susannah Harrison was sent for afterwards by the same convenience, tho' rather dark when she went. I cannot say, but it was by no means genteel in Mr Jeans to go thro' the Parish and not call. That they are gone, neither myself or Niece much lament — as the Children gave much unnecessary trouble, and Mrs Jeans too much affected. Sent Briton early to Norwich this morning in my little old Cart after News and many other things. Briton returned time enough to wait at dinner. He brought us some Whitings which we had for dinner, with boiled Beef, Beef-Stake Pye &c.

DECEMBER *8th, Saturday.* I breakfasted, dined, &c. again at home. Nancy breakfasted, dined, &c. again at home. Dinner to day Calfs-Fry and a rost Chicken. Our Newspapers brought by Bidewells People. Alarming Accounts on the Papers, Riots daily expected in many parts of the Kingdom, London &c. &c. A fresh Proclamation from the King on the present Affairs. The Tower of London putting in Order — Double Guard at the Tower and at the Bank ordered. Some People unknown sent to the Tower for high Treason. Meetings held in London by the

Lord Mayor Aldermen and Magistrates, at Norwich the same. Militia ordered to be embodied the ensuing Week. Meeting of the Norfolk Magistrates on Tuesday next at Norwich. Norfolk Militia to meet on Monday next, One Division at Yarmouth, the other at Lynn. Every appearance at present of troublesome times being at hand, and which chiefly are set on foot by the troubles in France. Pray God! however prevent all bad designs against old England and may we enjoy Peace. Parliament meets on Thursday next.

15th, Saturday. Billy Bidewells People brought our Newspapers. The Meeting at Norwich on Tuesday last was a very full one, almost all the Magistrates in the County attended, and very active measures taken to prevent any public disturbances from the different Societies or Clubs, respecting their late levelling behaviour. The Kings Speech* in the House of Lords, a very long one, but very good one, much liked. Most parts of the Kingdom have had general Meetings respecting the present threatening and levelling Principles, and fully attended. And proper measures taken to prevent any bad consequences from the levelling doctrines, dispersed among the poorer sort of People, by seditious publications &c. of late so much spread abroad every where. Every thing carried on at Norwich at the above meeting without the lest appearance of Riot or Disorder, and in other places the same, tho' it was rumoured about that it was the intention of many riotously disposed People, to have a rising of them this Week at Norwich, thank God it did not.

* The King's speech of 13 December referred to 'a design to attempt the destruction of our happy constitution and the subversion of all order and government'. He must 'therefore augment my naval and military forces for prevention and internal defence'. These strong words seemed to do the trick. Within a month Chauvelin, the French envoy in London, was writing that England was not ripe for revolution. On 1 February 1793 France declared war on England.

1793

JANUARY *26th, Saturday*. I breakfasted, dined, &c. again at home. Nancy breakfasted, dined, &c. again at home. Dinner to day Souse, Veal Pye and Calfs Heart rosted. Billy Bidewells People brought our Newspapers from Norwich. The King of France Louis 16 inhumanly and unjustly beheaded on Monday last by his cruel, blood-thirsty Subjects. Dreadful times I am afraid are approaching to all Europe. France the foundation of all of it. The poor King of France bore his horrid fate with manly fortitude and resignation. Pray God he may be eternally happy in thy heavenly Kingdom. And have mercy upon his Queen, 2 Children and their Aunt Princess Elizabeth, all of whom by the Papers are very ill indeed in their confinement. Their lives are in great danger now of being taken away by the French Assassins or Ruffians.

FEBRUARY *8th*. Mr Custance was so kind as to make us a long morning Visit tho' rainy most of the Morning. Mrs Custance and Family he left well at Bath. Mrs Custance sent Nancy by Mr Custance a small present of Tunbridge Ware, a kind of Vice with a Cushion to pin work to at a Table. Also a large wooden Spoon and a four-pronged wooden Fork for dressing up a Sallad, quite fashion. Mr Custance looked tolerably well after his Journey. My left side of my Face much swelled again.

MARCH *22nd, Friday*. Got up this morning with a comical kind of a sore throat, not much pain, had something of it Yesterday, rather worse to day—made use of Port Wine Yesterday pretty freely, and some black Currant Rob. Sent poor Frank Clarke, 1.0. Dinner to day Leg of Mutton rosted &c. Mr Custance was so kind as to drink Tea and Coffee with us this Afternoon, and stayed till near nine in the Evening, he sets off for Bath soon. Whilst Mr Custance was here, was seized with a violent pain in the small of my back, which continued the whole Evening, could not move from my Chair without great pain. To a poor travelling Woman going into Kent from Yorkshire gave to her to help her on 1.0.

APRIL *4th, Thursday*. About 2 o'clock this Afternoon two Men of Sudbury's at Norwich came with my Side-Board and a large New Mahogany Cellaret bought of Sudbury, brought on the Men's Shoulders all the way, and very safe. The Mens Names were Abraham Seily, and Isaac Warren. I gave them what ever they could eat and drink, and when they went away, gave them, 1.0 to spend either on the Road or at home and sent word by them to Sudbury to pay them handsomely for their Days work. Just as we were going to set down to dinner, Dr Thorne called on me, on my late poor Butcher's Account, as he is one of the Executors. I paid to him, due from me to Baker 9.2.0. I asked him to dine with us but he declined. Dinner to day, Neck of Mutton rosted &c.

19th, Friday. Fast-Day. This being a Day appointed to be observed as a publick Fast in these seditious times and France (the avowed Disturbers of all Peace in Europe) having declared War against us, unprovoked, I walked to Church about 11 o'clock and read Prayers provided on the occasion at Weston Church this Morning, a large Congregation attended Divine Service which I was very glad to meet on the Occasion. Pray God our Prayers may be accepted, the Hearts of all the Enemies to Peace converted, and a happy and general restoration to Peace, good Order and Government re-established to all the different Powers of Europe concerned. I found it very cold to Church and back again rough NE Wind with Hail and Snow &c. Dinner to day rost Loin of Pork &c.

333

MAY *2nd, Thursday*. Mr Du Quesne made us a long morning Visit in his one horse Chaise, came to meet Mr Priest of Reepham as per Note to him, and from hence Mr Priest was to return with Mr Du Quesne to dinner. Mr Priest however never came and Mr Du Quesne returned to his own home to dinner, though we asked him to dine with us more than once. He complained much of being terribly shook about in his Chaise by the badness of the roads more particularly those of his own Parish. Mr Du Quesne is very far advanced in Years but he will not own it. He is by no means fit to drive a single Horse Chaise. His Servant Man that came on horseback with him, was afraid that he would overturn coming along, he cannot see the ruts distinctly, he will not however wear Spectacles at all. He cannot bear to appear old, but must be as young in anything as the youngest Person.

24th, Friday. We breakfasted, supped & slept again at home. We got up soon after six this Morning, dressed and breakfasted, and at half past seven we got into our Curricle and drove to Norwich, found the road very dusty and the Air very cold both going and coming back. We called at both the Priests, saw John Priest & Wife, his Father & Mr Priest of Reepham. Nancy bought her a new black beaver hat with purple Cockade and band. She gave for it 1.3.0. She bought it of One Oxley in the Market place. I also bought a new hat of him, pd him for it 1.1.0. Whilst my Niece was at Barths, Stay & Habit Maker, I walked to Bacons and paid him for Knox's Sermons lately published, one Vol. Octavo 0.6.6.

To the Widow Studwell, at the China Shop, pd 0.8.0 for Basons &c.

To 4 Maccarel, pd 0.1.8.

Paid Sudbury for my new Cellaret &c. 4.4.6.

To 11 Dozen of Buttons Coat & Waistcoat, some Italian, some Clay's Paper ones, all black at Bakers pd 0.9.6.

Sent a Letter to my Niece Jane Pounsett. Called at my Mercers, Smiths, and bespoke a Coat, Waistcoat and Breeches of him. Then went to my Taylors Forster, and told him to make a Suit of Livery for Briton. About 2 o'clock we got into a snug Room at the Wool-Pocket in St Giles's where our Horses were, and eat some very nice pickled Salmon which we enjoyed, had a Pint of Port Wine besides Porter, pd for it 0.3.6. Nancy then went to try on a new Habit & Stays at Barths, at 5 o'clock called for her, walked with her to where St Bennets Gates lately stood, and at half past 5 got into our Curricle and drove back to Weston Parsonage, where we got thank God safe and well at half past 7 o'clock. It was very cold on our return, glad of our great Coats. Mr DuQuesne & Mr Stoughton called at my House to day whilst we were out.

JUNE *4th, Tuesday*. Sent Ben early to Norwich this morning after fish. Mr DuQuesne, Mr and Mrs Jeans, and with them a Miss Mist about 16 Years, and Mr Stoughton Rector of Sparham, dined & spent the Afternoon with us. We had for Dinner fryed Soals, Ham & 3 boiled Chicken, a Surloin of Beef rosted, Gooseberry Tarts &c. Mrs Jeans very affected, & talked very consequential. Mr DuQuesne looked very poorly, complained much, eat however pretty tolerably and was jocose. Whist played before and after Tea. I won at Whist with DuQuesne, Jeans & Stoughton 2s od. The Company did not leave us till half past 8.

24th, Monday. We breakfasted, and spent the morning at Weston Parsonage, after breakfast we were very busy in packing up things in our Trunks for our intended Journey into the West of England as We set off to day. About 2 o'clock this afternoon we left Weston, got into one of the Kings Head Chaises from Norwich, and went for Norwich, got thither about 4 and there dined & spent the Afternoon at the Kings Head. Briton went with us in my little old Cart. Ben went with him to have back the Cart to Weston. At 9 o'clock this Evening we got into the Angel Post Coach for London. Briton rode on the Top of the Coach.

Paid for our Dinners, Chaise &c. at the Kings Head 1.0.5.
To Chaise Driver & Servants at Norwich gave 0.4.0.
For extra Luggage, paid about 0.9.0.

25th, Tuesday. After travelling all Night and till 2 o'clock this Afternoon, we got safe & well (thanks to Almighty God) to London, to the Angel Inn at the back of St Clements near the Strand, where we dined, supped & slept. To extraordinaries in the Night, Coachman &c. pd 0.5.0. Nancy & self bore our Journey last Night very well. Nancys Brother Saml supped and spent the Even' with us at the Angel Inn, he looks thin & pale, but was in good Spirits.

28th, Friday. We got up about 4 o'clock this morning and at 5 got into the Bath Coach from the Angel and set off for Bath. Briton on the top of the Coach. The Coach carries only 4 inside Passengers. We had a very fat Woman with a Dog and many band boxes, which much incommoded us, and also a poor sickly good kind of a Man that went with us. We breakfasted at Maidenhead on Coffee & Tea.

For Strawberries at Maidenhead pd 0.1.0.

For our breakfasts pd 0.2.0.

We were very near meeting with an Accident in Reading, passing a Waggon, but thank God we got by safe and well. It was owing to the Coachman. As we went out of Reading we met a Regiment of Soldiers, some Militia going into Reading. At Reading there were two young Gentlemen by name Joliffe that got up on the top of the Coach, being going home from School for the Vacation. I remembered their Father at Winchester School. We dined at the Pelican Inn, Speanham Land. The young Gentlemen dined with us, I franked them. Their Father lives about 10 Miles beyond Bath. For our Dinners, Coachman &c. pd abt 14.0. Paid at Speenham Land for extra Luggage abt 4.0. About 10 o'clock this Evening, thank God, we got safe and well to Bath, to the White Hart Inn, where we supped & slept —a very noble Inn. Found our Friends Mr and Mrs Pounsett & Daughter at Bath, at Lodgings in the Orange-Grove, at one Roubelles, all tolerably well. Mr Pounsett better for being at Bath. They were very glad to see us. For Extraordinaries on the road to day pd abt 2.6. As soon as the young Jolliffes got to

336

Bath, they hired a Chaise immediately & set off for home. The fat Lady that came with us, supped with us. It was rather late before we got to bed. We were very happy to find that our friends were not gone from Bath. We are to have Lodgings to Morrow in the same house with them.

29th, Saturday. We breakfasted at the Hart and after breakfast paid at the Inn for our Suppers last Night &c. 0.9.6. To Servants at the Inn, Barber included 0.5.0. We then ordered our Trunks to Mr Roubelle's in the Orange Grove where our Friends were and then we dined, supped & slept. Mr Custance & two eldest Sons called on us about Noon & stayed ½ an Hour with us. After Nancy had dressed herself I walked with her to No. 1, Portland-Place and paid our respects to Mrs Custance and the rest of her Family. We found Mrs Custance very well indeed and all her eight Children. They were very glad to see us and desired us to dine with them to Morrow.

30th, Sunday. We breakfasted, supped & slept again at Roubelles. We dined & spent the Afternoon at Portland Place with Mr and Mrs Custance, & Family. Miss Custance Sister to Mr Custance also dined with us. My Niece Jane Pounsett went also with us to Portland Place. We spent a very agreeable Day with Mr & Mrs Custance &c. We had a very handsome Dinner.

JULY *8th, Monday.* We supped and slept again at Cole. At 7 o'clock this morning I took a Walk with Nancy to Mrs R. Clarkes at C. Cary, and there breakfasted, dined, & spent the Afternoon, with her, my Brother & Wife. Between breakfast & dinner I took a Walk to Gallhampton to Willm Woodfordes, stayed about an hour & half with him & Wife & returned to Cary to dinner. Willm & Wife behaved very friendly and kind. Willm has made a very pretty place of his little Cottage. Intensely hot indeed all day, sweated amazingly. Dinner to day, Peas & Bacon, boiled Beef, a Couple of Ducks rosted, and a Gooseberry Pye. We returned to Cole in the Evening about 9 as we went.

AUGUST *14th, Wednesday*. At Quadrille this Evening lost 0.0.6d. Had an unpleasant Letter this Evening from my Maid Betty Dade at Weston Parsonage in Norfolk, informing me that my other Maid Winifred Buderoy has turned out very bad, was with Child and so near her time that she was paid her Wages & sent away from my house which was very well managed by Betty. Poor Mr DuQuesne rather worse than better.

SEPTEMBER *26th, Thursday*. We were sorry to see on this Days Paper from Bath that our very valuable and worthy Friend the Revd Mr DuQuesne of Tuddenham was no more. It is a very great Loss to us, but I hope to him, Gain. Pray God he may be eternally happy. Dinner to day boiled Leg of Mutton & a rosted Rabbit.

OCTOBER *11th, Friday*. We breakfasted at Cole & spent part of the Morn' there. To Mr Pounsetts Servants gave 1.1.0. To Sybbil & Sally at the other house gave 0.5.0. About 11 o'clock this morning we took our leave of our Cole Friends, got into one of Bruton Chaises and went off for Frome, got to Frome by one o'clock, had some little refreshment there for which I paid about 0.3.6. For the Bruton Chaise, single Horse & Driver pd 1.2.0. About 2 o'clock we got into a Frome Chaise for Bath, but had not gone above 500 Yards from the Inn, going up Frome Hill, when on a sudden turn up the Hill we met with a large tilted London Waggon with eight Horses in it and very heavily loaden, and it being very narrow where we met it, the Driver of the Chaise in backing his Horses to avoid being drove over overturned the Chaise, but very providentially blessed be Almighty God for it! we received very little Injury, Nancys Face was a little bruised. It was a wonder that we escaped so well, as we were afraid that the Waggon would have crushed us. Briton got off his Horse & stopped the Horses in the Waggon, The Waggoner being rather behind. The Chaise Windows & Pole were broke, we therefore walked back to the Inn, stayed about half

338

an Hour till the Pole was mended, and then set off in the same Chaise for Bath. We got to Bath (thank God safe & well) about six o'clock this Evening, to the White Hart Inn in Stall Street, kept by one Pickwick, where we drank Tea, supped and slept, a very good, very capital Inn, everything in stile. Sent Briton this Evening with a Basket of Game to Mr & Mrs Custance No. 1 Portland Place. There were in it a brace of Pheasants & a Hare. For the Frome Chaise, single Horse & Driver pd 1.2.0.

Oxford

17th, Thursday. We breakfasted, dined, supped & slept at the Angel Inn. After breakfast we walked about the University by ourselves. A Meeting of the Warden & Fellows of New-College being this morning we did not call there. We went to Christ Church and called at Dr Bathursts but he and Family were in the Country. I called at New-College about 2 o'clock this

339

Afternoon saw Caldecot and Mr Cook who was last Year presented to the Living of Hardwiche, and also saw Mr Sissmore who behaved very kindly to me. They desired me much to dine at College to Morrow. Caldecot shewed me the improvements making in the Chapel, which when finished will be one of the finest Sights in the whole University. After Dinner I took another Walk with my Niece and shewed her more of the University. She went with me this Evening to Magdalen College Chapel to Prayers. We returned to our Inn to Tea, and after Tea I walked into St Giles's and called on my Friend Dr Holmes formerly of New-Coll. saw him, Wife & Sister, desired him to give my Niece a Dinner to Morrow at his House, as I am to dine at New-College then—rather formal reception. I called at Dr Walls in St Giles's but did not see him. In my return to my Inn called on the Head of Exeter College Dr Stinton who is bad in the Gout stayed about half an Hour and then went to my Inn. Called on my Friend Locke the Silversmith this Morning who behaved very obligingly and knew me at first Sight. I changed a ten Pound Note with him, he keeps a Bank and does great Business. Dr Holmes's Wife is a very agreeable Woman, and his Sister is very pleasant, exactly like him. The high Street of Oxford greatly improved since I last saw it all paved like London, and I think is one of the finest Streets in the Kingdom.

23rd, Wednesday. Soon after dinner we got into one of the Kings Head Chaises and went off for Weston, where we got safe and well & found all my People at Weston Parsonage very well & glad to see us, thank God! about 5 o'clock this Afternoon. Paid at the Kings Head for our Dinners Chaise &c. 1.1.4. Gave to poor lame Joe, the Boot Catch 0.1.0. Gave the Driver of the Chaise 0.2.0. We drank Tea, supped and slept once more at our old House, Weston Parsonage. Whilst we were at Norwich I wrote a Letter to my Sister Pounsett informing her of our safe arrival at Norwich, & put it into the Post Office myself. Accept O Almighty God! my sincere & unfeigned thanks for thy great goodness to us, in our late long Journey into the West & back again, and all the dangers we have escaped, particularly for that great & providential escape near Frome in Somersett. Lord! ever make us thankful, and may thy divine goodness ever protect us. Travelling Expenses and others from June 23, 1793 from the time we left Weston to our return back again this Evening to Weston, amounted in the whole — 78.19.7.

NOVEMBER *2nd, Saturday*. Sent Briton early this morning to Norwich in my little old Cart after News & many other things. Sent by him also a Letter to put into the Post Office for the Revd Mr Sissmore of New-College, Oxford, and in it a Norwich Bank Note of Gurneys of ten Pounds, to be presented to the Society of New-College, towards the improvements in their Chapel, which when finished will be great and will be well worth every observer 10.0.0.

4th, Monday. After breakfast I drove Nancy over to Witchingham being fine Morn' to Mr Jeans's and spent the remaining part of the Morn' with him & his Wife. We met with Mr Jeans in our Parish coming to us. Mrs Jeans is far advanced in pregnancy. We stayed there till almost 2 o'clock, they pressed us much to dine with them, but there being no Moon and likewise some Rain falling we could not, but borrowed an Umbrella and Mr Jeans's french Cloke for Nancy & returned home by three o'clock. It rained tho' very gently all the way. Dinner to day Knuckle of Veal boiled & Pigs face and a Neck of Pork rosted with apple Sauce. Mrs Jeans was pressing for us to dine with them more than was agreeable. It was rather beyond the Line of being pleasing.

19th, Tuesday. Got up very early this morning about half past five. Brewed a Barrel of Table Beer to day. We took a Walk this morning to Weston House, it being very pleasant, and walked over most part of it, we found it as well as could be expected but for want of fires, it feels rather cold, and some of the Paper in the Rooms, rather faded. We also walked over the Garden, which appeared in tolerable good order, kept by Knights & Son. Gave

Knight's Son, bringing some Strawberry Plants to us Yesterday Morning 0.1.0. I found myself very unwell this Aft. so very low. The Gout flying about me. Very much oppressed with Wind in my Stomach. Dinner to-day Neck of Pork rosted &c. I eat but little.

25th, Monday. Mr and Mrs Bodham made us a long Morning Visit, it gave us much pleasure to see them. Mr Bodham looked poorly & complained much. Mrs Bodham appeared rather thinner than usual. They were so kind as to bring us a profile Picture of our late worthy Friend Mr DuQuesne. They eat a Biscuit with us & drank a Glass of Wine. I am much afraid that poor Mr Bodham is not long one of this World, he is much altered. Soon after Mr and Mrs Bodham left us, Mr Priest of Reepham called on us in his way to Honingham Hall where he dines and sleeps at Mr Townshends. He is gone to settle Mr DuQuesne's Affairs with him. I privately baptized a Child of Hubbard's this Afternoon by name John at my House. Dinner to day, boiled beef &c. N.B. Blackbirds & Thrushes singing this Morn' in our Garden as if it was Spring, very mild. Thank God! that I continue bravely & can eat. N.B. Took 4 more of Nancy's Pills this Evening.

DECEMBER *11th, Wednesday.* My poor old Spanish Dog, by name Spring, was found this morning dead and stiff, under the hay Stack, worn out with age, being 14 Years old. He has looked very thin and poor some time.

25th, Wednesday also Christmas Day. We breakfasted, dined, &c. again at home. This being Christmas Day I walked to Church this morning, read Prayers and administered the Holy Sacrament, gave for an Offering 0.2.6. Had a very respectable Appearance at the Altar to partake with me of the H. Sacrament, 2 Rails. The Singers sang the Christmas Anthem and very well, between the Litany & Communion. The following poor People dined at my House or had their Dinner sent them & one Shilling each — Widow Case, my Clerk Tom Thurston, Christopher Dunnell, John Peachman, Tom Carr and Nathaniel Heavers. Nat. Heavers & Tom Carr had their Dinners sent them being ill. Gave to the above People in all o.6.o. Dinner to day, a boiled Rabbit and Onion Sauce, Surloin of Beef rosted, plumb Puddings and Mince Pies.

1794

JANUARY *19th, Sunday*. We breakfasted, dined, &c. again at home. I read Prayers & Preached this Morn', only few being there. Dinner to day, Breast of Veal rosted &c. Nancy made me very uneasy this Afternoon and does very often, by complaining of the dismal Situation of my House, nothing to be seen, and little or no visiting, or being visited &c. If we have of late lost our best Friends, by the removal of Mr Custance's Family to Bath, and the Death of Mr DuQuesne, must it not be affected by me as well as her? In short my Place has been too dull for her I am sorry to say for many Years—As things are so— infoelix!

25th, Saturday. We breakfasted, dined, &c. again at home. About Noon very high Wind indeed with some Snow. Barometer very low down to 28—7. I don't know that I ever saw it lower. Sent Briton to Norwich after News &c. he went in my little old Cart, and returned in very good time before 4 this Afternoon. A terrible Journey he had back, so very rough Wind, with Snow and intensely cold. He said, it almost took away his breath. Mem. The Barometer about 4 o'clock this Afternoon was down to 28—4, the lowest I ever remembered. The Wind so high that it greatly alarmed us. Part of my Barn uncovered by it, Thatch blown off, Many Tiles from my House blown down &c. Pray God: preserve all that are exposed to it particularly all poor Souls on board Ships. Dinner to day a Couple of Rabbits boiled and Onion Sauce, some beef Steakes &c. But the Wind was so very tempestuous at dinner time, that we made a very poor dinner. The Wind rather somewhat abated towards the Evening but still very high. Glass rather rose. I sat up in my Study the whole Night.

27th, Monday. Had but a very indifferent night of Sleep, having the Cramp in both feet great part of the Night owing I apprehend to the extreme cold Weather as it frose very sharp within doors last night. Very much indisposed all the Day, appetite very bad indeed, and Spirits greatly depressed for want of more natural rest. The last two Nights deprivation of Sleep, have much unhinged me. Dinner to day, boiled Tongue and Mashed potatoes and some rost Pork &c. Exceeding cold all day, froze within doors all the Day. The present severe cold Weather pinches me greatly. It snowed all the Morning but it was very small. Afternoon mostly clear but intensely cold indeed. Parliament met on Tuesday last January 21. Kings Speech very good and spirited one. Mr Pitt 218 — Majority in the House of Commons. I did not hear of any great damage being done by the High Wind Saturday, thanks to God for it.

28th, Tuesday. Thank God! had some tolerable Sleep last Night. Very severe frost indeed, freezes sharp within doors and bitter cold it is now. Two Women froze to death Saturday last going from Norwich Market to their homes.

30th, Thursday. Had a very indifferent Night of sleep scarce any at all. Recd of my Butcher for Tallow at 3d per lb 0.2.9. A Frost again but not so sharp as Yesterday. It did not freeze within doors last Night. Recd for Butter this Evening at 1s 0d, 0.2.6. It froze also in the Afternoon, and the Barometer still rising, but in the Evening it thawed and some Rain fell. I was saying before dinner that there would be alteration of Weather soon as I a long time observed one of our Cats wash over both her Ears — an old observation and now I must believe it to be a pretty true one. Dinner to day Peas Soup & rost Neck of Pork &c. Ben went out a tracing for a Hare this morning before breakfast, found one, and killed it, but the Greyhounds had eat full half of it, before Ben could get up to beat them off. After breakfast Ben & Briton went out a tracing till dinner time and they brought home a brace of fine Hares.

FEBRUARY *10th, Monday*. We breakfasted, &c. again at home. Between 11 and 12 o'clock this morning we took a Walk to Hungate Lodge, and paid our respects to Mr and Mrs Carbould, who came there to reside on Thursday last and were married that Morning at Talcolneston by Mrs Carbould's Father the Revd Mr Warren, and was the first time of our ever seeing either of them. They behaved very friendly to us as well as politely and appear to be very agreeable, pleasant People. We were treated with Chocolate & Wedding Cake. Mr Carbould is a Clergyman and Son of a Mr Carbould, many Years an Hatter at Norwich of whom I have had many a Hat. He has retired from business about 5 or 6 Years, and with a fortune of at least 15 Thousand Pound. He has only two Children one Son & one Daughter. We called on Mrs Peachman as we went there. Paid my Butcher (Billy Stoughton) this morning his Quarterly Bill for Meat the Sum of 10.8.6. The roads were very dry, but the Wind very rough indeed as we went to Mr Carboulds this morning and likewise on our return home.

11th, Tuesday. To 7 Yards of Cotton a mixed Colour of black, purple and Green, for a morning Gown for myself, this Morning of Aldridge at 2s 2d per Yrd pd 0.15.2.

Of Ditto for 7 Yrds of white Cotton for a lining to the above at 1s od per Yard, pd 0.7.0.

Of Ditto, for a Pr of Castle-Cary Stockings pd 0.5.0.

Dinner to day, Leg of Pork boiled & Peas Pudding. Mr Custance arrived at Weston House this Aft. from Bath, after being absent almost a whole Year. I sent to enquire for him in the Evening. To a poor Man of N. Tuddenham out of work and a very cleanly old Man, gave this Morn' 0.0.6.

12th, Wednesday. Mr Custance very kindly made us a morning Visit and stayed with us more than an Hour. He was in high Spirits & appeared happy to be again at Weston. But he looked very thin.

MARCH *7th, Friday*. Paid Robert Buck of Honingham for his

Father a blacksmith for Iron-Work done to Cart &c. o.16.o. Nancy drove out Rodney in the new Cart this Morning by way of an airing. Briton with her. I took a walk this morning by myself to Weston House to see Mr Custance, but he being rode out I walked on to Mr Jeans at Witchingham, and in my walk there, I called at Mr Fosters at Lenewade Bridge and spent about half an hour there with him, his Wife, her Mother Mrs Chambers, and I think her Sister. Got to Mr Jeans about 1 o'clock, stayed abt an hour with Mr & Mrs Jeans, & returned back to Weston-House about half past two, saw Mr Custance and chatted with him about half an hour and then returned home to dinner. Saw Mr and Mrs Copland at Mr Jeans. At Betty Cary's Shop this Evening for things pd o.1.o. Had 2 Tubbs of Geneva brought me this Evening by Moonshine, 4 Gallons each Tub. Sent a Note this Evening to Mr Carbould at Hungate Lodge to invite him, Mrs Carbould & Miss Carbould to dinner on Wednesday next. Recd a Note back that they would wait on us. Note shockingly bad wrote.

8th, Saturday. Busy this morning in bottling off Moonshine.

APRIL *11th, Friday.* One of my Greyhounds, young Fly, got to Betty Cary's this morning and ran away with a Shoulder of Mutton undressed & eat it all up. They made great lamentation & work about it. I had the Greyhound hanged in the Evening.

12th, Saturday. Newspapers brought by Bidewells People. A County Meeting held to day at Norwich concerning voluntary contributions for the internal defence of the Country in the present Crisis in case of a french Invasion, or any Riots &c. I did not go to it, neither did Mr Custance.

22nd, E. Tuesday. Hearing Yesterday that Mr Mellish, who succeeded Mr DuQuesne was come to reside at Tuddenham, I drove over to the old House and paid my respects to him this morning, stayed about half an Hour with him and returned home to dinner. Mr Mellish is quite a young Man, fair with flaxen hair, rather short & lisps, very much of the true Gentleman in his behaviour. There was another young Clergyman with him who was on a Visit for a few days there. In my return home I called at Mr Corboulds and took up my Niece who was there. Dinner to day boiled beef & mince Veal &c.

23rd, Wednesday. It being a very fine pleasant Morning I drove my Niece over to Mattishall to Mr Bodhams and made them a long Visit, but we returned home to dinner. Mr Bodham is I think better, but worse than ever with regard to his temper, for ever scolding & finding fault.

MAY *14th, Wednesday.* We breakfasted, and spent part of the Morning at home, about 11 o'clock I drove Nancy in my little Curricle to Norwich, and we got thither about 12 o'clock after a very pleasant ride, Briton went on horseback with us, put up ourselves and horses at the Kings-head in the Market-Place, our old Inn and there we dined supped and slept. Briton went with us on the Mare, Jenny. In the Evening we went to the Theatre and saw acted a Comedy called the School for Wives. The Entertainment, Midas, a very good house. It was for the benefit of one Jackson. The Song of God save the King was sung with great Glee. We did not return to our Inn till 11 o'clock. Dinner to day, fresh Salmon & Veal Cutlets &c. It was so hot at the Theatre, that Nancy was quite ill on her return to the Inn, could eat nothing for Supper. Soon after we got to Norwich, I walked about the City and paid many Bills that I owed, viz.

To Lock, Timber-Merchant, pd 1.3.0.
To Sudbury, Upholsterer, pd 5.7.0.
To Forster, Taylor, pd 4.9.6.
To Bacon, Bookseller, pd 0.16.3.
To Priest, Wine-Merchant, pd 2.4.0.
To Steward, Attorney, pd 6.7.1½.
To Buckle, Ironmonger, pd 0.9.6.
For two Box Tickets for the Play, pd 0.6.0. Gave Briton also to go to the Play 0.1.0.

To Ratifee-Cakes 2 oz, of Blacks, pd 0.0.3.

We called on both the Priests Families, this Morning. To Rum & Water at the White Hart, pd 0.0.3.

31st, Saturday. Mr Custance made us a Morning Visit to take his leave of us, being going to Bath very soon. He seemed very low on the thoughts of quitting Weston. I was quite sorry to see Mr Custance so dejected. I believe he goes from Weston to Morrow Morning.

JUNE *4th, Wednesday.* It being the Kings Birth-Day, I put the Ship into the Lagoon in my Garden, full dressed.

11th, Wednesday. Sent Ben early this morning to Norwich with my great Cart, after my new Garden Roller of Cast-Iron. He returned home with it before two o'clock and brought some Maccarel which we had for dinner with a very nice small Neck of Pork rosted &c. It is a very clever Roller and is called the ballance Roller, as the handle never goes to the Ground. It is certainly very expensive but certainly also very handy. The Roller amounts in the whole to 4.0.0 viz.: Cast-Iron 2 cwt 2 qtrs 26 lb, at $2\frac{1}{2}$d per lb, 2.17.6. Hammer'd-Iron, 40 lb at $6\frac{3}{4}$d, do. 1.2.6. Ben had leave to dine out, & to stay out all Night.

15th, Sunday. We breakfasted, dined, &c. again at home. I read Prayers, Preached and christened two Children this Afternoon at Weston Church. Nancy walked with me to Church being pleasant. Great News, Lord Howe has beat the French Fleet took seven Men of War with about 5,000 Men. Lord Hood also has beat the French in Corsica.* Dinner to day fore-Qtr of Lamb rosted &c. Between Tea and Supper Mr and Mrs Corbould in taking their Evening Walk called on us and stayed about an hour with us.

---

* Lord Howe had just defeated a French fleet (safeguarding a convoy of grain from America) off Ushant. Meanwhile Lord Hood (with Nelson's help) was engaged in the capture of Corsica.

JULY *17th, Thursday*. Soon after Eleven this Morning I drove Nancy over to Mr Mellishs at East-Tuddenham and paid our respects to Mr Mellishs Mother and his Sister, we stayed near an Hour with them and then returned home to dinner—They are very genteel, and fashionable Ladies—Miss Mellish very handsome indeed, and seemed very sensible & accomplished. Mrs Mellish a fine old Lady and very chatty—They are People of great Fortune I apprehend, and live quite in Style. We had a warm ride of it. Miss Mellish's Name is Nancy. Miss Woodforde likes Miss Mellish very much. Dinner to day Breast of Mutton rosted &c.

24th, Thursday. I reprimanded Briton this Evening for going to Bidewells and staying there unknown to me longer than he ought and am afraid was rather tipsy. At bed-time, which was full two hours after, he gave me notice that he had rather leave my Service at Michaelmas next. Such is the gratitude of Servants. He has been with me nine Years the 26 of April last, which I find is much too long for any Norfolk Servant for they will then get pert, saucy & do as they please. Such of late has been the behaviour of Briton. To Morrow Morning, I told him, I should speak to him.

25th, Friday. I told Briton this Morning that I should by no means keep him after Michaelmas—He did not care for he could get a Place he did not doubt, if not, he had a home to go to, his Fathers. After breakfast, he walked into the Garden to work singing out very loud, which was very impudent.* Thank God Almighty am brave to what I was.

AUGUST *21st, Thursday*. Finished Harvest this Evening. I cracked my Parlour Bell this Evening by giving it a very gentle Touch with my little Stick, and which I had done many times before without hurting it. It fretted me a good deal, but not at all abt the value.

* Briton did not leave at Michaelmas after all.

25th, Monday. To Knights for fruit from Weston House gave 0.1.0 which fruit I sent to Mr Corboulds at Hungate Lodge. Mr Corbould gave us a short morning Call. About one o'clock this Aft. I walked to Weston Church and buried poor George Warton, aged 65 Years. At three o'clock this Afternoon we walked to Hungate Lodge, and there dined & spent the Afternoon with Mr and Mrs Corbould, Miss Corbould, Mr & Mrs Day of Horsford, a Mrs Payne, Sister to Mrs Day, formerly Westons, and Mr and Mrs Jeans of Witchingham. Mrs Howman of Hockering drank Tea at Mr Corboulds. We had a very genteel Dinner—First Course at the upper End, stewed Tench, Veal Soup, best part of a Rump of Beef boiled, 2 rost Chicken and a Ham, Harrico Mutton, Custard Puddings, backed Mutton Pies, Mashed Potatoes in 3 Scollop Shells brown'd over, Roots 2 Dishes. Second Course. At the upper End, Rabbitts fricasseed, at the lower End Couple of Ducks rosted, Trifle in the Middle, blamange, Cheesecakes, Maccaroni, and small Rasberry-Tartlets. Desert of Fruit mostly that sent by me to them, Peaches, Nectarines and three kinds of Plumbs. We got home between 8 and 9 in the Evening. Mr and Mrs Jeans drove furiously by our House as they went to Mr Corboulds, Mrs Jeans took Miss Woodforde up pretty sharply, but Nancy silenced her very soon.

SEPTEMBER *1st, Monday.* We breakfasted, dined, &c. again at home. Herring, & his Nephew, Tuttle of Norwich & Peachman beat very early this Morning for Partridges all round my House, before anybody else, shot several times, and about Noon came again & did the same, went thro' my Yard, but never sent me a single Bird. A little before 2 Mr Corbould, with young Londale and John Girling Junr, Mr Custances Gamekeeper, called on us & Girling gave us a Leash of Partridges. Dinner to day, boiled Calfs Head, Pork & Greens, and one Partridge rosted, & Pigeon Pye. This being the first Day of Partridge shooting, Guns from all Quarters of Weston were heard, Morn' & Afternoon. Mr & Mrs Corbould with Miss Corbould & young

Londale gave us a call between Tea & Supper for about ½ an Hour.

14th, Sunday. I read Prayers & Preached this morning at Weston Ch. Miss Corbould with my Niece were at Church. In the Afternoon we took a Walk to Mr Courboulds and drank Coffee & Tea, with him, Mrs Corbould, Miss Corbould, a Mr Hastings, Rackham & his Wife of Hockering Park Farm, belonging to old Mr Berney of Brecon-Ash. Hastings appeared to be a modest well behaved young Farmer. Rackham & Wife very bold & high, and but low in the World neither.

15th, Monday. Took a ride this morning in my little Curricle to Mr Mellish's at E. Tuddenham, to make him a Visit after his return from London on Friday last, after the very late melancholy Event in his Family, the Death of his Mother, who was taken off very soon indeed, by a very violent Fever, she is much regretted by all that knew her. We never saw her but twice, once at Mr Mellish's & once at my own house and that not above two Months ago, and then she appeared as well & in as good Spirits as I ever saw any Person. Pray God! she may be happier and send Comfort to her much distressed Family—As so good a Parent must occasion on her decease such sorrow as is not to be described or felt but by those that have experienced it —The Loss of my dear Parents I feel to this Moment, and never can forget it during Life. I stayed with Mr Mellish about an Hour, and then returned home to dinner. I found him very low. Mr Jeans had been with him this Morning before. At Harwich all Day, having Masons white-washing my Study Ceiling &c. &c. Dinner to day, Neck of Pork rosted &c. Mr Collison sent us 2 brace of Partridges this Aft.

25th, Thursday. My ankle very painful in the night at times, which made me sleep but very little, dismal dreams. My ankle having given so much Pain last Night & having applied nothing at all to it but our Family Plaster, soon after breakfast I sent to John Reeves at the Heart who practises something in the doctoring way, for some Yellow Basilicum Ointment, which I immediately applied to my ankle, & wch Dr Buchan* recommends, pray God! it may do good—But I have my doubts of its turning out a very serious matter—I mean my ankle which I am afraid is much worse than it appears to be—very dangerous. It makes me I must confess very low. My Corbould made us a morning Visit. Dinner to day, boiled Tongue & Turnips &c.

26th, Friday. Had a better night of Sleep than the last Night and my Ankle not so painful, better I believe from my applying the Basilicum Ointment Yesterday, and it appeared better this morning on being fresh dressed. My Spirits (thank God) much better to day. Very busy all the morning from breakfast to dinner in cleaning my Study Pictures thoroughly. Dinner to day, Eels fryed & boiled, and boiled Beef. I relished my Dinner very well to day & eat hearty.

30th, Tuesday. Pretty busy this Morning at home having had thirteen young People come to me to be examined against Confirmation next Week. I gave them all Cake and a Glass of Wine. Dinner to day Knuckle of Veal boiled with Pork & Greens and a brace of Partridges rosted &c. In the Afternoon or rather Evening we walked to Hungate Lodge and drank Coffee & Tea with Mr and Mrs Carbould, Mrs Corbould's Brother, a Mr John Warren a Clergyman, and Mr Girlings eldest Son who had been shooting with Mr Corbould all the whole morning. We returned home to Supper.

OCTOBER *7th, Tuesday.* We breakfasted, supped & slept again at home. It being a fine cheery Morning tho' cool, we got up at 7 o'clock, dressed ourselves, and about 8 we got into my little Curricle, and I drove Nancy over to Witchingham to Mr Jeans's where we made a second tho late breakfast with Mr & Mrs Jeans, the Bishop of Norwich Dr Charles Sutton and his Chaplain,

* William Buchan (1729–1805) whose *Domestic Medicine; or the Family Physician* (first published 1769) went into nineteen editions during his lifetime and was translated into many languages, including Russian.

Mr Thoroton a young Man, and half Brother to the Bishop who married his Sister. We had for breakfast, Chocolate, green & brown Tea, hot Rolls, dried Toast, Bread & Butter, Honey, Tongue and ham grated very small. The Bishop did not come to Mr Jeans's till 10 o'clock having mistaken the road. He and his Chaplain came in a Post-Chariot & four, with three Servants. About a Quarter before 11, we attended the Bishop to Reepham to Mr Priest's, and when the Bishop had robed himself we attended him to Church in our Gowns, where he confirmed about 200 People. Mr Priest, Mr Jeans & self were with the Bishop in the Church, arranging the People in order as they came & the Chaplain recd the Tickets at the Church Gates. It was all finished by two Clock, and the Bishop walked back to Mr Priests, we attending him, and after drinking a Dish of Chocolate, the Bishop with his Chaplain drove back to Norwich to a late Dinner. A great Many Clergy attended on the Occasion, in their Canonicals, who most of them after their return from Church, went for their respective homes. Mr Jeans, Nancy & self dined at Mr Priests with him, Mrs Priest, Miss Mary & Miss Sally Priest, Robt & Charles Priest. Dinner to day Leg of Mutton boiled & a Couple of Ducks rosted, and a baked rice Pudding. About 5 o'clock we left Reepham and drove to our respective homes. We left Mr Jeans at Witchingham, did not get out being likely for Rain, which it did a little on the road from Mr Jeans's, and lucky we had not more, for our Umbrella was clung so fast that we had a hard matter to open it when at home. Mr Priest, Mr Jeans & self, went to the Kings Arms after the Bishop was gone, to dine with some of the Clergy, as there was a Dinner bespoke, but only meeting with Mr Atthill of Foulsham there, we returned to Mr Priests. As we did not dine at the Kings Arms we gave the Landlord, Bell, by way of compensation one Shilling each, with which he was very well satisfied. We got home safe & well, thank God for it before seven o'clock. The Rain that fell Yesterday rose the Water at Foxford & at Eads Mill quite high, Nancy very much alarmed & frightened therewith as it came almost into our little Cart. Every thing however passed over exceeding well to day and all conducted well throughout. Miss Woodforde much pleased with her Excursion and mightily so with the Bishop's very agreeable and affable, as well as polite & sensible behaviour.

20th, Monday. About 10 o'clock this morning I walked to Church and married George Barnard & Mary Girling by Licence, for which I received 1.1.0. Had but an indifferent night of Sleep last Night my Ancle being painful most part of the night, and also towards the Morning had a gouty Pain on the great Toe of the other Leg, but not bad. It made me hobble however between both this morning. Dr Thorne called on me about 1 o'clock and dressed my Leg. No discharge but kind of blood on the Lint appeared, the red precipitate Yesterday did more harm than good I apprehend and which occasioned so much pain in the night. The Doctor dressed it to day with yellow Basilicum only, except a little corner of the Wound where was a little speck of proud flesh on which he put a very small matter of red precipitate Powder, instead of Ointment & that covered with Basilicum Ointment. The red Precipitate Powder gave me much pain for a little time but after being dressed some time, my Ancle much easier. Busy most part of the Afternoon in making some Mead Wine, to fourteen Pound of Honey, I put four Gallons of Water, boiled it more than an hour with Ginger and two handfulls of dried Elder-Flowers in it, and skimmed it well. Then put it into a small Tub to cool, and when almost cold I put in a large gravey-Spoon full of fresh Yeast, keeping it in a warm place, the Kitchen during night. Dinner to day, Breast of Veal rosted &c.

26th, Sunday. We are afraid that our Maid, Molly, is with Child she looks so big, but she denies it very positively.

27th, Monday. My Ancle still continues very finely thank God. Dr Thorne called here about 1 o'clock, and dressed it as he did before. He was surprised to see it so well, it was almost healed. He said that it required but very little more to be done to it. No pain at all to signify. Very dull, wet, melancholy day, but mild. Dinner to day, Cottage Pye, and a Neck of Mutton rosted. Betty, both the Washer-women as well as ourselves say that our Maid Molly is with Child, but she persists in it that she is not.

NOVEMBER *2nd, Sunday.* I read Prayers & Preached this Aft. at Weston-Church. Had a pretty full Congregation at Church. My Maid Molly has declared herself with Child, more than half gone. Molly is with Child by one Sam Cudble, a Carpenter of the Parish of Coulton, and he says that he will marry her — The Man bears a fair Character — However, in her Situation, it is necessary for me to part with her as soon as possible. To Morrow therefore I intend at present to dismiss her. She is a very poor, weak Girl, but I believe honest. Dinner to day, Breast of Veal rosted &c.

3rd, Monday. After breakfast, I talked with Molly, paid her three Quarters of a Year and one Months Wages, which amounted in the whole to 4.7.0 and after packing up her things, about one o'clock she left my House, and walked off for Coulton where she is to be at Cudble's Father's, till such time that they are married. She says that Cudble made not the least objection to marrying her, she foolishly denied being with Child till the middle of last Week, and then obliged to, the Work becoming too much for her present Situation. I don't think that she is far from lying in by her appearance. For my own part, I have long thought her breeding. My Ancle, thank God, is now almost well, I dressed it in the same manner as the Doctor did Yesterday.

8th, Saturday. Sent Ben early this Morning to Norwich with ten Coomb of Wheat to Mr Bloomes at Trowse-Mills. A fine Sunshine Morning, small Frost, and cool. My Ankle so easy to day that I did not dress it. Sent by Ben a fine Cock-Pheasant to Mr Corbould who with his Wife are at old Mr Corboulds at Norwich. Ben did not return till after 6 this Evening, he brought back half a Chaldron of Coals. Mr Bloome gave for my Wheat 27 Shillings per Coomb, and Ben brought me home in Cash for the same 13.10.0. Sally Gunton (a Girl about 20 Years of Age) who is at present in Mr Townshends Service at Honingham Hall, came this Evening to offer her Service in the Room of my late Maid. The Townshend Family going to London next Week, wants her no longer. She appears to be a Girl that will do, and comes from honest Parents, tho' they are both dead. Dinner to day, Beef-Steak Pudding &c.

DECEMBER *16th, Tuesday*. Brewed a Barrell of common Beer to day. Mr Symonds of Reepham, cleaned both my eight day Clocks to day, almost the whole day after them, he breakfasted & dined with our folks. When he went away, which was in the Evening I paid him a Bill for cleaning Clocks & Watch from October, 1789, to Dec. 1794 1.0.6 cleaning my Clocks to day included in it. I did not take any change of him out of a Guinea. Dinner to day, fine Rump of Beef boiled &c.

25th, Thursday, Xmas Day. We breakfasted, dined, &c. again at home. It was very cold indeed this Morning, and the Snow in many Places quite deep, with an E. Wind. About 11 this Morning I walked to Church and read Prayers & administered the Holy Sacrament. Had but few Communicants the Weather so bad. Gave at the Altar for an Offering 0.2.6. Immediately after the Morning Service so far as before the administration of the H. Sacrament I was attacked with an Epileptic Fit, and fainted away in my Desk, but thank God! soon recovered and went through the remaining part of my duty. Mr & Mrs Girling, Mr & Mrs Howlett, Mr St Andrews, Mr Hardy &c. &c. were much alarmed and were very kind to Me, during the fit and after. The Weather being so severely cold, which I could never escape from feeling its effect at all times, affected me so much this Morning, that made me faint away, what I always was afraid off for some Winters past, having often had many fears. Mr Howlett after Service, very kindly offered to drive me home in his Cart, but as I was better I declined it, however hope that I shall not forget his civility. After Service was over, I walked into Mr Stephen Andrew's House, and having warmed myself, I walked home and thank God, got home very well. Mr Stephen Andrews & Family behaved very kindly. After I got home and had something warm to drink, I soon got tolerably well, but could only eat some plumb Pudding & a few Potatoes. Nancy was much alarmed when she first heard of it. Eliz. Case, Widow, Ned Howes, Thos Atterton Senr, Christ. Dunnell, Robert Downing, and my Clerk Thos Thurston, all dined at my House to day being Christmas Day, & each had a Shilling 0.6.0. A very fine Sirloin of Beef rosted and plenty of plumb Puddings for dinner & strong beer after. Took some Rhubarb going to bed.

26th, Friday. Thank God! had a pretty good Night last Night, and I hope am something better, but rather languid & low. Could eat but very little for dinner to day. Appetite bad.

To Weston Ringers, gave 0.2.6.

To Christmas Boxes &c. gave 0.4.0.

Dinner to day, Calfs Fry & a Rabbit rosted. I drank plentifully of Port Wine after dinner, instead of one Glass, drank 7 or 8 Wine Glasses, and it seemed to do me much good, being better for it.

1795

JANUARY *15th, Thursday*. Got up this morning very bad indeed in the Gout in my right foot, could scarce bare to put him on the ground, and so it continued the whole Day and night, not free one Minute from violent pain. The Weather Most piercing, severe frost, with Wind & some Snow, the Wind from the East and very rough. We had some boiled Beef & a Hare rosted for dinner. I could eat but very little indeed for dinner to day. I had my bed warmed to night & a fire in my bed-Room. I never was attacked so severe before in my life. Obliged to put on my great Shoe, lined with flannel. The Weather very much against me besides.

19th, Monday. Had a very restless Night last Night, much hurried in my dreams, & perspired a good deal. The Gout better, tho' much pain, but not swelled so much. Quite heavy, dull and low and listless. I privately baptized a Child of Thos Atterton Junr this Morning at my House, by name John.

Paid Briton, this Morning, for things 0.3.0.

Paid Betty, ditto for ditto 0.11.6.

Paid Ben, ditto for ditto 1.11.6.

Mr Corbould made us a Visit this Evening, but did not stay to drink Tea with us. Dinner to day a Couple of boiled Rabbits &c. I drank 6 or 7 Glasses of Port Wine after dinner and in the Evening, my foot pained me extremely and very much swelled, more than ever. The frost this Evening more severe than ever.

FEBRUARY *4th, Wednesday*. As cold a Night last night almost as we have had yet, it froze very sharp within doors, all the Milk & Cream froze. Extreme cold this Morning with cutting wind, and much Snow besides. Both Barometer & Thermometer very low. Many birds have been found dead, and the Rooks and Crows so tame that they come up to the Kitchen door where I feed my Poultry. Dinner to day, boiled Veal and Pork, &c.

5th, Thursday. Sent Ben this morning after breakfast down to Mr Girlings with a ten Pound Note for him to dispose of the same to the Poor of Weston as he should think Most to their advantage in this inclement Season. Very soon after I heard that Mr Custance arrived at Weston House last Night from Bath. As cold and as severe a Frost as Ever, and now not likely to alter, being very fair above. My Pain in my Foot rather worse this Morning. About 2 o'clock Mr Custance very kindly came on foot (tho' the Snow was deep on the ground) to our House, and spent an Hour with us. Mr Custance looks thin, but was in high Spirits. Miss Woodforde had a Note from Mrs Custance. Dinner to day, Leg of Mutton rosted &c.

15th, Sunday. There was no duty at Weston Church to day, tho' I am much better than I have been, yet not quite well enough to go to Church, for fear of a Relapse. Divine Service to day would have been in the Morn'. There was forty Shillings worth of brown bread given to the Poor of Weston on Tuesday last, and fifty Shillings worth of the same given this day, from the late Collection for the poor. Please God! I hope to be able to go to Church next Sunday. Dinner to day, Loin of Veal rosted &c. Britons Father dined with our Folks to day. As Britons Father is a Baker, I spoke for him to the Gentlemen of the Parish, to make part of the bread which is to be given away, and he is to make 50 Shillings worth against next Sunday.

MARCH *6th, Friday.* Mr Girling called on me this Morning and paid Me, for Tithe for Mr Custance for 1794 18.18.6. Mr Custance, Mr and Mrs Corbould, and Mr Stoughton of Sparham, dined & spent the Afternoon with us and stayed till after 9 o'clock at Weston Parsonage. We gave them for Dinner a Couple of boiled Chicken and Pigs Face, very good Peas Soup, a boiled Rump of Beef very fine, a prodigious fine, large and very fat

Cock-Turkey rosted, Maccaroni, Batter Custard Pudding with Jelly, Apple Fritters, Tarts and Raspberry Puffs. Desert, baked Apples, nice Nonpareils, brandy Cherries and Filberts. Wines, Port & Sherries, Malt Liquors, Strong Beer, bottled Porter &c. After Coffee & Tea we got to Cards, limited Loo, at 1d per Counter. I won at it abt 0.2.0. It turned out a very indifferent Day of weather as it rained Almost the whole Day, was very sorry for it. All our Dinner was very nicely cooked indeed. Mr Custance eat very hearty for dinner.

8th, Sunday. Mr Stoughton of Sparham did duty for me this Aft. at Weston-Church, being unable, tho' very desirous. Mr Custance at Church and a large Congregation.

22nd, Sunday. I walked to Weston-Church in the Afternoon and there read Prayers & Preached, which I have not been able to do before since Janry 11th. Had a very large Congregation at Church to day. Mr Custance at Church, as was my Niece. Fifty Shillings-worth of Bread given after Service to the Poor of Weston, out of the late Collection. Blessed be God! that I was able to do my Duty at Church again. I performed it with much more ease, than I thought myself able to day — The Day turning out very dry, though cold Air. Dinner to day, boiled Pork and a Turkey rosted. We did not dine till after Divine Service. I wore both of my largest gouty Shoes to Church to day. I think myself obliged to my Parishioners, for their expressions of kindness towards me in seeing me again at Church & performing My Duty there.

28th, Saturday. Mr Thorne waited on me again this morning and looked at my Ancle, applied a Caustic to it just touching the part with it with a small kind of fine hair Pencil in a Quill-Case. He much recommended again the resting of it. Briton returned between 4 and 5 this Afternoon brought a Letter for me from my Niece J. Pounsett acquainting us that Mr Pounsett was very bad in the Gout, and not likely to live long, unless he was soon better, intreating me to come into the Country. My Sister Pounsett also very poorly. The Letter greatly distressed me, as in my present Situation respecting my Leg, it would be almost Death to me to undertake such a Journey. Mr Custance sent us a brace of Snipes this Morning. Dinner to day, boiled Beef &c. My Ancle looked finely this Evening on dressing it. I took a little Rhubarb this Evening instead of the Pill.

APRIL *4th, Saturday.* Charles Cary's People brought my Newspapers this Evening with two Letters for me from Somersett one from my Brother and another from my Niece Jenny Pounsett, both announcing the Death of poor Mr Pounsett on Tuesday last, March 31st, entreating Me to come into the Country as soon as possible, but in my present Situation with so bad an Ancle, I cannot at present do it, and which I am very sorry for. As they have so many Relations near them is a Satisfaction to me. Am truly sorry for poor Mr Pounsett, pray God he may be eternally happy. His Sufferings for many Years have been very great. Pray God direct My Sister and Niece for the best under their Loss. I know nothing of Mr Pounsetts Affairs nor Will. He used to say that he had left my Sister & Niece all that he had, equally between them. It made us both low this Evening on the Occasion.

26th, Sunday. Thank God Almighty! got up this Morning very finely indeed, almost totally free from any pain whatever, either from Ancle or Gout. I walked to Church this Afternoon and there read Prayers and Preached. Had a very large Congregation. Mr Custance at Church. Fifty-Shillings worth of Bread given to the Poor again to Day after Divine Service. Dinner to day, Loin of Veal rosted &c. Mr Stoughton of Sparham sent us a fine Pike this Evening by his Servant Man John. Gave John for bringing it o.1.o. I took another Pill again to night.

JUNE *1st, Monday.* After half past 8 o'clock this Morning, just as we had breakfasted, who should come to our House in a Kings-Head-Chaise from Norwich but Mr Custance and his Butler, Rising, and they breakfasted at Weston Parsonage. Mr Custance with us and Rising in the Kitchen. The Driver also had his breakfast here. Mr Custance said that he had been near five Hundred miles, since last Friday se'ennight, he looked much jaded. He made a very good breakfast, had little or no refreshment Yesterday. He stayed with us about an Hour and half and then walked to Weston House by himself. He took Leave of us also, as he sets forth to Morrow Morn' about 8 o'clock, back for London where he stays a short time with his Son George and then both return to Bath, where Mr Custance remains for some time, after his Son is settled. To the Woman, Lancaster of Tuddenham, having lost some things which she had bought at Norwich, on her way home from a Waggon, gave 0.2.6. Mr Custance brought us this Morn' two Maccarel. Dinner to day, Maccarel & a Shoulder of Veal. Mr & Mrs Bodham sent over to enquire after us this Morning from Mattishall—Want to see us. Mr Custance sent us this Evening a large Piece of a fine Wedding Cake sent from London to Mr C. on the Marriage of Miss Durrant (Daughter of Lady Durrants) and Captain Swinfen of Swinfen-Hall in the County of Stafford, eldest Son of — Swinfen, Esq. Very curious devices on the Top of the Cake.

3rd, Wednesday. I drove Nancy over to Mattishal to day about Noon, and we dined & spent the Afternoon at Mr Bodhams, with him, Mrs Bodham, & Miss Anne Donne, Daughter of the late Revd Castres Donne who is about thirteen Years of Age, a very nice Girl. We found Mr Bodham very bad indeed, much altered, As helpless almost as an Infant, being led about and also fed, besides being almost blind. He looks fresh, and eats and drinks heartily, he complains at times of violent pains, and very sleepy by day, but very restless at nights, is had out of bed often in the Night. Poor Mrs Bodham does everything for him, poor Woman I heartily pity her, she bears it up wonderfully well. We had for Dinner a few Maccarel, some Veal Cutlets and a small Green-Goose & Asparagus, and some Gooseberry Tarts. No Potatoes, Greens &c. Mr Bodham is very hasty & often swears at People. He is certainly at times deranged & talks wildly. Tho' he has been so ill & so long, yet is continually having Workmen about him & spends great Sums that way, in building up and pulling down, besides buying Carriages to go out in, but will get into none of them. We saw a prodigious handsome new full-bodied Coach, sent from London half a Year ago. He behaved very civil indeed to us & glad to have us. We stayed till about 7 in the Evening & then returned home. In our way to Mattishall, we called on Betty England at Tuddenham & had some Chat with her, but we did not get out of our Carriage. We got home about half past 8 o'clock, & soon after Mr Corbould with Miss Sutcliffe called at the Gate in their Carriage & we had some Chat with them there.

4th, Thursday. We breakfasted, dined, &c. again at home. About half past 9 this Morning I got into my Curricle and drove over to Norwich, it being the Kings Birth Day. Nancy would not go—So I took Briton. Got there about a Quarter after Eleven. Saw all the Soldiers both Horse & Foot drawn up in the Market Place about one o'clock, and the foot fired three Vollies, and the Cannon on the Castle Hill also fired thrice. Soon after the Soldiers fired, they marched off. And those Soldiers lately returned from the Continent, marched to Coe's late Quantrille's Garden, where a Subscription Dinner was provided for them, of rost Beef & boiled Beef &c. Pies, and plenty of rost Legs of Mutton. I walked thither on purpose to see them at dinner, & a pretty Sight it was. They all had Porter to drink. A great deal of Company were in the Gardens to see them. I gave to go into the Gardens 0.1.0. Paid there for refreshment 0.0.3. The Soldiers dined at 3 & at 4 marched off for the Barracks, all things conducted very well. About one Thousand Soldiers were supposed to be there. The Subscription for them was said to be 100 Pound.

7th, Sunday. I read Prayers & Preached this Morning at Weston C. Miss Woodforde at Church this Morning. Thirty-Shillingsworth of Bread given to the Poor of the Parish this Morning at Church. Dinner to day, Loin of Veal rosted &c.

After Tea this Evening we took a Walk to Hungate Lodge to enquire after Mr & Mrs Corbould, they having been nearly killed last Night coming from Norwich in their high Gig—Some part of the Carriage breaking let down the same, which frighting the Horses, they ran away. Mr and Mrs Corbould both jumped out, and very fortunately neither of them recd any injury. The Horses ran two or three Miles before they were stopped. The Gig very much shattered. It happened between the Turnpike & Cossey. We met Mr & Mrs Corbould going to take a Walk, just by their own House, we walked back with them, stayed about half an Hour and then they walked back with us to the Parsonage, stayed abt 10 Minutes, drank a Glass of Mead apiece, and then returned home to Supper.

8th, Monday. Mr Corbould sent to borrow a Horse for to Morrow, but we could not lend him one, as poor Rodney is badly. They are fond of borrowing, but rather forgetful to return what is borrowed. I lent him some Hay for his Horses being distressed in April, but never sent any back as yet. Am not well by any means, every day almost about Noon I feel odly, great depression of Spirits, owing I think to Gouty Wind flying about me.

16th, Tuesday. After breakfast I got into my Curricle and drove to Norwich, taking Briton with me. We got there about Noon—And it being Guild-Day when the new Mayor is sworn in, there were great doings, the Court going in Procession to the great Church and from thence to the Guild-Hall, & then to St Andrews Hall to dinner. Old Mr Alderman Ives is the new Mayor, and it is the second Time of his succeeding to that Office. Some of the old time doings exhibited to day such as he did the last Time of being Mayor—A fine & curious Triumphal Arch of green Box intersped with many Flowers & variegated Lamps hung in the Centre of the Arch, near Mr Ives's House and by St Clements Church near Fye Bridge. At the Mayors Door there was a similar Arch with three golden Crowns on it and the Prince of Wales's Feather in the middle, of Gold, with a continual Firing of Cannon & Guns. Flaggs flying throughout the Mayors Parish &c. A vast Number of People at Norwich to day indeed. At 3 o'clock I went to the Wool-Pocket and eat part of Mutton Chop quietly, but very tough.

For a Lobster to carry home 3 lb 3 Qtrs, pd 0.2.6.

To Gingerbread Nuts &c. &c. paid & gave abt 0.1.0.

For my Dinner paid and gave 0.2.0.

About 6 o'clock this Evening I got into my Curricle & drove home to Weston by 8 to Supper. The Main Spring of my Watch being broke I left it at Amyots to be repaired by Saturday next. I fagged about a good deal to day.

JULY *13th, Monday.* We breakfasted & spent the Morning at Cole. Gout almost gone. Leg where I scratched it, indifferent. Nancy paid me this morning the Guinea she borrowed. About Noon, I walked with Nancy, and Miss Pounsett to Castle-Cary, and there we dined & spent the Aft. at Mrs Richd Clarke's with her, my Brother and Wife, and my Sister Pounsett. My Sister Pounsett rode there. In the Evening I walked back to Cole with Miss P. and supped, spent the Evening and slept there. My Sister being afraid to ride back, walked home rather late and Mr Robt White with her and he supped and spent the Evening at Cole. We left Nancy at Cary to spend a few Days at Mrs R. Clarkes. Dinner to day a Couple of Chicken boiled & a Pigs face, Peas, a Leg of Mutton rosted and Tarts. Paid my Brother to day for Carriage which he paid for me for our large Trunk from Norfolk 0.10.0.

15th, Wednesday. My Sister P. complains a good deal, more so than I think she ought. She eats too gross things, too rich for her Stomach.

20th, Monday. I supped and slept again at Cole. Leg bravely. At 8 o'clock this Morning I walked with my Niece Pounsett to Castle-Cary, and there we breakfasted at Mrs R. Clarkes with her, my Brother & Wife, Nancy Woodforde and my Sister Pounsett, who rode on horseback behind Phillip. After breakfast I walked with my Brother to Gallhampton and spent an hour with

366

Willm Woodforde and Wife. Saw the Hermitage which Willm lately built in which he has shewn great Taste.* From thence we walked to the Parsonage at Ansford and spent half an Hour with Mr Frank Woodforde & Wife. Then we walked to Mr Robt White's where we dined and spent the Afternoon with him & Wife, Sister White, My Brother's Wife, Mrs R. Clarke, my Sister Pounsett & Daughter and Nancy Woodforde. In the Afternoon I walked over to my Uncle's and made him & his Wife a Visit, both of whom considering their Age, my Uncle being in his 90th Year and his Wife in her 84th were very well. My Uncle can see and walk without a Stick and has all his faculties remarkably well. I stayed about half an Hour with them, & returned to Mr Whites. I called in at many Places in Cary. We all walked back to Cole after Tea, got home abt 9 o'clock. My Niece Pounsett was crying, & fretting all the way back to Cole which made it very unpleasant. She never enjoys herself in Company, and does not like to go from Cole, very uncommon in one so young.

27th, Monday. Had a very bad Night of rest last Night, very ill, in the Gout indeed in my right hand, very much inflamed & very much swelled, so bad at dinner that I could not cut my Victuals, and so continued all the whole Day, at times in most violent pain. Had my hand bound up in flannel, very low. Appetite very indifferent, rather unfortunate.

31st, Friday. It being a fine Morning and Haymakers all at work, My Sister ordered a Leg of Pork to be dressed for them, but Rain coming about Noon they were obliged to leave off and go to their respective homes. The Pork had been boiling for them two Hours, we had it taken up and put by for them against another Day. Dinner to day, boiled Salmon & cold rost Beef &c.

AUGUST *6th, Thursday.* My Sister Pounsett is greatly altered to what she used to be, she is vexing, fretting & complaining all the day long. Nothing can please her. The Folks busy in making

* A folly or perhaps summer-house.

Cheesecakes &c. to day. To Hannah Arnold & her Sister gave 0.1.0.

28th, Friday. I breakfasted, dined, supped & slept again at Gallhampton. After breakfast, I desired Willm to drive me over in his one horse Phaeton to Sandford-Orcas, where I have a small Estate* which I have not seen for many Years, accordingly we took a ride thither and had very fine Weather for it, tho' very rough road and a great way, near eight Miles from Gallhampton. We got thither about 12 o'clock, and viewed all the Premises. Farmer John Downe has taken to it, and has let one of the Tenements to one Thomas Marks, a Husbandman, and the other Tenement to one Saml Bullen, a Carpenter. The whole has been put in very sufficient repair, and a new blacksmith's Shop erected upon it, all done by the above Farmer John Downe, the Orchards near the Tenements have been dug up and set to Potatoes, which should not have been done. I did not see either the Farmer or his Tenants. I have recd no Rent for the above Premises since Lady Day, 1787. Last Lady Day therefore had eight Years Rent due from my Estate at Sandford. We returned home about 3 o'clock to dinner. Dinner to day, 3 boiled Chicken and a Pigs Face, a Bullocks Heart rosted & a rich plumb Pudding. After Coffee and Tea this Evening we got to Whist again the same as last Night, won 0.1.0 but did not receive the Cash either to night or last Night, so that Mary stands indebted to me 0.2.6. I had an exceeding good bed & Room indeed last Night.

SEPTEMBER *8th, Tuesday.* Mr Frank Woodforde and Wife & Daughter Fanny with her Brother Tom dined and spent the Afternoon with us. They came & returned in Captain Johnsons Carriage. Fanny Woodforde was left behind to spend a Day or two with Jane Pounsett. Jane behaved quite rude this Evening, I never saw a Girl in my Life of such a

* Now in Dorset, then in Somerset. JW was left an estate here by his great-uncle John Collins, who died in 1744.

Disposition, she is never easy, & always disturbing other People.

14th, Monday. Farmer John Downe of Sanford Orcas my Tenant came to Cole about 2 o'clock this Afternoon to settle some Matters with me. William Woodforde came with him. He brought me in Bills for repairs for the last four Years, to the Sum of 31.18.9¼. Mr Pounsett let him have the whole for four Guineas a Year, 4 Years due from Downe at last Lady Day, from last Lady Day for the future He is to give five Guineas per Annum, till the whole Expences of the late Repairs are paid. The last four Years being deducted from the above Expences, that is 16.16.0, there then remains to be paid 15.2.9¼. The Farmer eat some Victuals & had some Cyder.

OCTOBER *26th, Monday.* About Eleven o'clock this Morning, Nancy and self took leave of our Friends at Cole, and sat off for Bath. Briton went with us on an hired Horse. We had one of Ansford Inn Chaises. Gave to my Sister Pounsetts Servants 1.1.0. We went thro' Bruton, Evercreech, Shepton Mallet to old Downe Inn, about 13 Miles from Bruton. We got thither about one o'clock, eat a bit of cold Beef, and then got into a fresh Chaise and Horses and off for Bath. We left our Friends at Cole very low, we were so also.

27th, Tuesday. We breakfasted, supped & slept at the White-Hart. I took a long Walk early this Morning about Bath. To a Barber shaving me & dressing my Wig 0.1.0. After breakfast whilst Nancy was dressing I walked to Sydney Gardens, very pretty, gave there &c. 0.1.0. Mr Custance called on us this Morning about 11 o'clock and stayed a full hour with us. He desired us to dine with them to day. As we were at our Inn Window opposite the Pump Room this Morn' we saw John Dalton coming from the Pump-Room way on foot. We did not call to him, as he was with Company. About 2 o'clock I walked with Nancy to Portland Place where we dined & spent the Afternoon with Mr & Mrs Custance, their Children, Willm, Miss Custance, Emily, John, Neville & Charlotte. Poor Nancy was greatly chagrined & mortifyed going up to Portland Place which stands very high & the Wind much Power. The Wind was unluckily very high with some Rain just before we got thither, and directly opposite Mr Custance's Front Windows, the Wind took Nancy's riding Hat & Feathers with a green Vail entirely off and was blown some little way, and her Hair tho' but just dressed, quite destroyed, the Family at Portland-Place, seeing it all. The Family were extremely glad to see us. A Mrs La Mair, Governess, dined with us. We had for Dinner, some Soals rather stale, a Saddle of Mutton rosted, Pork Steaks, Soup &c. We returned to our Inn about 8 o'clock & had a better Walk back, tho' Windy & cold.

29th, Thursday. As we heard when we got to London that the Sessions of Parliament was to be opened this Day—At one o'clock I walked with Nancy to St James's Park about half a Mile, where at two o'clock or rather after we saw the King go in his State Coach drawn with eight fine Cream-Coloured Horses in red Morrocco-leather Harness, to the House of Lords. The Park was uncommonly crouded indeed, never was known a greater Concourse of People before, and I am very sorry to insert that his Majesty was very grossly insulted by some of the Mob, and had a very narrow escape of being killed going to the House, a Ball passing thro' the Windows as he went thro' old Palace-Yard, supposed to be discharged from an air Gun, but very fortunately did not strike the King or Lords. On his return from the House to James's Palace he was very much hissed & hooted at, and on his going from St James's to the Queens Palace in his private Coach, he had another very lucky Escape, as the Mob surrounded his Coach and one of them was going to open the Door but the Horse Guards coming up very providentially at the Time, prevented any further danger. The State-Coach Windows going from St James's to the Mews were broke all to Pieces by the Mob, but no other damage done to the Coach. We had very difficult work to get out of the Park, the Croud still increasing, however at about 4 o'clock we got out thro' a narrow Passage between Marlborough House and St James's Palace into Pall-Mall, and when we got to Charing-Cross in going up the Strand We Met such a Mob of the lowest Class that quite alarmed us, they were going to the Park. We crossed the Street under the Heads of Horses that were in the Coaches which stood quite close one to another all up the Strand. The Mob was composed of the most violent & lowest Democrats. Thank God the King received no Injury whatever, neither did we as it happened. Every Person attached to his Majesty was very much alarmed and concerned for him to-day. It was said that there were near two hundred thousand People in St James Park about 3 o'clock. I never was in such a Croud in all my Life. By the Horse Guards the whole Area of the Parade was entirely filled up and all the Park quite to the Queens Palace very much crouded besides. Soon as ever the King got thro' the Horse Guards the Gates were shut as he went & as he returned. We were glad to get back to our Inn safe. Dreadful Work was expected to be done to night. Three or four of the Rascals that insulted the King were taken into Custody & had before Parliament. Both Houses of Parliament were very busy almost the whole night in consultation concerning the shameful Insult his Majesty received,* but nothing done as we heard off when we went to bed which was very late to night. Dinner to day, Whitings & some Veal Cutlets.

30th, Friday. We breakfasted, dined, supped & slept again at the Angel-Inn. Thank God! no bad work done last night tho' much was expected. Soon after breakfast I walked with Nancy to Miss Sally Popes in Newgate-Street, and from thence to Miss Webbs in Tudor-Street, but neither Miss Webb or her Brother

* A mass meeting on 26 October organised by the London Society in Copenhagen Fields was followed three days later by mob violence. The complaints were that prices had risen steeply and famine threatened. The King's opening of Parliament was greeted with cries of 'Give us peace and bread'. Shortly afterwards Parliament passed measures to defend the King's person and to prohibit assemblies of the tumultuous kind witnessed by JW.

or Miss Hussey were at home, but as they were expected soon I left Nancy there and walked back to my Inn. About 3 o'clock I sent Briton after her whilst I was dressing. Nothing talked of to Day but the happy Escape from the danger the King had Yesterday. His Majesty nevertheless with the Royal Family go this Evening to Covent Garden Theatre. Every Well-Wisher to them, is very anxious for their Welfare to night. Pray God! defend them.

To 2 pair of Silk Stockings, partly Cotton pd 17.0.

To 3 pair of white worsted Boot-Stockings, pd 6.0.

To Cakes & other refreshment in the Morn', pd 0.6. Dinner to day, Soals & Pork Stakes. Mr Webb called on us about 10 o'clock this Night, smoked a Pipe with me & had Brandy & Water.

31st, Saturday. We breakfasted, dined, &c. again at the Angel Inn. Took a long Walk this morning by myself abt the Court End of the Town long before breakfast. In my Walk for a Pair of Gloves, pd 0.2.0. For a Ladies Pocket Book for 1796, pd 0.2.0. Mr and Miss Webb drank Coffee and Tea with us this Evening, after which we all got into an Hackney Coach and went to New-Drury-Lane Theatre where we saw performed a very pretty new Comedy called, First-Love. Entertainment: Lottery Ticket. Both pretty things and extremely well performed. Principal Actors & Actresses were Palmer, Bannister Junr, King, Mrs Jourdan, Miss Farren, Miss Pope, Signiora Storace &c. For 2 Tickets, pd 0.7.0. To Coach hire from the Theatre &c. pd 0.2.0. I walked about with Nancy after breakfast, to Miss Popes Miss Webb &c. Dinner to day fryed Herrings and some Beef Steaks &c. Cyder, Wine & Porter to drink. His Majesty with the Queen and most of the Royal Family were at Covent Garden last Night, and very graciously received, God Save the King was played six Times—Every thing pleasant. Thank God! that they met with nothing disagreeable.

NOVEMBER *4th, Wednesday.* We had I thank God! a good night

of Weather all last night, good Lights to our Coach the beginning of the Night, and a good Moon early in the Morning. It was very cold in the Night being a smart Frost. We did not breakfast till we got to Tivetshall Ram in Norfolk about 8 o'clock this Morning, and only fifteen Miles from Norwich.

Gave to Coachmen & Guard from London 0.5.0.

For our breakfast this Morn' & on the Road 0.4.0.

About 11 o'clock this Morn' we got to Norwich safe & well, blessed be God for it. We stayed at Norwich at the Kings Head about an Hour then off in one of their Chaises for Weston and got home to Weston Parsonage between 3 and 4 o'clock in the Afternoon, and found all my Family well & all things in order —accept O Lord my Thanks for the same.

Paid for Refreshment at Norwich & Chaise to Weston and Horse for Briton & given to Servants 1.1.7.

To the Norwich Driver, gave 0.1.6.

Gave my Barber at Norwich, Frank 0.1.0 as he brought me a new Wig to carry home. We drank Tea, supped & slept at our comfortable quiet, happy, thatched Dwelling. Our People had been expecting us some time.

6th, Friday. We breakfasted, dined &c. again at home. There was a most violent Gale of Wind this Morn' early about 3 o'clock, continued More than an Hour. It waked me. It also shook the House. It greatly frightened our Maids in the Garrett. Some Limbs of Trees blown down in my Garden. Many Wind-mills blown down, and a good deal of Damage done to Weston House-Tiles. Mr Girling called on us this Morning. Mr Maynard, my Curate in my absence, called on me also this Morning. I thanked him for serving my Church and gave him 10.0.0. He served Weston from June 24 to Nov. 5th being 19 Sundays. He stayed about half an Hour. Mr Corbould & the Revd Mr John Warren made us also a Morning Visit. Mr Girling sent us a Leash of Partridges this Even'. Gave to the Servant that brought them 0.1.0. Dinner to day a boiled Chicken and a Pigs Face and some beef Steaks.

16th, Monday. Mr and Mrs Corbould made us a late Morning Visit. I engaged Mr Corbould this Morning to be my Curate for the ensuing six Months, to begin on Sunday next, at the rate of thirty Pounds per Annum with all Surplice Fees.

22nd, Sunday. Mr Corbould read Prayers & Preached for me this Morning at Weston Church, for the first time on being appointed by me for my Curate. He called on us as he rode to Church. We did not go to Church this Morning. Dinner to day, Neck of Veal rosted &c. Mr Smith of Mattishall sent over his Servant Lad this Morning to enquire for us after our Journey. It is somewhat strange, as he has not sent a Servant to enquire after us for Years—No Note.

24th, Tuesday. Mrs Bodham sent Nancy a Note this Morning by their Servant Willm Ward, to enquire after us. Poor Mr Bodham rather worse than better, Senses almost gone. The Servant stayed some time on Account of the Rain. Soon after the Servant went, Aldridge who goes abt with Cottons &c. called here, and whilst I was dealing with him, Mr Mellish of Tuddenham made us a Visit and stayed about half an Hour with us, I asked him to dine with us & meet Mr & Mrs Corbould but he said that he expected his Sister from London. To Aldridge for 14 Yards of Cotton, at 2s 3d pd 1.11.6 which I gave to my two Maids, a Gown each. To Aldridge also, for 8 Yrds of Cotton, at 2/6, 1.0.0 which I gave to Miss Woodforde. Also for 7 Yards of Cotton for a Gown for myself, at 2s 2d, pd 0.15.0. Pd him likewise for a Marcella-Waistcoat Piece Yellow Ground ¾ yrd square, for Ben 0.8.0. To Aldridge also, for 2 Silk Handkerchiefs from Spittal Fields, Chocolate Ground & Yellow Spots, pd 11.0. One of which I gave to Ben & the other to Boy, Tim. Paid Aldridge in the whole 4.5.2. It being late almost dinner time, before I had finished with Aldridge, I asked him to dine with our Folks but he could not stay for that, he eat some cold rost beef and had some Table-Beer. Before I had quite dressed Mr & Mrs Corbould came to dine with us, which they did in a friendly way and stayed till near 8 in the Evening. We gave them for dinner, Hashed-Calfs Head a boiled Chicken & some Bacon, a Leg of Mutton rosted, and a Norfolk batter-Pudding & drippings after that, we had a Duck rosted, Maccaroni & Tarts. By way of Desert, we had white Currants, Pears & Apples, and Filberts. After Coffee & Tea we played one Pool of Quadrille at 2d per fish, very little lost, I neither won or lost.

DECEMBER *25th*, *Friday*, Christmas Day. We breakfasted, dined, &c. again at home. This being Christmas-Day, the following poor People dined at my House & had each one Shilling apiece given to them by me 0.6.0. Old Tom Atterton, Ned Howes, Robin Downing, old Mrs Case, old Cutty Dunnell, and my Clerk Tom Thurston. They had each a Glass of strong Beer after they had dined. The Holy Sacrament was administered this Morning at Weston Church by Mr Corbould. It hurt me to think that I could not do it myself, but suffering so much the last Christmas Day by the cold, am afraid since to go to Church during the Winter Season. Nancy might have gone, but did not. It turned out a very fine Day indeed, no frost. Dinner to day, a Surloin of Beef rosted, a fine Fowl boiled & Bacon, & plumb Puddings.

26th, Saturday. We breakfasted, dined, &c. again at home. Sent Ben early this Morning to Norwich with 10 Coomb of Barley to carry to Mr Bloome. Ben returned about 5 this Evening, all safe & well thank God. He brought a Note of the Barley as he did not see Mr Bloome, but Ben told me that Barley was at 17s 6d and 18s 0d per Coomb. If at 18/0, Mr Bloome owes me 9.0.0.

To Charles Wibley, Blacksmiths Man 0.1.0.
To Tom Short, Wheel-wright's Son 0.1.0.
To Weston Ringers 0.2.6.
To Weston Singers 0.2.6.
Dinner to day, Souce fryed & boiled Beef &c. Recd for Butter to day at 1s 1d 0.2.8½. Wheat amazingly dear indeed 3 Pound, & three Guineas, per Coomb given it is said.

1796

JANUARY *1st, Friday*. We breakfasted, dined, &c. again at home. To my Butcher's Lad, Peter Sharman, gave this Morning a Christmas Gift of 0.1.0. To my Malster Man, Jos Edwards, Xmas Gift 0.1.0. Dinner to day, boiled Pork, hash Mutton & a Pudding. Gave Nancy this Afternoon being New Years Day her annual Gift of the Sum of 10.0.0 but her pleasing me to day I added to it 0.10.0 which made it ten Guineas.

FEBRUARY *9th, Tuesday*. Widow Greaves Junr who in the last Summer lost a Cow, waited on me this morning with the Petition that was drawn up for her on the Occasion with the List of the Subscribers. She had collected near Six Pounds, had bought another Cow for four Pounds, so that she was a great Gainer by her loss. I gave her, this Morning (as I happened not to be at home at the time) 0.5.0. Dinner to day, fryed Pork & Turnip Green, a Duck rosted and some Apple Fritters being Shrove-Tuesday.

MARCH *9th, Wednesday*. Very ill this morning, having had little or no Sleep all last Night, so very cold. A general Fast this Day. Mr Corbould read Prayers only this morning at Weston-Church. Mr Custance at Church, we were not. Mr Corbould called on us as he went to Church. Dinner to day, boiled Veal & Pork &c.

APRIL *3rd, Sunday*. We breakfasted, dined, &c. again at home. Mr Corbould called here this Morning in his way to Weston Church. I walked with him to Church, where Mr Corbould read Prayers and administered the Holy Sacrament at which I was present. I gave for an Offering 0.2.6. It gave Me Much pleasure & Satisfaction in my Attendance this day on Divine Service. It was ever my greatest Pleasure to pay that homage to our great Creator which even only from Gratitude, it demands. It gave me also pleasure to see so many Communicants—25 or 26—present. Mr Custance, was not at Church, neither were Mrs Corbould or Miss Woodforde. Dinner to day, Loin of Veal rosted &c. Sent a Note this Afternoon to Mr Custance to desire the favour of his Company to dinner on Friday next or Thursday, and he fixed on Friday next.

8th, Friday. We breakfasted, dined, &c. again at home. Recd for Butter this Morning at 1s 0½d, 0.4.8½. Mr Custance, Mr and Mrs Corbould, Mr Mellish of Tuddenham, and Mr Stoughton of Sparham, dined and spent the Afternoon with us, and did not leave us, till after 9 in the Evening. Each Gentleman had a Servant with him. It was very near 4 o'clock before we sat down to dinner, Mr Corbould coming very late to us. Mr Custance was with us by half past two. He brought us a brace of Cucumbers, very fine ones, and the first we have seen this Year. It was extremely kind of Mr Custance. We had for Dinner, a fine Cod's Head and Shoulders, boiled, and Oyster Sauce, Peas-Soup, Ham and 2 boiled Chicken, and a fine Saddle of Mutton rosted, Potatoes, Colli-Flower-Brocoli, and Cucumber. 2nd Course, a rost Duck, Maccaroni, a sweet batter Pudding & Currant Jelly, Blamange, and Rasberry Puffs. Desert, Oranges, Almonds & Raisins, Nutts, & dried Apples, Beefans. Port & Sherry Wines, Porter, strong Beer & small. After Coffee & Tea, we got to Cards, limited Loo, at which I neither won or lost. Nancy lost 5s 6d, Mr Custance won abt 12s 0d. Mr Mellish having no Silver, lent him 0.2.0. Every thing very well conducted to day. My Company seemed well-pleased &c. We spent upon the whole a very agreeable Day.

20th, Wednesday. We breakfasted, supped & slept again at home. Mr Corbould made us a Morning Visit, soon after, Mr Thorne, my Doctor, called on me and stayed a considerable time with us after Mr Corbould was gone. I paid him a Bill of

3.13.6. It was after two o'clock before Dr Thorne left us, and both of us quite undressed, so that we had to dress ourselves (being going to Mr Mellish's to dinner) and to be at Tuddenham by half past three o'clock, if we could. At 3 o'clock I drove Nancy over in my little Cart to Mr Mellishs, and did not get there till 4 o'clock, owing to Briton's being on foot. Mr Corbould overtook us near Mouses House and went with us, he being going to dine there. The Party we met there was Mr Mellish, Mr and Mrs Eaton, Mr and Mrs Howman and Mr Corbould. All the Company met within ten Minutes of each other. Dinner was soon announced after our Arrival, which consisted of the following things, Salmon boiled & Shrimp Sauce, some White Soup, Saddle of Mutton rosted & Cucumber &c., Lambs Fry, Tongue, Breast of Veal ragoued, rice Pudding the best part of a Rump of Beef stewed immediately after the Salmon was removed. 2nd Course. A Couple of Spring Chicken, rosted Sweetbreads, Jellies, Maccaroni, frill'd Oysters, 2 small Crabs, & made Dish of Eggs. N.B. No kind of Pastrey, no Wheat Flour made use of* and even the melted Butter thickened with Wheat-Meal, and the Bread all brown Wheat-Meal with one part in four of Barley Flour. The Bread was well made and eat very well indeed, may we never eat worse. After Coffee & Tea we got to Quadrille, that, is Mr Mellish, Mr Corbould, Miss W. and self. Neither Mr or Mrs Eaton, nor Mr & Mrs Howman played at all at Cards, but were setters by. About half past eight we all took our Leave of Mr Mellish and returned to our respective homes as we went, we got home about half past nine, as we went very slowly on Account of Briton's walking, who muttered very much about walking and when he got home was very impudent indeed, but I believe he had been making too free with Mr Mellishs Beer &c. Mr & Mrs Howman are both high and consequential, the Latter remarkably so, if a Dutchess (by which

* A patriotic effort by Mr Mellish perhaps—Pitt was said to have suggested that people should eat meat to save bread, now excessively expensive.

name she is by some called) could not give herself more consequential Airs. Mr Mellish is a very worthy Man I verily believe. No Affectation or Pride, but seems to have every good Quality that can belong to Man.

MAY *8th, Sunday*. We breakfasted, dined, &c. again at home. By particular desire of Billy Gunton, & which I promised him on friday last, as this day to administer the H. Sacrament to him, himself with his Mistress Mrs Michael Andrews, came to my House about 11 o'clock this Morning and I then had them into the Parlour and there administered the H. Sacrament to them and which I hope will be attended with due effects both to him, Mrs Andrews & myself. I put on my Gown and Band on the Occasion. Mrs Andrews appeared to pay as much Attention to Billy Gunton, tho' her Servant, as if it was really her own Son —very good of her. It gave me great pleasure, tho' far from well in doing what I did, as it will ever give me pleasure to do any thing in my power, that may give any satisfaction or ease to any person whatever, especially to the distressed. No Service at Church this Afternoon, the Church not being fit. Next Sunday I hope there will. Dinner to day, Leg of Mutton rosted &c.

10th, Tuesday. On going to bed to Night, our Boy Tim Tooley who was supposed to have been gone to bed was not to be found —All his Cloaths gone also. It is thought that he is gone to Norwich to enlist himself, as his Head has long run on a Soldiers Life. His being at Norwich last Saturday & then offered ten Guineas if he would go for a Soldier, determined him.

11th, Wednesday. My Boy Tim Tooley was supposed to have slept in my Barn last night, and that very early this Morning he marched off for Norwich to enter into his Majesty's Land Service. Richmonds eldest Son is likewise gone. They both agreed last Sunday to leave Weston and enlist. Both our Maids being gone most of the Morning to Church, to clean it against Sunday next, we helped dressing our Dinner which was a piece of rost

Beef & Suet Pudding. Gave Willm Nelson, my Carpenter this Even' 0.1.0.

16th, Monday. My late Servant Lad, Tim Tooley, called on us this Morning. He came from Norwich with a Cockade in his Hat, and says he has entered himself in the thirty third Regiment of Foot. Poor Fellow, he appeared happy & looked well. I paid him what Wages were due to him and half a Crown extraordinary, in all 17.6. Dinner to day, some more Eels fryed, mince Veal and some boiled Pork &c. Merry doings at the Heart to day being Whit-Monday.

JUNE *4th, Saturday.* Still very rough, tempestuous Weather, not quite so much Rain. We are quite flooded in the Yard. I promised to send for Nancy this Morning from Norwich, but the Weather proving so very bad prevented me, tho' I wish for her home. I told Nancy before Miss Corbould on Thursday last, that I would send for her on Saturday. Miss Corbould was totally silent on the Occasion, did not express the least desire of Nancy's staying any longer. Miss Corbould they say, is like her Father, rather penurious and stingy. Mr Custance drank Tea with me this Evening and stayed till after 8 o'clock. He came walking. He goes for Bath on Monday next. Mr Custance quite sorry to leave Weston House. Dinner to day, boiled Beef & a rost Chicken &c.

8th, Wednesday. Sent Ben, to Norwich this Morning early, with my great Cart, to bring home some Wine for me. He returned home by 4 o'clock with the same. Had 3 Dozen of Port Wine 13 to the Dozen this Morning of Johnny Reeves at the Heart for wch I paid him, at 29s od per Dozen 4.7.0. I likewise had of him one Gallon of Rum for which I also paid him 0.16.0. Dinner to day, Rabbit Pudding & a Goose rosted. Finding myself rather poorly to day, I took some Rhubarb this Evening on going to bed.

15th, Wednesday. I breakfasted, supped & slept again at home. Miss Woodforde, breakfasted, dined &c. again at home. It

being a very bright Morn' I got up early, shaved & dressed myself, and immediately after breakfast abt 8 o'clock, I got into
my little Cart and drove off for Norwich, taking Briton with me.
We got thither before ten o'clock. I got out of my Cart just before we entered the City, and walked down to Trowse-Mills to
speak to Mr Bloome, whom I found at home. He promised to
call on me at the Kings Head and settle all Accounts at 3 o'clock
this Afternoon. I stayed about half an Hour with Mr & Mrs
Bloome and then walked back to Norwich thro' Kings Street to
Tombland, and to my Taylors, Willm Forster, to whm I paid a
Bill for the last Year, of the Sum of 4.11.6. From thence Went
to Mrs Brewster's in Cockey Lane and paid to Miss Gillman,
for Tea &c. 3.18.0. From thence went to Mannings my Brazier
in the same Street but nearer the Market & paid him 3.6.4 for
a new Washing Copper. Recd of him for the old one, 29 lb at
9d per Pd 1.1.3. So that I paid him on the balance 2.5.0. From
thence went to Oxley's, Hatter, in the Market Place and paid
him for a New Hatt 1.1.0. From thence went to my Mercers,
Smith, almost next Door to Oxley's, and paid him a Bill 6.18.0.
From thence went to my Wine Merchant, Mr Robt Priest, and
paid him for a Qtr of a Pipe of Port, had last Week, Discount for
ready Money included 17.0.0. Corks and Cooperage &c.
0.6.6. Paid him also for 2 Gallons of Rum, had at the same
time, at 16s od per Gallon 1.12.0. So that I paid him in the
whole 18.18.6. I paid him the above at his Son John's House,
who asked me to dine with him at his Sons, which I promised if
I could—they dine at 2 o'clock. I then called at Mr Corboulds,
went in, but saw only a Servant, Mrs Corbould and Miss Corbould were at home but above Stairs, but did not make their
appearance, sending word down that they were dressing. Mr
Corbould Junr was just walked out, it was said. Old Mr Corbould I knew was at Weston. I never saw any thing at all of
them all the time I was at Norwich which was till 5 in the Afternoon. I was obliged to go many times by their Door, my Cart
being put up almost directly opposite their House, which is in

St Giles's. At 2 o'clock I went to Mr John Priests and made a very good dinner on a fore Qtr of Lamb, with him and his Father only, Mrs J. Priest in the Country. Paid Thos Burroughs, Breeches Maker in London Lane, for a Pr of Breeches for Briton &c. 1.4.0. At three this afternoon, I went to the Kings Head and there waited till near 4 o'clock before Mr Bloome came. When he was come we soon settled Accounts. I paid him for Coals 15.13.6. And I received of him for Corn 43.10.0. So that I received of him on Balance 27.16.6. To my Barber, Frank Lofty, for a new Wigg 1.1.0. For a Glass of white Wine & Water at Ravens, pd 0.6. At Nosworthy's, for 2 Rolls of Pomatum, pd 2.0. For three Coombs also there, pd 1.8. To my Taylors Men, gave as a free Gift 1.0. For some Cakes & Porter &c. pd & gave 0.6. At 5 this Evening got into my Cart and went for home. Almost immediately after we got out of the City, we had a very heavy Storm of Rain which made us wet thro' but it did not last long, having a new Hat on, it did it no benefit or good. We had very little or none after till we got home, which was about 7 o'clock, thank God safe & well.

25th, Saturday. We breakfasted, dined, &c. again at home. This Morning about 9 o'clock, got into my Cart and drove to Mattishall to attend at the funeral of Mr Bodham, an old acquaintance. I got thither about half past ten o'clock, and there stayed at the House till near half past two in the Afternoon before the Corpse was carried to Church. It was a very handsome Funeral indeed. Two mourning Coaches and four, one Mourning Chariot and pair, two Post Chaises, besides other Carriages. Poor Mr Bodham was fifty five Years of Age. Mr George Smith, Curate of Mattishall, buried him. A great Number of People attended indeed. Chocolate, cold Ham, Veal &c. at the side Tables in the Room we were in, the best Parlour. We returned back to the House after the interment, took some little refreshment, and then each went to their respective homes. I did not get home to Weston to dinner till 5 o'clock this Afternoon. I took Briton with me. He had a black Silk Hatband and a pair of Gloves. I brought Nancy a pair of the best white Kid Gloves which was orderd by Mrs Bodham. Nancy had saved me for Dinner a few green Peas & Bacon, and some rost Chicken. I was quite jaded when I got home and very hungry. I was very glad when I got home, for I much dreaded the Day, my Spirits being but indifferent, thank God however, I got thro' it extremely well.

JULY *14th, Thursday*. Called at Betty Englands at E. Tuddenham late a Servant to poor Mr Du Quesne. When at Tuddenham we went to the Church and saw the Monument put up lately by Mr Townshend for his Friend & Relation Mr Du Quesne. It was the plainnest I ever saw, it is Marble, but nothing more than a mere Slab, only wrote on. The Character given of him is very great. We got home before 3 o'clock. Had for dinner a large Piece of Beef boiled &c.

AUGUST *7th, Sunday*. We breakfasted, dined, &c. again at home. Mr Corbould read Prayers & Preached this Morning at Weston Church. Mrs Corbould at Church as were Miss Woodforde & self. Mrs Corbould was so frightened at Church by a Bat flying about the Church, that she was obliged to leave the Church.

Nancy went out also to attend her. They went to the Parsonage where Mrs Corbould stayed till we returned. Mrs Howlett was at Church and exhibited for the first time, a black Vail over her

Face. Mem. Times must be good for Farmers when their Wives can dress in such stile. Dinner to day Loin of Veal rosted &c. Very fine and pleasant Day. Mr & Mrs Corbould with young Longdale, Miss Woodforde & self took a Walk this Evening after Tea, to Farmer John Buck's. Himself & Wife behaved very hearty & generous, we staid abt half an Hour there, & returned home.

SEPTEMBER *10th, Saturday*. We finished Harvest this Afternoon, and thank God! had a fine Time for it, & all well. Sent a Note this Morning early by Briton to Mr Anson at Lyng, to desire his and Brothers Company to dinner on Wednesday next, had a genteel Answer back, but they are engaged. Bidewell's Folks, got the Newspapers for us. The Austrians have beaten the French smartly of late, killed 5000, and taken 2000. Serious apprehensions are entertained by many in high rank of the French invading England some time this Autumn.* Preparations are making.

12th, Monday. We breakfasted, dined, &c. again at home. I dreamt last Night that I was at an Entertainment given by Mr Coke at his House, amongst other Dishes there was a Faun rosted but cold, and plenty of Hares rosted, and cold also, &c. Mr Coke very civil to me, on coming away I lost my Hat, some one had taken it, & I thought a Soldier. I thought however that I bought a second hand one of old Mr Corbould, with many other things, all forgot. A Raven fled over my House this Morning. All which tokens are said to bode no good. To Largesses to day, gave 0.2.0. Dinner to day, boiled Beef &c.

24th, Saturday. We breakfasted, dined &c. again at home. The

* The Archduke Charles, brother of the Austrian Emperor, had just heavily defeated the French, who had crossed the Rhine in June and invaded Bavaria. By the end of October the invader had been driven back across the Rhine. At the same time (and for some time) the French had been organising an expedition to invade Ireland with the help of Wolfe Tone and similarly disaffected natives. This eventually set sail for Bantry Bay on 15 December; the preparations were known in advance to the Government, but not the destination.

Morning was cool. Afternoon fair. Evening cold with a kind of Scotch Mist. Dinner to day, Bullocks Cheek stewed, and a Neck of Mutton rosted &c. James Peggs brought our News for us to day, & likewise two Letters, One for me from my Niece Jane Pounsett, and one for Nancy from her Brother Saml now at Stourhead. Miss Pounsett informs me that she and Mother had been lately at Weymouth for six Weeks, during the Time of the Royal Family being there, and that my Sister Pounsett was much better by going. And also she acquainted me that during her stay at Weymouth, a Mr Grove a young Man & a Clergyman (and a quondam Admirer of Janes) had again paid his Addresses to her, and that she accepted of him & hope it will meet my Approbation. Nancy's Letter from her Brother informs her that he is at Sir Colt Hoares at Stourhead with a full House of Company, Lord & Lady Bruce, Lady Hoare &c.

OCTOBER *10th, Monday.* My Boy, John Brand, left my Service to day, as he had proper Notice so to do, being the most saucy swearing Lad that ever we had, and am afraid that if he does not soon do better, he will bring his poor Mother with sorrow to her Grave. He can do his Work well if he pleases, but cannot be trusted out of Sight, but the worst is, he is profligate. Ben paid him his Wages due to him for four Months Service, due this Michaelmas at the Rate of two Guineas per Annum. He went before Dinner, and in the Evening my new Boy of this Parish by name Barnabas Woodcock between 11 and 12 Years of age, succeeded him. Dinner to day, Hash-Mutton &c. Pudding and a Goose rosted, being old Michaelmas Day.

14th, Friday. Just as we had dined Mr Girling with one of the Chief Constables by name Copeman called on me to subscribe my name to an agreement, to prevent Riots or any publick disturbances that may happen by being active in suppressing such. I told them that I heartily concurred in it, and would do all in my power, but did not think it consistent with the Character of a Clergyman to put his name to it, therefore I did not.

NOVEMBER *6th, Sunday.* We breakfasted, dined, &c. again at home. Mr Corbould read Prayers & Preached this Aft. at Weston Church. He called on us as he Went to Church & young Longdale with him. They each eat a Cake and drank a Glass of Wine. We did not go to Church, Nancy having a bad Cold, and myself but poorly, and it being very cold, there being a smart Frost this Morning. The general talk is now concerning an Invasion from the French — Mr Pitt having Mentioned in the House of Commons that he had substantial reasons for believing it, but such as at present improper to mention. As Mr Pitt is prime Minister, it is much credited throughout the whole Country, and creates a general alarm. The Militia are to be doubled, and new Cavalry to be raised. Dinner to day, Skaite & a fine Hare rosted.

7th, Monday. We breakfasted, dined &c. again at home. There being a Justice Meeting to day at Reepham, respecting Militia Men, and those inrolled concerning this Hundred in defence of it, against any Riots or disturbances that might happen — I sent my two Men, Ben and Briton (whose Names were put down some time back) this Morning to Reepham & there they stayed all Day but returned in good Time in the Evening abt six o'clock, with two black Staves in their Hands with a black Leather-Guard for the Hand, and on the Staff were painted these Letters in white and figures 58, 59. E.H.L.A., viz: Eynesford Hundred Loyal Association.

12th, Saturday. We gathered some white Currants from a tree in the walled Garden this Day about Noon. Dinner to day, Giblet-Soup, with odds & ends. Bidewell's People brought our Newspapers. Admiral Elphinston's Squadron off the Cape of Good Hope had fell in with a Dutch Squadron and captured every Ship without firing a single Gun — 9 Ships, 342 Guns, 1972 Men. Admiral Elphinstone's Fleet consisted of 14 Ships, too great a Match for the Dutch. The Dutch Admirals Name is Lucas. They took our Fleet for the French Fleet, Admiral Richery's, which were to have joined them there and to have retaken the Cape of good Hope.*

DECEMBER *24th, Saturday.* We breakfasted, dined, &c. again at home. Very hard Frost indeed, last Night, froze above Stairs in the Stair-Case window quite hard. It froze the whole day within doors in a few Minutes—very severe Weather indeed—So cold last Night that it was a long time before I could get any sleep at all. I am much afraid that the Turnips will suffer greatly by the present severe Weather, being almost entirely uncovered—We want Snow. Dinner to day, Neck of Mutton boiled & a Fowl rosted. Betty Cary went to Norwich to day and brought our News &c. She brought a Letter for me from my Brother and another for Nancy from Jenny Pounsett now at Cole Place, Somersett. We were obliged to have Hulver-branches† without berries to dress up our Windows &c. against Christmas, the Weather having been so severe all this Month, that the poor Birds have entirely already stript the Bushes.

31st, Saturday. We breakfasted, dined, &c. again at home. Very Mild but dark and damp. Dinner to day, a boiled Rabbit & Onion Sauce, Peas-Soup and a breast of Mutton rosted &c. to John Shorten, Miller's Man, by Jon Lillistone 1.0. Mrs Bidewell brought our Newspapers to day and likewise a Letter for Miss Woodforde from her Brother Saml, now at Sir Thos Champneys at his Seat at Orcherly near Frome in Somersett giving her some Description of a late Masquerade Ball, given at the House, upwards of one Hundred & fifty genteel People at it. It was said on the Papers, that it was of the first Degree of Taste. Saml was at it, being there to paint some Portraits. The Treaty on Peace, between England & France, which has been some time transacting, broke off very suddenly last Week by the

* After the Franco-Dutch alliance against England in early 1795, the English fleet captured the Dutch colonies and made short work of the Cape of Good Hope and Ceylon. The victory here described took place in August of this year, but the news had only just arrived.
† Holly.

French & our Negociator, Ld Malmesbury ordered to leave Paris in 48 Hours—bad News indeed.* The French in short, are afraid of making Peace, for fear of the Consequences which might arise from their dismembering their great Armies. Tho' very unfavourable the present aspect of public Affairs throughout Europe, at the Conclusion of the Year 1796—May God so direct the Minds of Men before the Conclusion of the ensuing Year, that a general Peace and every blessing attending it, may be felt in every Nation of Europe & over the whole World and whenever such Blessings arrive, May we all with one Heart & one Mind give our Most hearty thanks to that God for the same, and not unmindful of him Now or for ever.

* Pitt, forced to sue for peace, sent Lord Malmesbury to Paris for that purpose. England's allies had dropped away, indeed the Dutch and Spaniards had become enemies. Thanks to Bonaparte Italy was by now almost a French dominion. Ireland seethed with disaffection. Hefty taxation made the war unpopular at home. In the Paris negotiations England asked for Belgium to be restored to Austria; otherwise France was to retain her conquests and regain the colonies in the East and West Indies which the Royal Navy had conquered. England wished, however, to retain the captured Dutch colonies. On 19 December these terms were rejected by the victorious Directory. Lord Malmesbury was summarily sent home from France.

1797

JANUARY *15th, Sunday*. We breakfasted, dined, &c. again at home. Mr Corbould read Prayers & Preached this afternoon at Weston-Church, he called on us as he went, and told us that one of his Pointer Dogs, by name Tony, was gone mad and had got out in the Night when confined by making a Hole in the door, after loosening his Chain, and went over great part of the Parish & the Parish of Ling, biting many dogs, Pigs, &c. But was killed this Morning at Mr Corboulds, as he returned home. Mr Corbould hung all his Greyhounds & other Dogs immediately, except a favourite Pointer by name Juno, which is close confined & Antidotes given her, and is to be removed to Bracon, soon. The mischief done by the Dog, as known, is this, 2 Piggs of Mr Howletts, Michael Andrews Yard Dog, Mr Girlings ditto. 2 Pigs of Cases, and what is worse than all, is, that Jermyn's Son was bit in the hand—so far known, but what other Mischief has been done, God knows. I hope we shall not hear of much more. Mr Corbould is very uneasy about it. We did not go to Church, being rather dirty &c. Dinner to day, rost Beef & a Rabbit boiled &c.

FEBRUARY *3rd, Friday*. We breakfasted, dined, &c. again at home. To a poor French emigrant Woman, very short, who came to my House this Morning to ask Charity, being in very great distress—gave 0.1.0 and also a Mince Pye & some Beer. She told me as far as I understood her (as she talked but little English) that her Husband with 2 or 3 Children were killed in the late Bloody Commotions in France. Dinner to day, boiled Leg of Mutton & Capers &c.

26th, Sunday. We breakfasted, dined, &c. again at home.

Nancy near the same as Yesterday. Sent Ben this Morning to Dr Thorne's at Mattishall to desire the Dr to come to Morrow Morn to see Nancy. The Dr sent Word that he would call this Afternoon. Dr Thorne came to see Nancy this Afternoon about three o'clock, stayed near an Hour with us, I asked him to dine with us, but he could not. He said, that her complaint proceeded from a feverish kind, and had affected a weak part. He told her to live as usual, by no means lower, to poultice her Knee by Night with a Milk Poultice, and to keep a bandage on it by Day. Not to walk on it but little, no cold Water whatever to be applied. To take some Camphor &c. Pills some of which he left with her, 10 of them to be taken at 2 different times between 5 o'clock this Evening and before she went to bed. To Morrow he said he should send something for the Knee to be bathed with. He said he did not think it of any great consequence. Mr Willins did duty again at Weston Church for Mr Corbould. Mr Custance not there. I did not go, being very damp, Nancy could not. Mrs Corbould was not at Church either. Mr Corbould sent us this morning a small Codling about half a Pound — Value about 3 pence. We did not dine to day till after 4 o'clock. Dinner to day, the Codling boiled and a very fat Turkey Hen rosted &c.

March *29th, Wednesday.* Mr Corbould called on us this Morning, as did Mr Stoughton of Sparham. Mr Thorne came to see Nancy this Morning. He strongly recommends Port Wine and to drink rather More than less. She drank to day between a Pint & a Quart without having the lest effect upon the Brain. She has not drank less than a Pint for many Days. Dinner to day, Tripe boiled & cold Beef &c. Mr Stoughton brought us some good news. That we had taken the Island of Trinidad in the West Indies from the Spaniards, had taken some of their Ships &c. Admiral Harvey's Fleet gained the above Victory. Nancy continues near the same as Yesterday.

April *27th, Thursday.* We breakfasted, dined, &c. again at

home. About Noon, Mr Suckling of Aylsham with his Brother Horace from London, came to my House in a Post-Chaise and a Servant on Horseback and they stayed and dined & spent the Afternoon with us. They came to see Hungate-Lodge and to treat with Mr Custance about the same. I went with them in the Chaise to Hungate and immediately after to Weston House, but Mr Custance was gone to his Brothers at Lyng. We saw Mr Willm Custance who shewed them some of the Rooms. I left Compts for Mr C. and should be glad to see him in the Afternoon. We returned home by 3 o'clock to dinner. Dinner a Piece of rost Beef, hashed Calfs Head, a plain Pudding, Rasberry Puffs &c. About 5 o'clock Mr Custance came to us and drank Coffee and Tea with us. A little after 6 Mr Suckling & Brother went for Aylsham having settled all Matters with Mr Custance to the Satisfaction of all Parties. Mr C. stayed with us afterwards till after 8 o'clock. He approves much of the Messrs Sucklings. They are fashionable young Men, and Horace who is to be my Curate, appears to be a good natured, sensible, easy Man—rather fat & short. He is to enter on my Curacy & Hungate Lodge at Michlms. Mr Custance sent us half a dozen young Pigeons by Knights. Gave him o. 1. o.

MAY *12th, Friday.* We breakfasted, dined, &c. again at home. Had but an indifferent night of Sleep last Night. My cold being very troublesome wch made me cough. Very ill indeed towards bed-time &c.

Memorandum. Being taken extremely ill on 12th May 1797 declined entering any thing in this Book.*

13th, Saturday. Had a very indifferent Night last night. This Morning taken very ill, could scarce get down Stairs. Sent for Mr Thorne, who ordered me immediately to bed, having had a fit in the last Night and there I laid all night in a very bad State scarce sensible all the Night long. In the Night had a Blister put between my Shoulders which discharged very much indeed in

* While ill JW continued his diary on loose sheets.

the night and which made me soon better. But before that was put on was all but dead quite senseless. Nancy & Betty up with me most part of the night.

20th, Saturday. Had a good Night again last night thank God and got up very early. N.B. Sally a bad Sitter up at Nights. My Brother & Wife from Somersett, came to us just before Dinner to day, and they dined, supped & slept there. They were much fatigued indeed. I was very glad to see them. Nancy had very properly informed them of my Illness. Dr Thorne called on me again to day, found me better. Briton & Betty sat up with me to night.

21st, Sunday. Had a good Night again last Night. Got up this Morning much better thank God—was below stairs very early. My Brother & Wife breakfasted, dined &c. here again. About 11 o'clock this Morning Willm Woodforde of Gallhampton came in a Post Chaise to my House from Somersett having heard of my being ill—and he dined &c. here. Ben & Sally sat up with me to Night but an indifferent night.

22nd, Monday. We breakfasted &c. again at home. My Brother & Wife breakfasted, dined &c. &c. here again. Somewhat better to day thank God had a tolerable night.

Memorandum. Ben Leggatt & Sally Gunton sat up with me last Night. N.B. I have a particular reason for making this remark which made me uneasy—not to sit up with me on any account. Time will shew the cause of my Uneasiness and Suspicion. Slept but very indifferent all the night long—rather uneasy.*

JUNE *13th, Tuesday.* Mr & Mrs Custance with all their Family from Bath arrived at Weston-House about 5 o'clock this Afternoon. They went by our House in a new Coach & four Horses

* Much of this entry was scored out, but happily Beresford found it just decipherable, so was able to transcribe it. There are many similar cases of crossing out odd sentences or sections of the text which either JW on reflection or some member of the family after his death found embarrassing, offensive or simply too private.

and a Post-Chaise with Servants attending on the same. Great Rejoicings on their Return to Weston made on the occasion. Mr Maynard called on us about Noon & stayed about an Hour with us. He brought me & Nancy a Couple of Books which we subscribed to some time back of Newtons Poems a young man of Norwich Son to Newton, Minor Canon of Norwich C. a small affair—Mr Maynard is Curate to his Father at Attlebridge. I would have paid for both Books but Mr Maynard would not take for Nancys Book as he intended to give it to her. So that I paid him only for one Book & that was o.3.o. Paid him also, for paying for me at the late Generals etc o.1.o. Mr Corbould gave us a Call this Morning but did not stay long. During his stay with us, we recd a Letter each of us from Revd Ben Suckling of Aylsham, respecting Furniture at Hungate Lodge, what his Brother would chuse to take at Michaelmas &c.

19th, Monday. We breakfasted, dined &c. again at home. My Brother & Wife & My Nephew Willm breakfasted &c. here again. Had a tolerable good Night last Night. After breakfast between 11 and 12 My Brother's Wife & Nancy went in my little Curricle or taxed Cart to Weston House, My Brother & Willm walked with me thither, we stayed there till near 2 o'clock. We returned as we went—saw all the Family but Mr George who is in the E. Indies. All the young Folks much grown and much altered but Emily who is just the same but much grown. On our return home found Mrs Thorne & daughter Mary Anne at my House, had been there some time. They stayed & dined with us & spent the Afternoon. They came in a one horse Chaise a Servant Boy driving them. A Mantua Maker from Mattishall Burgh by name Burroughs came here early this Morning, and she breakfasted, dined & stayed the Afternoon at Weston Parsonage. Miss W. by desire of her Aunt sent 3 Maccarel to Weston-House (having bought 1 doz this Morning before we went out) before our return home—Mrs Custance wishing the Man had called there also. I was quite tired out almost by the time that Dinner came in. Very much vexed indeed on going up

393

to Weston H. to see a Clay Pit of mine in the Field in the path thro which we go thither (occupied at present by Jon Baker) so much Clay having been of late taken from thence by him & carried away, as to make the foot path very dangerous indeed for Passengers, in some places the foot path entirely taken away. I sent to him directly to leave that Glebe at Michelmas next— It greatly hurt me. In Parlour & Kitchen to day we had 14 People at Dinner. I was quite tired out almost before I got to bed to Night. Dinner to day, Maccarel & fore Qtr of Lamb rosted &c.

JULY *20th, Thursday*. We breakfasted, dined, &c, again at home. My Brother and Wife breakfasted, dined &c. here again. I find myself rather getting strength but very slow indeed. Have at times uncommon sinkings within me—tho' I constantly take Cake and a Glass of Port Wine every Morn' about 11 o'clock and strengthening Cordial twice a Day the first thing before breakfast and at 2 in the Afternoon being an Hour before Dinner —which I have constantly been taken for the last Month if not longer. Finished my last Dose this Afternoon and now am to drop it. Dinner to day, fryed Soals and boiled Beef &c.

21st, Friday. We breakfasted, dined, &c. again at home. My Brother & Wife breakfasted, dined &c. here again. A Mr Cotman a young Man & a Clergyman (Son also of a Mr Cotman well known by late Mr Du Quesne) called on me this Morning concerning the Curacy of Weston in case Mr Suckling does not take it after Mr Corbould at Michelmas next & I cannot get a resident Curate. He did not stay long with me, would not walk in. Dinner to day Leg of Mutton rosted &c.

AUGUST *12th, Saturday*. We breakfasted, dined, &c. again at home. My Brother & wife breakfasted, dined &c. here again. Sent Ben to Norwich this Morning after Coal &c. Holland the Chimney Sweeper, swept my Study Chimney, Parlour ditto— and their Chamber Chimneys, with Kitchen and Back-Kitchen ditto—in all six. He had a new Boy with him who had likely to have lost his Life this Morning at Weston House in sticking in one of their Chimnies. I gave the poor Boy a Shilling, Dinner Shoulder of Lamb rosted &c.

SEPTEMBER *22nd, Friday*. We breakfasted, dined, &c. again at home. My Brother & Wife breakfasted, dined, &c. here again. Mr Stoughton of Sparham sent us a Leash of Partridges. Mr Cotman, called on me this Afternoon soon after dinner to talk with me about being my Curate—I soon settled with him— That is, he is to have it and enter upon it when Mr Corbould leaves it which will be in November. He did not stay long with me having 2 Ladies with him at ye Gate. Dinner to day, fryed Eels, Calfs Pluck or Fry &c.

23rd, Saturday. We breakfasted, dined, &c. again at home. My Brother & Wife breakfasted, dined &c. here again. Bidewells People brought our News-papers—No Letters. Dinner to day, a Couple of Chicken boiled & Pork, & Leg Mutton rosted. My Brother but indifferent, Inflammation in one of his Eyes and much of the flying Gout in his Constitution. Since I have taken to the Flannel Waistcoat, think myself better & stronger for so doing. No good News. Less appearance of Peace than ever. Lord Malmesbury sent home in a hurry from France.*

OCTOBER *10th, Tuesday*. We breakfasted, dined, &c. again at home. Dinner to day boiled Fowl & Pork &c. Brewed a Barrel of Table Beer to day. Very weak indeed to day. No Appetite whatever. Unless I get better soon I cannot long survive it. Pray God! have mercy on me a poor, weak Creature. Lent Mr Corbould

* From early July Lord Malmesbury had again been in France negotiating for peace. Pitt was prepared to recognise all French conquests in Europe, including Belgium, and acknowledge French dominance in Holland and Italy. Of British naval conquests only the Cape, Ceylon and Trinidad would be retained. In the end this was unacceptable to the French. Malmesbury was ordered to quit France within twenty-four hours.

my common Cart with harness for 2 Horses, Waggon Line &c. to go to Norwich with Goods.

11th, Wednesday. We breakfasted, dined, &c. again at home. Mr Mellish sent us about 12 lb of Honey—rather old. Paid young Mr Girling for his Father for a half yrs poor Rate at 11d, 1.13.2½. Dinner to day, Leg of Mutton boiled & Capers &c. Very poorly & very weak all the whole day. Mr Corbould sent home the Cart &c. this Afternoon. Mr Corbould carried away every thing from Hungate Lodge that could be, every Nail & every Vegetable in the Garden.

15th, Sunday. We breakfasted, dined, &c. again at home. Weaker this Morning than I have been yet. Scarce able to make a Walk of it to day. No Appetite still. Mr Corbould did duty this Afternoon at Weston Church. He made us a Visit on his return from Church. He went to Norwich afterwards, they having left Hungate-Lodge. Dinner to day, rost Beef & Plumb Pudding &c. I eat some plumb Pudding for Dinner but nothing else. In the Evening thought Myself a little better. The Medicine that Mr Thorne sent me seem to do good. For the last two days I have been very bad indeed not able to put on some of my Cloaths or pull them off. Great News on the public Papers, Admiral Duncan having completely beaten a large Fleet of the Dutch.*

24th, Tuesday. Thank God! I had a good Night of rest last Night and found myself pretty strong & hearty this Morning without any Assistance or Attendance whatever I got up. Dinner to day fryed Beef & Potatoes & a rost Chicken.

NOVEMBER *17th, Friday.* We breakfasted, dined, &c. again at home. Thank God! found myself rather better this Morn' not so bewildered or so weak as Yesterday, Senses better & stronger —still however very, very poorly. Appetite better, made a very

* The French were again expected to invade Ireland, convoyed by the Dutch fleet. Bad winds and tides stopped the Dutch fleet sailing until 8 October. The engagement at Camperdown took place on 11 October.

good Dinner considering what I have done of late. Eat pretty hearty of a fresh boiled Tongue & mash Potatoes. Smoaked my Pipe this Afternoon better than of late. Paid my Blacksmith John Buck his Annual Bill—3.8.6.

26th, Sunday. Quite mild this Morning with some Rain. Found myself better to day, but still cannot gain strength. Dinner to day, a Loin of Pork boiled & a Hare rosted &c. My Appetite is pretty good, Made a very good dinner. Mr Cotman entered upon the Curacy of Weston this day and therefore read Prayers & Preached here this Afternoon. None of Mr Custance's Family at Church to day being wet. Mr Custance's People have taken up some Poachers that were found in ipso facto on his Premises.

DECEMBER *3rd, Sunday.* Mr Cotman did duty this Morning at Weston Church. Mr Custance and his eldest Son, called on us this Morn' after Divine Service—They had been at Church. A smart Frost this Morning which rather affected me, but upon the whole think myself rather stronger than of late. Dinner to day, Neck of Veal rosted &c. The present times seem to prognosticate e'er long very alarming circumstances. No appearance of Peace, but on the contrary the French reject every Proposition of it and so inveterate are they against our Government, that they are determined to make a descent on England & the Taxes therefore on the above account are talked of being raised trebly to what they were last Year.

17th, Sunday. We breakfasted, dined, &c. again at home. I found myself rather weaker to day than of late; but very little. I can eat pretty well and thank God sleep very well. Mr Cotman did duty this Afternoon at Weston Church. It grieves me much that I am rendered unable to do it myself or to attend at Church being so very infirm. Dinner to day, Shoulder of Veal rosted &c. Very windy all the Day, obliged to be in the Parlour as our Study smoaked so very much. Wind WNW. Ben went to Crownthorp on my Horse to day, returned in very good time in the Evening.

397

1798

JANUARY *15th, Monday.* We breakfasted, dined, &c. again at home. After breakfast I paid my Servants their Year's Wages due Janry 5th 1798 as follows.

To Benj. Leggatt, my farming Man pd 10.0.0.

To Bretingham Scurl my Footman pd 8.0.0.

To Betty Dade, my House-Maid pd 5.5.0.

To Sally Gunton, my Cook & Dairy Maid pd 5.5.0.

To Barnabas Woodcock my Yard-Boy pd 2.2.0.

Dinner to day, a boiled Fowl & Pork, & Beef-Steaks &c. To a poor Man, lately a Marine, by name Cleveland, gave 1.0. Sally Gunton's Brother, Billy Gunton, a Grenadier and Corporal in the Norfolk Militia, a very fine looking young Man, called here in the Evening to take leave of his Sister to join his Regiment at Colchester on Wednesday next or Thursday without fail having been absent near 3 Weeks. I gave him on his going away 0.2.6. Nancy sent a Letter by him to Norwich, to Miss Pounsett.

FEBRUARY *3rd, Saturday.* We breakfasted, dined, &c. again at home. Sent Briton this Morning to Norwich in my old Cart after many things. He returned home about 4 in the After. brought a Letter to Nancy from her Aunt Jon Woodforde announcing the Marriage between my Niece Jane Pounsett and the Revd Frederick Grove to have taken place on Thursday the 25th Day of January last past, at Pitcomb Church in Somersett. Immediately after the Ceremony they set off for Bath with my Sister Pounsett and Mary Woodforde of Taunton who was bride-Maid where they are to spend some Days. Mrs Woodforde's Letter also mentions that the Settlement on Jane Pounsett is a very bad one & a very cunning one for in case she dies without Issue, every thing whatever goes to Grove immediately on her demise. Dinner to day, rost Pork &c.

16th, Friday. We breakfasted, dined, &c. again at home. Paid John Reeve for 2 doz. of Port Wine 3.6.0. 13 Quart Bottles to the Dozen—an amazing Price indeed, 33s 0d per Dozen.* In the Year 1774 we had Port Wine at New-College at 1s 6d per Qt Bottle. A Pipe of Wine then to be had at about £30 per Pipe. Now it cannot be had under near £70. Dinner to day boiled Pork & a rost Rabbit &c.

19th, Monday. Michael Andrew's Wife called on me this Morning upon Mrs Mann's Account she being dangerously ill and informed me that she was desirous of having the Sacrament administered to her on Wednesday next. I sent to Mr Maynard directly to desire him to do it. A more officious, busy-bodied, Woman in all Cases relating to other People's Concerns I know not. More particularly when ill—a true Jobish Friend. Dinner to day, fryed Pork & Potatoes &c. Sent Mrs Mann to day, she having Company at her house a Couple of ready trussed Chicken, a nice Duck and three Mince Pies—by my Maid Betty. Poor Woman she now keeps her bed I am afraid she cannot last long. The only Company I hear that is at Mrs Manns is only Johnny Rose's Wife, late Miss Temple, whose Father marry'd Johnny Rose's Mother who formerly lived here.

MARCH *14th, Wednesday.* Js Pegg called on me this Morning and left me an account of the new additional Taxes per annum exclusive of the old, which amount to my Share 25.5.6. Very heavy indeed are the new Taxes on the Clergy in short. How the new taxes will go down with the People in general I know not, I hope they will not create more new Taxes after these, tho' at present are talked of.

27th, Tuesday. Gave my Maid, Sally Gunton, for sitting up with me when ill, 2 Yards of black Silk, being a hatband sent

* In the previous two years Pitt more than doubled the wine duties, which readily accounts for the increased price.

me by John Mann on the Death of his Mother. Dinner to day, Neck of Veal rosted &c. Mr Hambleton Custance drank Tea with us this Evening.

APRIL *1st, Sunday*. We breakfasted, dined, &c. again at home. Mr Cotman read Prayers & Preached this Morn' at Weston C. Mr Hambleton Custance called on us this Morning after Divine Service and spent near an Hour with us. Dinner to day, Fillett of Veal rosted &c. Very cold indeed to day & severe Frost—very unusual. By the publick Papers, every thing in them appears very distressing & alarming. French Invasion daily expected.* Made a very good dinner to day, but cannot gain Strength.

6th, Good-Friday. We breakfasted, dined, &c. again at home. My Parishioners were much disappointed in not having Divine Service this Morning at Church as usual on G. Friday. Mr Cotman promised me that he would attend this Day and declared the same last Sunday at Church. Mr Custance with most of the Family with a great many of my Parishioners were at Church, and much displeased. It vexed me a great deal, as I told him of having Divine Service in the Morning of Good-Friday as usual on this Day. It hurt me very much to hear of it in my Weak State. Young Mr Girling brought us a small Pike this Morning. Dinner to day, Salt Fish, Eggs, & Fritters &c. Between one thing and another was made very uneasy.

25th, Wednesday. Nothing talked of at present but an Invasion of England by the French. Great Preparations making all over England &c. against the said intended Invasion, especially all along the Sea Coasts every where.

27th, Friday. We breakfasted, dined &c. again at home. Dinner to day, hash Mutton and a Suet Pudding, I made a very

* Such entries reflect the deep anxiety in England at the plans for invasion France was pursuing. An English spy met Bonaparte on 13 February on his way to Ostend to inspect the port and commisson flat-bottomed boats for the crossing.

great Dinner to day indeed, was rather afraid I had eat too much but I recd no Inconvenience from it. A Meeting of the Parish this Afternoon at the Heart, respecting a sudden Invasion from the French &c. what was necessary and proper to be done on a sudden attack. Mr Custance attended as did most of the Parish —I could not.

JULY *20th, Friday*. We breakfasted, dined, &c. again at home. Mrs Custance with her two Daughters & Son John called here this Morning and stayed near an Hour with us. They took Miss Woodforde back with them to Weston-House to spend the Day with them. The young Ladies looked but poorly as did Master John—they have been too free with fruit I shd suspect. They looked dull and pale—by no means Well. Dinner to day, Shoulder of Mutton rosted &c. I made a tolerable good Dinner tho' by myself. Miss W. returned home about 8 o'clock this Evening. She was brought back in their Coach. A Mr Whitbread from Suffolk & Mr Press Custance dined there. Mr Whitbread is a very old Acquaintance of Mr Custance. It rained again to day and so it has more or less on the Day of St Swithin and every day since.

AUGUST *7th, Tuesday*. My poor Cow is a good deal better to day, Put her in my Garden. The old Gander very weak and lame and very poor indeed, had him into the Garden and gave him plenty of Barley.

SEPTEMBER *14th, Friday*. Mr Custance made us a Morning Visit, he came on foot. To one Largess to day, Emeris's Men gave 0.1.0. Dinner to day, Pigs Fry & Pork Steaks &c. I fancy myself rather stronger of a few days past than of late tho' at times I feel myself rather hurried and alarmed. Mr Willm Custance sent us a brace of Partridges, which was very kind of him, this being the first Day of shooting Partridges. Great News said to be recd from London, concerning Ireland; viz. that the

French who had landed there, had been defeated, and that the Irish were in a fair Way, of being made quiet.*

NOVEMBER *8th, Thursday*. Very poorly and very weak this Morning as I was taken in a kind of fainting Fit, getting into bed, last Night. I had just time to open my Bed-Room Door before I fell down, wch Miss Woodforde hearing, came to my assistance and our Betty also came soon after. I fell down and being so extremely weak could not get off my Breeches or get on my Legs. Dinner to day, rost Beef &c. Mr Custance made us a Morning Visit, he had been to Mr Townshend, alias, Lrd Baynings.

11th, Sunday. We breakfasted, dined, &c. again at home. Getting up this Morning I was taken very ill, with a giddiness in my Head, could not get down Stairs without Assistance (after some little time I got better) — owing to great Weakness & relaxation. Mr Cotman being gone into Kent to a Living that he has got there, Weston Church was not served this Morn' as it ought to have been. Mr Cotman should have got a Substitute. It is not using me well by neglecting it. Dinner to day, the other fore Qtr of Pork rosted &c. Miss Woodforde had a Letter last Night from her Aunt John Woodforde from Bath, informing us that they had left Castle-Cary and had gone to Bath to live, himself and Wife — Her Sister Patty Clarke having married Jeans. They left Castle-Cary, the third of October. They have hired Lodgings in Chatham-Row No. 8 — at a Widows House with only a Servant. They carried with them, a Girl only as a servant. I cannot say that I approve of their living there.

12th, Monday. We breakfasted, dined, &c. again at home. Very poorly, very giddy & weak again this Morn'. Mrs Bodham sent a Note by her Man, Willm Ward, to enquire after us, and

* The rebellion planned by the United Irishmen to coincide with the arrival of a French fleet had broken out on 23 May — but the French never turned up. A small French force arrived on 22 August. They surrendered on 8 September.

402

also respecting the Curacy of Weston for a Young Man by name Dade, Nephew of the Dean of Norwich, but tho' I had partly promised him before, but recollecting that Dr Baker's Son of Cawston had applied prior to him, in case one by name Brown of Norwich refuses it—wch I had entirely forgot to mention to her here—I desired Nancy to acquaint her of the same. Mr Maynard also called this Morning, and he had scarce left us, before Mrs Custance and her two Daughters called on us in a Walk and stayed upwards of an Hour with us. Dinner to day, boiled Leg of Mutton & Capers &c.

29th, Thursday. We breakfasted, dined, &c. again at home. Great Rejoicings at Norwich to day on Lord Nelsons late great & noble Victory over the French near Alexandria in Egypt. An Ox rosted whole in the Market-Place &c. This being a day of general Thanksgiving Mr Cotman read Prayers this Morning at Weston-Church, proper on the Occasion. Dinner to day, Leg of Mutton rosted &c. I gave my Servants this Evening after Supper some strong-Beer and some Punch to drink Admiral Lord Nelson's Health on his late grand Victory and also all the other Officers with him and all the brave Sailors with them, and also all those brave Admirals, Officers and Sailors that have gained such great & noble Victories of late over the French &c. &c.* Miss Woodforde recd a Letter this Morning from Richardson & Goodluck in London, informing her of her having a Prize in the Irish Lottery which was entirely done unknown to me. It was a 16th Share in the Irish Lottery of a nine Pound Prize. She paid for the Share elevn Shillings & sixpence and she will receive for her Share only 11 Shillings and 3 pence, by which Prize, she will be out of Pocket 3d if not more when it is received. No rejoicings at all at Weston. I should have been very glad to have contributed towards some, if Mr Custance had come forward.

---

* Nelson was born at Burnham Thorpe—some miles to the north-west of JW's village—where his father was rector. Between 1787 and 1793, when on half-pay, he lived at the parsonage.

DECEMBER *16th, Sunday.* We breakfasted, dined, &c. again at home. Nancy had two Letters this Morning brought from Weston House by Briton, which they brought Yesterday from Norwich, some of the Family being at Norwich then. Both very melancholy ones indeed, One was from Cole from Mrs Grove at Cole, the other from Nancys Brother William. The former giving us the dismal Account of the Death of my dear Sister Pounsett on Tuesday last in the Afternoon of a putrid Fever at her House at Ansford. Nancys Brother did not mention her Death only that she was very dangerously ill. The melancholy News of the Death of poor dear Sister Pounsett made me very miserable indeed. It is our great Loss—but to her I hope great Gain. We thought her quite well and happy at her little Palace at Ansford —and we were informed in a late Letter from Miss Hussey, that her Aunt Mrs Webb had been very lately into Somersett and at my Sister Pounsett's—and that my Sister Pounsett with her Aunt talked of going to Bath and also to London together very soon. I don't know after all things considered whether it is not happier for her, her Son in Law, Grove, having of late behaved to her rather unkind on all accounts—Oh! Tempora quo modo mutantur!—In his Temporibus, Quid desiderandum!* Dinner today, a Turkey rosted etc.

22nd, Saturday. We breakfasted, dined, &c. again at home. Betty Dades Father called here this Morning. Dinner to day, a boiled Rabbit & Beef Steaks &c. Nancy had a Letter this Evening from her Brother William at Gallhampton confirming the bad News of my dear Sister Pounsetts Death and the unfeeling behaviour of her Son in Law, Grove respecting the burial of my poor Sister, none of her Relations invited to attend her to her last home. No Pall-Bearers & also even a Pall partly refused. From such unfeeling & base Hearts which Grove hath shewn to so deserving a Woman may we never more hear of such. What a miserable Prospect has my Niece his Wife before her! She

* 'How times have changed! In these times what should we wish for!'

would have him, and every device from her Friends respecting a proper Marriage-Settlement was thrown away upon her, So that Grove had everything not only all Janes' but her Mothers also—which now comes to him, every thing of my late poor Sister Pounsetts.

28th, Friday. We breakfasted, dined, &c. again at home. Frost last Night & this Morning & all the Day intense—it froze in every part of the House even in the Kitchen. Milk & Cream tho' kept in the Kitchen all froze. Meat like blocks of Wood. It froze in the Kitchen even by the fire in a very few Minutes. So severe Weather I think I never felt before. Even the Meat in our Pantry all froze & also our Bread. I think the Cold was never more severe in my Life. Giblett Soup & Piggs Fry for Dinner to day &c. This Evening, if anything, Frost more severe.

1799

JANUARY *31st, Thursday*. We breakfasted, dined, &c. again at home. Paid Js Pegg this Morning a Qtrs Land-Tax 3.0.0. John Norton was Yesterday committed to Aylesham Bridewell for a Breach of the Peace. Dinner to day, boiled Veal & Pork &c. Many People are glad that Jon Norton is sent to Bridewell as he was so unruly. His Wife & Daughter, as well as Neighbours were afraid almost to go to bed at Nights afraid of being burnt in their beds, as he took so little care of fire—scarce ever went to bed, and his behaviour to a poor-bed-ridden Wife and a good Daughter, was almost beyond example, distressing. Bitter cold again to day with some Snow. Frost very severe, froze sharp within doors.

FEBRUARY *2nd, Saturday*. We breakfasted, dined, &c. again at home. Still very severe Weather, much Snow & hard Frost. The Turnips have lost all their Tops and now look like so many large Bowls or foot-Balls. I was taken very ill last Night on going to bed fell down in a fit, but Nancy hearing me fall came kindly to my Assistance with Betty. The cold quite overpowered me, going from a warm Room to a cold Room above without fire, and after walking round below in seeing all things safe—the cold was too much for me. The Snow so drifted in some Places as to make the Roads almost impassable. Scarce ever known such severe Weather for the last forty Years and still likely to continue. It affects me extremely indeed, have scarce any feeling, am almost benumbed both in Mind & Body. Bidewells People brought our Norwich Paper, the Ipswich Paper not come to Norwich owing to the Severity of the Weather—The Roads being impassable almost to any Place on Account of the Snow being drifted in almost every Road. Such severe Weather has not been known for the last 6o Years till the present. Snow drifted in some places uncommonly high. Dinner to day, boiled Pork and a roast Duck &c.

7th, Thursday. We breakfasted, dined, &c. again at home. The same cold Weather prevails with very severe Frost accompanied with some Snow. Water froze in the back-house quite hard within, in less than four hours after it had been brought in from the Well to day abt Noon. Such severe Frost to day, as scarce was known. Mr Custance obliged to Norwich to send to day after Coal being quite out. Two Waggons went this Morning after some and obliged to come by my House to France-Green and so on to Honingham to get to the Turnpike Road there, and three or four Men went with the Teams. It is also even thought that when they get there, that they could not get any, as no Coals can come from Yarmouth, No Barges stirring—all bound fast by the Frost on the River. This very severe Weather almost kills me. I am much affected by it for the worse. Dinner to day, boiled Leg of Pork &c.

16th, Saturday. Early in the Morn' there was a small Frost but it thawed again fast about 8 o'clock after. I felt pretty well & strong this Morning. Dinner to day, Shoulder of Mutton rosted &c. No News Papers &c. came to hand to day, Tho' my Butcher promised me faithfully to bring them which very much disconcerted me.

17th, Sunday. We breakfasted, dined, &c. again at home. Our Newspapers &c. we received this Morning by Sarah Grant of the Poor House on Hungate Common. My Butcher having left them there last Night. Had a Letter from Mrs Grove in Somersett. No Duty at Weston Church this Morning, Mr Cotman attended but it was late when he got there. Dinner to day, boiled Pork & a Turkey rosted &c. My Strength rather better, Spirits also, and my Appetite very good but feel however feverish. I eat five times a day—at breakfast, abt Noon, Dinner, Afternoon at Tea, and at Supper—and at all times with a proper relish. Mr William Custance called on us this Morning. Very dismal Accounts on the Papers respecting the last severe Weather—many, many People having lost their Lives thro' the inclemency of the same. Mail Coaches &c. unable to travel. The Roads in very, very many Places impassable. The long continuance of so severe cold Weather having scarce been ever known for the last Century. It has lasted now (with scarce any intermission) from the 17th of December last past & still likely.

26th, Tuesday. We breakfasted, dined, &c. again at home. Sent Ben, this Morning, to Norwich, on purpose to pay off two Bills for me, having been wrote to by the People, here mentioned. Messrs Smith, Woolen-Drapers, and Forster, Taylor. I told Ben to take a stamp Receipt of each of them in full of all Demands having done with them. Dinner to day, a boiled Fowl & Pork & Beef-Steaks. Ben returned about 4 o'clock this Afternoon with proper Receipts on paying the said Bills. It pleased me much on the said Bills being paid but the remembrance of their being sent me by them, will not be by me so soon forgot having dealt with them for at least 23 Years. Smith the Mercer is a Presbyterian and I suppose, Forster, the Taylor, is of the same Persuasion. I have now done with them for ever for their late shabby, ungentleman-like behaviour. Fish at Norwich very scarce and very dear.

MARCH *22nd, G. Friday.* Mr Cotman called on me this Morning before he went to Weston Church to read Prayers being Good-Friday. He also wished to leave the Curacy of Weston at the expiration of the present Quarter. I cannot say that I was displeased at it, as he has been rather too inattentive to duty. Dinner to day, Salt Fish, Eggs & Fritters. I was rather a little giddy in my Head to day a little before dinner—but only a few minutes.

31st, Sunday. We breakfasted, dined &c. again at home. Mr Cotman read Prayers and administered the H. Sacrament this Morn' at Weston Church. Nancy had a Letter from her Brother William this Morning brought Yesterday from Norwich by Mr Custance Servant—a most melancholy one indeed to us, as it announced to us the Death of our dear Friend my dear Brother John Woodforde, who died very suddenly at Mrs Patty Clarkes at Castle-Cary on Saturday last, having come from Bath. He came from Bath with Ralph Woodforde on the Sunday before, Ralph coming from Allhampton on the Death of his Mother— Ralph being executor. I sincerely pity poor Mrs Woodforde my poor Brothers Wife for so dreadful a shock & not being with him at the time.

APRIL *2nd, Tuesday.* Bitter cold again to day, hard Frost, but less Wind. There being but few sound Turnips, the poor Stock such as Bullocks, Cows, Sheep &c. are shockingly distressed, few Farmers have scarce anything to give them. Scarce ever known such distressed times for Stock of all kinds, nothing growing, no vegetation, every thing almost dead in the gardens, Beans & Peas &c. almost all gone dead. It is grievous to behold how every Vegetable is hurt—Not even a Daisy or any kind of flower seen. What dismal, dreary Aspect have we at present.

22nd, Monday. Sally's Brother, Willm Gunton, called on her this Morn'. He is still in the Norfolk Militia. He looked very well indeed, he is now a Serjeant. Dinner to day, boiled Calfs Head &c. Nancy busy to day in answering her Brother Willm Woodfordes Letter. Rather low-spirited to day, all Family Affairs in the Country contrary to my desire or wish and those People which ought to be Friends by blood turn out the greatest Enemies on Earth.

MAY *26th, Sunday*. We breakfasted, dined, &c. again at home. Mr Cotman read Prayers & Preached this Afternoon at Weston Church for the last time as he leaves the Curacy this Day of Weston. He called on me (by my desire) this Afternoon and I paid him for his last half Year's Curacy, before Miss Woodforde the sum of 15.0.0 in full of every demand from me to him. He drank a Glass of Port Wine and soon left us. Young Mr Dade (who is to succeed Mr Cotman in the Curacy of Weston) called on me also this Afternoon, and informed me that he would enter upon the Curacy of Weston by my desire on Sunday next, and therefore will read Prayers and Preach at Weston-Church on Sunday morning next—to begin at a Qtr before Eleven. When Duty in the Afternoon at Qtr before three. Mr Dade drank a Glass of Port Wine whilst here. Dinner to day a Calfs Head boiled & Pork &c. I was pretty well to day, not so very nervous. Young Baker of Cawston was to have succeeded Cotman in my Church as Curate, but was very lately preferred to a Readers Place at Bury. I cannot say that I am very sorry for it, as of late I heard that Dr Baker and whole Family are very violent Democrats indeed.

JUNE *10th, Monday*. We breakfasted, dined &c. again at home. Mr Maynard called on us this Morning. To a Man of Shearingham by name Hull for six small Crabs paid him 0.1.0. Dinner to day, a small Leg of Mutton rosted and remarkably fine flavoured—Scotch Mutton. Mr Custance called on us in his Evenings Walk about 7 o'clock & spent an Hour with us. Michael Andrews Wife has met with a very bad Fall and very dangerously strained her Ancle. Washing Week with us this Week. We wash every five Weeks. Our present Washerwomen are Anne Downing and Anne Richmond. Washing and Ironing generally take us four Days. The Washerwomen breakfast and dine the Monday and Tuesday, and have each one Shilling on their going away in the Evening of Tuesday. Mr Custance brought us great News, that the French had been entirely driven out of Italy by the Austrians & vast Numbers of them had been killed and taken Prisoners in the late battles.*

JULY *6th, Saturday.* We breakfasted, dined &c. again at home. We had another Swarm of Bees to day about Noon and out of the same Hive that we had the last Swarm from. So very hot to day that makes me very faint. Willm Woodcock hived the Bees for us again, for which I gave him o.1.o besides Victuals and drink. Paid him also for a new Straw-Hive o.1.o. Nancy sent a Letter to her Brother Willm by Betty Cary who brought our News for us from Norwich this Week. Dinner to day, green Peas for the first this Season and plenty of them & some Pork &c. Mr Custance spent more than an Hour with us this Evening. He came walking. He eat 2 or three of our small sweet Cakes. He complains of a cold inwardly which gives him a good deal of Pain, especially when he coughs, but he wont doctor himself. Sir Edmund Bacon hath been at Weston-House lately. Heard little or no News by Mr Custance. Betty Cary came early this Evening from Norwich.

SEPTEMBER *3rd, Tuesday.* We breakfasted, dined, &c. again at home. Our Wheat remarkably fine & heavy but very much beat down by the late Winds & Rain which makes it very bad for shearing. I hired, Yesterday, one Henry Daines, a Boy of 13 Years old, in the place of Barnard Woodcock, who leaves me at Michaelmas next being too old for his Place & can better himself. I liked the Boy very well, having an open, honest countenance to all appearances, his Mother who came with him, seemed to be a good kind of Woman & very Motherly. I gave the Boy, on hiring him o.1.o. Dinner to day, rost Beef & Plumb Pudding as our People are busy, in shearing of Wheat. I was but

* JW is referring to the victorious campaign of the combined Austrian and Russian forces in the north of Italy. They entered Milan on 28 April, Turin on 27 May, and shut up the French in Genoa.

indifferent all day, very weak, tho' I made a very good Dinner on the Beef.

11th, Wednesday. Very fine Day again for the Harvest &c. 'Lord make us all truly thankful for the same and give us gratefull Hearts in return.' Dinner to day, Beans & Bacon & Partridges. Thank God! I was very finely to day & eat hearty. All my Wheat but a very few Sheaves carried and put into Barn without any Rain at all upon it during the whole time of cutting, &c. Uncommonly fine Weather indeed have we had for the last 6 Weeks past.

25th, Wednesday. We breakfasted, dined, &c. again at home. Mr Maynard called here this Morning. Just before Dinner, Nancy's Brother William from Somersett came riding into our Yard, and he dined, supped & slept here. His coming upon us so sudden affected us at first, but after dinner we were better. William slept in his usual Room. We had for Dinner to day boiled Eels &c.

OCTOBER *6th, Sunday.* We breakfasted, dined, &c. again at home. Andrew Spraggs brought a Box for me this Morning to my House, which he brought Yesterday from Norwich, in which was a fine large Somersett Cheese, a present from my Nephew now with me, from a Relation of his Wife's at Mew near Stowton by name James Jules, a great Dealer in Cheese and employed for Government in that way and is getting a good fortune by it. It was a very kind Present from my Nephew. The Cheese was about a Qtr of a Hundred Wht with the Kings Arms on the side of it. The Cheese was made near Wells in Somersett, Mr Dane read Prayers & Preached this Morn' at Weston-Church. It being rather damp & inclined to wet Nancy & Brother did not go. Dinner to day, Breast of Veal rosted &c.

1800

JANUARY *24th, Friday*. We breakfasted, dined, &c. again at home. Very busy all the Morning in looking over Family Accounts & Goods relating to Somersett that my Nephew Willm Woodforde might take a Copy of the same with him into Somersett. After which I made him a Present of a Bank of England Note of 5.0.0. Also two Guineas, to be laid out in Town for things in remembrance of me to his Wife and Children — 2.2.0. Dinner to day, Leg of Mutton rosted &c.

26th, Sunday. Mr Dade read Prayers & Preached this Morn' at Weston Church. Few People there. It was a dark wet Morning and mild. Dinner to day, Shoulder of Mutton rosted &c. We were rather dull and flat to day, as to Morrow Nancy's Brother Willm Woodforde leaves Weston Parsonage for Somersett.

MARCH *24th, Monday*. We breakfasted, &c. again at home. Nancy dined & spent the Afternoon and great part of the Evening at Weston-House, with Mr & Mrs Custance & their two Daughters, with their Sons Hambleton and William Custance, Lady Bacon with her Daughters Anne, and Maria Bacon, Miss Mary Anne Bacon from Devonshire, and Edmund Bacon eldest Son of Sir Edmund & Lady Bacon. Nancy did not return till after 9 o'clock this Evening as the young folks at Weston House had something of a Masquerade-Ball this Evening. Dramatis Personae, Miss Custance in the Character of an old Woman, Emily Custance a flower Girl, Devonshire Miss Bacon a Fortune-Teller alias Gipsy, Miss Bacon in the Character of a Fool, Miss Maria Bacon, a Ghost — None of the young Gentlemen acted at all or were dressed. I had for my Dinner to day a boiled Chicken &c.

APRIL *15th, Tuesday*. We breakfasted, dined, &c. again at home. Paid James Hardy, Landlord of Weston-Heart, this Morning, for Liquors 2.13.0.

viz, to two Gallons of Rum at 16s od, 1.12.0.

To one Gallon of Brandy at 21s od, 1.1.0.

Dinner to day, Leg of Pork boiled &c. I eat very hearty for Dinner to day & feel stronger inwardly, but right hand very weak & swelled wch I attribute to Gout. It is with great Pain that I write this.

JUNE *22nd, Sunday*. Mr Dade read Prayers & Preached this Afternoon at Weston-Church. Stormy Weather about Noon with Thunder & Hail and Rain, but we had not much of it. Dinner to day, boiled Leg of Lamb & Loin fryed. Betty continues but poorly & weak still. Nancy thinks that it is owing to a Love Affair with my farming Man & Servant, Ben Leggatt who hath for a long time taken notice of her. They have a long time been talked of. Whether he now slights her or not, I cannot say. I hope he hath not been too intimate with her. Thank God! I felt myself pretty well to day.

27th, Friday. We breakfasted, dined, &c. again at home. I was finely to day thank God for it! and this Day I entered my sixtieth Year being born (old Stile)* the sixteenth of June in the Year, 1740. Dinner to day, Shoulder of Mutton rosted &c. Accept my thanks O! Almighty God! for thy great Goodness to me in enabling me (after my Late great Illness) to return my grateful thanks for the same.

29th, Sunday. We breakfasted, dined, &c. again at home. Mr Dade read Prayers & Preached this Morning at Weston Church —None of Weston-House there. Nancy intended to be there, but prevented by Rain. Dinner to day, a Sculphling of Lamb rosted (viz.) a Breast and Neck joined together. The Weather being Muggy with gentle soft Rain made me rather dull and

* Britain had adopted the Gregorian calendar in 1752 and also moved New Year's Day from 25 March to 1 January.

spiritless to day. Delightful Weather however for all kinds of Vegetables, particularly so for all kinds of Grain. Thanks to the Almighty Creator for the same.

JULY *12, Saturday.* Nancy had another Swarm of Bees about Noon from the same old Hive which the last Swarm came from. It should have been mentioned Yesterday instead of to day as Yesterday it happened unknown to me and our Maids hived them. They settled in our Wall-Garden on one of the Sticks put into the Ground to prop up and for Peas to twist round & keep from the Ground. The Swarm of Bees happened very suddenly. Our Maids hived them very well indeed and they seemed to settle very well this Morn'. I think Nancy very lucky with her Bees. Dinner to day, Peas & Bacon &c.

AUGUST *27th, Wednesday.* Our tame Hawk that we had so long in the Walled Garden fled away Yesterday and hath not been heard of since. The Lapwing also we had so long, have not been heard of some Days. Harvest quite at a Stand at present. Mr Hambleton Custance drank Tea with us in the Evening. He came riding, stayed till near 8. Mr Foster sent us some Eels this Morning. Dinner to day, fryed Eels, boiled Pork & Greens &c. I was but poorly to day, weak, giddy & faint.

OCTOBER *10th, Friday.* We breakfasted, dined, &c. again at home. This being old Michaelmas Day, I paid my Servant Boy, Henry Daines, three Quarters of a Years Wages due this Day at two Guineas per Annum 1.11.6 and dismissed him from my

Service not behaving in a manner that I expected from him, as he could not be trusted to do any thing if not overlooked, and also a very saucy, foul-mouthed Lad. Mr Custance made us a Morning Visit he came walking & had been to Hungate-Lodge where his Brother is coming to reside this Day. Dinner to day, Mutton Soup & a rost Goose &c.

NOVEMBER *27th, Thursday*. We breakfasted, dined, &c. again at home. Dinner to day, fryed Pork & a Rabbit rosted &c. Mr and Mrs Shrimpton (late Betsy Davy) who are on a Visit at Mr Thornes of Mattishall made us a Morning Visit and stayed with us upwards of an Hour, Mrs Shrimpton looked remarkably well & of good Spirits. They live in a genteel Way in Suffolk and have one Child; a little Boy, by name Joseph, his Father's Name, about 2 Years old. Mr Shrimpton is a Dissenter, I believe a Presbyterian, he is rather plain and I should take him to be about 35 Yrs old. They came in a genteel Whiskey and had a Servant to attend them. They stayed with us upwards of an Hour, had some refreshment & returned back to Mattishall. They leave Mattishall to Morrow and return home to Walpole in Suffolk not a great many Miles from Beccles, where Mr Shrimpton's Father (who is lately dead) lived, and the Estate now comes to his Son. Mr Maynard called on us this Morning whilst Mrs Shrimpton was here — and during the time that Mr Shrimpton went in his Whiskey to see Weston-House. Mr Shrimpton had a Gun & a Pointer with him. I was rather hurried at first seeing them. I sent Ben, round this Morn' to my Farmers to meet at Parsonage on Tuesday next to pay me their Composition for Tithe for 1800 & dine here. Ben returned about 9 o'clock quite drunk which made me rather uneasy being rather ill.

DECEMBER *11th, Tuesday*. We breakfasted, dined, &c. again at home. A cold, raw, foggy, and dark day. Dinner to day, Giblet-Soup & a rost Rabbit. A Man called here this Evening about

5 o'clock had Trowers on and had he said been a Sailor. He walked as if he was lame, he asked Charity. He appeared rather a suspicious Character & that he had other things in view than mere asking Charity, this time of the Day. I rather suspect of his being after Poultry. As he might however be in want, gave him 0.1. I was finely this Morning when I came down Stairs, but being soon after made rather uneasy discomposed me the whole day after.

22nd, Monday. We breakfasted, dined, &c. again at home. Yesterday being Sunday & St Thomas's Day the Poor deferred going after their Christmas Gifts till this Morning, I had at my House fifty five, gave only to 53, the other two not living in the Parish. Gave in the Whole this Morn' at 6d each in Number 53 1.6.6. Dinner to day, boiled Beef & a rost Chicken. I was but poorly to day after dinner, giddy &c. Sitting too long to day at one time I think. The Poor to day behaved extremely well indeed tho' times were extremely hard for them—They all appeared very patient & submissive. Mr Press Custance sent us a Pheasant this Even'. Very fine and open Weather for the Season. I cannot remember a finer day (I think) for St Thomas's Day, than this Day proved. Pray God! make us all thankfull for the same.

24th, Wednesday. We breakfasted, dined &c. again at home. Recd of Betty for Butter to day—½ Pint 0.8½. Dinner to day, Skaite & broiled Mutton &c. This being Christmas Eve we dressed up our Windows with Hulver Branches as usual.

1801

JANUARY *31st, Saturday*. We breakfasted, dined, &c. again at home. Sent Ben this Morning to Norwich with eight Coomb of Wheat to Mr Bloome. Thank God! I was finely to day. Dinner to day, Pork and Peas &c. Ben returned home from Norwich about 5 o'clock this Evening, safe & well (thanks to God for it) and brought me Cash for my Wheat from Mr Bloome at 3.15.0 pr Coomb 30.0.0 an enormous Price I must confess indeed and sincerely wish that it might be cheaper e'er long for the benefit of the Poor who are distressed on that Account—tho' much alleviated by the liberal Allowance to them of every Parish.* Pray God! send us better Times and all People better. Fine mild Weather for the Season, thank God for it.

FEBRUARY *5th, Thursday*. Very fine Weather indeed for the Season. Bees quite brisk. Crocus's & Snow Drops out in full blossom. Gooseberry Trees coming into Leaf very fast indeed.

6th, Friday. We breakfasted, dined, &c. again at home. Had my Study, Kitchen, and Back-Kitchen Chimnies swept by Holland & his Boy, Hunt. To a Man of Sparham having lately lost a Cow, gave him 0.1.0. Received of Betty this Morning for 4 Pints and half of Butter at 1s 5d pr Pt 0.6.4½. Nancy got up early this Morning and walked to Weston-House before I was down Stairs, and there breakfasted, and soon after went with

* The relief given by the Government during this period against the steady rise in prices (which reached famine levels in 1795 and 1801) was considerable. JW's poor rate in 1794 for half the year was £1.10.3; two years later it was £2.5.4½; it rose in 1800 to £5.8.0¾. The problem arose from a bad harvest in 1800 and the temporary closure of the Baltic whence England imported grain.

Mr & Mrs Custance & Daughters to Norwich and did not return till after 5 this Evening about which time they brought her home. The Weather rather unfavourable, as it rained most part of the Day tho' not a heavy Rain. She was well pleased however with her Jaunt. Bought a new Pair of Stays &c. Dinner to day, a Leg of Mutton rosted &c. Miss W. did not dine till after return home. Thank God! they all went & returned home safe.

APRIL *16th, Thursday*. We breakfasted, dined &c. again at home. Mrs Custance with her two Daughters made us a Morning Visit & stayed upwards of an Hour. Brought us great News, that Lord Nelson had taken several Men of War from the Danes, had demolished Copenhagen, a great Part of it at least.* The Danes defied him. They have of late behaved very shabby towards us. The Emperor of Russia also is said to be dead supposed to have been put to death. He had long behaved bad towards England. Dinner to day, Breast of Mutton rosted &c.

MAY *9th, Saturday*. We breakfasted, dined &c. again at home. Dinner to day, 2 blade-bones of Pork rosted &c. I was rather better to day than Yesterday. Our Kitchen &c. White-washed to day by Js Hardy Junr but neither Parlour or Study. Mr Jeans of Whichingham, who has been gone from thence from the Year 1795 is reported to have been at Wichingham for many days and is still there — Mr Beevor being in the Kings-Bench-Prison and is to continue there for some little time yet for challenging Capt. Pain.†

* The Battle of Copenhagen brought the Armed Neutrality of Russia, Prussia, Denmark and Sweden to an end, thus reopening the Baltic to British trade.
† The Revd Mr Beevor had apparently been doing duty for the now non-resident Revd Dr Jeans. Although prime ministers were still fighting duels as late as this (Pitt with Tierney in 1798, the Duke of Wellington with Lord Winchelsea in 1829) it was unusual, not to say shocking, for a clergyman. In July of this year Beevor almost did duty at Weston, but JW countermanded it.

29th, Friday. We breakfasted, dined, &c. again at home. Nancy got up this Morning quite ill and much Fever about her of the low kind. After however taking a Glass or two of Port Wine She felt herself much better and made a tolerable good Dinner after on a boiled Leg of Lamb. I was very poorly myself all Day. I dare say the full Moon much affected us. Dinner to day, boiled Leg of Lamb and Spinage.

JUNE *22nd, Monday.* We breakfasted, dined, &c. again at home. Mr Maynard made us a Morning Visit. Stephen Andrews Junr called on me this Morn' being Church-Warden for a Copy of the Terrier and of the Registers for the Year 1800. I recd of him for the same 0.13.0 that is, for the Terrier 0.10.6 for the Registers 0.2.6. About 11 o'clock this Morning who should call on us but Mr Jeans from London in a single-Horse-Chaise. He slept last Night at Colonel Lloyds of Bawdeswell. He stayed about half an Hour with us and then went off for Norwich, and either to Morrow or the next day returns back to London, he looked remarkably healthy and well. He would take no refreshment with us. There was a Man with him but did not come in. Dinner to day, Pork & Peas & Neck of Mutton rosted. I was but poorly to day, Spirits very low.

26th, Friday. It being a fine Day, I had all my Hay carried, only five Cart Load from four acres, very well made indeed & without a drop of Rain. It makes but little Show but smells like a Violet.

JULY *14th, Tuesday.* We breakfasted, dined &c. again at home. Sent Briton this Morn' to Mr Ansons of Ling after a Puppey promised me by him, and a very nice little bitch he sent me back of a reddish Colour, all over—quite of the Fairy Size, therefore we named her Mab. Mrs Custance with Lady Bacon made us a Morning Visit, they came walking and were much frightened by a Cow coming across the Field. They appeared much agitated, they had each a Glass of Port Wine & other refreshment. They came about 2 o'clock and stayed till 3 as they stayed till we could send to Weston House after the Coach. Briton went to order it directly. It came in about an Hour after it was ordered. They were pretty well composed when they went. Mr Maynard dined & spent the Afternoon with us. Mrs Custance and Lady Bacon met him as they came near my House and he appeared to them disguised in Liquor; which I heard afterwards was the Case—he having been to Mr Mann's to name a Child, they perhaps urging him to drink. To James Rope of Ringland, losing Stock 0.2.6. Dinner to day, a Couple of boiled Chicken and a Chop, rost Beef & a Currant Pudding &c. Mr Maynard left us about 7 this Evening and perfectly sober & well. I would not by no means push the Glass on fast as I was uneasy about his drinking too much this Morn' at Manns he having been there to name Mann's Child.

AUGUST *10th, Monday.* Begun cutting Peas this Morn' in the Field. A Parish Meeting held this Evening at the Heart to take into consideration the Papers lately recd concerning what is to be done in case of an Invasion of the French on this Country. Dinner to day, Beans and Bacon &c. I was very nervous and weak to day, much agitated not knowing what to do at the present Crisis & wanting Health & Strength am scarce able to do even the most trivial action.

25th, Tuesday. Mr Maynard called on us early this Morning during the time we were at breakfast, We asked him to drink a dish of Tea with us, but he declined it, having breakfasted. He looked very sadly I thought. He said that he had been much hurried & fatigued concerning the Papers he lately recd in case of an Invasion by the French and Dutch on this Coast which is talked of at present. Dinner to day, Pork and Greens, &c. Busy in carrying Barley all day again.

SEPTEMBER *27th, Sunday.* We breakfasted, dined, &c. again at home. Mr Dade read Prayers & Preached this Morning at

Weston-Church. Mr Dade read the new Thanks giving Prayer to Almighty God! for his late blessing to us in a fine & plentiful Harvest. Mr and Mrs Custance at Church to day. Miss Woodforde also at Church. Dinner to day, Loin of Veal rosted & a Pudding. Ben abused Betty this evening on his hearing that she had accepted his Cousin Thos Leggatt of Ringland for a Paramour.

OCTOBER *3rd, Saturday*. We breakfasted, dined, &c. again at home. Recd of Betty for Butter this Week 6 Pints made, $3\frac{1}{2}$ sold at $1/5\frac{1}{2}$ per Pint $0.5.2\frac{1}{4}$. Dinner to day, Pork & Greens & a Pheasant rosted &c. Great Rejoicings we heard this day at Norwich on a report of there being Peace proclaimed in London. Briton heard of it this Morning at Mr Press Custance's. I hope it is a true report.*

21st, Wednesday. We breakfasted, dined, &c. again at home. Great Rejoicings to be to day on Account of Peace. A bullock to be rosted in the Market-Place &c. It raining all the Morning rather against them. About 6 in the Afternoon it cleared up and many went from Weston. Ben went about that time and had my Mare, Jenny, to go thither. Dinner to day, Ham & 2 Fowls boiled &c. Whilst we were at Dinner to day, there was a large flash of Lightning and one loud Clap of Thunder. The Lightning shone on Nancy's Plate. It rained hard for about an Hour afterwards. N.B. No Bullock rosted at Norwich as talked of.

DECEMBER *7th, Monday*. I was very indifferent & very unwell indeed to day so blown up with gouty Wind & strange feelings. Dinner to day, boiled Beef &c. Towards the evening I got something better. Cow, Beauty had a Cow-Calf.

17th, Thursday. Had a Letter this Morning (by Mr Custance's

* The preliminaries of peace, signed in London on 1 October, confirmed by Bonaparte on 5 October, were finally incorporated into the Peace of Amiens on 27 March 1802. In these early October days the public relief and joy were enormous.

Servant) from Robt Clarke of Castle-Cary, concerning some Money lent by him to my late Brother Heighes of 12£—dated March 24, 1783—unknown of by any of the family before now. Dinner to day, Giblet-Soup & cold rost Turkey. N.B. The above Robt Clarke (tho' very ingenious) hath greatly injured himself by following too Many Schemes one after the other to better himself. Mr Maynard buried poor old Widow Case this Afternoon at Weston-Church aged 78 Years.

25th, Friday. We breakfasted, dined, &c. again at home. Mr Dade read Prayers, Preached and administered the H. Sacrament this Morn' at Weston Church, being Christmas-Day. None from Weston-House at Church to day. Old Thos Atterton, Robt Downing, Roger Sherwood, Eliz. Ward Widow and the Clerk Willm Large, dined at Weston-Parsonage to day, being Christmas Day and had each in Money 1/0—5.0. Poor old Mary Heavers, Widow, very old & infirm I sent her Dinner to her and likewise—0.1.0. Dinner to day, Surloin of Beef rosted & plumb Puddings boiled for both Parlour & Kitchen. We had also in Parlour some Mince-Pies.

1802

JANUARY *1st, Friday*. We breakfasted, dined, &c. again at home. The New Year came in with Frost & Snow and with it very cold Weather indeed, which pinched me much—being an invalid. Dinner to day, Peas Soup & a Breast of Mutton. Our Servants being invited to Weston-House to Dinner to day, Briton & Sally went, but returned in good time about 10 o'clock at Night Much fatigued & tired, it being very bad & cold walking—The Snow in places quite high and No Moon. I hope they will not be ill after it.

FEBRUARY *1st, Monday*. We breakfasted, dined, &c. again at home. Mr Maynard called on us this Morning and stayed with us near an Hour. Paid Ben this Morning for divers things— 3.7.11. Paid Taylor Cary this Morning for a great Coat for my Servant, Bretingham Scurl, of a brown-Drab narrow Cloth at 5/0 per Yard, 7 Yards—1.5.0—Making &c—12/6½—1.17.6½. Dinner to day, Neck of Mutton, boiled &c. Being hurried a good deal this Morning, disconcerted me & made me very nervous. Lent my little Cart to Mr Ham. Custance to go to Lord Wodehouse's at Kimberley for a Day or two.

20th, Saturday. Very low, faint and very unwell all the Morn'. I don't know that I ever felt myself so depressed and so spiritless as this very day. Nancy out of Temper all the Whole day, very saucy.

MARCH *18th, Thursday*. We breakfasted, dined, &c. again at home. I was taken very giddy this Morning before I came down Stairs whilst I was washing my Face & Hands in the Passage next my Room and afraid to go down Stairs without help. After

424

breakfast I got something better. Betty's Father (Willm Dade of Mattishall) came here this Morning abt breakfast time to see his Daughter. Briton's Father from Reepham by Name Robert Scurl, Baker, called here this Morning to see his Son and inform him, that his poor weak consumptive Brother was released from his Misery—died on Thursday. His name was John, only 20 years of Age. Dinner to day, boiled Neck of Mutton &c. Nancy not liking boiled Neck of Mutton, had a Mutton Stake taken from the Neck before it was boiled—on wch she dined. I continued but poorly all the day, tho' better in the Afternoon and Evening—About Noon time almost every Day I feel poorly.

APRIL *13th, Tuesday.* We breakfasted, dined, &c. again at home. To James Pegg this Morn' by Betty, pd 3.6.8 being two Months Income Tax—at twenty Pounds Per Annum—Valued at 200£ per Annum N.B.—The above Tax to be repealed this Month —is now pretty generally believed if not already done—it being universally disliked. Very cold to day with Hail, Snow and Rain at times. Dinner to day, Leg of Mutton rosted &c. Had a Note this Evening from Mr Press Custance of Hungate-Lodge, informing us that Mr Stoughton of Sparham who is now at Norwich under Dr Beevor is better and declared out of danger— Mr P. Custance having been at Norwich to day. I was very indifferent all day, the Weather being severely & bitterly cold to day. To Will Richmond being very ill sent—0.2.6.

MAY *20th, Thursday.* We breakfasted, dined, &c. again at home. Paid Robert Cary, Taylor, for a new Pair of brown striped Velveret Breeches for Briton, every thing included whatever 1.1.6. I came down Stairs this Morn' very weak but more giddy, and obliged to have some Assistance, therefore had Betty to help me down the Stairs. Brewed a Barrell of common Beer to day. About Noon and after dinner somewhat better I felt myself, and Spirits better than in the Morn'. Brewed a Barrel of Table-Beer.

30th, Sunday. Mr Dade read Prayers & Preached this Afternoon at Weston Church — Mrs Custance there. There was Bread given to the Poor at Church this Afternoon by Briton from Money which he had received for that Purpose from some Person who desired that it may not be known from whom it came in value abt 1.5.0. Dinner to day a brace of Trout & a Fillet of Veal &c.

JUNE *1st, Tuesday*. We breakfasted, dined, &c. again at home. This Day being appointed for a general Thanksgiving for Peace, Mr Dade read Prayers and Preached this Morning at Weston-Church. Mr and Mrs Custance at Church, Miss Woodforde also there. I was rather poorly this Morning, so very cold & giddy & weak. It was very cold this Morn'. Many complained of it. Dinner to day, Knuckle of Veal, Pork and Greens & a large boiled plumb-Pudding. Mem. great Doings in many Places to day. At Weston nothing at all — Mr Custance against it.*

2nd, Wednesday. We breakfasted, dined, &c. again at home. Rather odd feelings about me immediately after breakfast this Morning, just as was going to shave, attended with the Cramp in my right hand, thank God! it did not last long, but alarmed me. Mrs Custance by herself called on us this Morning and made us a long Visit. Miss Woodforde shewed her a new Bonnett (by name Pick-Nick) which she had sent her from London by Miss Rider and came home by Mrs Stephen Andrews Junior who (with her Husband) returned from London on Saturday. Mrs Custance said it was very handsome and had seen nothing like it at Norwich as yet, tho' only at Norwich last Week to see the new Fashions. Dinner to day, boiled Beef &c. Very unwell and giddy & weak to walk. But still tolerable to what I have been.

18th, Friday. This Morn a Person by name Richard Page,

* Though the Peace of Amiens was popular with the mass of people it was strongly criticised by individuals, notably by Windham — who profoundly mistrusted Napoleon. Windham represented Norwich from 1784 to 1802 and was War Secretary between 1794 and 1801. Mr Custance was plainly very sympathetic to his views.

dressed as a Clergyman, walked up boldly to our Front Door through the Garden and knocked. I went and let him in, and walked into my Study and there informed me before Nancy, that he was a reduced Clergyman from Oxfordshire, was born at Bath in Somersetshire, had read Prayers &c. at the Abbey Church there for 12 Years. That a Dr Lawrence of Doctors Commons was his great Friend &c. He seemed well acquainted with Oxford and with many of my old Contemporaries there, was formerly of Baliol College or at St Edmund Hall, a short Man and thin, talked rather fast and made a plausible Story. Shewed me his Letters of Orders, signed by the late Dr Lowthe when Bishop of Oxford &c. He stayed about half an Hour with us, drank a Glass of Table Beer and then walked away. I gave him before he went, half a Guinea o.10.6. After he was gone we heard by Ben, that he had a Companion who talked with Ben all the time the other Man was with me, and that he saw the Man that was with me give the other the Money that I had given to him. That Man asked Ben many Questions about me. I do not know what to make of them. I saw Mr Maynard's Name on his Petition. Marquiss Townsend's Name was also on the same.

JULY *16th, Friday.* We breakfasted, dined &c. again at home. A Dr Ogilvie from Norwich came post haste in a Post Chaise after me to go back with him to Norwich to vote for Colonel Wodehouse. Sir Jacob Astley is running him hard—but I was too ill to go any where at present therefore was obliged to decline going. He stayed about half an Hour, came here about five o'clock in the Afternoon. It hurried me a great deal indeed. Dinner to day, Leg of Mutton rosted &c.*

* The diary entries from 18 July to 28 August have been torn out. JW has evidently been very ill during that period with a throat infection or worse. He nonetheless kept his diary, as is proved by the fragments of the clumsily torn pages remaining in the booklet—as well as by the faithfully recorded weather conditions for each of those missing days on the interleaved blotting paper.

AUGUST *29th, Sunday.* We breakfasted, dined, &c. again at home. I felt finely this Morning thank God! & stronger. Very hot indeed to day, especially at Noon. Dr Thorne was with us to day between 12 and 1 o'clock. He stayed some little time with us. My Throat is daily getting better he says. Mr Dade read Prayers & Preached this Afternoon at Weston-Church—Nancy at Church to day. Dinner to day, rost Beef & Plumb Pudding &c. Mrs Custance and Daughters at Church to day.

SEPTEMBER *1st, Wednesday.* We breakfasted, dined &c. again at home. Mr Salisbury very good-naturedly brought us about Noon, a Leash or three nice young Partridges of his own shooting this Morning early. Dr Thorne here again to day about 2 o'clock. Dinner to day, a Couple of Ducks rosted &c. The fine Weather still continues. It relaxes me a good deal & makes me quite weak.

2nd, Thursday. We breakfasted, dined &c. again at home. Fine Weather still continues (thank God for it), finer Harvest Weather scarce ever known. As our Folks were carrying a Cart-Load of Barley into the Barn this Morning before Dinner, with the Boy (Bob Case) upon it, the Load or great Part of it slipt off and fell into the Pond almost close to the Barn. The Barley being so very dry it slipt all at once and fell off but thank God! no great damage at all sustained, but a little Barley wetted. The Boy not hurt

at all. Dr Thorne here again near the same time as Yesterday. Dinner to day, boiled Beef & a Partridge rosted &c.

4th, Saturday. We breakfasted, dined, &c. again at home. No Doctor to day, Nancy put a Plaister to my Throat this Morning, nothing more being required. I saw my Throat this Morning for the first time and it frightened me indeed, to think, what it must have been at first, as it now appears (tho' almost well) very frightfull and disagreeable. Dinner to Day, Beef-Steak-Pye &c. I eat very hearty for Dinner to day, and have done so for many days last past, but still I continue very weak, & dont seem to gain much more strength if any at all for many days last past. Sometimes I think, that I rather get weaker & weaker.

6th, Monday. We breakfasted, dined, &c. again at home. Very ill indeed to day having had a very indifferent Night of rest last Night, owing to the Night Candle filling the Room in being so long going out with intolerable Smoke & Stink. Recd of Betty for Butter at $1/3\frac{1}{2}$, o.9.o$\frac{1}{2}$. Mrs Custance with her eldest Daughter made us a Morning Visit, as did Mr Custance who came soon after they were here, on foot. Dinner to day, Part of the Breast of Veal broiled &c. Dr Thorne called here about Noon. I left off all dressings to my Throat to day. Mr Press Custance sent us three Partridges.

9th, Thursday. We breakfasted, dined, &c. again at home. Very unwell & very weak indeed when I came down Stairs this Morn' having had a very bad Night of Rest. Very little if any sound Sleep during the whole time I was abed or in bed. Dinner to day, boiled Mutton & a brace of Partridges. Thank God! made a very good Dinner of Mutton.

12th, Sunday. We breakfasted, dined, &c. again at home. Very weak still, if not weaker, had a hard Matter to get down Stairs this Morn', tho' help'd. So tired after I got down, that I panted for breath. Mr Dade read Prayers & Preached this Afternoon at Weston-Church. Miss Woodforde at Church. Mr Custance at Church this Afternoon but none of the rest of the Family. Mrs Custance with her Daughters & Hambleton Custance, being gone this Morning for Sir Edmund Bacons at Rainingham. Dinner to day, Calfs-Head boiled, Pork & Greens &c.

13th, Monday. We breakfasted, dined, &c. again at home. Very weak, but a small matter better than Yesterday. All my weakness seems to proceed from my Belly just below my Stomach — a great tightness there. The lest Exercise also now, fatigues me greatly. A great coldness prevails all over me also. Mr Custance made us a Morning Visit. He came on horseback and without a Servant. Dinner to day, Fillett of Veal rosted &c.

17th, Friday. We breakfasted, dined, &c. again at home. Thank God! that I rather think, I am somewhat better than I felt myself Yesterday, and I hope stronger. Mr Stoughton of Sparham called on us this Morn' since his return from Cromer, having been there some time for his Health, it being close to the Sea. To a travelling Woman by Name (Falling), a married Woman, who sold divers things, for a Pound of different kinds of Thread for the use of the Family — paid 0.7.0. Dinner to day, Shoulder Mutton rosted &c. Mr Salisbury brought us a brace of Partridges this Evening — very weak towards bed-time. Briton still sleeps in my Room upon the Sofa, and a Candle burning all Night in the Chamber.

18th, Saturday. We breakfasted, dined, &c. again at home. Betty's Father (Willm Dade) of Mattishall was here this Morning early tho' on foot & I believe breakfasted with our Folks in the Kitchen. I was very poorly indeed this Morning, so faint & weak, scarce able to come down Stairs, my breath almost gone when I got down. My Legs also much swelled indeed to day. Mr Custance made us a Morning Visit, on foot. Dinner to day, Calfs' Fry & a brace of Partridges.

19th, Sunday. We breakfasted, dined, &c. again at home. Mr Dade read Prayers & Preached this Morning at Weston-Church. Nancy was at Church. None of Weston-House Family at Church. Mrs Custance & Daughters still at Sir Edm. Bacons. Dinner to day, Shoulder of Veal rosted &c. My Ancles rather swelled more than Yesterday. It made me quite uneasy & unhappy. However it made no one else so, but myself. Thank God! my Appetite is very good indeed. Rain is greatly wanted at this present time especially in this County, which is almost burnt up.

21st, Tuesday. We breakfasted, dined, &c. again at home. Very ill indeed all the Day, having had the blind-Piles very bad from my rising this Morn. Could neither sit, stand or Walk without a great deal of Pain indeed. The Pain was so great, that it put me quite in a Fever. Very warm Weather still prevails. Dinner to day, a Pike & cold rost Beef &c. Mr Emeris brought us this Evening a Basket of black Damson-Plumbs fit for preserving.

23rd, Thursday. We breakfasted, dined, &c. again at home. I sent Ben this Morning after Dr Thorne being very ill. The Doctor came about 2 o'clock and stayed with us, near an Hour. I am to have some Medicine to Morrow Morn' sent me. My Legs and also Thighs swelled to day. The blind Piles also very bad to day and discharged a great deal of thin watery nature. Dinner to day, Leg of Mutton rosted &c. I made a very good dinner upon the same. Mr Press Custance sent us a Leash of Partridges.

25th, Saturday. We breakfasted, dined, &c. again at home. I was very poorly again this Morn' so very weak. Sent Briton early this Morning in my little Cart after divers things wanted in House. Mrs Custance made us a Morning Visit. Dr Thorne called on me this Morning again. Dinner to day, a Partridge Pye &c. A very nice Pye indeed it turned out to us. Briton returned from Norwich abt 5 this Evening. Mr Emeris brought us 3 nice young Pigeons. My Feet & Legs swelling so much makes me uneasy.

29th, Wednesday. We breakfasted, dined, &c. again at home. I seemed finely this Morn' tho' both my Legs & Thighs were swelled rather more. Dr Thorne called here about Noon, and was rather surprised to see both my Legs swelled. Hambleton Custance called here this Morning in his Walk with his Gun and Dogs. Dinner to day, a Goose rosted being Michmas Day. The Piles being painful, still make me uneasy.

431

30th, Thursday. We breakfasted, dined, &c. again at home. Had a very good Night of Sleep (thank God) last Night, but my Legs & Thighs appeared more swelled (I think) this Morning than Yesterday. Dinner to day, Giblett-Soup & boiled Mutton &c. Our Oldest Sow had a Litter of 14 Piggs.

OCTOBER *1st, Friday*. We breakfasted, dined, &c. again at home. Recd of Betty this Morning for Butter sold last Week to Betty Cary at 1/5½ per Pint 0.8.0. Very poorly still, Legs &c. much swelled yet. I continue taking Medicine, but do not find, I confess, any great relief from the same. The Piles continues on me still, tho' not so bad. They are not of the bleeding kind but rather watery. Dinner to day, boiled chicken with Pork & Greens. Sent Mr Press Custance this Evening some Filberts. Mr Girling sent us half a Doz. Pigeons this Evening. Harry Baker made me a small low Stool to day to rest my Legs upon, as they swell so. No Appearance whatever yet of Rain.

2nd, Saturday. We breakfasted, dined, &c. again at home. I was rather better this Morning when I got up I think, than I was Yesterday Morning. Mr Custance sent us a brace of Partridges. Dry Weather still continues to prevail. Dr Thorne called here about 4 o'clock this Aft. Dinner to day, boiled Calfs Head, Pork & Greens and a Pigeon-Pye hot. My Legs & Thighs still continue much swelled, if any thing rather more and higher. Spirits much depressed to day upon that Account.

3rd, Sunday. We breakfasted, dined, &c. again at home. Mr Dade read Prayers & Preached this Morning at Weston-Church —Nancy at Church. Mr and Mrs Custance at Church and Daughters. Sent Ben this Morning early to Mattishall after Medicine for me from Dr Thornes. Ben returned home to breakfast. Dinner to day, Breast of Veal and a Plumb Pudding boiled &c. Britons Sister, Lydia Scurl, came here this Morning by herself on horseback & dined here. She is a fine young Woman about 24 Yrs of Age. Mr Foster of Lenewade Bridge, sent a Servant this Afternoon to enquire after me, very kind.

4th, Monday. We breakfasted, dined, &c. again at home. Mr Maynard called on us this Morning and I paid him for my not attending the Generals at Reepham on Friday last as usual 0.2.0. Dinner to day, hash'd Calfs Head & Partridges.

11th. Our New Boy Jon Lane about 13 Years old, came to his Place to Night and slept here. I continue very indifferent indeed. Pain so great scarce able to walk.

15th. Mr Emeris brought us some Damson Plumbs.

16th. Eliz. Grey (an Infant) was buried this Afternoon by Mr Maynard, aged 12 Years. Rather weaker & full of Pain all over me.

17th, Sunday. We breakfasted, dined, Very weak this Morning, scarce able to put on my Cloaths and with great difficulty, get down Stairs with help. Mr Dade read Prayers & Preached this Morning at Weston Church—Nancy at Church. Mr & Mrs Custance & Lady Bacon at Church. Dinner to day, Rost Beef &c.*

* On 'Rost Beef &c.' JW suitably ended his diary. Thereafter, though he did not die until New Year's Day 1803, he was silent.

Brief Biographies

BACON, Sir Edmund, of Earlham, was the premier baronet of England. He married in 1778 Anne Beauchamp-Proctor, for whom JW expressed almost as affectionate a regard as for her sister, Mrs Custance.

BODHAM, the Revd Thomas, was one of JW's closest Norfolk friends, and, after the departure from the district of the Revd Castres Donne, a member of the Monday Rotation dining club. Born at Swaffham in 1742, he was admitted pensioner at Caius, Cambridge, in July 1759, the same month and year in which JW became a Scholar of New College. BA 1764, MA 1767, Fellow of his college 1769–79. In 1770 he was ordained deacon at Norwich, but thanks to some unexplained 'nervous disorder' he never proceeded beyond Minor Orders; after the deaths of his father and brother he became very rich. In 1781 he married Anne Donne, sister of Castres Donne, curate of Mattishall. They lived at South Green Lodge, Mattishall. He died in June 1796.

BEAUCHAMP-PROCTOR, Sir Thomas and Mr George, Mrs Custance's brothers.

BURGE FAMILY. One of the prosperous and respectable Cary families who formed part of the Woodforde social circle. (They were, indeed, related to the disreputable Ansford family of the same name, though the connection was not recognised.) William Senior had four sons, one of whom (also William) was a cloth manufacturer, and the family had other commercial interests. Thomas Austin Burge and Seth Burge were their cousins. Seth was churchwarden with D. Maby in the year of the gallery quarrel at Castle Cary.

CLARKE, Anna Maria (1759–1794), 'Nanny', third child of Dr Richard Clarke and Sobieski (Woodforde). A mental invalid, in later life she was boarded out with a Betty Lancashire at Ansford.

435

CLARKE, Jane (1754–1836), 'Jenny'. She married her cousin Francis Woodforde and thus became mistress of Ansford Parsonage for sixty years.

CLARKE, Dr Richard (d. 1785), was a specialist in inoculation treatment as a preventative against smallpox. He ran a hospital for the reception of seriously ill patients, though he put up in his own home many of those who were only slightly affected. He married first Martha, half-sister of JW's mother, and by her had James (1744–91) and Richard (1745–84); his second wife was Sobieski, JW's eldest sister, by whom he had three more children.

CLARKE, Samuel (b. 1756), the son of Dr Richard Clarke and Sobieski (Woodforde), showed signs of mental instability from boyhood. With his mother he visited Weston in 1780, when occurred the disturbing incident of the stolen purse, later found burnt in the kitchen grate, recalling an episode in 1769 when JW writes with relief: 'the Ring which I had lost was unaccountably found in little Sam Clarke's breeches.' By 1793 he was living in London, having been brought there by his mother for treatment. JW paid them a visit in Hackney. Presumably he died in London.

CLARKE, Sobieski (1725–1821), 'Sister Clarke', was the eldest child of Samuel and Jane Woodforde, and outlived all the others, dying at Ansford at the age of ninety-six. Her last appearances in the diary see her living in distressed circumstances in Hackney where she is caring for her son Sam. Dr Clarke was reckoned by JW a year or two before his death to be worth not far short of £16,000.

CLARKE, Sophia (1761–1839), daughter of Dr Richard Clarke and Sobieski, eloped with her cousin Robert White in 1780. They had ten children, and for most of their married life lived at Ansford Lodge.

CLARKE, William, 'Painter', no relation of the above Clarkes, was a man of many talents—undertaker, carpenter, decorator, tailor, auctioneer and valuer, even tax collector. Though his social status would not have been above that of a skilled workman, he was accepted as an equal by the professional men of the district.

COOKE, Washbourne (1745–1804), an Oxford friend, accompanied

JW on his inspection visit to Weston Longville in 1775. He was a Fellow of New College from 1767 to 1793, when he became rector of Hardwicke, and later of Hatford, Berkshire, which were in the gift of his own family.

CORPE, William, for many years manservant of the Woodforde family, dropped dead in the street in Castle Cary on the evening of his wedding day, aged forty-five.

CREECH or CRITCH, Mary, was housekeeper at Babcary Parsonage when JW was curate there in 1764–5. She moved to Ansford with him when, having got a taste for independent living (or 'house-keeping', as he put it), he took up residence in the Lower House. She left the service of the family after JW had moved back to the Parsonage and his brother John remained at the Lower House. Her daughter, Elizabeth (Betty), became housekeeper at the Parsonage in 1772. Mary Creech died at Ansford in 1782 aged seventy-five.

CREED, Mr (Sr) (1688–1774), was already an old man during the early years of the diary. The Creeds lived at South Cary House. He outlived his son by only a couple of months.

CREED, Justice (1707–1774), by whom JW was taken up after 1764, when they met at the Melliars' house. Thereafter the diarist dines frequently with the Justice and his old father. The Creeds were very well connected and lived in style; Mr Creed took JW to dine with the Hoares at Stourhead, for instance. That he was a man of strong opinion is evident from the stand he took over the church gallery affair, when his man was refused entrance by the church singers. He made himself so unpopular in this matter that he was burnt in effigy by the people of Cary. JW seems to have been much in awe of him, yet flattered by Mr Creed's condescension.

CUSTANCE FAMILY. The founder of the family fortunes was John Custance (1673–1752), who as a younger son went into trade in Norwich and prospered as a cloth manufacturer. He was Mayor of Norwich in 1726, and again in 1750. He bought the Weston Longville estate for £5,000 from the Rookwood family. The estate included Weston Old Hall, although no member of the Custance family seems to have lived there.

John Custance, JW's squire, grandson of the above John Custance, was born in 1749. In his youth he had travelled—he once told JW about his adventures in Turkey—but when he married, in 1778, he immediately came to live in Norfolk. At first he and his wife lived at the Manor House, Ringland, until they were able to move into the newly built Weston House, in 1781. His wife was Frances Mary Beauchamp-Proctor (1756–1836), daughter of William Beauchamp-Proctor of Epsom. They had eleven children, all born between 1779 and 1791, three of whom died in infancy. Of the seven who survived to adulthood William lived to be eighty, Fanny and John to eighty-one, while Emily and Neville reached ninety. The Custances left Norfolk, and went to live at No 1 Portland Place, Bath, between 1793 and 1797, for the purpose of sending their daughters to school in that city.

Press Custance, the squire's younger brother, lived with his mistress, Esther Sherman, for many years. Soon after the Custances came to live in Norfolk he had to ask her to refrain from using his seat in the chancel at Weston Church. As soon as John Custance expresses his disapproval of Miss Sherman, JW starts to refer to her as 'Press Custance's woman'.

DAVIE or DAVY, Mrs Elizabeth, née Roupe, born in 1747, married Lancelot Davie of Southwold, a surgeon, in 1769. He died in 1773, leaving her with two surviving children—Betsy (b. 1770) and Nunn (b. 1771). She was thus a youngish widow when JW met her in 1775. At this time she was living in lodgings in Norwich and later moved to Hockering to look after Mrs Howes, who was her aunt. Later still she lived in Foulsham and Mattishall. JW was charmed by and attracted to her at first, but her behaviour was 'fast' and by 1790 he sees her and her daughter Betsy as being 'very cunning, close and not without much Art'.

DONNE, the Revd Castres (1744–1789), was curate for the non-resident vicar of Mattishall, living there with his mother in 'a very small poor Cottage house' until his marriage in 1780. His sister married Mr Bodham. They were cousins of the poet William Cowper.

DU QUESNE, the Revd Thomas Roger, was born in 1717, educated at Eton and King's College, Cambridge, where he matriculated in 1738. BA 1742–43, MA 1746, Fellow of King's 1741. Most of his considerable preferment in the Church came to him through the influence of his cousin and patron, Charles Townshend of Honingham Hall. He became vicar of Honingham with East Tuddenham in 1753; and of Scole, alias Osmundeston, in 1756, the last-named no the presentation of Lord Cornwallis. He was appointed Prebendary of Lichfield, 1765, Chancellor Canon of St David's, 1776, and Prebendary of Ely, 1783, the stall 'worth £300 a year' according to JW. Very close to the diarist, in spite of the difference of age, he was the only friend to be invited to meet and stay with the Somerset relations. Unmarried, generous to his servants, fond of music (he was a violinist), he appears as an excellent type of cultivated eighteenth-century man.

GEREE, John (1740–1774), the closest of Woodforde's Oxford friends, had also been at Winchester with him. Geree stayed at New College until 1772, when he exchanged his Fellowship for one at Winchester. In 1773 he was given the tied living of Milborne Port, but died before he had been inducted. He and JW remained firm friends until his early death.

HOLMES, Robert, one of JW's closest Oxford friends, was a Fellow of New College 1769–83, when he became vicar of Stanton St John. He was Dean of Winchester in 1804. Between 1783 and 1793 he had been Professor of Poetry in the university.

HOOK or HOOKE, John (1738–1810), was JW's defeated opponent in the New College election of December 1774 for the vacant living of Weston Longville. In the previous year their interests had clashed also over the vacant Mastership of Bedford School, when JW was disappointed. Presumably Hooke fell back on Bedford School, which Woodforde had heard was 'the third best thing in the gift of New College'.

HOWES, the Revd George (1709–1786), was vicar of Honingham from 1738 to 1753 when Mr Du Quesne took it over, and of Mattishall Burgh from 1742 when that parish was consolidated with Hockering. He was licensed as curate of Weston Longville from 1760 and was serving that parish when JW arrived in Norfolk. Once the question of dilapidations was settled JW was on friendly enough terms with Howes. In 1776 Howes was living with the third of his

439

four wives, Catherine *née* Roupe (the aunt of Mrs Elizabeth Davie). Within two months Mrs Howes confided to JW that she 'lived very uneasy with her Husband', who wanted her to make a will in favour of his relations. She lived until 1782. Howes rapidly married again, and relations between him and JW soon cooled. He appears to have been irascible and eccentric, as quick to give social offence as to take it.

JEANES, the Revd Thomas (1749–1835), a Fellow of New College in the mid-1770s, was in 1785 appointed rector of Witchingham and so became a neighbour of JW. He was also vicar of St John's Maddermarket in Norwich, retaining both livings until his death. JW took a somewhat dry view of his wife's airs and graces.

KERR, Mr and Mrs, lived at France Green, East Tuddenham, and were part of the immediate social circle with whom JW had frequent contact. Mr Kerr is often sending him presents: 'a fine woodcock' or a greyhound even. The Kerrs even sit in the rector's seat in the chancel, presumably with permission. They lived in some small style —their dinners were most elegant, and it was noted that dinner and supper were served on Chelsea dishes and plates. In 1781 JW feared Mr Kerr was going mad. He died in 1782.

MABY or MABEY, David (d. 1798), parish clerk of Ansford and Castle Cary, was also churchwarden in 1769 during the quarrel over the singing gallery. Unlike the parish clerks at Weston Longville, who were poor working men, Maby would appear to have been a man of substance. JW reports in 1791 that he is building himself a grand house in Castle Cary.

MASTER, William, 'Master Senior' (b. 1740), was at Winchester and New College where he was a Fellow from 1758 to 1776. He had the first option of the living at Weston Longville but he turned it down after his inspection visit. Shortly afterwards he accepted another New College living, that of Paulerspury, Northants. JW seems to have lost contact with him, as with most of his Oxford friends, after he moved to Norfolk.

MELLIAR FAMILY. James Melliar, 'Counsellor Melliar', and his wife, Mary, lived at Galhampton, a mile or two south of Ansford.

They had five children, four of whom were sons. The other Melliars are William (1720–72) of South Cary, who at the beginning of the diary is a widower living with his one daughter, Priscilla (b. 1751). William Melliar was married again, to Joanna Cheeke of Bruton. These two families were very friendly with the Woodfordes and are constantly mentioned in the early part of the diary. There is a certain cooling off, however, on the part of JW when he is taken up by Justice Creed; during the feud over the gallery singers he doesn't see them at all. Relations are eventually restored, but on a somewhat touchy basis.

PARR, Elizabeth (1699–1771), Aunt Parr, second daughter of Heighes and Mary Lamport, was a childless widow living next to the church at Ansford. She died the day before JW's father.

PEW FAMILY. Another of the families who take part in the social comings and goings of the Somerset diary. William Pew owned the carriers which ran between Cary and Bristol. He was a sometime miller and had been prosecuted for selling adulterated flour in 1757; he was later exonerated. His subsequent history is obscure, but he died in a debtors' prison at Ilchester in 1784. His wife, Mary, died in 1776, just after JW had gone to Norfolk. They had ten children, all born between 1746 and 1760.

POUNSETT, Jane (1734–1798), 'Sister Jane', JW's youngest and favourite sister, was married at the age of forty to John Pounsett of Cole. She had one daughter, Jane (1775–1820), who married the Revd Frederick Grove.

POUNSETT, John (1733–1795), was the son of a formidable mother (Mrs Pounsett of Cole was the sister of Mr Guppy, frequently mentioned in the diary). Mr Pounsett courted Jane Woodforde for a long period, but JW had to speak to him sharply before he would come to the point. In due course all was well, however, and Sister Jane became Mrs Pounsett before the diarist left Ansford for good in 1775. They lived first at Ansford Parsonage and later at Cole Place which they had built for themselves by 1781.

POWELL, Mrs, Lady of the Manors of Ansford and Castle Cary, had in her gift the livings of those parishes. JW did not approach her until 1771, shortly before his father's death, to try to secure the livings for himself; indeed only in 1767 had his father made a single and inconclusive visit to Harpenden where she lived. Meanwhile Thomas Woodforde, having ousted Heighes Woodforde as steward to the lady of the manor, managed to persuade her to make over the living of Ansford to his son, Frank. The whole affair shows how dilatory JW was in pursuing his own interests.

PRIEST, the Revd Richard, was born in 1733 in Norwich. After taking his BA at Hertford College, Oxford, he spent 1755 in Cambridge and on being ordained priest in 1757 became rector of Reepham, a small town a few miles to the north of Weston Longville. By his first wife, who died aged twenty-nine, he had two sons and three daughters, by his second three sons and two daughters. He died in June 1799. His brother Robert, who died in 1825, aged eighty-eight, was a Norwich wine-merchant of whom JW was a regular customer.

RIDLEY, Mrs, widow of JW's predecessor at Weston Longville, was at the time of his preferment living in Greenwich. Woodforde's first months in Norfolk were clouded by a dispute with her over the sum due to him for dilapidations. In the end he won.

TOWNSHEND, The Hon. Charles, of Honingham Hall (1728–1810), married Annabella Smith-Powlet of Sombourne, Hants. He represented Great Yarmouth in Parliament and became the first Baron Bayning of Foxley in 1797. Mr Du Quesne was first cousin once removed to him. Mr Townshend was patron of both Mr Du Quesne and Mr Howes.

WHITE, Betsy (b. 1754), daughter of Lawyer White of Shepton Mallet, thus the niece of JW's brother-in-law Robert White, was the only girl he ever considered marrying. He was charmed by her even as a small girl, and sporadic references to her show how his attachment developed. For his part he thought there was some kind of understanding between them. That she was dismissed as a 'mere jilt' on the occasion of her marriage to Mr Webster, a rich man living in Devon, shows that the understanding was probably more on his side than on hers. Most likely JW's usual timidity and lack of assertion were the cause. He was in any case in no position to marry until he could secure a benefice for himself. Fellowships of Oxford colleges could not be held by married men. Weston Longville came a year or two too late.

WHITE, James (1763–1791), was the son of Robert and Mary White, afterwards a lawyer in Shepton Mallet and partner of his uncle, Lawyer White.

WHITE, Mary (1729–1804), 'Sister White', third child of Samuel and Jane Woodforde, married Robert White of Ansford. They had seven children, only one of whom, Robert, survived his mother. Molly died aged six in 1761 and the invalid 'Little Jacky', their eldest son, survived to the age of eighteen, though he suffered appallingly.

WHITE, Robert Junior (d. 1831), the only child of Robert and Mary White to survive his mother, eloped with his cousin Sophie Clarke.

WHITE, Samuel, the younger brother of Robert and James (Lawyer) White, appears to have been a butcher. He went bankrupt in 1764.

WOODFORDE, Anne (1691–1773), was JW's Aunt Anne, the eldest child of Heighes Woodforde (1664–1724), rector of Epsom, and of his wife, Mary Lamport. Anne never married. As she received a £10 annuity from the Countess of Derby, she may have been some kind of paid companion. She also had a nest egg of £600. Latterly she lived in a house by Ansford churchyard.

WOODFORDE, Anna Maria (1757–1830), was always known as Nancy. Eldest daughter of JW's brother Heighes, Nancy was the niece who came to live with him in Norfolk.

WOODFORDE, Francis (b. 1748), was the cousin who succeeded to the living of Ansford instead of the diarist. He married his cousin, Jane (Jenny) Clarke.

WOODFORDE, Heighes (1726–1789), the second child and eldest son of Samuel Woodforde DD, was an attorney in Ansford and sometime clerk to Justice Creed. He had an allowance of £20 a year from his father and enjoyed the income from the Sussex estate brought to the family by Mary Lamport. Always short of money, he was constantly lent or given it by JW. He married Ann Dorville of

Allhampton, near Ditchleat. They had four children, Anna Maria (JW's companion, Nancy), William ('Nephew Bill'), Juliana and Samuel. By 1764 the marriage was in trouble, and in 1768 Ann Dorville gave birth to the first of three sons of whom Heighes was almost certainly not the father.

WOODFORDE, Jane (1706–1766), born Miss Collins of Ansford, married Samuel Woodforde in 1724. Her half-sister, Martha, was the first wife of Dr Richard Clarke, so the families were already closely connected before Sobieski became the second Mrs Clarke.

WOODFORDE, John (b. 1703), 'Uncle John', was a younger brother of Samuel Woodforde, and became rector of North Curry in Somerset until 1760. By his marriage to Rebekah Hamilton he had two sons, Robert and Thomas.

WOODFORDE, John (1744–1799), JW's 'Brother Jack', was apprenticed in 1759 to a Bristol merchant ironmonger, but he returned to Ansford and joined his brother when JW moved to the Lower House. During this period the low company he kept and his drinking habits were a constant source of worry and irritation to the diarist. JW was hopeful that he might marry several times before Melliora Clarke of Evercreech took him on in 1774.

WOODFORDE, Juliana (1760–1788), third child of Heighes and Ann Dorville, died of tuberculosis in May 1788. Nancy Woodforde was extremely distressed not to be with her sister during her illness.

WOODFORDE, Robert (1675–1762), 'My uncle at Wells', was JW's great-uncle and the family patron. He figures in visits in the earliest parts of the diary. He was a canon of Wells and Treasurer of the Cathedral.

WOODFORDE, Robert (1738–1825) and Thomas (1743–1828), were sons of JW's uncle, John Woodforde. These cousins were frequent companions and visitors during the Ansford period. Robert, after various unsatisfactory medical posts, ended as an apothecary in Bath. His brother was distinctly more successful; working in Taunton, he built up a highly successful and lucrative medical practice and latterly became partner in a bank.

WOODFORDE, Samuel DD (1696–1771), rector of Ansford and vicar of Castle Cary, the diarist's father.

WOODFORDE, Samuel RA (1763–1817), the most distinguished of Heighes's children, was a considerable artist in his day. He was elected ARA in 1800 and RA in 1807. Through the patronage of the banker Henry Hoare of Stourhead, at which house many of his portraits may be seen, he was able to visit and study in Italy.

WOODFORDE, Thomas (1706–1800), 'Uncle Tom', was the youngest child of Heighes and Mary, JW's grandparents. He married Sarah Adams. He was to become the diarist's 'greatest enemy' because of the way he intrigued to obtain the living of Ansford for his son, Francis, at the expense of James.

WOODFORDE, William (1758–1844), 'Nephew Bill', was the son of Heighes and Ann Dorville. Bill accompanied his uncle to Norfolk in 1776 as companion (his sister Nancy being prevented by illness) and stayed at the parsonage from May 1776 until December 1778, apart from a long visit to Somerset. He had some ambition to join the Navy, but he was already too old for a midshipman. He left to join a ship through the good offices of a Norfolk acquaintance. He was an energetic and restless young man with too little to do; no wonder he strained the patience of his middle-aged and rather stuffy uncle. The lowest point of the visit is reached when Sukey Boxley, JW's favourite maid, becomes pregnant: 'He is the occasion of nothing but troublesomeness to me.' However, he subsequently did well as a naval officer.